D1826416

Negotiating Identities
in Modern Latin America

Negotiating Identities

in Modern Latin America

Edited by Hendrik Kraay

UNIVERSITY OF
CALGARY
LATIN AMERICAN
RESEARCH CENTRE

TURNING POINTS SERIES:

Occasional Papers in
Latin American Studies

UNIVERSITY OF
CALGARY
PRESS

University of Calgary Press
2500 University Drive NW
Calgary, Alberta
Canada T2N 1N4
www.uofcpress.com

The University of Calgary Press
acknowledges the support of the
Alberta Foundation for the Arts for
our publications. We acknowledge the
financial support of the Government of
Canada through the Book Publishing
Industry Development Program
(BPIDP) for our publishing activities.
We acknowledge the financial support
of the Canada Council for the Arts for
our publishing program.

Canada

Printed and bound in Canada
by AGMV Marquis
∞ This book is printed on Silva Enviro 100

Cover design by Melina Cusano
Page design and typesetting
by Jason Dewinetz

LIBRARY AND ARCHIVES OF CANADA
CATALOGUING IN PUBLICATION

Negotiating identities in modern Latin
American / edited by Hendrik Kraay.

(Turning points : occasional papers in
Latin American studies no. 3)
Chiefly originating from papers
presented at a conference held at the
University of Calgary, Jan.
30-31, 2004.
Includes bibliographical references
and index.
ISBN 978-1-55238-229-5

1. Identity (Psychology) – Latin
America.
2. Group identity – Latin America.
3. Social change – Latin America
– History.
4. Latin America – Ethnic relations.
5. Latin America – Social conditions
– 19th century.
6. Latin America – Social conditions
– 20th century.
I. Kraay, Hendrik, 1964–
II. Title: Negotiating identities.
III. University of Calgary. Latin
American Research Centre
IV. Series.

HN110.5.A8.N43 2007   305.098
C2007-903201-X

Contents

Preface

IDENTITY HAS SURGED TO THE FOREFRONT of scholarly interest among Latin Americanists, as a quick glance at recent titles published in the field reveals. The demise of old political certainties in the aftermath of the Cold War and the rise of political movements that draw their strength not from class but from other politicized social identities – notably the black movement in Brazil and the indigenous movements in Andean countries – urge closer attention to the ways in which groups collectively define themselves as different from others. The apparent weakening of the nation-state, never very strong to begin with in Latin America, and the recognition that nationalist claims are inherently unstable and inevitably contested points to the need to consider other collective identities that are important to people.

These broad concerns inform the chapters that follow, which focus not on the "high" politics of identity but on its day-to-day negotiation. Their authors hail from different disciplines (history and anthropology) and work throughout the region of Latin America. Their subjects are different social groups, ranging from privileged European and North American expatriates to poverty-stricken rural Maya and black residents of urban Brazil's slums. The contributors share a common interest in how identities are constructed; they eschew essentialist notions of primordial identities and rather focus on the fundamentally political acts of identities' social construction or their negotiation.

Most of the chapters in this book were first presented at the confer- ence, "Negotiating Identities in Latin American Cultures," convened by Elizabeth Montes Garcés and Hendrik Kraay at the University of Calgary on 30–31 January 2004. It turned out to be the coldest weekend of the winter but, undeterred, about three dozen scholars from Canada, the United States, Mexico, and Brazil, representing a variety of disciplines and approaches, presented papers on the ways in which people in Latin America have shaped their identities. This conference proved to be a stimulating and exciting event for the participants, many of whom read- ily agreed to continue working on their papers in light of the conference discussions.

Two books have resulted from this conference: this volume, with its historical and anthropological approaches; and a companion volume on literature, *Relocating Identities in Latin American Cultures*, edited by Elizabeth Montes Garcés (published in 2007 by the University of Calgary Press).

Special thanks go to Stephen J. Randall (then dean of the Faculty of Social Sciences, University of Calgary), Pierre-Yves Mocquais (then dean of the Faculty of Humanities, University of Calgary), and the University Research Grants Committee, whose generous financial support made possible the conference and, ultimately, this book. Christon I. Archer, Jane Kelley, and Elizabeth Montes Garcés deserve thanks for their en- couragement and help at various points in the editing process. Two anon- ymous reviewers for the University of Calgary Press provided helpful comments on the manuscript. During parts of the editing process I held a Professor Visitante Estrangeiro fellowship from Brazil's Coordenação de Aperfeiçoamento de Pessoal de Nível Superior at the Universidade Federal do Rio de Janeiro and a Killam Resident Fellowship at the University of Calgary. I thank both institutions for their support.

1 Introduction:

NEGOTIATING IDENTITIES IN MODERN LATIN AMERICA

Hendrik Kraay[1]

INTRODUCTION

Contemporary Latin America presents a complex field of identity politics. The 2001 demand of neo-Zapatista militants that the Mexican constitution be rewritten to recognize that "we Indians are Mexicans but have different cultures and traditions" has been repeated by countless other mobilized identity groups. Comandante Moisés, identified on a Zapatista website as a Tzeltal, continued: "We have today's great Mexico thanks to our ancestors. We Indians have our way of understanding the world around us and for this reason have resisted for almost 509 years."[2] With their mix of particularistic Indian identity, appeal to Mexican nationalism, and consciousness of a shared Americas-wide indigenous experience, Moisés's remarks exemplify the multiple levels on which contemporary identity politics operate.

This book steps back from the highly visible and overtly politicized identities whose advocates jostle for attention and struggle to make their claims known to examine the equally important day-to-day negotiation of identity in Latin American societies. Despite the long-standing academic interest in identity, it remains a slippery concept. Few scholars today accept essentialist or primordial definitions of identity; most instead agree that identity is a social construct, that it is malleable, and that peoples' identities are fluid and multiple, or even "fluidly multiple."[3] The contributors to this volume adhere to such a constructivist view of identity and seek to understand how groups of people in Latin America create, maintain, and modify collective identities in the face of changing social, political, and economic circumstances. Such "negotiation" of identity underscores its relational and political nature.

IDENTITY IN THE SOCIAL SCIENCES

The term "identity" was originally popularized out of its use in psychology through the work of Erik Erikson, who coined the phrase "identity crisis," and it took firm root in North American academe in the 1960s. While Erikson's ideas about the deep psychic structures of individuals were essentially primordialist, sociological understandings of identity presented it as the product of individuals' interaction with society, a constructivist approach. However, the increasingly widespread use of the concept led to decreasing rigour in its definition. Already in 1983, Philip Gleason could argue that "as *identity* became more and more a cliché, its meaning grew progressively more diffuse, thereby encouraging increasingly loose and irresponsible usage. The depressing result is that a good deal of what passes for discussion of identity is little more than portentous incoherence." Gleason's concern was that theoretically eclectic discussions of identity did not fully take into account the very different assumptions that underlay the social-science approaches to it.[4]

Since then the use of identity has continued to proliferate and the constructivist position has won the day in academe, but identity is often used in an unproblematic way. Sometimes, scholars opt for loose definitions that lack academic rigor, yet capture key points. "Identity," writes one sociologist, is "who you are, what you represent or stand for, whence you derive your self-esteem"; an anthropologist treats "identity as the way(s) in which a person is, or wishes to be, known by certain others."[5] Others take the term as a given and do not define it; however, as Rogers Brubaker and Frederick Cooper have recently argued, this runs the risk of using the term as it is understood in nonacademic practice, "in an implicitly or explicitly reifying manner … that implies or asserts that 'nations,' 'races,' and 'identities' 'exist' and that people 'have' a 'nationality,' a 'race,' an 'identity.'" The problem that they identify is the "dual orientation of many academic identitarians" as analysts and as protagonists of identity politics. As analysts, they recognize the constructed nature of identity, but as protagonists they find essentialist claims to be necessary "if appeals to 'identity' are to be effective in practice."[6]

To address this problem and to better interrogate the concept of identity, Brubaker and Cooper disaggregate it into three major components which, they argue, more effectively describe what is conflated under the rubric of identity, and assist in more critical analysis of the concepts and assumptions underlying it: (1) "identification" or "categorization" by individuals themselves or by others (or the state); (2) "self-understanding"; and (3) a cluster of terms, "commonality, connectedness, and groupness," to describe the sense of affiliation to others which operates at different levels of intensity and in different ways. Working with these distinctions among the different elements often subsumed under the category of identity, they argue, makes possible a more critical analysis of the concept of identity (and of the claims of identity politics), and also avoids the implications of unchanging sameness connoted by the etymology of the term "identity."[7]

Few go so far as Brubaker and Cooper to reject an overarching concept of identity altogether. Instead, Charles Tilly proposes "that we get identity right" by "recognizing that people regularly negotiate and deploy socially-based answers to the questions 'Who are you?' 'Who are we?' and 'Who are they?' ... Their answers are identities, always assertions, always contingent, always negotiable, but also always consequential." He then proceeds to define the four sociological components of identities: (1) a boundary that separates "me from you or us from them," (2) relations among those within the boundary, (3) relations across the boundary, and (4) a set of stories about the boundary and the relations. Identities, he continues, become political when governments take them up; moreover, "identity claims and their attendant stories constitute serious political business."[8] As Tilly implicitly does, the editors of *Identities*, a journal devoted to its study, distinguish between "identity politics," which involves the institutional practices of states or transnational entities, and the "politics of identity," which involves personal and group power and takes place within all social and political institutions.[9] This latter distinction is difficult to deploy in practice, given the prominence of the modern state and the multiple forms of its power,[10] and it is best to understand as broadly as possible the politics in the "serious political business" of identity.

The contributors to this volume regularly resort to the term "identity," yet they are well aware of the problems with simplistic use of the concept. Through analysis of the ways in which some in Latin American societies – usually those in power – have identified their nations as distinct imagined communities, the contributors point to the political nature of identity and the often exclusionary nature of national identity politics – in other words, the drawing of boundaries against Others. The focus on how members of groups understand and present themselves in relation to dominant ideologies and top-down social reform projects underscores that self-understandings and self-identifications often differ fundamentally from categorizations by others. Other contributors trace the senses of affiliation and connectedness that are profoundly important to people, yet recognize that they are the product of peoples' actions and that they are far from immutable.

Scholarly discussions of Latin American identity and identity politics have tended to focus on the nation and people's identities as negotiated in relation to the nation-state. In part, this derives from the prolixity (and relative success) of those who, since independence, have sought to define their nations, but it also reflects both the nation-state's claim to an all-encompassing loyalty from its members and the long-term growth in state power and capacity until at least the 1980s. The proliferation of identity politics in the last two or three decades has, on some levels, profoundly challenged the nation-state paradigm, but the state still remains a powerful force in moulding the contours of identity negotiation.

Since the conquest of the sixteenth century, people in Latin America have produced numerous answers to the age-old question, "Who are we?" Colonial intellectuals laid the groundwork for what David Brading has called "creole patriotism," an "idiosyncratic amalgam of Marian devotion, hatred of Spanish immigrants, and identification with the Aztec past" that defined the American-born of European ancestry as different from Spaniards. As the conquest faded into the past, Mexican creoles claimed for themselves the glories of the Aztec past; in the Viceroyalty of Peru, a stronger indigenous elite clung to the Inca heritage until well into the eighteenth century.[11] The ideals of colonial and independence-era intellectuals scarcely reflected those of the indigenous masses (defined by the colonial state as Indians), the enslaved population, or the growing mixed populations of mestizos or *mestiços* (in Portuguese), for whom myriad new categories were invented. Given the overwhelmingly oral culture in which these people lived, most of their understandings of self are lost to us, yet they were certainly complex. Indigenous communities (and free blacks) knew very well how to present themselves as loyal vassals of the king when dealing with the government; at other times, notably moments of rebellion, indigenous Andeans derided Spaniards as *puka kunkas* (rednecks) who deserved to be killed. Yet by the eighteenth century, the people whom the Spaniards labelled "Indians" might also see themselves as devout Christians, deeply committed to, if not the (Spanish) priest, then certainly the parish church and the institutions of the cargo system that surrounded it.[12]

Independence brought creole elites to power in nine republics and one monarchy by the early 1820s; subsequent divisions saw the birth of seven more republics on the mainland. The wars for independence – fought with greater or lesser intensity throughout Latin America during the 1810s – and the appeals to nativism with which elites mobilized the masses were crucibles of identity formation. Popular anti-Spanish and anti-Portuguese sentiment proliferated: Mexico went so far as to expel natives of the former mother country, other countries contemplated such drastic action, and anti-Portuguese appeals effectively mobilized urban Brazilian crowds.[13]

Everywhere, nineteenth-century governments and elites imagined homogenous nations and struggled mightily to invent them out of the wreckage of Spanish and Portuguese colonial rule. Through "reconciliations and amalgamations of national constituencies cast as lovers destined to desire each other," novelists created "foundational fictions" that sought to overcome deep divisions in the new nations.[14] Historians endowed their countries with suitably heroic national histories and poets sang the praises of distinctive flora and fauna.[15] Geographers mapped the national territory and thereby gave physical form to the idea of nation.[16] Civic rituals expressed official forms of nationalism and sought to transfer loyalties from the old monarchy to the new republics in Spanish America (and from the old monarch to the new one in Brazil). In these rituals, "Indianesque" rhetoric and symbolism celebrated a long past – and often physically remote – indigenous heritage even as existing Indians figured as obstacles to the new nations.[17] Romantic literary indigenismo played a prominent role in defining national identity among the literate elite in Brazil and elsewhere.[18] The proliferation of newspapers after independence helped build the "imagined communities" that Benedict Anderson wrongly attributed to the late-colonial press.[19] Successful government institutions, notably in Brazil but also in Chile and a few other countries, cemented nationalism, or at least a "state-based patriotism," a commitment to the state on the part of elites (whose class interests lay in ensuring an effective central power).[20]

But the great mass of the population stubbornly resisted the Latin American versions of what Eric Hobsbawm has called the "salesmen of national politics," especially when it seemed that such ideologues envisaged nations that ultimately offered little to improve most peoples' way of life.[21] More than a few Latin American statesmen despaired; Domingo Faustino Sarmiento saw Argentina (and by extension, the rest of Latin America) as engaged in a struggle between civilization and barbarism; gauchos and Indians had to be exterminated so that European civilization could be implanted in his country.[22] When Sarmiento and the rest of the Generation of 1837 came to power in Buenos Aires in the early 1860s, they had their chance to impose their vision of a modern nation-state on recalcitrant provinces and reluctant lower classes. By 1870, Sarmiento and his ilk had triumphed, although not without providing the occasion for one of the most dramatic manifestations of nineteenth-century Latin American nationalism – Paraguayans' determined resistance to invasion by the Allies (Argentina, Brazil, and Uruguay) during the War of the Triple Alliance (1864–70) – which derived not from modern ideas of nationhood but from a very traditional identification with the locality and that country's Hispano-Guaraní culture.[23]

Notwithstanding the Paraguayan case, Latin America's nineteenth-century interstate wars failed to produce powerful modern nationalisms. Miguel Angel Centeno argues that the conflicts in the region were the wrong sort for that purpose. They were not profound enough to require massive mobilizations and the associated citizenship that military service often implies; in any case, Latin American elites did not desire such a mobilized, nationalistic citizenry whose claims might upset the social order.[24] Peru's experience in the War of the Pacific (1879–82) nicely underscores this point. The country's utter defeat has often been attributed to the nationalistic Chilean soldier who knew why he was fighting, while the Peruvian indigenous peasant conscript cared not who won.[25] The discovery of significant Andean peasant resistance to the Chilean occupation, which continued as resistance to the Lima-based Peruvian government until the 1890s, led Florencia Mallon to argue that peasants were, in fact, nationalist and that they had conceived a national project for Peru, one that was more attuned to their interests than that of the government in Lima. Unlike in Mexico, where such peasant projects were partially incorporated into the ultimately victorious liberal movement, Peruvian peasant nationalists were brutally suppressed and the Aristocratic Republic (1895–1914), like so many contemporary Latin American regimes, envisaged itself as a European country.[26]

To cast nineteenth-century Latin American history in terms of the failure to create nations runs the risk of naturalizing national identity and making nationalism the only legitimate public identity. Other identities were far more salient for most people in the region; again, given the limited written records, we can know little about them. While some lament the failure of people of African descent to develop a "unifying socio-racial identity" after independence,[27] such an approach directs attention away from the rich variety of neo-African nations, Afro-Cuban *cabildos*, and Afro-Brazilian religions that fostered creolized or hybrid African-American identities. Such identities stood out as obstacles to elite views of the nation. At other times, however, some black Brazilians publicly presented themselves as true patriots, not unlike the Peruvian peasants.[28] The Maya in the Yucatan turned their backs on Mexico and, in the aftermath of the Caste War (1847–50), developed an identity as Cruzob (followers of the so-called speaking cross cult); they held off all comers until the early twentieth century.[29] And we should also take note of the regional identities that, while they did not necessarily reject the nation-state, nevertheless revealed the importance of other loyalties as they celebrated local folkways and regional heroes. Arequipa as Peru's "white city" and Antioqueños as the hardest-working Colombians are but two of the many examples that could be cited. Scholarship on sprawling Brazil has called attention to the numerous such identities that, for the most part, reveal less a rejection of Brazil than different ways of being Brazilian.[30]

The rise of the United States in the last decades of the nineteenth century, and particularly its victory over Spain in 1898 (which secured Cuba a constrained independence and Puerto Rico an eventually even more ambiguous status), reinforced Latin American elites' adherence to their Latin, European heritage, which they then conceived of as a fundamental Other to the materialistic Anglo-Saxon culture. In his classic *Ariel* (1900), Uruguayan José Enrique Rodó wrote that "North American prosperity is as great as its inability to satisfy even an average concept of human destiny," contrasting it unfavourably to what he saw as Latin America's superior humanism.[31] The Peruvian statesman, Francisco García Calderón, called on Latin Americans to develop "the European influences which enrich and improve them," which required "the purging of the nation from the stains of miscegenation, and immigration of a kind calculated to form centers of resistance" against the United States.[32] By the end of the 1910s, the Día de la Raza (October 12) was a widespread pan-Spanish-American holiday; its commemorations publicly celebrated the connection to Spain and presented an Hispanic Latin America. Thus, for a relatively brief period around the centenary of independence, Spanish-American elites declared that their nations were Hispanic and creole, not Indian (even in a romantic or rhetorical way), and much less mestizo.[33]

Such elite visions of national identity could have little appeal to the mass of Latin American populations. Indeed, like García Calderón, Europhile elites throughout the region saw black, indigenous, and mixed-race peoples as obstacles to progress and deliberately sought to remake their nations. The dominant scientific racism of the day reinforced this disdain for the native-born and the preference for European immigrants. Argentina and Uruguay literally remade their populations during the decades of massive immigration before World War I – and thereby laid the foundations of their identities as white nations – and Brazil attempted to do so as well.[34]

Even as many celebrated the ties to Spain and sought European immigration, new readings of Latin American countries' pasts and futures emerged. By the 1910s, with gauchos long gone and Indians safely marginalized, conservative Argentine intellectuals, preoccupied with the threat of so many immigrants (and especially militant anarchist workers), came to valorize once-despised "traditional" customs and the gaucho became a symbol of the "true" Argentine nation. At about the same time, Chilean literary *criollismo* likewise focused on the rural lower classes, now seen as exemplars of *Chilenidad* (Chilean-ness).[35] Elsewhere, the issues were cast somewhat differently. Already in 1891, Cuban patriot José Martí castigated "those born in America who are ashamed of the mother who reared them because she wears an Indian apron" and denied the significance of racial differences.[36] In 1925, in the aftermath of the Mexican Revolution, José Vasconcelos envisaged that mestizo Latin America would form the basis of a transcendental cosmic race that would usher in a new era in world history.[37] Indigenistas in Peru and elsewhere traced national origins back to idealized indigenous pasts; Victor Raúl Haya de la Torre's APRA party rhetoric characterized Latin America as "Indoamerica" and lamented its citizens' fascination with Europe.[38] In the 1930s, through the works of Gilberto Freyre, Brazilians discovered the virtues of miscegenation; he rejected the determinism of scientific racism (which relegated those of mixed race to inferior status) and argued that the Portuguese benefited from their contacts with Africans and Indians.[39]

By the second half of the twentieth century, the ideal of a mestizo/mestiço Latin America had triumphed over the Europeanizing or Hispanophile project of the early twentieth century (although echoes of the latter can still be heard).[40] The ideologues of racial mixture (*mestizaje* in Spanish, *mestiçagem* in Portuguese) generally did not claim to speak for Latin America as a whole (as Vasconcelos had); rather, they spoke about the identity of their nation. Brazil, Colombia, and Venezuela became putative racial democracies; Mexico, Nicaragua, and others became mestizo nations.[41] On the one hand, mestizaje and racial democracy were powerful ideologies of nation-building that linked people of mixed and European ancestry in opposition to foreign, indigenous, and black Others. On the other hand, explains anthropologist J. Jorge Klor de Alva, mestizaje "has been effectively used to promote national amnesia about or to salve the national conscience in what concerns the dismal past and still colonized condition of most indigenous peoples of Latin America."[42]

It seems today virtually impossible to speak of racial democracy or mestizaje without qualifying them as "myths."

On many levels, the criticism of racial democracy and mestizaje is well-taken, for enormous inequalities persist in Latin America; census research in Brazil, to cite one example, reveals the numerous ways in which people classified as *preto* (black) and *pardo* (brown) suffer from lower quality of life than those defined as *branco* (white).[43] Indigenous peoples and those of African ancestry remain at the bottom of the social ladder, their cultures denied a space to survive, reduced to quaint folklore, or appropriated by others as part of the national or regional cultures. Moreover, mestizaje and racial democracy are often seen as cruel tricks that effectively keep the downtrodden in their place by hindering claims for redress on the basis of ethnic or racial identity.

Such, at least, is the critique expounded by black and indigenous activists in the last two decades or so. Brazil's black movement seeks to valorize a black identity; in addition to defining all those of African ancestry as *negros* (blacks), some of its most vigorous advocates reject the syncretism that mestiçagem celebrates and look to restore African cultural purity.[44] Indigenous movements have become powerful forces in Andean countries and the neo-Zapatistas have firmly placed indigenous questions on the Mexican national agenda. On many levels, such identity politics have been remarkably successful, notwithstanding the sometimes bitter criticisms levelled against its advocates.[45] Constitutions have been rewritten to guarantee indigenous land rights and some form of multi-culturalism has become official policy in many countries; governments in Ecuador and Bolivia have fallen in the face of indigenous movements.[46] Brazil's black movement has fundamentally changed the terms of debate about race and racial discrimination in the country; the one-time racial democracy has seen fit to initiate programs of affirmative action – called "quotas" – for blacks in university admissions and government hiring.[47] Nevertheless, it remains to be seen how effective such policies will be; in some countries, changes thus far have been relatively limited.[48] Moreover, as we will see, some have argued that the entire project of multicultural-ism is inherently restrictive.

In the headlong rush to reject racial democracy, to spurn mestizaje, and to redefine nations as neither homogenous nor becoming homoge-nous, but rather as composed of groups bearing specific identities deserv-ing of specific rights and redress for past wrongs, it is easy to lose sight of the extent to which these ideologies were originally powerful rejections of prevailing early-twentieth-century ideologies of scientific racism and European superiority. Not only did mestizaje and mestiçagem take place in biological and cultural terms – in this sense they were profoundly real – but the ideal of a mestizo or mestiço nation offered avenues for social mobility to many.[49] And in Brazil scholars have found much evidence to suggest that ordinary people see (and have long seen) racial democracy as a desirable ideal to be achieved, though they certainly recognize that reality falls short of the ideal.[50]

Even as the protagonists of identity politics have come to question the bases of many Latin American nations, we should also recognize the continuing successes of national projects among significant sectors of the population. Important cleavages persist between nations whose middle and upper classes define themselves as white, rejecting the ideologies of mestizaje and mestiçagem and looking down on their non-white neighbours (a rejection which extends to their countries' non-white populations).[51] Indeed, one of the lesser-known byways of national identity politics in the region is the sometimes aggressive and brutal construction of national difference and boundaries between nations. The 1937 massacre of Haitians ordered by Dominican dictator Rafael Trujillo in the then fluid Haiti-Dominican Republic frontier firmly marked the differences between a black Haiti and an Hispanic Dominican Republic and realized the anti-Haitian project of many Dominican nationalists.[52] Migration between Latin American countries has also been a flashpoint for assertions of difference, as in the case of Nicaraguan immigration to Costa Rica.[53] Throughout the twentieth century, the presence of non-European immigrant groups challenged dominant discourses about nationalities, as they struggled to maintain ethnic identities within societies often hostile to hyphenated ethnicities such as Japanese-Brazilian.[54]

In short, while identity politics on the part of indigenous peoples and people of African descent has profoundly challenged existing narratives of national identity, the nation-state remains an important focus for loyalty and identity, and a powerful force in shaping the contours of identity politics and the politics of identity.

ASSESSING IDENTITY POLITICS

The rise of identity politics in Latin America during the last decades of the twentieth century coincided with the decline of class-based politics in the aftermath of the Cold War's end and the perceived failure of Marxism. Where once class-based movements organized around an idealized national-popular alliance characterized the Latin American left, now a kaleidoscope of groups contest on a more complex and less-clearly defined political terrain opened by the region's democratization since the 1980s. The postwar left saw class struggle as the irreducible core of political contest and subordinated other issues to class; ethnicity, race, gender, and sexual orientation – to name but a few of the politicized identities – provide the basis for political claims today, and few adhere to the teleological certainty of Marxism.[55] Academic scholarship on identity has proliferated in response to this transformation in regional politics, but many issues remain unresolved.

Most agree that globalization has played an important role in the rise of identity politics. The ever deeper international economic integration, the structural adjustments required by international financial institutions, and the increasing rapidity of communication as well as the lengthening reach of global media have had varied impacts on Latin America. While some profit, many more have seen their livelihoods threatened by sometimes ruthless neo-liberal reforms. Mexico's neo-Zapatistas effectively timed their revolt to take place on the day on which the North American Free Trade Agreement was to go into effect (1 January 1994) and explicitly declared that NAFTA amounted to a "death sentence for the indigenous ethnicities of Mexico."[56] Although critics decry globalization's tendency to homogenize cultures and societies, it has opened new spaces for indigenous and Afro-Latin American activism, as well as for that of other groups. New models of politics, new ways for people to envisage their struggles, and broader international alliances are as much the product of globalization as the wrenching economic dislocations. To paraphrase Alison Brysk, local villages now connect to the global village.[57]

In the 1980s and 1990s, many foresaw that such economic developments and the increasing ease of communication would lead to the decline of the nation-state and nationalism. In what Arjun Appadurai then characterized as an emerging "transnational, deterritorialized world," the nation-state loses much of its former power, and new "ethnoscapes" of group identity emerge out of the complex interactions of people in an interconnected world shaped by new electronic media and relatively much easier migration.[58] The strong personal, cultural, and economic connections that many Latin Americans living in the United States maintain with their home communities exemplifies the processes that Appadurai identified elsewhere.[59] While it is true that modern technologies make possible very different kinds of connections among far-flung groups of people, Appadurai's transnational and deterritorialized world may not be so new after all. It has important precedents in the cultural forms and new identities produced in the "black Atlantic" or the "Atlantic world" created by the enforced migration of millions of Africans to the Americas from the 1500s to the mid-1800s, until its end the largest intercontinental migration in history.[60] Latin America's complex social structures and

innovative cultural bricolage displayed many of these processes well before they were discovered by students of globalized cultural forms. Homi
Bhabha's "'in-between' spaces" that "provide the terrain for elaborating
strategies of selfhood – singular or communal – that initiate new signs
of identity, and innovative sites of collaboration, and contestations" can
be found in virtually any period of Latin American history. "Hybridity,"
as Néstor García Canclini notes, "has a long history in Latin American
cultures."[61]

Notwithstanding a certain shrinkage in state capacity under the impact of neo-liberal reforms, the nation-state and national identities have
not simply withered away, and tragic events around the world have shown
that the nasty features of nationalism and other forms of collective identity politics are alive and well. Furthermore, the state's adoption of many
of the aims of identity politics' proponents has changed the dynamics of
identity negotiation itself in significant ways. Scholarship on Colombia,
where the 1991 constitution enshrined land rights for rural indigenous
and black communities, is beginning to address this question. One anthropologist has traced how Law 70 of 1993, which defined the terms
under which Pacific coast black communities can claim collective land
titles, set off a "strange merry-go-round of identity" construction as individuals and groups adjusted their public personae to obtain these benefits.[62] Such an approach, of course, assumes that there is a "true" identity
for these groups and runs the risk of dismissing new developments in
identity politics as artificial creations. It fails to recognize that identities
are continually negotiated, that some conjunctures are more conducive
to change than to continuity, and that people construct and reconstruct
identities in a constantly changing environment.

The extent to which the state can and does shape identity politics raises
the question of its interests in doing so. A recently developed scholarly
critique holds that the espousal of multiculturalism and respect for indigenous rights by governments and by international institutions such
as the World Bank is a Trojan horse. Charles R. Hale warns that multiculturalism menaces popular movements when state policy defines the
limits of what is acceptable or appropriate activism. Through this inser-
tion of state power, collective mobilization against structural inequities
can be delegitimized and identity politics can be reduced to little more
than the search for spoils within the (unjust) existing social, economic,
and political order. In this view, recent institutional changes recognizing indigenous rights amount to little more than the state's exercise of
its remaining power to defuse conflict by making selective concessions
to preserve hegemonic social relations.[63] Still others worry that inter-

national alliances lead to foisting U.S. ideas about, for example, the appropriate forms of racial politics, onto Latin America – a new form of imperialism.[64]

Moreover, identity-based political movements have troubling features. Their tendency toward "essentialism" – justified as a necessary "strategic essentialism" – and their assumptions about "coherent and bounded common culture" fly in the face of the hybridity and contingency posited by contemporary anthropological understandings of culture and sometimes naturalize other social hierarchies such as those based on gender.[65] As in the study of any political movement, we must be careful not to assume that activists, however laudable we may find their aims, necessarily reflect the views of the constituents. Moreover, as another anthropologist has warned, we must also not assume that the scholarly discourse about identity automatically provides the "relevant analytic categories and parameters," and we must listen closely to what our subjects tell us.[66]

What is needed, in short, is careful attention to the full range and complexity of identity and its negotiation on multiple levels. Some recent works seek to do this. Livio Sansone's sensitive analysis of the "failure" of Brazilian blacks to adopt an ethnic identity as blacks along the lines of that in the United States offers a sophisticated understanding of the meaning of blackness in that country that respects the uniqueness of the Brazilian racial formation.[67] María Elena García's study of Peruvian Quechua parents who reject the intercultural and bilingual education offered to their children by the ministry of education – apparently one of the victories of the international indigenous movement – likewise points the way to more nuanced thinking about identity politics and its relationship to peoples' senses of self and their interests.[68] Writing about Mixtec migrants to Baja California, Carmen Martínez Novo describes a Mexican state that funds indigenous groups but whose agents insist that people subscribe to the prescribed indigenous identity, which serves to mark them as "different and subordinate," much to the benefit of commercial agriculture. Grassroots migrants, however, "forcefully reject the stereotypes of both their foes and their advocates" and stress their right to education and social mobility, "whether or not they choose Mixtec language and identity."[69] Such studies offer more nuanced assessments of the full complexity of identity politics and the politics of identity.

BEYOND NATIONAL IDENTITIES AND IDENTITY POLITICS

The very different assessments of the current wave of identity politics together point to the need for empirical work on how identities were and are constructed and reconstructed – negotiated – in Latin Americans'

Cartography by Robin Poitras, 2006

1.1. Map of Latin America

day-to-day lives. This is the aim of the chapters that follow, which deal with four broad issues: the nation, foreigners, race, and community identity. The authors seek to understand the complex mechanisms through which groups (and sometimes individuals) identify themselves as similar or different to others (or are so identified), how their members come to understand themselves as different from others, and how they come to see commonalities between themselves and other members of their groups. They underscore the continuing importance of identity and of the socially-constructed differences in peoples' lives.

The three chapters in the first section return to the question of nation, approaching it not as a given but as an identity constructed through a long process of debate in which the state and intellectuals played key roles, but always had to contend with the rest of the population. Hendrik Kraay examines the civic rituals prominent in Brazilian elites' efforts to win loyalty for the newly-independent empire. Celebrating independence on 7 September and constructing Emperor Pedro I's 1822 cry of "Independence or Death" as the moment of independence provided a suitably conservative and monarchist myth of origin for the new nation-state. Despite proclaiming that they celebrated a nation to which all Brazilians belonged, the commemorations of the 1840s and 1850s on which Kraay focuses expressed a circumscribed understanding of the nation. Numerous groups could not be part of the nation envisaged by those who controlled the celebrations.

The next two chapters turn to the period around 1900 when, at least to elites in power, Latin American countries were rapidly modernizing and progressing and when elites hewed closely to a European identity for their nations. Using the concept of masculinity, Stephen Neufeld examines the state's efforts to modernize the Mexican army during the long administration of Porfirio Díaz (1876–1911). While new masculine models gained some purchase among the officers, they had but limited impact on the rank-and-file soldiers whose rough-and-ready masculinity had little use for the dandified ideals spreading through the officer corps. Moreover, like so many other efforts at modernization during this period, its advocates wanted a façade of the new, without significant changes to the social order or to structures of power. Díaz, in short, wanted an army that would look good on parade, but not one whose generals might harbour ambitions on the presidential palace nor one whose officers might come to see themselves as leading agents of political or even social and economic reform.

Gregg Bocketti examines the early history of Brazil's participation in international football (soccer). Today, of course, soccer is thoroughly diffused throughout Brazilian society and the participation of all Brazilians in the sport epitomizes the ideal of racial democracy. In the years before the First World War, however, football was an elite sport and, through hosting elite British teams, the patricians who controlled Brazilian soccer could identify themselves with the paragons of European civilization. They presented a white, European Brazil; their accounts of the matches only hint disdainfully at plebeian engagement with the game. Such silencing and exclusion, however, did not last, and in the 1920s, Brazilian football changed significantly; nonwhite and lower-class players were admitted to national teams and soccer developed into a national sport.

The following section turns to the question of foreigners in Latin American countries. In most of the nineteenth century, the British were the quintessential foreigners and Louise Guenther examines the contradictions of the British place in Brazil's second city of Salvador. Without formally segregating themselves from local society, the British constructed a tight-knit, visibly-different community. Even as Brazilians admired British mercantile success and technical prowess (and respectfully ceded to British naval power), they maintained a healthy suspicion of these peculiar foreigners. Satires in which clever Brazilians got the better of obtuse Englishmen constituted one Brazilian strategy, while vigorous anti-British sentiment during London's long campaign against the slave trade reveals the continued distance between British expatriates and their Brazilian hosts. Here there was little or none of the mindless imitation of the foreigner for which so many twentieth-century intellectuals castigated their forebears.

Ronald Harpelle turns to a classic early twentieth-century enclave society, the American community sustained by a U.S. oil company operating in Peru. Exhaustively analyzing a single source – a cookbook produced by the wives of the company's American employees – he shows how these women constructed their identity as white Americans by distinguishing themselves from their nonwhite Peruvian domestic help. We may not literally be what we eat, but what we eat is often a fundamental mark of collective identity. Imported, canned, and otherwise processed foods, readily available at the company stores, dominated the ingredient lists of the recipes submitted by company wives. They eschewed local Peruvian ingredients and, through this bilingual cookbook, sought to train their domestic help to produce meals indistinguishable from those to which they were accustomed in the United States. In so doing, the company wives firmly marked themselves as Americans against the Other of the Peruvian domestic servant, whom they nonetheless had to admit into their homes (or at least into their kitchens).

Not all foreigners in Latin America come from outside of the region. In the second half of the twentieth century, hundreds of thousands of Bolivians have found work in Argentina, mostly in the capital, Buenos Aires. There, as María Eugenia Brockmann Dannenmaier describes in her chapter, these men and women live under a legal regime strikingly similar to that under which Mexican and other Latin American immigrants live in the United States. Like the United States, Argentina has resorted to periodic amnesties to grant residence status to illegal immigrants. Argentines construct Bolivians as racially different; Bolivians without legal status are often doubly exploited by more successful fellow

Bolivian migrants. Brockmann analyzes the migrant experience through the narratives told by Bolivians who returned home to Cochabamba in the aftermath of the 2001 Argentine economic crisis.

The two chapters in the following section focus on race and identity in Brazil, an issue already raised by Kraay in his discussion of racial politics during Brazilian independence celebrations and by Bocketti in his discussion of the exclusion of black players from Brazil's international football teams in the 1910s. Maria Cecília Velasco e Cruz turns her attention to a violent conflict among members of a Rio de Janeiro dockworkers' union in 1908. Usually characterized as a struggle between black Brazilian and white immigrant workers, this and other similar instances are held up as examples of ethnic and racial rivalries that weakened the country's nascent labour movement. Cruz questions the essentialising assumptions about racial and ethnic identities that lie behind this interpretation and shows that the conflict was considerably more complex. Union members forged a collective identity that stressed the equality of all workers and, in fact, the adoption of government regulations that banned foreigners from holding union office set off the conflict. The union easily survived the incident, but collapsed in the face of employer reaction in late 1908. In short, as she warns us, racial and ethnic identities are not necessarily as salient in peoples' lives as scholars have sometimes suggested.

Jennifer Manthei responds to the call for qualitative research on race in contemporary Brazil, particularly the negotiation of its meaning in everyday life. Manthei focuses on the image of the *mulata* (mulatto woman) among teenage girls and young women in a nontourist city. The sexy mulata, so prominent in Brazil's carnival and tourist industries, played a central role in discussions of national identity by writers such as Gilberto Freyre and Jorge Amado and continues to serve as a discursive resource. However, Manthei finds that girls speaking from different social locations (of class and colour) define and deploy the mulata image in different manners according to their particular projects of identity negotiation.

The final three chapters in this book focus on the classic subject of anthropological research – the (usually indigenous) small village community. Once characterized as static "closed corporate communities" or dismissed as obstacles to progress, liberal equality, and national projects, such communities have proven remarkably resilient. Denise Fay Brown traces how the Maya residents of Chemax define themselves as *eetcahal*, or members of their community, in opposition to Others, the non-Maya residents of the town and the rest of the Mexican nation. Maintaining a house plot in the town and participation in the annual festival are essential components of identification with Chemax. Despite the rapid changes of the past decades, which have led more and more members of the community to seek work in the tourist enclaves of the Mayan Riviera, identification with Chemax remains strong, not because it is something primordial, but rather because it remains meaningful and significant.

Like Brown, Marjorie Snipes examines an indigenous community distant from the centres of national power; while Brown's subjects emerge as defenders of a community identity to which the Mexican state is irrelevant, the residents of El Angosto, on the Argentine-Bolivian border, define their community in direct relationship to the state. They see themselves as more patriotic than the Argentine government: Angosteños present themselves as staunch defenders of the remote frontier, determined builders of a school (to which the state contributed only sporadically), and guardians of a road built during the military dictatorship (1976–83) that demonstrates their importance to the nation-state. El Angosto's community identity, at least as strong as that of Chemax, rests on fundamentally different bases from its Maya counterpart.

Historian Julie Gibbings turns to another Mesoamerican community, the culturally diverse Uaxactún, located in northern Guatemala. In this country, a fundamental reorientation in state policy has led to significant changes in how the people of Uaxactún articulate their collective identity. The militaristic state of the early 1980s that waged a brutal campaign of terror against the Maya gave way to an oligarchic democracy that adopted the international rhetoric of environmentalism in the 1990s. Instead of obstacles to progress or sanctuaries for Marxist guerrillas, forest communities are now held up as guardians of the environment. The creation of the Mayan Biosphere Reserve, however, came at the cost of heavy, if benignly intended, state control over the community. Uaxactecos readily adopted the rhetoric of environmentalism but adapted it for their own purposes. Gibbings theorizes these developments and shows how Uaxactecos used environmentalism to subvert the state project and to force state officials to respond to community demands.

Thus the chapters that follow point to the numerous ways through which people define their membership in groups and their collective identity. Participation in rituals (whether national or community-based), shared food, involvement in community institutions, identification with place, support for the national football team, and numerous other practices cement relationships on one side of the boundary that demarcates identity groups. Migration challenges understandings of identity and brings people into contact with new groups, sometimes forcing redefinitions of identity. Boundaries within nations or societies make for daily contact with Others against whom identity is continually defined and redefined. In some chapters, the state looms large as it sets the terms for identity negotiation or seeks to force changes that elicit resistance or creative engagement. In others, the state remains in the background, yet it is almost never wholly absent from the politics of identity. Finally, the authors underscore the importance of listening to our subjects, whether they speak to us indirectly through the written sources with which historians work or directly through anthropologists' interviews and participant observation. What they tell us about who they are is the starting point for any analysis of the negotiation of identity.

NOTES TO CHAPTER 1

1 I thank Denise Fay Brown and Jennifer J. Manthei for their helpful comments on an earlier version of this chapter.

2 Statement of Comandante Moisés, "Delegación zapatista a la ciudad de México," 2001, http://www.ezlnaldf.org/static/delegacion.htm (12 Aug. 2005).

3 For such approaches to identity in Latin America, see (among many others) Luis Roniger and Mario Sznajder, eds., Constructing Collective Identities and Shaping Public Spheres: Latin American Paths (Brighton: Sussex Academic Press, 1998); Luis Roniger and Tamar Herzog, eds., The Collective and the Public in Latin America: Cultural Identities and Political Order (Brighton: Sussex Academic Press, 2000); Mercedes F. Durán-Cogan and Antonio Gómes Moriana, eds., National Identities and Sociopolitical Changes in Latin America (New York: Routledge, 2001). Jean E. Jackson and Kay B. Warren use the phrase "fluidly multiple" in their "Indigenous Movements in Latin America, 1992–2004: Controversies, Ironies, New Directions," Annual Review of Anthropology 34 (2005): 561.

4 Philip Gleason, "Identifying Identity: A Semantic History," Journal of American History 69:4 (March 1983): 931; for useful introductions to the range of scholarship on identity see Linda Alcoff and Eduardo Mendieta, Identities: Race, Class, Gender, and Nationality (Oxford: Blackwell, 2003); Heidrun Friese, ed., Identities: Time, Difference and Boundaries (New York: Berghahn Books, 2002).

5 Anton Blok, "The Narcissism of Minor Differences," European Journal of Social Theory 1:1 (1998): 48; Anthony Cohen, "Culture as Identity: An Anthropologist's View," New Literary History 24:1 (Winter 1993): 195.

6 Rogers Brubaker and Frederick Cooper, "Beyond Identity," Theory and Society 29:1 (Feb. 2000): 6; see also Cohen, "Culture as Identity."

7 Brubaker and Cooper, "Beyond Identity," 14–21.

8 Charles Tilly, Identities, Boundaries, and Social Ties (Boulder: Paradigm Publishers, 2005), 209–10.

9 Jonathan D. Hill and Thomas M. Wilson, "Identity Politics and the Politics of Identities," Identities 10:1 (Jan.-March 2003): 1–8.

10 For a recent survey, see Begoña Arextaga, "Maddening States," Annual Review of Anthropology 32 (2003): 393–410. A classic work in this vein is Philip Corrigan and Derek Sayer, The Great Arch: English State Formation and Cultural Revolution (Oxford: Blackwell, 1985).

11 David A. Brading, The First America: The Spanish Monarchy, Creole Patriots, and the Liberal State, 1492–1867 (Cambridge: Cambridge University Press, 1991), 602; Anthony Pagden, "Identity

Formation in Spanish America," in *Colonial Identity in the Atlantic World, 1500–1800*, ed. Nicholas Canny and Anthony Pagden, 51-93 (Princeton: Princeton University Press, 1987); Stuart B. Schwartz, "The Formation of a Colonial Identity in Brazil," in *Colonial Identity*, ed. Canny and Pagden, 15–50; Carolyn Dean, *Inka Bodies and the Body of Christ: Corpus Christi in Colonial Cuzco, Peru* (Durham: Duke University Press, 1999).

12 Jan Szemiński, "Why Kill the Spaniard? New Perspectives on Andean Insurrectionary Ideology in the 18th Century," in *Resistance, Rebellion, and Consciousness in the Andean Peasant World, 18th to 20th Centuries*, ed. Steve J. Stern, 166–92 (Madison: University of Wisconsin Press, 1987); Sergio Serulnikov, *Subverting Colonial Authority: Challenges to Spanish Rule in Eighteenth-Century Southern Andes* (Durham: Duke University Press, 2003).

13 Harold Dana Sims, *The Expulsion of Mexico's Spaniards, 1821–1836* (Pittsburgh: University of Pittsburgh Press, 1990); John Charles Chasteen, "War to the Death: Nativism and Independence in Latin America," in *The Concept of the Foreign: An Interdisciplinary Dialogue*, ed. Rebecca Saunders, 223-36 (Lanham: Lexington Books, 2003); Robert Rowland, "Patriotismo, povo e ódio aos portugueses: Notas sobre a construção da identidade nacional no Brasil independente," in *Brasil: Formação do Estado e da nação*, ed. István Jancsó, 365-88 (São Paulo: HUCITEC, 2003); Gladys Sabina Ribeiro, *A liberdade em construção: Identidade nacional e conflitos antilusitanos no Primeiro Reinado* (Rio de Janeiro: Relume-Dumará, 2002).

14 Doris Sommer, *Foundational Fictions: The National Romances of Latin America* (Berkeley: University of California Press, 1991), 24.

15 Nicolas Shumway, *The Invention of Argentina* (Berkeley: University of California Press, 1991).

16 Raymond B. Craib, *Cartographic Mexico: A History of Social Fixations and Fugitive Landscapes* (Durham: Duke University Press, 2004), chap. 1; Klaus-John Dodds, "Geography, Identity and the Creation of the Argentine State," *Bulletin of Latin American Research* 12:3 (1993): 311–31; Demétrio Magnoli, *O corpo da pátria: Imaginação geográfica e política externa no Brasil (1808–1912)* (São Paulo: Editora UNESP and Moderna, 1997).

17 William H. Beezley and David E. Lorey, eds., *!Viva Mexico! !Viva la Independencia! Celebrations of September 16* (Wilmington: Scholarly Resources, 2001); Rebecca Earle, "Creole Patriotism and the Myth of the Loyal Indian," *Past and Present* 172 (Aug. 2001): 125–45, and "'Padres de la Patria' and the Ancestral Past: Commemorations of Independence in Nineteenth-Century Spanish America," *Journal of Latin American Studies* 34:4 (Nov. 2002): 775–806.

18 Renata R. Mautner Wasserman, *Exotic Nations: Literature and Cultural Identity in the United States and Brazil, 1830–1930* (Ithaca: Cornell University Press, 1994); Dave Treece, *Exiles, Allies, Rebels: Brazil's Indianist Movement, Indigenist Politics, and the Imperial Nation-State* (Westport: Greenwood, 2000).

19 Benedict Anderson, *Imagined Communities: Reflections on the Origins and Spread of Nationalism*, rev. ed. (London: Verso, 1991), 62–64; Fernando Unzueta, "Periodicos y formación nacional: Bolivia en sus primeros años," *Latin American Research Review* 35:2 (2000): 35–72; François-Xavier Guerra, "Forms of Communication, Political Spaces, and Cultural Identities in the Creation of Spanish-American Nations," in *Beyond Imagined Communities: Reading and Writing the Nation in Nineteenth-Century Latin America*, ed. John Charles Chasteen and Sara Castro-Klarén, 3–32 (Baltimore: Johns Hopkins University Press, 2003).

20 Roderick J. Barman, *Brazil: The Forging of a Nation, 1798–1852* (Stanford: Stanford University Press, 1988); Richard Graham, "Constructing a Nation in Nineteenth-Century Brazil: Old and New Views on Class, Culture, and the State," *The Journal of the Historical Society* 1:2–3 (Winter 2000): 17–56; Patrick Barr-Melej, *Reforming Chile: Cultural Politics, Nationalism, and the Rise of the Middle Class* (Chapel Hill: University of North Carolina Press, 2001), 54–57.

21 Eric Hobsbawm, *Nations and Nationalism Since 1780: Programme, Myth, Reality*, 2nd ed. (Cambridge: Cambridge University Press, 1990), 79.

22 Domingo F. Sarmiento, *Facundo: Or, Civilization and Barbarism*, trans. Mary Mann (1845; repr., New York: Penguin Books, 1998).

23 Shumway, *Invention of Argentina*; Thomas L. Whigham, "The Paraguayan War: A Catalyst for Nationalism in South America," in *I Die with My Country: Perspectives on the Paraguayan War, 1864–1870*, ed. Hendrik Kraay and Thomas L. Whigham, 177-98 (Lincoln: University

of Nebraska Press, 2004); John Hoyt Williams, "Race, Threat, and Geography: The Paraguayan Experience of Nationalism," *Canadian Review of Studies in Nationalism* 1:2 (Spring 1974): 173–89.

24 Miguel Angel Centeno, *Blood and Debt: War and the Nation-State in Latin America* (University Park: Pennsylvania State University Press, 2002).

25 Heraclio Bonilla, "The War of the Pacific and the National and Colonial Problem in Peru," *Past and Present* 81 (Nov. 1978): 92–118.

26 Florencia Mallon, *Peasant and Nation: The Making of Postcolonial Mexico and Peru* (Berkeley: University of California Press, 1995). See especially pages 2–5 for her reformulation of the concept of nationalism.

27 Aline Helg, *Liberty and Equality in Caribbean Colombia, 1770–1835* (Chapel Hill: University of North Carolina Press, 2004), 193.

28 Philip A. Howard, *Afro-Cuban Cabildos and Societies of Color in the Nineteenth Century* (Baton Rouge: Louisiana State University Press, 1998); Rachel E. Harding, *A Refuge in Thunder: Candomblé and Alternative Spaces of Blackness* (Bloomington: Indiana University Press, 2000); Mieko Nishida, *Slavery and Identity: Ethnicity, Gender, and Race in Salvador, 1808–1888* (Bloomington: Indiana University Press, 2003); Hendrik Kraay, "Patriotic Mobilization in Brazil: The Zuavos and Other Black Companies," in *I Die with My Country*, ed. Kraay and Whigham, 61–80.

29 Nelson Reed, *The Caste War of Yucatan* (Stanford: Stanford University Press, 1964).

30 Sarah C. Chambers, *From Subjects to Citizens: Honor, Gender, and Politics in Arequipa, Peru, 1780–1854* (University Park: Pennsylvania State University Press, 1999), 1–3; Emiro Kastos, "Antioquia and Its Customs," in *Nationalism in Latin America*, ed. Samuel L. Baily, 58-62 (New York: Albert A. Knopf, 1971); Hendrik Kraay, "Between Brazil and Bahia: Celebrating Dois de Julho in Nineteenth-Century Salvador," *Journal of Latin American Studies* 32:2 (May 1999): 255–86; Evaldo Cabral de Mello, *Rubro veio: O imaginário da restauração pernambucana*, 2nd ed. (Rio de Janeiro: Topbooks, 1997); Ruben Oliven, *Tradition Matters: Modern Gaúcho Identity in Brazil*, trans. Carmen Chaves Tesser (New York: Columbia University Press, 1996); Barbara Weinstein, "Racializing Regional Difference: São Paulo versus Brazil, 1932," in *Race and Nation in Modern Latin America*, ed. Nancy P. Appelbaum et al., 237-62 (Chapel Hill: University of North Carolina Press, 2003).

31 José Enrique Rodó, *Ariel*, trans. Margaret Sayers Peden (Austin: University of Texas Press, 1988), 79.

32 Francisco García Calderón, *Latin America: Its Rise and Progress*, trans. Bernard Miall (London: T. Fisher Unwin, 1913), 312.

33 Ilan Rachum, "Origins and Historical Significance of Día de la Raza," *European Review of Latin American Studies* 76 (April 2004): 61–81; Earle, "Padres de la Patria," 801–5.

34 Nicholás Sánchez-Albornoz, *The Population of Latin America: A History* (Berkeley: University of California Press, 1974), 146–81; George Reid Andrews, *Blacks and Whites in São Paulo, Brazil, 1888–1988* (Madison: University of Wisconsin Press, 1991), 54–89.

35 Carl Solberg, *Immigration and Nationalism: Argentina and Chile, 1890–1914* (Austin: University of Texas Press, 1970), 132–68; Barr-Melej, *Reforming Chile*, 77–101.

36 José Martí, "Our America," in *Our America: Writings on Latin America and the Struggle for Cuban Independence*, trans. Elinor Randall, Juan de Onís, and Roslyn Held Foner; ed. Philip S. Foner, 85, 93-94 (New York: Monthly Review Press, 1977).

37 José Vasconcelos, *The Cosmic Race: A Bilingual Edition*, trans. Didier T. Jaén (Baltimore: Johns Hopkins University Press, 1997).

38 Robert J. Alexander, ed., *Aprismo: The Ideas and Doctrines of Victor Raúl Haya de la Torre* (Kent: Kent State University Press, 1973), 255–57. On indigenismo and its complexities in Peru, see Marisol de la Cadena, *Indigenous Mestizos: The Politics of Race and Culture in Cuzco, Peru, 1919–1991* (Durham: Duke University Press, 2000).

39 Gilberto Freyre, *The Masters and the Slaves: A Study in the Development of Brazilian Civilization*, 2nd English ed., trans. Samuel Putnam (Berkeley: University of California Press, 1986); Thomas E. Skidmore, *Race and Nationality in Brazilian Thought* (New York: Oxford University Press, 1974).

40 Mario Vargas Llosa, "Questions of Conquest: What Columbus Wrought and What He Did Not," *Harper's* 281 (Dec. 1990): 45–53.

41 Emilia Viotti da Costa, "The Myth of Racial Democracy: A Legacy of the Empire," in *The Brazilian Empire: Myths and Histories*, rev. ed. (Chapel Hill: University of North Carolina Press, 2000); 234–46; Peter Wade, *Blackness and Race Mixture: The Dynamics of Racial Identity in Colombia* (Baltimore: Johns Hopkins University Press, 1993); Winthrop R. Wright, *Café con Leche: Race, Class, and National Image in Venezuela* (Austin: University of Texas Press, 1990); Jeffrey L. Gould, *To Die in This Way: Nicaraguan Indians and the Myth of Mestizaje, 1880–1965* (Durham: Duke University Press, 1998); Alan Knight, "Racism, Revolution, and Indigenismo: Mexico, 1910–1940," in *The Idea of Race in Latin America, 1870–1940*, ed. Richard Graham, 71-113 (Austin: University of Texas Press, 1990); Jeffrey Pilcher, *Que Vivan los Tamales! Mexican Cuisine and National Identity* (Albuquerque: University of New Mexico Press, 1997).

42 J. Jorge Klor de Alva, "The Postcolonization of the (Latin) American Experience: A Reconsideration of 'Colonialism,' 'Postcolonialism,' and 'Mestizaje,'" in *After Colonialism: Imperial Histories and Postcolonial Displacements*, ed. Gyan Prakash, 257 (Princeton: Princeton University Press, 1995).

43 Edward Telles, *Race in Another America: The Significance of Skin Color in Brazil* (Princeton: Princeton University Press, 2004), chapters 5–8.

44 For a recent discussion of this issue see Matthias Röhrig Assunção, "Brazilian Popular Culture or the Curse and Blessing of Cultural Hybridism," *Bulletin of Latin American Research* 24:2 (April 2005): 157–66.

45 Kay B. Warren, *Indigenous Movements and Their Critics: Pan-Maya Activism in Guatemala* (Princeton: Princeton University Press, 1998).

46 For introductions to these topics see David Maybury Lewis, ed., *The Politics of Ethnicity: Indigenous Peoples in Latin American States* (Cambridge: David Rockefeller Center for Latin American Studies, Harvard University, 2002); Rachel Sieder, ed., *Multiculturalism in Latin America: Indigenous Rights, Diversity and Democracy* (Houndmills: Palgrave Macmillan, 2002); Xavier Albó, "Ethnic Identity and Politics in the Central Andes: The Cases of Bolivia, Ecuador, and Peru," in *Politics in the Andes: Identity, Conflict, Reform*, ed. Jo-Marie Burt and Philip Mauceri, 17–37 (Pittsburgh: University of Pittsburgh Press, 2004).

47 There is still very little scholarship on the new policies; for introductions see Mala Htun, "From 'Racial Democracy' to Affirmative Action: Changing State Policy on Race in Brazil," *Latin American Research Review* 39:1 (2004): 60–89; and Telles, *Race in Another America*, chapter 3.

48 Juliet Hooker, "'Beloved Enemies': Race and Official Mestizo Nationalism in Nicaragua," *Latin American Research Review* 40:3 (Oct. 2005): 14–39; Rebecca Overmyer-Velázquez, "The Self-Determination of Indigenous Peoples and the Limits of United Nations Advocacy in Guerrero, Mexico (1998–2000)," *Identities* 10:1 (Jan.-Mar. 2003): 9–29

49 This argument has been forcefully developed by Alejandro de la Fuente, "Myths of Racial Democracy: Cuba, 1900–1912," *Journal of Latin American Studies* 34:3 (1999): 39–73; and John Charles Chasteen, *National Rhythms, African Roots: The Deep History of Latin American Popular Dance* (Albuquerque: University of New Mexico Press, 2004), 197–204. See also Alejandro de la Fuente, *A Nation for All: Race, Inequality, and Politics in Twentieth-Century Cuba* (Chapel Hill: University of North Carolina Press, 2001), and Peter Wade, "Rethinking Mestizaje: Ideology and Lived Experience," *Journal of Latin American Studies* 37:2 (May 2005): 239–57.

50 Hebe Maria Mattos de Castro, *Das cores do silêncio: Os significados da liberdade no sudeste escravista, Brasil, século XIX* (Rio de Janeiro: Arquivo Nacional, 1995); Robin E. Sheriff, *Dreaming Equality: Color, Race, and Racism in Urban Brazil* (New Brunswick: Rutgers University Press, 2001).

51 Emanuela Guano, "A Color for the Modern Nation: The Discourse on Class, Race, and Education in the Porteño Middle Class," *Journal of Latin American Anthropology* 8:1 (2003): 148–71.

52 Richard Lee Turits, *Foundations of Despotism: Peasants, the Trujillo Regime, and Modernity in Dominican History* (Stanford: Stanford University Press, 2003), chapter 5.

53 Carlos García Sandoval, "Contested Discourses on National Identity: Representing Nicaraguan Immigration to Costa Rica," *Bulletin of Latin American Research* 23:4 (Oct. 2004): 434–45. See also María Eugenia Brockmann Dannenmaier's chapter in this book.

54 Jeffrey Lesser, *Negotiating National Identity: Immigrants, Minorities, and the Struggle for Ethnicity in Brazil* (Durham: Duke University Press, 1999).

55 For a discussion of these developments, see Charles R. Hale, "The Cultural Politics of Identity in Latin America," *Annual Review of Anthropology* 26 (1997): 567–90.

56 Nicholas P. Higgins, *Understanding the Chiapas Rebellion: Modernist Visions and the Invisible Indian* (Austin: University of Texas Press, 2004), 152

57 Alison Brysk, *From Tribal Village to Global Village: Indian Rights and International Relations in Latin America* (Stanford: Stanford University Press, 2000).

58 Arjun Appadurai, *Modernity at Large: Cultural Dimensions of Globalization* (Minneapolis: University of Minnesota Press, 1996), 54, 48, and passim.

59 For examples, see Mary Louise Pratt, "Why the Virgin of Zapopan Went to Los Angeles: Reflections on Mobility and Globality," in *Images of Power: Iconography, Culture, and the State in Latin America,* ed. Jens Andermann and William Rowe, 271-89 (New York: Berghahn Books, 2005); Jorge Duany, *The Puerto Rican Nation on the Move: Identities on the Island and in the United States* (Chapel Hill: University of North Carolina Press, 2002).

60 Paul Gilroy, *The Black Atlantic: Modernity and Double Consciousness* (Cambridge: Harvard University Press, 1993); John K. Thornton, *Africa and Africans in the Making of the Atlantic World, 1400–1800* (Cambridge: Cambridge University Press, 1998); Philip D. Morgan, "The Cultural Implications of the Atlantic Slave Trade: African Regional Origins, American Destinations, and New World Developments," *Slavery and Abolition* 18:1 (April 1997): 122–45.

61 Homi K. Bhabha, *The Location of Culture* (London: Routledge, 1994), 1–2; Néstor García Canclini, *Hybrid Cultures: Strategies for Entering and Leaving Modernity* (Minneapolis: University of Minnesota Press, 1995), 241.

62 Odile Hoffmann, "Collective Memory and Ethnic Identities in the Colombian Pacific," *Journal of Latin American Anthropology* 7:2 (2002): 118–39. For different approaches see Joanne Rappaport, "Redrawing the Nation: Indigenous Intellectuals and Ethnic Pluralism in Contemporary Colombia," in *After Spanish Rule: Postcolonial Predicaments of the Americas,* ed. Mark Thurner and Andrés Guerrero, 310-46 (Durham: Duke University Press, 2003); Peter Wade, "The Colombian Pacific in Perspective," *Journal of Latin American Anthropology* 7:2 (2002): 2–33.

63 Charles R. Hale, "Does Multiculturalism Menace? Governance, Cultural Rights and the Politics of Identity in Guatemala," *Journal of Latin American Studies* 34:3 (Aug. 2002): 485–524; Charles R. Hale, "Neoliberal Multiculturalism: The Remaking of Cultural Rights and Racial Dominance in Central America," *Political and Legal Anthropology Review* 28:1 (May 2005): 10–28. See also Virginia Q. Tilley, *Seeing Indians: A Study of Race, Nation, and Power in El Salvador* (Albuquerque: University of New Mexico Press, 2005); Juliet Hooker, "Indigenous Inclusion/Black Exclusion: Race, Ethnicity and Multicultural Citizenship in Latin America, *Journal of Latin American Studies* 37:2 (May 2005): 285–310; José Vinueza Almeida, "The Ecuadorian Indigenous Movement and the Gutiérrez Regime: The Traps of Multiculturalism," *Political and Legal Anthropology Review* 28:1 (May 2005): 93–111; and Julie Gibbings's chapter in this book.

64 Pierre Bourdieu and Loïc Wacquant, "On the Cunning of Imperialist Reason," *Theory, Culture, and Society* 16:1 (1999): 41–58. See also the critique by John D. French, "The Missteps of Anti-Imperialist Reason: Bourdieu, Wacquant, and Hanchard's *Orpheus and Power,*" *Theory, Culture, and Society* 17:1 (2000): 107–28.

65 Kay Warren and Jean Jackson, "Introduction: Studying Indigenous Activism in Latin America," in *Indigenous Movements, Self-Representation, and the State in Latin America* (Austin: University of Texas Press, 2002), 8–9; Jackson and Warren, "Indigenous Movements," 559–60. For impassioned critiques of this tendency in other contexts see Paul Gilroy, *Against Race: Imagining Political Culture beyond the Color Line* (Cambridge: Belknap Press of Harvard University Press, 2000), and Jean-François Bayart, *The Illusions of Cultural Identity,* trans. Steven Rendall et al. (Chicago: University of Chicago Press, 2005).

66 Les W. Field, "Beyond Identity? Analytic Crosscurrents in Contemporary Mayanist Social Science," *Latin American Research Review* 40:3 (Oct. 2005): 284.

67 Livio Sansone, *Blackness without Ethnicity: Constructing Race in Brazil* (New York: Palgrave Macmillan, 2003).

68 María Elena García, *Making Indigenous Citizens: Identity, Development, and Multicultural Activism in Peru* (Stanford: Stanford University Press, 2005), especially chapter 4.

69 Carmen Martínez Novo, *Who Defines Indigenous: Identities, Development, Intellectuals, and the State in Northern Mexico* (New Brunswick: Rutgers University Press, 2006), 4–6, 156–62.

Part 1:

Definging Nations

2

"Let Us Be Brazilians on the Day of Our Nationality":

INDEPENDENCE CELEBRATIONS IN RIO DE JANEIRO, 1840S−1860S

Hendrik Kraay[1]

INTRODUCTION

Before dawn on 7 September 1853, José Maria do Amaral "and some distinguished Brazilians" ascended the Corcovado peak and, at daybreak, resolved to found the Sociedade dos Cavaleiros do Ipiranga (Knights of Ipiranga Society). Its purposes were to commemorate Brazil's independence each 7 September, to construct "a grandiose monument" in honour of independence, "to develop and sustain the nationality," and to acquire documents and artifacts related to the "declaration of independence."[2] This patriotic society was formally established in 1855 as the Sociedade Ipiranga (Ipiranga Society); its first board of directors explained that its "patriotic and philanthropic ends are not limited to the puerile pastimes of a people without ideas, but are to immortalize the anniversary of the empire's independence each year with a significant act, in this way awakening patriotism, and with it, love of liberty and hatred of slavery." By 1856, the society counted almost 900 members, each of whom had paid six mil-réis (US$3.36) in dues.[3]

For a few years, the society stood in the forefront of major changes in the commemorations of Brazilian independence in the capital of Rio de Janeiro, which turned them into a large-scale street festival. Several other similar societies joined the Ipiranga in promoting commemorations. The size of these patriotic manifestations surprised contemporaries and raises important questions about the nature of mid-nineteenth-century Brazilians' engagement with the imperial state, the scope of the Brazilian nation constructed through these rituals, and the content of the Brazilian identity publicly expressed on the capital's streets and squares.

The celebrations of 7 September recalled the day in 1822 when Pedro, the son of the king of Portugal, publicly declared his break with the government in Lisbon. On the banks of the Ipiranga River in São Paulo, he responded to correspondence from Lisbon with a declaration of "Independence or Death," an event subsequently interpreted as the proclamation of independence and the founding moment of the Brazilian nation. In 1822, however, few paid much attention to this episode but, the following year, the ill-fated constituent assembly judged 7 September to be the "anniversary of independence." In 1826 it was included among the new empire's national holidays and, by the end of the decade, it had become firmly established as the premier "day of national festivity" in the capital.[4] Like all successful symbols, 7 September's strength lay in its polyvalent nature. On the one hand, it offered a suitably monarchical origin for the empire, celebrating the acts of the prince who proclaimed independence and, in 1824, granted a constitution. On the other hand, beginning in the late 1820s, radical liberals could interpret Pedro I's actions as his response to popular demands for a break with Portugal. In this view, the monarch was merely the Brazilian nation's servant and 7 September celebrated the people's role.[5]

Civic rituals offer rich perspectives on the complex processes of state- and nation-building and the formation of collective identities. They are at once "rites of power," liturgies through which authorities express and enact their claim to legitimate rule and potentially spaces in which opponents of the existing order of things make their claims publicly.[6] In newly-independent Latin American countries, civic rituals were important tools for elites who sought to create new nations.[7] But civic rituals also pose complex problems of interpretation. As Claudio Lomnitz-Adler explains, "national rituals and myths do indeed reveal general principles that operate in political society, but they cannot easily show the ways in which these principles articulate different social classes and groups within the nation." In other words, it remains difficult to assess the "effectiveness" of civic rituals in building nations or in fostering loyalty to the state.[8] Nevertheless, a close reading of both the practice of 7 September celebrations and, more important, the discourse surrounding them reveals much about Brazilians' understanding of their collective identity as members of the nation.

This chapter focuses on Rio de Janeiro during a relatively brief period from the 1840s to the early 1860s. The capital of the Brazilian empire was then a major commercial metropolis with a population of 206,000,

according to an 1849 census; two-thirds of the 79,000 slaves who laboured in the city were Africans.[9] A complex racial hierarchy, for the
most part not sanctioned by law, structured social relations among the
free. As the seat of government and of the Brazilian monarchy, Rio de
Janeiro had a strong state presence in comparison to the rest of Brazil.
In 1840, the fourteen-year-old Pedro II came to power; most of this
decade was dominated by campaigns against regional rebellions in the
far-flung empire. In 1849, the last of these movements was defeated and
the peaceful years of the 1850s and early 1860s are usually seen as the
imperial regime's apogee, a time when a general acceptance of imperial
political institutions prevailed.[10]

By the 1840s and early 1850s, 7 September celebrations had become
routine, state-run affairs with little space for the populace or for civil
society to participate. Only dim echoes of the early debates about 7
September's meaning could still be heard. The Sociedade Ipiranga and
the dozen or so similar societies founded in the mid-1850s transformed
the holiday, turning it into a three-day street festival that involved a significant proportion of the capital's population. Although short-lived, this
period of reinvigorated 7 September celebrations offers ample material
to analyze the understandings of the Brazilian nation publicly expressed
on city streets and in the more restricted spaces of commemoration such
as the theatre. In its public ritual manifestations, the Brazilian nation
was a "civilized" one, whose superior political institutions ensured the
country's orderly progress. The nation embraced a relatively broad spectrum of the urban population, but the celebrations nevertheless marked
clear boundaries between Brazilians and those excluded from the nation
– Africans, vagrants, Indians, and slaves (although the latter, if Brazilian-
born, might be incorporated in subordinate fashion).

IN THE CUSTOMARY WAY:
COMMEMORATIONS IN THE 1840S AND EARLY 1850S

By the 1840s, there was a well-established routine for major civic rituals
and newspapers regularly recorded that 7 September celebrations took
place "in the customary way." The city awoke to artillery salutes from its
forts and warships, which were repeated at noon and at dusk. In 1842,
Prussian Prince Adalbert accompanied the young Emperor Pedro II for
the entire day and provided a lengthy description of the official celebrations. He watched the green-and-yellow-uniformed National Guard form
up on the "somewhat desolate-looking" Santana field, a large square and
parade ground on the city's outskirts. That day, Pedro laid the cornerstone for an orphanage, after which Adalbert accompanied him in the

procession into the city from his suburban palace. The streets were "filled with people; at all the corners were gathered groups of black slaves, to greet the emperor; all shades of colour were here seen collected, from the negro and mulatto to the half-brown or white dandy." After the Te Deum mass in the imperial chapel, Pedro reviewed the troops from the downtown palace's balcony as they filed by and fired salutes. This was followed by a levee, during which "the military and civil authorities … advanced in different corps to kiss the emperor's hand," the so-called *beija-mão*, or hand-kissing. The official celebrations ended with a theatre gala, which Adalbert also attended (see below).[11]

Through the early 1850s, 7 September celebrations followed this pattern. The procession, Te Deum, military parade, and levee and beija-mão were repeated year after year (except when heavy rains, as in 1850 and 1855, or elections caused the government to cancel the parade), as were the usual morning, noon, and night artillery salutes. Such rites of power offered little space for most of the city's population, reduced to spectators. The citizenry – males who earned above a minimum income – were carefully regimented in the National Guard. The monarch played a central role in all of the ceremonies and formally received obeisance from the city's elite during the levee; less formally, he received it from the crowds that greeted him as he entered the city. Many aspects of this ritual derived from old-regime practices, yet surprisingly few historians have connected colonial monarchical rituals to those of the independent empire.[12]

At least as important as the actual ritual practice was the discourse about it. Lengthy newspaper essays explained 7 September's significance and thereby gave meaning to the ritual, as well as contributing to the creation of an "imagined community" of Brazilians.[13] From the mid-1840s to the early 1850s, there was relatively little press debate about 7 September's meaning. Newspapers placed more or less emphasis on Pedro I's actions, but rarely questioned his role. They repeatedly proclaimed that 7 September celebrated both independence and the constitution. It was the day, explained one newspaper, on which "a magnanimous prince . . . inaugurated a [nation's] life of independence and liberty."[14] Independence was, according to another, the "magnificent work of a truly liberal prince, aided in his heroic efforts by the patriotism and enlightened [actions] of many distinguished Brazilians."[15] Brazil's success at avoiding anarchy and revolution through constitutional monarchy was an example for her unfortunate republican neighbours, exulted still another newspaper in 1854.[16] That year, the campaign to erect a monument to Pedro I as founder of the empire, which had sputtered along since the 1820s, finally resumed in earnest, and would result, eight years later, in the inauguration of the

2.1. Equestrian Statue of Emperor Pedro I (Inaugurated in 1862), 2001
Source: Photo by Hendrik Kraay.

equestrian statue on Constitution Square (today Tiradentes Square). The monument's design – Pedro I on horseback holding up the constitution – reflected the dominant view of the first emperor as both proclaimer of independence and grantor of the constitution (Figure 2.1).[17]

A second theme in discussions of 7 September's meaning was the importance of progress. In 1845, shortly after the negotiated end to the long-running Farroupilha Rebellion in Rio Grande do Sul, *O Mercantil* proclaimed that Brazil, under its constitutional monarchy, now advanced along the "road of progress toward peaceful conquests in the arts, in civilization, and in moral and material prosperity."[18] The opening of a new waterworks in 1851 provided the occasion for congratulatory rhetoric about Brazil's progress; not even London, explained one columnist, had as sophisticated a water system.[19] Others might lament that Brazil had not progressed sufficiently. In 1843, *O Echo do Rio* declared that Brazil was still "very far from where she should be" and, two years after its optimistic assessment of Brazil's prospects, *O Mercantil* lamented the lack of material progress and called on Brazilians to unite to raise their country to the status of the "cultured nations of Europe."[20]

Since the 1820s, radical liberals had tended to downplay Pedro I's role in the achievement of independence; rather, they stressed its popular origins and argued that the monarch had merely followed the popular lead (and that, in fact, popular pressure obliged him to grant the constitution). *O Mercantil* expressed this view in moderate form in 1845, when it explained that Pedro had "adhered to Brazilians' ardent desires" in 1822.[21] In their heyday of the early 1830s, radical liberals had mounted elaborate 7 September celebrations that largely ignored the monarch. They found anti-Portuguese nativism to be a powerful means of popular mobilization – the gouging Portuguese shopkeeper was a favoured target of lower-class opprobrium – and, for radical liberals, popular involvement in 7 September celebrations demonstrated true patriotism.[22]

In 1848, radical liberals took to the streets on 7 September during bitterly contested municipal elections. According to conservative newspapers, their demonstrations amounted to little more than "sinister shouts of 'long live' and 'death to' by a torch-lit mob of rabble." Apparently the demonstration had been planned in advance, for the protesters had arranged for bands to accompany them as they paraded through downtown parishes. The following day, this turned into isolated nativist patriot attacks on Portuguese nationals, to which the police quickly put a stop. The moderate liberal *Correio Mercantil* claimed that the crowd simply cheered "the objects of our veneration" on 7 September, condemned the isolated "imprudent shouts," and denied that anti-Portuguese agitation was justified. A few days later, this newspaper lamented that the government had invoked a law that banned illicit gatherings in order to "disperse those who were celebrating 7 September with cheers and music," a view that ephemeral radical liberal newspapers expressed much more vigorously than the *Correio*.[23]

At stake on 7 September 1848 was the role of "the people" – a vaguely-defined category – in the Brazilian nation. For conservative newspapers, it was too dangerous to have uncontrolled groups of people, however patriotic, on the streets on national holidays, for they might gain control of the symbolic expressions of the nation, not to mention perpetrate violent acts. Two stalwarts of Rio de Janeiro political journalism debated this issue once more in 1854. Antônio Borges da Fonseca, an old radical liberal, lamented that 7 September had passed "with neither commemoration nor enthusiasm," to which the conservative Justiniano José da Rocha retorted that Borges da Fonseca only saw as true national festivals those on which "bands of common people run the streets shouting, among vivas, death threats." Brazil had last seen such a festival on 7 September 1848 but now the nation recognized the need for peace and progress. Today no one believed the "revolutionary treachery" that had convinced the youth that "absurd recolonization plans were afoot," so there were no pretexts nor justifications for "noisy demonstrations."[24] Borges da Fonseca responded that, in fact, Brazil was still not free of the Portuguese and pointed out that the United States celebrated its independence enthusiastically, as did Bahians on 2 July. In Rio de Janeiro, "not a single lantern was set out, for this city belongs to the Portuguese."[25]

A STRAW BLAZE? CELEBRATIONS IN THE 1850S AND 1860S

Within a year or two of Borges da Fonseca's lament, 7 September celebrations in the capital experienced a remarkable resurgence. The Sociedade Ipiranga led the way, followed by at least a dozen other societies that took on the task of rejuvenating traditional forms of commemoration and instituting new traditions. In 1855 and subsequent years, the Sociedade Ipiranga requested that residents once again illuminate the windows of their houses in honour of independence, the traditional colonial custom whose disappearance Borges da Fonseca had lamented.[26] In 1856 and 1857, the Sociedade Ipiranga prepared detailed programs for the celebrations. At dawn on 7 September, a band would play the independence anthem on Constitution Square, the locale designated for the equestrian statue of Pedro I. At the same time, fireworks from the city's hills would announce the start of the festivities, along with artillery salutes from the forts and ships in the harbour. This would be repeated at 1:00 pm and at dusk. A deputation from the society was designated to attend the levee, and at 4:00 pm the society would hold a Te Deum at the Ordem Terceira do Carmo's chapel. After this, the entire society would parade to the city council chambers to pay homage to the portrait of Pedro I. The society hired bands to play outside the council building and, in 1856, planned a fireworks display for after the theatre gala. The following year, it planned fireworks for 9 September.[27] Other societies did similar things. The Sociedade Independência Brasileira (Brazilian Independence Society) claimed São Domingos Square as the locale of its festival and raised temporary monuments (*iluminações*) in 1857 and 1858, by which time it was calling them customary celebrations.[28]

The newspaper accounts of the second half of the 1850s all concur that these societies' efforts transformed 7 September. Whereas a *Jornal do Comércio* columnist judged the 1855 celebrations as "insipid, very insipid," the following year he could barely contain himself as he described the "din of happiness," led by the Sociedade Artista Nacional (National Artisan Society) and the Sociedade Ipiranga. The artisans' society constructed a triumphal arch on the Largo do Paço (the square outside of the downtown palace), while the Sociedade Ipiranga celebrated on Constitution Square. Numerous public and private buildings were illuminated. The usual official ritual took place, with the exception of the traditional National Guard parade, but all eyes were on what newspapers called the "popular festivals."[29] In 1857, explained one newspaper columnist, Rio de Janeiro enjoyed "three nights of illuminations, salutes, girandoles and rockets until we couldn't stand them anymore, philharmonics in band shells and on the streets, dinners and patriotic gatherings, and finally, a fireworks display in front of city hall, in the presence of their imperial majesties."[30] In 1858, the entire royal family visited many of the monuments and street festivals on foot.[31] The celebrations began even earlier in 1859. At midnight, hundreds of girandoles lit up the sky; "thousands of citizens of all classes and stations" rose well before sunrise "to greet the dawning of the nation's greatest day." On Constitution Square, one society had constructed a fountain, topped by a bust of Pedro I, and supported by the four great rivers of Brazil (the Amazon, Plata, Tocantins, and São Francisco), surrounded by twenty pillars with stars representing the provinces. Other societies likewise put up ephemeral allegorical structures. Bands and delegations from patriotic societies circulated through the streets, visiting each other's celebrations and attracting crowds.[32]

At the same time, neighbourhood committees began raising funds and organizing 7 September celebrations. In 1858 and 1859, residents of several districts requested permission from the city council to construct monuments and fireworks platforms in city streets; others set up band shells and arranged for music.[33] Criticism of the neighbourhood committees' efforts occasionally surfaced; in 1857, "O Oprimido" (The Oppressed One) complained that too many of these subscriptions were organized by city councillors and other officials who, backed by a detachment of municipal guards, intimidated residents into contributing to the celebrations.[34] Still others worried that the proliferation of celebrations was diluting the commemorations, while a satirical newspaper announced – tongue-in-cheek – in 1859 that a triumphal arch would be erected between the Santa Cruz and São João forts, located on opposite sides of the entrance to the bay![35]

The dominant discourse of these celebrations denied divisions among Brazilians. The author of a 7 September proclamation called on his fellow countrymen "to be Brazilians on the day of our nationality," and the *Jornal do Comércio*'s columnist explained that it was "a day to recall the most beautiful achievement, a day in which all party differences disappear ... a day in which all are truly brothers in the fatherland (*pátria*)."[36] Several small and short-lived opposition newspapers repeated familiar radical liberal themes of government despotism and anti-Portuguese nativism during these years, but apparently had no impact on the celebrations. In 1857, *O Tirano* denounced the violence visited on National Guardsmen by their officers, complained that the police arrested people indiscriminately "during the three days of celebrating liberty," and lamented the fate of "the poor citizens, enslaved by [the government's] despotism," incarcerated on the *Presiganga* (prison hulk), itself decorated in honour of Brazilian independence. Condemnations of foreign (Portuguese) control of commerce and the lack of a free franchise were also wrapped in 7 September patriotism.[37]

For no apparent reason, this outburst of patriotic commemoration declined almost as abruptly as it had burst onto the scene. The celebrations of 1860 were "less brilliant" than those of previous years, but the *Jornal do Comércio*'s columnist consoled himself with the peaceful elections of that day, proof of the country's orderly progress.[38] In 1861, the *Revista Popular* declared that, "sad and dispirited, the greatest Brazilian day has descended into the abyss of the past." Those who, only a few years earlier, had doubted the durability of the "false flame of improvised patriotism" had been right when they dismissed it as a "straw blaze."[39] The following year, things were little better. One newspaper castigated the Sociedade Ipiranga for doing little more than putting up two band shells beside the newly-inaugurated equestrian statue and hastily dismantling them the next day. More charitably, another newspaper reported that a few diehards from this society and the Sociedade Festival Sete de Setembro (7 September Festival Society) rose early to greet the statue at dawn. Even Emperor Pedro II marvelled at the "indifference with which today was celebrated this year, in light of the enthusiasm of a few years ago." *O Espectador da América do Sul* agreed with this assessment in 1863: "We no longer have those popular festivals of independence in which, formerly, the people, all heart, remembered, almost with tenderness, the birthday of their collective mother." That year, the Sociedade Ipiranga ceased to collect dues and announced that it would not promote any further commemorations.[40]

REMAKING STREETS AND SOCIETY:
ENVISIONING BRAZIL, 1856–1859

The sudden rise and fall of these 7 September commemorations remain as mysterious today as they were to contemporaries. Clearly these celebrations differed in important ways from the radical liberal demonstrations of 1848; popular participation there was, but it did not challenge the government. A close analysis of the celebrations of the late 1850s reveals key aspects of the Brazil envisioned by the festival's organizers which, newspapers implicitly suggested, received popular approbation through participation in the celebrations.

Virtually nothing is known about the leaders or the rank-and-file of the societies who led the celebrations of the late 1850s. I have found no membership lists and only a few indications of who their directors were. To judge by its name, the Artisans' Society included men from that class of the population; the membership dues levied by the Sociedade Ipiranga, though relatively modest, would have excluded most of the city's population. Prominent figures in this society included Manoel de Araújo Porto Alegre, director of the fine arts academy and a leading figure in the city's cultural elite who enjoyed Pedro II's patronage; he repeatedly served as the society's official orator. Antônio Borges da Fonseca also supported the society by printing its statutes for free.[41]

Further indications of the class to which these celebrations appealed – and thereby the limits of the nation envisioned in them – can be found in the 7 September newspaper coverage. Above all, the press stressed that the celebrations were orderly and peaceful. Scarcely a year passed without newspapers commenting that the large crowds had behaved in orderly fashion, a back-handed indication of how worrisome large gatherings could be. Moreover, there were no manifestations of the "dangerous theories of a poorly-understood liberalism," such as those of 1848.[42]

Closely related to the concept of order was that of respectability. Nighttime street celebrations required major changes to this public space, normally neither safe nor considered appropriate places for "respectable" middle- and upper-class members of society.[43] Those who lived and worked on the streets were also obstacles. The female food-sellers (likely Africans) of Capim Square had to move in 1858 to make way for the erection of a triumphal arch and one newspaper hoped that the government would make their removal permanent.[44] Light figured prominently in this transformation of public space. The illuminations, both the temporary monuments and the practice of lighting candles and lanterns in front windows, made it possible for gentlemen and ladies (*senhores* and *senhoras*) to frequent the celebrations. Their impact in an era of inadequate street lighting was much greater than we might suppose. In the week leading up to 7 September, stores did brisk business in a lush variety of lamps carefully described in detailed newspaper advertisements. Manoel Olegário Abranches's shop was the leading "innovator in good taste" to replace the "wretched oil lamp" with "an elegant light" like that used in Paris.[45] Accounts of experimental demonstrations of electric lighting reveal a fascination with new technologies that could turn night into day.[46]

But only new and modern forms of lighting were acceptable. Plans for massive bonfires on the hills surrounding the city elicited a vigorous condemnation in 1856. The author of a letter to the editor condemned this "insane plan," for 7 September should never be celebrated, he concluded, "with bonfires like those [holidays] of savages or country bumpkins (*gente da roça*)."[47] Not surprisingly, bonfires were never again lit during this period. Other types of celebration that belied the image of civilization so painfully being constructed in the capital were also unwelcome. In 1845, the *Jornal do Comércio* complained of the bands of *capoeiras* (practitioners of violent forms of this Afro-Brazilian martial art) who joined the crowds and terrorized respectable citizens, but no amount of police repression could put an end to this practice and occasional arrests of *capoeira* practitioners were recorded during the celebrations.[48] What underlay these concerns was the fervent desire that "the foreigners who share our enthusiasm have no reason to find fault with our knowledge, civilization, and progress."[49]

The transformation of public space was, however, only temporary and, during the early-morning liminal period as the celebrations wound down, the street returned to its former condition. Respectable celebrants who failed to return home on time ran risks. In 1857, a group of shop clerks insulted a woman as she was returning home with her husband.[50] A more serious incident took place in 1859 when the police arrested a Spaniard who had been making "offensive jokes" and insulting "ladies" (*senhoras*) who were leaving the celebrations on Constitution Square. He offended one "woman" (*mulher*) with an "indecent act"; before her escort could respond, police arrested the Spaniard. A crowd numbering about two hundred people gathered, some shouting for the man's release, others cheering the police's actions. As the crowd dispersed, one group proceeded to vandalize the darkened fountain constructed for the celebrations, amid shouts of "death to the chief of police." Members of the society that had built the monument were enjoying a late-night dinner at a nearby house and rushed to protect their handiwork. They tried unsuccessfully to calm the mob by explaining that it was wrong to destroy "a structure raised in celebration of independence." Finally the police cavalry moved in and arrested twenty-five men: "thirteen Brazilians of low condition," ten unemployed Portuguese shop clerks, one Frenchman, and one slave. The *Jornal do Comércio* denied any political significance to the vandalism, explaining that it had been perpetrated by "vagrants and rowdies of the sort that abound in all cities in order to give the police something to do." Another newspaper condemned the police's excessive use of force against the populace.[51]

As the newspaper made clear, the Brazilian nation necessarily excluded many, and they needed to be controlled by the police. The issue of slavery also raised questions about the Brazil envisaged by the 7 September celebrants. Back in 1855, the Sociedade Ipiranga's founders had declared that they would promote the "love of liberty and hatred of slavery." At the time, no active antislavery movement existed in Brazil, although British subventions had made possible the publication of abolitionist newspapers and some small antislavery societies had existed early in the decade.[52] News that the society planned to free slaves on 7 September 1856 caused a stir in the city. Rumours spread among the "lowest classes" that all slaves would be freed that day.[53] Undeterred, the society drew five names by lot from "the large number of slaves" whose names had been proposed by the membership and whose owners were willing to part with them on easy terms. All were women, something that the society had stipulated, and three were identified as *pardas* (mulatto women); in these respects they were typical of the slaves who gained manumission.[54] Dubious about the proceedings, the *Correio da Tarde*'s columnist worried that, without continued support, the women would fall into prostitution.[55] His counterpart at the *Correio Mercantil*, however, wholeheartedly supported the manumissions, for the newly-freed would forever associate "the greatest day of their lives with the greatest day in the history of a people."[56]

Despite the controversies of 1856, the following year, the Sociedade Ipiranga and the parish committees that it organized managed to raise sufficient funds to free twenty-two slaves who, as the *Jornal do Comércio*'s columnist exulted, "thus entered into the great assembly of this nation for which the philosophical and Christian dogma of brotherhood and human equality is not a theory questioned by prideful prejudice."[57] The Sociedade Independência Nacional (National Independence Society) was founded that year with the express purpose of freeing slaves (and promoting "popular festivities") on 7 September.[58] Despite the enthusiasm of 1857, patriotic manumissions did not continue and would not become a major feature of civic rituals until the 1880s when a resurgent abolitionist movement sensed that slavery's end was near. No society, in fact, freed slaves in 1858 or in the next three years (and only one newspaper commented on their failure to do so). The last 7 September manumission took place in 1862, when the cash-strapped Sociedade Conservadora Sete de Setembro (7 September Conservation Society) found itself with insufficient funds to put on a public celebration and opted to spend its last monies on freeing a slave boy.[59] In short, freeing slaves was too dangerous an action at a time when slavery was still flourishing.

Civilization, respectability, worry about foreigners' perceptions, concern to exclude anything that smacked of African or Indian Brazil, and doubts about manumission, all suggest that the large-scale celebrations of 1856–59 remained firmly under the control of Brazil's elite. To be sure, there was popular participation of a sort, but the rhetoric of nationality excluded Africans and Indians and anything that did not live up to the standards of an idealized civilization. Only orderly, apolitical crowds were welcome at the commemorations; at best, the people could be subordinate members of the nation. A closer look at middle- and upper-class activities on 7 September provides another way of approaching this question of what the celebrations meant for those involved.

FROM HOME TO THEATRE:
MIDDLE AND UPPER-CLASS SOCIABILITY

During the 1850s, opportunities for respectable middle- and upper-class 7 September activities proliferated. Advertisements for flute and piano music, including variations on the independence anthem and a "triumphal march for piano," complete with a portrait of Pedro I, indicate domestic celebrations.[60] The Hotel da França, located on the Largo do Paço, offered specials on its veranda for "respectable (*honradas*) families and society" to watch the "celebrations and magnificent illuminations" in security and comfort.[61] Some of the patriotic societies of the 1850s put on balls, as did private establishments.[62]

A series of tongue-in-cheek articles in the *Periódico dos Pobres* offers glimpses into a middle-class family's activities on 7 September in the early 1850s. Living on the parade route, they were frequently importuned by relatives who wanted to watch from the windows and ended up staying for dinner. The parade was the occasion for much flirting, as windows overlooking the streets were "crammed with the fair sex." "It was all merriment [and] conversation, sometimes about this or that fellow who marched by ... or about fashion and courting, etc." Buildings along the parade route were, in 1851, "elegantly decorated with rich tapestries and very pretty girls dressed in their finest." In 1850, a year in which the parade was rained out, "D. Mathias" attended the levee, after which he and his wife had dinner with a "glass of good wine to toast the independence of Brazil."[63]

That night, he resolved to attend the gala at the São Pedro de Alcântara Theatre (Figure 2.2), but much to his disgust, had to pay three mil-réis

2.2. São Pedro de Alcântara Theatre, *ca.* 1835
Source: G.^{me} Theremin, *Saudades do Rio de Janeiro dedicadas a S.M.D.n Pedro II, Imperador Constitucional e Defensor Perpetuo do Brazil* (Berlin: L. Schase, n.d. [*ca.* 1835]).

(US$1.74) instead of the two mil-réis (US$1.16) advertised ticket price. The ticket booth was nothing more than a "fish-market booth for mocking and ripping off the people at will," a repeated complaint about the city's theatres.[64] "D. Mathias" nevertheless paid the scalpers' premium and joined the imperial family, most of the city's elite, and a good part of its middle class in one of the most traditional aspects of 7 September sociability. While upper-class women viewed the theatre gala from their boxes, most of the audience was, like "D. Mathias," male, and paid the relatively modest price for seats on the floor, from which women were excluded.[65]

Back in the 1810s, the theatre had emerged as a key locus of political activity, and while its importance diminished somewhat in the 1820s as parliament and a free press emerged, the theatre gala remained an important barometer of the political mood.[66] All of the city's theatres put on special gala spectacles on major civic holidays, but the one attended by the royal family enjoyed the most prestige. The basic program changed little during these years. Upon the monarchs' arrival at their box, the orchestra would play the national anthem or the independence anthem to accompany the prima donna (or the entire opera company) who sang the words. The anthem was apparently not sung collectively by the audience. After this, a series of cheers involved the entire audience; in 1850, they unanimously hailed the Brazilian nation, the constitution, the monarch, and the imperial dynasty.[67] The cheers might be interrupted by poets who recited verse in honour of the day, either from the floor or from boxes. The centrepiece of the evening was usually a European opera or drama, but it might be preceded or followed by a short allegory in honour of 7 September or a dance intermezzo.

The cheers and the poetry were, to some degree, unscripted. Often, poets distributed leaflets with their verses beforehand, and these later appeared in the press. In 1850, "D. Mathias" heard Antônio José Nunes Garcia's cloying sonnet, which included the following lines:

> Se de PEDRO nós veio hoje a existência
> Outorgando o Brasil melífluo favo
> De nossas plagas exime o ser d'escravo
> Dando-nos o renome, a Independência
> . . .
> O Filho de PEDRO herói!! PEDRO Segundo!!
> Brasileiro Monarca! Egrégio, forte
> De virtudes tantas, de saber profundo
> Eternisará a Independência do Sul té o Norte.

> If our existence came from PEDRO
> Granting Brazil the sweet honeycomb
> Removing from our shores the condition of slave
> Giving us prestige, independence
> . . .
> The son of PEDRO the hero!! PEDRO the second!!
> Brazilian monarch! Illustrious, mighty
> Of many virtues, of profound wisdom
> Will eternalize independence from South to North.

Garcia stumbled over his words, "but concluded very well."[68] Eight years earlier, Adalbert commented that some of the five poets "seemed to have learned their task by heart imperfectly."[69] The opera performances varied in quality. In 1852, Gaetano Donizetti's *Betly* "was good for nothing," and narrowly escaped "a tremendous boo" from the disgruntled audience (spectators contained themselves out of respect for the royal family), but Giuseppe Verdi's *Attila* was more successful the following year, as was his *Il Trovatore* in 1854.[70] The audience's restraint in 1852, part of a tradition of not applauding performances on 7 September, so that cheers and applause be reserved solely for the glory of the day itself, fell by the wayside in 1855. Fans of the prima donnas loudly called for them to return to the stage after the performance of Vincenzo Bellini's *Norma*. The Teatro Lírico's manager permitted them to do so and was immediately arrested by the police delegate, prompting a flood of letters to the editor of the *Correio Mercantil*. Some claimed that there had been a plot to have the manager, himself a Portuguese native, applauded, which would have been an insult to Brazilians.[71]

Amid this debate, the *Correio Mercantil*'s columnist pointed out that, in fact, the arts had not yet been "nationalized." That year all of the city's theatres had put on foreign productions for 7 September and most of the performers (including the prima donnas) were foreigners. Was it not ridiculous, he wondered, that foreign performers sang the independence anthem with its lines, "Or leave the fatherland free/Or die for Brazil" (*Ou deixar a pátria livre/Ou morrer pelo Brasil*)? Moreover the man who sang the line, "Brave Brazilian people" (*Brava gente brasileira*), laughed as he did so – the "rascal" knew that, in Italian, the phrase "*brava gente*" could mean "imbeciles."[72] Enrico Tamberlick, the Italian tenor who sang the anthem the following year, had better patriotic bona fides; the audience erupted in cheers as he pronounced the words "homeland" (*pátria*) and "independence," for he had fought for Italian independence.[73] The first Brazilian opera to be staged on 7 September in Rio de Janeiro was Carlos Gomes's *A Noite do Castelo* in 1861.[74]

Much less well-known than these operas were the occasional "dramatic laudations" (*elogios dramáticos*) that sought to make a political point or express patriotic values.[75] In 1853, the Teatro Provisório's performance of *Attila* would be followed by a new "allegorical divertissement" or "allegorical dance," entitled *A glória do Brasil* (*The Glory of Brazil*). It featured a male portraying Brazil and five female dancers playing the parts of Liberty, Philosophy, Ignorance, Treason, and Despotism, along with numerous furies and nymphs. The plot involved Brazil being freed from the clutches of Ignorance, Treason, and Despotism by the timely intervention of Liberty and Philosophy, a transparent celebration of the elite view of the imperial regime. The *Correio Mercantil*'s columnist derided it as a "ridiculous little farce," in which Brazil was played by "a big guy dressed in shreds with tin handcuffs on his wrists and a rag on his head." The "strumpet" (*menina loureira*) who played the part of Philosophy looked like one of those women who impoverished many a Brazilian man as she danced around Brazil "displaying her legs [and] showing a delicate little foot."[76]

Only once during the 1840s and 1850s did the theatre gala include a play directly based on historical events. In 1840, the São Pedro de Alcântara Theatre staged G. J. de M. Pimentel's *A expulsão dos holandezes ou O*

heroismo brasileiro (*The Expulsion of the Dutch or Brazilian Heroism*).
The only description of the performance comes from a critic whose account suggests that the playwright had presented an interpretation that
challenged Brazilian social hierarchies. He disliked the prominent role
given to Henrique Dias, the black hero of these seventeenth-century wars
in Pernambuco, for he was an African, and not a Brazilian, and because
"some of what he said at the start on behalf of blacks (*pretos*) appeared
to be a bit subversive." Moreover, the play portrayed Indians as uncor-
rupted until the arrival of Europeans. The critic declared that Brazilians
were neither black nor Indian and thanked God for the "European blood"
in his veins. Statements that the land belonged to Indians were tanta-
mount to inviting Botocudo chiefs to rule over Rio de Janeiro. All of this,
concluded the critic, was an insult to the royal family, "whose grandeur
and majesty all come from its European lineage (*sangue*), illustrious and
ancient."[77] More explicitly than virtually anyone else, the critic expressed
the view of Brazilian society enacted during the theatre gala. To be sure,
the elite etiquette about race meant that such explicit assertions of racial
identity rarely found public expression in the press, but it was latent in
much of the 7 September commemoration.[78]

The theatre thus served several purposes. It offered an occasion for
members of the elite to be seen publicly and to associate with the emperor.
Together they participated in European high culture and expressed their
political allegiances. The clumsy allegories and pompous poetry reflected
the view that the theatre was a didactic institution whose task was to
improve the people's culture and civilization. Just as this project, most
closely associated with realism, ultimately failed, the allegories' didactic
effect was probably limited for the capital's sophisticated theatre-going
audiences.[79]

CONCLUSION

Writing in the late 1880s, folklorist Alexandre José de Melo Moraes Filho
declared that, about thirty years earlier, "the celebrations of Independence
... were ostentatious and were distinguished by popular devotion" to them.
But the Paraguayan War (1864–70), "the liquidation of Brazilian patriotism," started a decline in patriotic culture and only silence remained.[80]
While no doubt Melo Moraes had seen many changes during his lifetime,
what he described as typical 7 September celebrations were, in fact, the
distinct commemorations of the late 1850s, and their decline had preceded the war.

Officially, the 7 September commemorations of the 1840s and 1850s
presented an argument about Brazilian national identity that stressed

the country's superior monarcho-constitutional institutions granted by Pedro I, secured by Pedro II, and embraced by its orderly population. What Africans, slaves, and the lower classes who struggled to survive in the city thought about the celebrations (which they could not have missed) remains difficult to elucidate. We can only speculate on the inconveniences suffered by the food-sellers evicted in 1858 (and wonder whether they profited from sales to the evening crowds). Similarly, we can only speculate on the motives of those who vandalized the temporary fountain. Brazilian historians have argued that there was a reciprocal influence between popular festivals and civic rituals, especially in understandings of the monarchy.[81] While highly suggestive, this interpretation remains difficult to demonstrate through the 7 September celebrations, which clearly differed from popular festivals. Still, the rapid decline of the 7 September commemorations in the early 1860s may well indicate the limits of this nationalism's appeal.

NOTES TO CHAPTER 2

1 Research for this chapter was supported by the Social Sciences and Humanities Research Council (Canada), the University Research Grants Committee (University of Calgary), a Killam Resident Fellowship (University of Calgary), and a Professor Visitante Estrangeiro fellowship from Brazil's Coordenação de Aperfeiçoamento de Pessoal de Nível Superior (held at the Universidade Federal do Rio de Janeiro). Sonya Marie Scott provided research assistance in 1999–2000. I thank José Murilo de Carvalho for his comments on an earlier version, which was also presented at the Conference on Latin American History, Washington, January 2004; and at the history departments of the Pontifícia Universidade Católica do Rio de Janeiro (October 2004) and the Universidade Federal de Minas Gerais, Belo Horizonte (November 2004). All of the newspapers cited were published in Rio de Janeiro.

2 *Correio Mercantil*, 7 Sep. 1854.

3 "Relatório dos trabalhos da directoria provisoria," *Correio Mercantil*, 23 March 1857.

4 Sessions of 5 and 9 Sep. 1823, *Diário da Assembléa Geral Constituinte e Legislativa do Império do Brasil, 1823*, vol. 1, facsimile ed. (Brasília: Senado Federal, 1972), 722, 733; Lei, 9 Sep. 1826, *Coleção das Leis do Império do Brasil*. See also Lúcia Maria Bastos Pereira das Neves, *Corcundas e constitucionais: A cultura política da Independência (1820–1822)* (Rio de Janeiro: FAPERJ and Revan, 2003), 369–70.

5 Maria de Lourdes Viana Lyra, "Memória da Independência: Marcos e representações simbólicas," *Revista Brasileira de História* 15:29 (1995): 173–206; Hendrik Kraay, "Nação, Estado e política popular no Rio de Janeiro: Rituais cívicos depois da Independência," in *Nacionalismo no Novo Mundo*, ed. Don Doyle and Marco Pamplona, forthcoming.

6 Sean Wilentz, ed., *Rites of Power: Symbolism, Ritual, and Politics since the Middle Ages* (Philadelphia: University of Pennsylvania Press, 1999); John R. Gillis, ed., *Commemorations: The Politics of National Identity* (Princeton: Princeton University Press, 1994); David I. Kertzer, *Ritual, Politics, and Power* (New Haven: Yale University Press, 1988).

7 William H. Beezley and David E. Lorey, eds., !Viva Mexico! !Viva La Independencia! Celebrations of September 16 (Wilmington: Scholarly Resources, 2001); Rebecca Earle, "'Padres de la Patria' and the Ancestral Past: Commemorations of Independence in Nineteenth-Century Spanish America," Journal of Latin American Studies 34:4 (Nov. 2002): 775–806.

8 Claudio Lomnitz-Adler, Exits from the Labyrinth: Culture and Ideology in the Mexican National Space (Berkeley: University of California Press, 1992), 6. On this point, see also Ângela Miranda Cardoso, "Ritual: Princípio, meio e fim. Do sentido do estudo das cerimônias de entronização brasileiras," in Brasil: formação do Estado e da nação, ed. István Jancsó, 549–602 (São Paulo: HUCITEC, Ed. UNIJUÍ, and FAPESP, 2003).

9 Mary C. Karasch, Slave Life in Rio de Janeiro, 1808–1850 (Princeton: Princeton University Press, 1987), 66.

10 On the political history of this period, see the relevant chapters in Roderick J. Barman, Brazil: The Forging of a Nation, 1798–1852 (Stanford: Stanford University Press, 1988); see also his Citizen Emperor: Pedro II and the Making of Brazil, 1825–1891 (Stanford: Stanford University Press, 1999).

11 Prince Adalbert, Travels of His Royal Highness Prince Adalbert of Prussia, vol. 1 (London: David Bogue, 1849), 270–79. See also Jornal do Commercio, 8–9 Sep. 1842.

12 On colonial rituals, see István Jancsó and Iris Kantor, eds., Festa: Cultura e sociabilidade na América portuguesa, 2 vols. (São Paulo: EDUSP, 2001); on the continuities between late-colonial and early-imperial civic rituals, see Iara Lis Carvalho Souza, Pátria coroada: O Brasil como corpo político autônomo, 1780–1831 (São Paulo: Editora da UNESP, 1998).

13 Benedict Anderson, Imagined Communities: Reflections on the Origin and Spread of Nationalism, rev. ed. (London: Verso, 1991).

14 O Americano, 8 Sep. 1849. See also Correio do Brazil, 7 Sep. 1852; O Pavilhão Nacional, 7 Sep. 1850.

15 O Social, 9 Sep. 1845. See also O Tempo, 10 Sep. 1846.

16 O Brado do Amazonas, 7 Sep. 1854. See also O Brasil, 10 Sep. 1850.

17 Maria Eurydice de Barros Ribeiro, "Memória em bronze: Estátua eqüestre de D. Pedro I," in Cidade vaidosa: imagens urbanas do Rio de Janeiro, ed. Paulo Knauss, 15-28 (Rio de Janeiro: Sette Letras, 1999); James N. Green, "The Emperor on His Pedestal: Pedro I and Disputed Views of the Brazilian Nation, 1860–1900," in Brazil in the Making: Facets of National Identity, ed. Carmen Nava and Ludwig Lauerhass, Jr., 181-202 (Lanham: Rowman and Littlefield, 2006).

18 O Mercantil, 8 Sep. 1845.

19 "Ao amigo ausente," Jornal do Commercio, 7 Sep. 1851. See also Correio da Tarde, 9 Sep. 1851.

20 O Echo do Rio, 9 Sep. 1843; O Mercantil, 7 Sep. 1847.

21 O Mercantil, 8 Sep. 1845.

22 Gladys Sabino Ribeiro, A liberdade em construção: Identidade nacional e conflitos antilusitanos no Primeiro Reinado (Rio de Janeiro: Relume-Dumará, 2002); Jeffrey C. Mosher, "Political Mobilization, Party Ideology, and Lusophobia in Nineteenth-Century Brazil: Pernambuco, 1822–1850," Hispanic American Historical Review 80:4 (Nov. 2000): 881–912; Kraay, "Nação."

23 Correio da Tarde, 9 Sep. 1848; Jornal do Commercio, 11 Sep. 1848; Correio Mercantil, 9 and 12 Sep. 1848; O Farricoco, 10 Nov. 1848.

24 O Velho Brasil, 14 Sep. 1854.

25 O Republico, 18 Sep. 1854. On 2 July celebrations in Salvador, see Hendrik Kraay, "Between Brazil and Bahia: Celebrating Dois de Julho in Nineteenth-Century Salvador," Journal of Latin American Studies 32:2 (May 1999): 255–86.

26 See the advertisements in Jornal do Commercio, 7 Sep. 1855, 7 Sep. 1856, and 6 Sep. 1857.

27 "Programa dos festejos que a Sociedade 'Ypiranga' tem deliberado fazer," 1856, Arquivo Geral da Cidade do Rio de Janeiro (AGCRJ), 43-3-64, fol. 3r-v; "Programa dos festejos que a Sociedade Ypiranga pretende [sic] fazer no dia 7 de Setembro de 1857," Biblioteca Nacional, Rio de Janeiro, Seção de Manuscritos (BNRJ/SM), II-31, 33, 19; Correio da Tarde, 9 Sep. 1856.

28 Sociedade Independência Brasileira to Câmara Municipal, Rio de Janeiro, 29 July 1857, 31 July 1858, AGCRJ, 43-3-64, fols. 6, 10; "Chronica da Semana" and "Chronica da Quinzena," 1 and 20 Sep. 1859, Revista Popular 1:3 (1859): 333, 396.

29 "Folhetim," *Jornal do Commercio*, 9 Sep. 1855; *A Semana*, 28 Sep. 1856; *Jornal do Commercio*, 9 Sep. 1856; "Folhetim," *Jornal do Commercio*, 14 Sep. 1856; "Paginas Menores," *Correio Mercantil*, 7 Sep. 1856.

30 "Folhetim," *Jornal do Commercio*, 14 Sep. 1857. See also *Jornal do Commercio*, 8–9 Sep. 1857.

31 "Folhetim," *Jornal do Commercio*, 13 Sep. 1858.

32 "Chronica da Quinzena," 20 Sep. 1859, *Revista Popular* 1:3 (1859): 394–95; *Correio Mercantil*, 8–9 Sep. 1859; *Jornal do Commercio*, 8–9 Sep. 1859; *Correio da Tarde*, 9 Sep. 1859.

33 See the petitions in AGCRJ, 43-3-64, fols. 11, 15, 16, 20; *Correio da Tarde*, 15 July 1858, 5 Sep. 1859; *Correio Mercantil*, 5 and 6 Sep. 1859.

34 Letter from "O Oprimido," *O Tyranno*, 12 Sep. 1857.

35 "Paginas Menores," *Correio Mercantil*, 14 Sep. 1857; *A Marmota*, 14 Sep. 1858; *O Charivary Nacional*, 4 Sep. 1859.

36 D. C., "Saudação ao dia 7 de setembro," *Correio Mercantil*, 7 Sep. 1859; "Folhetim," *Jornal do Commercio*, 7 Sep. 1856.

37 *O Tyranno*, 12 Sep. 1857; *O Carapuça*, 6 Sep. 1857; *7 de Setembro*, 7 Sep. 1859; *O Clamor Publico*, 7 Sep. 1860; *A Crença*, 6 Sep. 1863.

38 "Folhetim," *Jornal do Commercio*, 8–9 Sep. 1860.

39 "Chronica da Quinzena," 10 Sep. 1860 [sic = 1861], *Revista Popular* 3:11 (1861): 377. See also *A Marmota*, 6 Sep. 1861.

40 *O Espectador da América do Sul*, 10 Sep. 1863; *Jornal do Commercio*, 3 Sep. 1863. See also *O Constitucional*, 7 Sep. 1863.

41 *Jornal do Commercio*, 10 Sep. 1856; *Correio Mercantil*, 8–9 Sep. 1858; "Relatório dos trabalhos da directoria provisoria."

42 *Correio da Tarde*, 6 Sep. 1858.

43 This perception of the streets draws on Roberto DaMatta's interpretation of "house" and "street" in Brazilian culture. See his *A casa e a rua: Espaço, cidadania, mulher, e morte no Brasil* (São Paulo: Brasiliense, 1985).

44 *Jornal do Commercio*, 5 Sep. 1858; *Correio da Tarde*, 9 Sep. 1858.

45 *Correio Mercantil*, 5 Sep. 1858.

46 *Jornal do Commercio*, 12 Sep. 1858, 7 Sep. 1859, 7 Sep. 1860, and 7 Sep. 1861.

47 Letter from "O cego que vê, o surdo que ouve," *Jornal do Commercio*, 2 Sep. 1856. On the bonfire plans, see *Correio Mercantil*, 6 Sep. 1856; "Páginas menores," *Correio Mercantil*, 7 Sep. 1856.

48 *Jornal do Commercio*, 9 Sep. 1845; *Correio Mercantil*, 10 Sep. 1857; *Correio da Tarde*, 9 and 10 Sep. 1859. On capoeiras in public festivals, see Carlos Eugênio Líbano Soares, *A negregada instituição: Os capoeiras na corte imperial, 1850–1890* (Rio de Janeiro: Access, 1999), 79–83; Thomas H. Holloway, "'A Healthy Terror': Police Repression of *Capoeiras* in Nineteenth-Century Rio de Janeiro," *Hispanic American Historical Review* 69:4 (Nov. 1989): 665, 670; Maya Talmon Chvaicer, "The Criminalization of *Capoeira* in Nineteenth-Century Rio de Janeiro," *Hispanic American Historical Review* 82:3 (August 2002): 531–32; Matthias Röhrig Assunção, *Capoeira: The History of an Afro-Brazilian Martial Art* (London: Routledge, 2005), 80–83.

49 *A Semana*, 28 Sep. 1856.

50 *Correio Mercantil*, 8–9 Sep. 1857.

51 There are two different accounts of this incident: *Jornal do Commercio*, 11 Sep. 1859; *Correio Mercantil*, 11 Sep. 1859. The condemnation of the police appeared in *7 de Setembro*, 18 Sep. 1859.

52 Leslie Bethell, *The Abolition of the Brazilian Slave Trade: Britain, Brazil, and the Slave Trade Question* (Cambridge: Cambridge University Press, 1970), 313; Robert Conrad, *The Destruction of Brazilian Slavery, 1850–1888* (Berkeley: University of California Press, 1972), 27.

53 *Correio da Tarde*, 1 and 5 Sep. 1856.

54 Karasch, *Slave Life*, 345.

55 *Jornal do Commercio*, 7 and 9 Sep. 1856; "Relatório dos trabalhos da directoria provisoria"; "Carta de João Fernandes a seu compadre Manoel Mendes," *Correio da Tarde*, 6 Sep. 1856.

56 "Paginas menores," *Correio Mercantil*, 7 and 21 Sep. 1856.

57 "Folhetim," Jornal do Commercio, 14 Sep. 1857; Correio da Tarde, 15 July 1857; Correio Mercantil, 12 Sep. 1857.

58 Correio Mercantil, 8–9 Sep. 1857.

59 A Marmota, 14 Sep. 1858; O Constitucional, 10 Sep. 1862.

60 Jornal do Commercio, 5 Sep. 1857; Correio Mercantil, 6 Sep. 1856. On pianos in Rio de Janeiro society, see Cristina Magaldi, Music in Imperial Rio de Janeiro: European Culture in a Tropical Milieu (Lanham: Scarecrow Press, 2004), 8–12.

61 Jornal do Commercio, 4 Sep. 1856.

62 Jornal do Commercio, 5 Sep. 1851; 6 Sep. 1856; 7 Sep. 1856; 6 Sep. 1864; Correio Mercantil, 8–9 Sep. 1859.

63 "Carta de D. Mathias ao seu compadre Pitorra," Periodico dos Pobres, 7 Sep. 1850; "Visita das priminhas," ibid., 9 Sep. 1854; 9 Sep. 1851.

64 "Carta de D. Mathias . . .," Periodico dos Pobres, 10 Sep. 1850; "A directoria do Theatro Lyrico e a policia," Correio Mercantil, 8 Sep. 1855; "Theatro Lyrico," Correio da Tarde, 10 Sep. 1855.

65 Luís Antônio Giron, Minoridade crítica: A ópera e o teatro nos folhetins da Corte (São Paulo: Editora da Universidade de São Paulo; Rio de Janeiro: Ediouro, 2004), 98. Evidence on the social composition of theatre audiences is sketchy and contradictory. While Silvia Cristina Martins de Souza notes that ticket prices were low enough that skilled artisans could have afforded to attend theatre spectacles, she does not indicate that such members of the working classes did so. Shop clerks and students, however, were assiduous theatregoers; see her As noites do Ginásio: Teatro e tensões culturais na Corte (1832–1868) (Campinas: Editora da UNICAMP, 2002), 128n68, 279–82. Cristina Magaldi vacillates between stressing the socially-exclusive nature of theatre-going and its social breadth; see her Music, xxi, 13, 17, 31n45, 38–39, 54, 60nn13–14.

66 On these changes, see Marco Morel, As transformações dos espaços públicos: Imprensa, atores políticos e sociabilidades na cidade imperial (São Paulo: Hucitec, 2005). On the theatre as a political space, see also Jurandir Malerba, A corte no exílio: Civilização e poder no Brasil às vésperas da Independência (1808 a 1821) (São Paulo: Companhia das Letras, 2000), 91–124; Lorenzo Mammi, "Teatro em música no Brasil monárquico," in Festa: Cultura e sociabilidade na América portuguesa, István Jancsó and Iris Kantor, eds., vol. 1, 48–49 (São Paulo: EDUSP, 2001); Magaldi, Music, 12–13.

67 O Brasil, 10 Sep. 1850.

68 "Carta de D. Mathias" and "Soneto recitado no theatro na noite de Sete de Setembro," Periodico dos Pobres, 10 Sep. 1850.

69 Adalbert, Travels, 279.

70 "Visita das priminhas," Periodico dos Pobres, 9 Sep. 1852; "Folhetim," Jornal do Commercio, 11 Sep. 1853; Jornal do Commercio, 10 Sep. 1854.

71 "Carta de João Fernandes," Correio da Tarde, 10 Sep. 1855; Letters to the Editor, Correio Mercantil, 8, 10, and 11 Sep. 1855. On the so-called theatre "parties or "factions" and police efforts to control them, see Giron, Minoridade, 14, 73–75, 82–83, 89, 97–99, 134, 147; Souza, Noites, 58–59, 289–91; Magaldi, Music, 47.

72 "Paginas menores," Correio Mercantil, 8 Sep. 1855. On the campaign for a national opera, see Giron, Minoridade, 158–63, 190–97.

73 Correio Mercantil, 8–9 Sep. 1856; "Paginas menores," Correio Mercantil, 21 Sep. 1856.

74 Jornal do Commercio, 4 Sep. 1861; Correio da Tarde, 8 Sep. 1861. On this opera, see Giron, Minoridade, 197–201.

75 On such laudations, see Malerba, Corte, 100–111; Mammi, "Teatro," 46–47.

76 "137ª pacotilha, Carijó e Comp.ª," Correio Mercantil, 11 Sep. 1853.

77 Letter from "Hum Irmão da Caridade," Jornal do Commercio, 10 Sep. 1840.

78 On imperial racial etiquette see Emília Viotti da Costa, The Brazilian Empire: Myths and Histories, rev. ed. (Chapel Hill: University of North Carolina Press, 2000), 241–44.

79 On the theatre's civilizing mission, see Souza, Noites.

80 [Alexandre José de] Mello Moraes Filho, Festas e tradições populares do Brasil, 3rd ed. (Rio de Janeiro: F. Briguiet, 1946), 147, 152. This article was first published in Gazeta de Noticias, 7 Sep. 1887.

81 Lilia Moritz Schwarcz, *As barbas do imperador: D. Pedro II, um monarca nos trópicos*, 2nd ed. (São Paulo: Companhia das Letras, 1999), 257–59; Martha Abreu, *O império do Divino: Festas religiosas e cultura popular no Rio de Janeiro, 1830–1900* (Rio de Janeiro: Nova Fronteira, 1999).

3

Performing the Masculine Nation:

SOLDIERS OF THE MEXICAN ARMY, 1876—1910

Stephen Neufeld[1]

INTRODUCTION

Mexican elites, along with those in much of the Western world, became increasingly concerned with the notions of appropriate masculine behaviour and image in the late nineteenth century; they sought to shape the subject in new ways in conformity with modern ideals. Under the regime of Porfirio Díaz, who dominated Mexico from 1876 to 1910, the military began to professionalize and to modernize, while remaining a tightly-controlled "paper tiger" unable to threaten the stability of the regime. Pragmatism dictated that the military could be expected to fulfill only a limited role within the nation, so rather than building an effective armed force, the regime spent almost half the national budget on an institution that, for the most part, did little more than parade and perform for chosen audiences. The visual presentation of the soldier and officer of modern Mexico demonstrated and, in a less direct sense, built upon specific conceptions of masculinity. As such, the military was displayed as a fetish object along with railways and the *rurales* (the paramilitary rural police), all of which exemplified the Porfirian agenda of order and progress in the nation.[2] The regime directed the military's performances in public spaces and in contact zones where interactions between citizens, foreigners, and government agents occurred. From this visual and symbolic space emerged a multiplicity of ways to see and be seen as male, shaping cultural understandings for the new century.

49

At the end of the nineteenth century, the practices and discourses that made up real lived experiences, including masculinity, were articulated in novel ways. These experiences were defined, discussed, depicted, and put into practice in ways self-reflexively labelled either modern or traditional, concepts created simultaneously and in tension with each other.[3] These concepts informed Porfirian perspectives on gender roles and presentations of self, and framed the way that practices could be discarded or embraced.[4] With the increasing power of the nation-state to intervene against and discipline gendered identities, from simultaneously forbidding and demanding duels to regulating hygiene among prostitutes, recourse to invented traditions that reinvested value and meaning into gendered identities could become life-or-death matters. At the same time, there was a widely recognized crisis of masculinity in this era, exemplified internationally by events as disparate as the Oscar Wilde trial, the Dreyfus Affair, and the Baden-Powell movement in reaction to the Boer War.[5] Change in Mexico followed suit. While the nineteenth century foundational narratives of nation in Mexico strongly emphasized the homosocial bonding of its protagonists, changing sexual anxieties shifted this emphasis to clearly heterosexual tropes from the time of the Porfiriato onwards.[6] The 1901 scandal over transvestites at a Mexico City ball (the Famous 41 case) reinforced this transforming discourse, and scientific explanations for criminality and the body presented citizens with "evidence," and hence solutions, for modern deviance. As society changed around them, Porfirian subjects looked to new spaces and the images of the modern world around them to make sense of themselves.

The army and its institutions became arenas of performance where conceptions of masculinity and nationhood were created, contested, interiorized, and "projected" to society. The *rurales* as an institution conveyed a new masculine national image, but the Porfirian elite also looked to the federal military to set a similar example, particularly due to its older traditions, greater presence, and established social significance. The historiography of the Mexican military, nonetheless, remains relatively mute on this period, with no comprehensive or theoretical studies addressing the armed forces or their significance to the formation of identities and nation.[7] In contrast, historians have addressed these issues for many other Latin American nations, and especially for Brazil.[8]

Masculinity and male ideals in the federal military were experienced and articulated differently for the lower ranks and for the officers. These differences represent a more variegated conception of gender than is usually assumed, especially for military men. Masculinity describes the performance of a politicized and persistent stereotype of gender norms, behaviours, and appearances that entail manliness in a specific context and to a specific audience.[9] Never a homogenous vision of the masculine, the Porfirian military exhibited a variety of competing and alternative masculinities that, far from exhibiting stability, changed and adapted over time. These subjective identities varied along the lines of class and national, regional, and cosmopolitan idealizations, and were framed by racial and positivist preconceptions.

Masculinity therefore represents a contingent identity and, at the same time, a lens through which to examine facets of social experience. As an umbrella concept, it allows an analysis that accounts for race, ethnicity, and class as the lesser elements in a discursive environment that sought to shape a national manhood. For contemporary viewers, the military as an institution represented a masculine image that overlapped and articulated with other identities; soldiers were universally male while other descriptors had secondary importance. The regime displayed the disciplined soldier as an archetype to which the poor should aspire, intending to civilize them through a mitigated and tamed manliness. Similarly, officers would represent the "better" classes' masculine ideal, emulating the fashions and sharing the perspective of Porfirian high society.[10] As a public spectacle, the military as an institution enacted an ideal of what the nation should be, constructing an identity through its interaction with the gazes of the nation's subjects and privileged foreign viewers.[11] This is not to argue that there were no other motivations or concerns that shaped the military image, nor to say that all male activity is inherently about masculinity. Rather this frame of analysis serves to suggest how the rough contours of a negotiated and gendered identity formed in the particular context of the federal army. In a most general sense, two different masculinities formed within this ideal, one typical of the common soldier and another for the officer.

TRANSFORMING THE COMMON SOLDIER

Foreign observers' perspectives on the Mexican military, while skewed in many ways, offer a useful entry point into an investigation of common soldiers, as they frequently highlighted extreme images in encounters with the exotic Other, and in so doing, provide a contemporaneous sense of what foreigners considered normal. One such outsider was the highly influential American author William Henry Bishop. He traveled extensively through Mexico as a guest of the Porfirian regime from 1881 to 1882, attending senatorial dinners, touring with a military escort, and visiting salons and *pulquerías* (crude bars selling agave alcohol) alike. His book, *Old Mexico and Her Lost Provinces* (1883), is a detailed travelogue taking the reader through much of Mexican geography.[12] Bishop did not hold Mexico or its people in particularly high esteem, once proclaiming about a decrepit town jail that "no self-respecting American prisoner could be induced to stay in a place so easy to escape from. But there is no accounting for tastes."[13] Nonetheless, his work offers important, if anecdotal, starting points for the investigation of a military extremely concerned with its image.

Recruits for the Mexican federal army faced a long march, and a rough one. Soldiers experienced a strict regime of discipline, training, and drilling, and yet their identity and behaviour remained, or became, considerably less controlled than their military superiors envisioned. Bishop described an incident in 1881 in which a trainload of soldiers and *aguardiente* (hard liquor), en route to Cuautla, derailed. It was a dark night and officers were not present, so the troops, shrugging off the effects of the crash, seized the opportunity to loot the liquor from the wrecked train, and became "drunk and excited." At this point, according to Bishop, they began to shoot and stab one another, drunk, in the dark, in the wreckage – a scene of terror and barbarism. In the chaos, accidental fires ignited the alcohol and the ammunition cartridges, resulting in tremendous carnage: 156 killed and a further 68 wounded.[14]

This example highlights what the author saw as the base and depraved nature of troops who, in his opinion, were little better than savages. This image of the soldier corresponded to the worst stereotypes propagated by both Mexicans and foreigners, many of whom remained convinced of the inferiority of the common recruit. Far from exhibiting any type of disciplined masculinity or military pride, these troops seemed perpetually a hairsbreadth away from violent and chaotic animalistic behaviour. At night they were locked in barracks and on the march surrounded by armed officers, leading many contemporary viewers to assume that these men were criminals; in fact, many entered the army bound in chains and shackles. The typical recruit appeared, according to another American author, "half wild, half starved, half naked, and ridiculously armed," an image that readily corresponded with the worst stereotypes that some Mexican civilians themselves held.[15] Many, especially in the newly aware and increasingly vocal middle classes, perceived the military as the complete antithesis of the family home, an institution of moral endangerment and vice in which men became, among other things, marijuana users. There were few supporters for this continued recruitment of the "worst elements of society" into the federal army. One Porfirian minister of war admitted that "it would do incalculable good to the morality, discipline, and economy of the army" if the *leva*, the current system of forcibly recruiting "bums, the vicious, or criminals," were eliminated.[16] As a vision of *mexicanidad* (Mexican-ness) and manliness, these soldiers were widely viewed with derision, and certainly did not present the image that the elite desired.

The Mexican soldier was always intended to be something much better than this; the elite, the middle classes, officers, and even critics of the regime had all envisioned a different motivation for military service, and far better results. Spending time in the military would, they hoped, rid the lowest classes of their criminal and unhygienic habits, inculcate nationalism and patriotism and, significantly, make proper men of them. With an elegant uniform as well, one officer wrote, "the army [would] ... give an elevated idea of the country's culture to the masses."[17] Although the creation of an orderly army mattered as well, at the heart of this effort, the intention of elite and middle-class society was the remoulding of lower-class masculinity. Although the lower classes might be *muy hombre* (very manly), the upper and middle classes desired to mitigate the brutish and unpredictable nature of this other masculinity.[18] Equally, they desired to reinforce their own ideal of masculinity, one that stressed sexuality and power in different ways, and was inherently both nationalist and cosmopolitan. This ideal set their chosen traits such as wealth, manners, and education on top of the social hierarchy, and kept brute strength and violent passions in check. Yet typical lower-class masculine identities little resembled this ideal, and they were not easily given up. While violence does not necessarily equate to manly behaviour, for soldiers from the lower class, aggression, competition, and subordination of women figured as prominent characteristics of a previously learned gender role.[19] For the recruit, military service was simply an onerous task; he considered himself a man long before he put on a uniform.

The elite argument about the inculcation of the soldiers' sense of duty and citizenship closely linked ideals of the nation to ideals of masculine identity. They identified military service with manly duty, yet at the same time, questioned conscription as an unwarranted invasion of the government into private life. Central to this debate was the failure of the recruitment system, proposals for universal service for men, and the militarizing of education. These questions were extensively debated among elite factions including the *Científicos* (positivist advisors to the president), retired officers, politicians, and serving military men such as General Bernardo Reyes. In an influential 1910 book, retired general Eduardo Paz examined no fewer than eight separate systems of recruitment or universal service that had been proposed or enacted during the Porfiriato.[20] Among his many reforms, Reyes (who served as secretary of war from

1900 to 1903) created a largely middle-class and urban Second Reserve that brought some 30,000 new men into service by 1902.[21] Although short-lived, the Second Reserve was an attempt at reforming a recruitment system gone horribly wrong, but was disbanded by Díaz because of his quite justified anxiety over arming and training the middle classes in Mexico City.

Reforming recruitment was more complicated an affair than might be assumed. Governors used impressment not only to meet state recruitment quotas, but also to cull the political opposition and to rid themselves of criminals, vagrants, and even those maimed too badly to be workers.[22] These abuses were exemplified by the impressment of prisoners-of-war during the Sonoran uprisings of 1880–1901; Yaqui rebels were at times immediately forced to serve in the very federal army unit that had captured them.[23] While some governors favoured the existing system for their own reasons, others advocated universal service, of the poor at any rate, as a means to spread education, literacy, and patriotic duty among the men of Mexico. Nevertheless, the forced nature of soldiers' service vitiated any attempts to instil patriotic duty, and further complicated attempts at discipline. Despite some efforts to remedy recruiting practices, the lower ranks continued to be pressed into service as prisoners of the state, and not surprisingly, the annual desertion rate approached 50 per cent.[24] The result was an impossibly chaotic army that desperately needed to find an alternative to impressment.

One alternative was universal military service by men, on the model of the German military system. As a preliminary step toward this end, military training in primary and secondary schools began in 1908 with the additional intention of inculcating nationalism.[25] One educator, Francisco Vázquez Gómez, believed that if secondary schools developed the physical, intellectual, and moral quality of students, it would be possible to "make men of them," and in time "inculcate [values of] the Mexican man" whose new primary loyalty was to the state.[26] The idea of true universal service faced a major obstacle in the reluctance of the wealthy to serve as soldiers; they argued that the "decent classes" better served the nation by working on improving the economy, not hefting rifles. They also worried that young middle- or upper-class men would be corrupted if put in direct contact with lower-class recruits. Vázquez Gómez clearly articulated this fear in his worried remarks on universal service and barracks:

> We must consider that there are three classes, whose limitations
> are not well determined, … and it is impossible to have decent
> and well-educated youths (rich or poor) share a barracks, let

alone a room with the promiscuity and moral dangers of the drunk, the petty thief [*ratero*] and the criminal. A parent would spare nothing in his power to pay for a replacement, and [this] changes a sacred honourable duty into a disgrace, because barracks life would extinguish the youth's not very well cemented habits of work and morality.[27]

The ideal Mexican man was not, according to contemporary opinion, to be found among the soldiery. General Reyes himself was gravely concerned over the use of marijuana in the barracks, and as secretary of war, he attempted to remedy what he saw as pervasive immorality in the ranks. His efforts to enforce existing regulations with greater vigour included increased pay for non-commissioned officers, frequent inspections, and removing temptations from troops, for example, by closing certain barracks found to be serving as bars.[28] Among the lower and middle classes, the presumed inability of the regime to police this restricted space raised further doubts about the credibility of Porfirian rule.

The efforts made to transform the recruit into the "modern" and nationalist soldier largely failed to alter his behaviours and indigenous self-identity. To be sure, habits of clothing, speech, and postures were taught, drilled, and enforced, but they were promptly discarded whenever officers with disciplinary powers were absent. This apparent regression, well supported by descriptions, photographs, and sketches of the day, should not be seen only as a failure of the officers and drill instructors, but also as a sign of successful resistance by lower-class men with a more robust sense of masculine self than that offered by the army. The Porfirian elite anticipated that discipline, the European panacea for military and industrial malaise, would be a powerful lathe for shaping men out of rough material. Instilling discipline in raw recruits required breaking down and rebuilding senses of self, and this required experienced sergeants and time. It also required some motivation on the soldiers' part, whether through nationalism, a shared enemy, or meaningful traditions. Recruits experienced these processes, though the degree varied greatly between different locations and different units. This harsh "boot camp" was designed to erase or break down identities; only once stripped of self could the new disciplined and national man be moulded.

Porfirian troops also faced sexualized humiliations, as depicted in Francisco Urquizo's novel *Tropa Vieja* (*The Old Troop*, 1930) in which the recruits are stripped naked for their officer and one veteran remarks: "They castrate you and you are ready, you are a soldier."[29] Common nicknames for federal soldiers in the Revolutionary era such as *mochos* (dehorned bulls) and *pelonas* (shaved or shorn) allude to this removal of essentially male features.[30] Rather than being strictly emasculating, it is more accurate to label this treatment of new soldiers as infantilization – being stripped of independence and agency. They were shorn of their hair, dressed in an anonymous national uniform, taught where to sleep, how to walk, how to speak, how to clean, and how to live in the military. Subjected to the dominant male gaze of the sergeant, the objectified recruit would ideally internalize the discipline and values instilled by training. In keeping with this, officers reviewed soldiers incessantly and troops participated in various power rituals including a ritual pledging of allegiance to the national flag in dialogue with an officer, and having the penal codes of the army read to them each day.[31] Over time, this infantilized soldier, with group bonding, shared experience, and a modicum of training, was to take on a new and guided masculinity, becoming a disciplined subject with masculine features in keeping with the national ideal.[32]

Contrary to elite hopes, between the infantilization and remasculinization of recruits, the inculcation of the new masculinity never occurred. With too few sergeants, unappealing and alien military traditions, little belief in official nationalism, and often too little training, any apparent disciplined masculinity was only superficial. Perhaps most of all, lack of money for a proper training regime left the majority of federal army units with troops so unreliable that officers only issued them a minimum of ammunition. This, officers reasoned, would discourage soldiers from deserting their units in hostile territory, as they would be fleeing virtually unarmed. There are numerous other examples, though none as extreme as the train wreck observed by Bishop, indicating that the ordinary soldiers fell short of the paragons of "spit-and-polish" military discipline that their officers hoped to create.[33] More than simply offending their standards, this further implied a sharp break in the progression from "dregs" to men that proper training was to instil. In another example, photos in Reyes's own official history of the military reveal soldiers on a break during manoeuvres napping on the ground or gathering for what appears to be gambling.[34] Given the circumstances and photographic technology of the day, the soldiers certainly knew that the picture was being taken, and the use of the picture (also distributed for publication in the United States and exhibited at the World's Fair in Paris, notwithstanding the image presented) suggests several possibilities. It may be that discipline was so completely lacking that this was the best picture available, or that the photographer selected these prints out of a sense of irony or ignorance. It is also possible that, since this was just prior to Reyes' tenure as minister of war, the photos were chosen to illustrate the need for his reforms. In any case, a distinct lack of military decorum is evident.

An important facet of professionalizing the military that further shaped masculine values was the exclusion of women from the daily experiences of the soldier's life. Reducing contacts with women for morality and the enhancement of homosocial bonding were as important as reducing the traditional dependency of military men on *soldaderas* (female camp followers), who were seen as unmodern and an immoral influence.[35] These women had long been a part of the Mexican military and continued to play a critical role in the daily function and supply of an army that had yet to modernize along European standards. The maintenance of the male-only isolation of the soldier was therefore impracticable; not only did women have access to the barracks, but they were integral to the operation of the military unit, accompanying the men on marches, cooking, washing clothing, selling goods and services, and on occasion fighting.[36] While Porfirian officers made certain that these women were invisible in military reviews, parades, or rhetoric, their continued presence in the soldiers' lives offered yet another distraction from the formation of a purely military identity. On the other hand, practicality combined with anxiety over the all-male barracks as the antithesis of the family home and potential locus for homosexual and immoral behaviour encouraged officers to overlook the female presence.[37] Although army regulations provided for the removal and punishment of "women of a bad life," *soldaderas* were never specifically banned from the barracks or the battlefield.[38] In practice, officers tolerated the *soldaderas'* presence and allowed them to accompany troops in the field, and they evidently held to a fairly broad interpretation as to what did or did not constitute prostitution. From the disciplinary problems created by the presence of *soldaderas* in revolutionary armies, ranging from rivalries to assassination attempts, one might speculate that similar difficulties complicated the task of training the soldier.[39]

Masculinity, as seen by the higher classes of society, was contingent on the ability of the military to instil discipline and inculcate a new subject identity on the lower-class recruit. But military experience was often incongruent with Mexican understandings of patriarchal duty and service, and the recruit frequently found himself exploited, mistreated, and dishonoured by officers. Typically, he reacted through an assertion of his own masculinity while dismissing officers as at best an obstacle, at worst an enemy.[40] Some officers may also have represented a distastefully effete image to their troops. The 1890 painting by Frederic Remington of *The Mexican Major*, for instance, depicts a major in what appears to be a rather ostentatious silvered outfit and a large gaudy sombrero.[41] Given the differences in dress, consumption, education, and culture between them, certain officers appeared to their troops to be dandies, and working-class homophobia already had its own language and understandings of that masculinity.[42] The typical recruit, satisfied with his own masculinity and reinforcing it in his own ways within the environs in which he found himself, was highly successful at resisting the infantilization and remasculinizing attempts of the state. For these men, the effeminacy ascribed to officer and upper-class masculine behaviours and the inherent emasculations of military service forced a hardening of their own masculine self-perceptions and conservatism. Largely rural in origin, the recruits' manliness, in as much as it may be generalized, focused on autonomy and self-mastery, on hard work and stoicism.[43] Presented with demands for obedience to often-exploitative officials, insubordination and incivility became a manly affectation. This presented a change in tone that would inform machismo in the century that followed.

CIVILIZING THE OFFICER

If a modern militarized and masculine construction did not filter down to the lower ranks, it had a significant influence on the officer classes, whose hypermasculine constructions stood in marked contrast to the attempted infantilization of the troops. Bishop provided an insightful example of this. On the dangerous road to Acapulco, he had the escort of a colonel, a "veritable military man" with twenty years' experience and the "bullet holes to prove them." The colonel had been ordered to the northern frontier as a reprimand for having

> lately fought a duel ... in which the weapons were sabres and had so slashed his opponent, a brother officer, that the latter was laid up in grievous state in the hospital. A vacant barracks had been set apart, by the War Department, for this proceeding. Army duelling, as on the Continent, is contrived at. The case seems to be that, if you fight, you are afterwards reprimanded; but if you do not, you are likely to be cashiered as pusillanimous.[44]

He went on to describe the two generals who had come to see the colonel off, providing a description of the connection between masculine behaviour, violence, and honour among the highest ranks. One general, a thickset black-bearded man with a conspicuous scar on his face had, while in command in the Yucatan in the 1870s, ordered a shooting on "some of the ordinary revolutionary pretexts" of a member of the powerful

Gutiérrez Estrada family. Perhaps insinuating a motive beyond politics, Bishop remarks that this family was noted for its intelligent and beautiful women. The victim's brother then returned from Paris to avenge the family, duelling with the general and leaving him on death's door.[45] As Bishop saw it, the Mexican army went to great, though quixotic, efforts to promote a code of behaviour that set "traditional" masculinity and honour into the context of discipline in a "modern" military system. Writing about Brazil, historian Peter Beattie points out that "manliness in societies of honor demands an audience," and that this demand encouraged confrontations based on "traditional" notions of honour that conflicted with "modern" military discipline.[46]

The approximately three thousand officers in the federal army embodied both the traditional male warrior figure and the modern technocratic professional.[47] Many entered their profession in their teens, and learned to perform as modern military men at an early age. Successfully inculcated with suitable masculine behaviours, most officers held to a particularly stringent sense of masculine behaviours when in public: appearing brave, respecting peers, and preserving dignity. Discipline was regulated through the *Junta de Honor* (Honour Board), a regulatory body within the military, whose function in large part was determining appropriately manly behaviours, from regulating sexuality to controlling duelling practices.[48] Here, in particular, conservative and traditional values of honour and the new cosmopolitan masculine clashed with the discipline and legalistic outlook of modern and scientific values.

The practice of duelling thus became a classic catch-22 for military officers – required (Article 1440) and punished (Article 3607) at the same time.[49] It was a necessary practice to prove one's upper-class masculinity; a shared sense of language and access to the codes and means of duelling increasingly embedded the military officer within the elite.[50] Setting themselves apart from men of the lower classes, officers sought to emulate not only the Porfirian upper class but also respected foreign militaries, particularly the French and German. Given the strong German influence on the Mexican military in the early twentieth century, it is not too surprising that while most civilian duels used the pistol, it was not unusual for the military duel to involve sabres, a very Prussian practice.[51] This reflected hypermasculine norms; there are few metaphors as obvious as a sabre for emphasizing male sexuality. In his 1903 novel, *Santa*, Federico Gamboa describes a young officer as irresistibly sexual, "having the air of a swordsman and a womanizer."[52] In some ways, the duel was a creature of fashion; the upper-class Jockey Club itself saw a number of what Bishop described "fashionable duels."[53] An extreme case of enacting a specific masculine code and a carefully protected practice, the duel existed as a potential recourse only for the honourable, meaning the wealthy, the higher classes, and the powerful. It represented appropriate manliness for the *hombre de bien*, the gentleman.

Framing this idea in positivist and Comtean language, elite men literally conceived of themselves as a better breed of men. With pressures from an emulative and encroaching middle class, and with a pseudo-scientific justification to look down on the lower classes, the Porfirian elite sought to maintain the duel as a strictly masculine practice that was solely available to their peers. Although poor men, and to an extent women, were equally likely to duel over slights to their honour, to the Porfirian elite and Mexican law these were merely criminals knife-fighting in the gutters; the lower class had no honour to fight over. Of course, the lower classes likewise viewed their social betters as dishonourable; they merely had fewer venues to express this and no legal rights to do so.[54]

The drive for inclusion into the upper classes and the concurrent professionalization of military officers also meant that officers had to learn the range of tastes and behaviours appropriate for men of their class. Contrary to expectations set for the lower ranks, officers were encouraged to have appropriate relations with women of good breeding as part of their self-improvement and as a means to enhance their social and cultural capital. For a good number of men, including Porfirio Díaz himself, learning modern manners was a civilizing mission best left to wives taken from wealthy homes. These civilizing pursuits ranged from the highly ambitious, such as cultivation of opera and symphony and the closing of the bull fighting rings, to the basic, such as teaching the president not to spit indoors (for which his wife received the credit). In other cases, military men emulated upper-class fashions through their conspicuous consumption of clothing, cosmetics, and other luxury goods.[55]

The incorporation of military men into the middle and upper classes also resurrected older attempts to teach manners within the military college. As far back as 1854, the regulations for the Military College of Chapultepec revealed an abiding concern for military morality and public image.[56] Officers were seen as a "distinguished class," to be set apart from rough society. Highly regulated, officers underwent a masculinizing discipline that partially mirrored the experiences of regular troops. Unlike at midcentury, however, military codes and penal laws were drastically overhauled during the Porfiriato, and taught as an essential element of military professionalization. Similar to earlier conventions, new regulations stated that men found incapable of "acquiring a good military carriage, vigour in command, discipline, and general aptitudes of the officer," or who were not of "irreproachable customs and manners," or who lacked "character, or spirit," could be judged by the *junta* to be unfit for a career in the military.[57] Even personal hygiene was a matter of regulation, and clean underwear was expressly required. The definitions of military honour in the codes remained the same, but the *juntas* that interpreted such things as "intimate friendships with badly received people," now did so in the atmosphere of turn-of-the-century sexual morality.[58] The vague regulations seemed deliberately flexible enough in application to allow the *junta* to widely police masculine behaviours, including sexuality, refusing or frivolously offering duels, or simply not meeting a manly standard.

Reopened in 1867 after a long closure, by the 1880s, the military college was well on its way to becoming a modern, professional institution that could reposition military officership as a national and elite masculine identity. Under the directorship of General Sostenes Rocha (1880–86), it gained a new curriculum and instructors well-versed in science and European military education; by the turn of the century, it was considered a world-class institution. There the cadet learned positivist science, modern hygiene, and appropriate manners.[59] The students who partially acquired upper-class tastes in the college avidly pursued them as graduates; all but 14 per cent left the military upon graduation to pursue better paying civilian work, thereby joining a militarized civilian elite to the detriment of a professionalizing army in great need of trained officers.[60] Yet even so, the majority of graduates had interiorized the value sets of military manhood, and retained their sense of institutional loyalty, if not necessarily loyalty to the government, in the years to come.

Taking military honour very seriously, students figured in some of the most discussed duels of the Porfiriato. In 1887, General Pacheco begged the president's permission for a duel between two young students over a girl. Although the military college director had refused his consent, Díaz acceded to Pacheco's request on the basis that, since Porfirio Díaz Junior was also a cadet, it would reflect poorly on the president not to allow an honourable fight. Eventually, José Sáenz Botello exchanged ten pistol shots with a fellow cadet at ever shorter ranges, resulting in his opponent's slight wounding and everything forgiven between them.[61] Back in the early 1880s, Rocha had no such scruples as director, for he viewed the duel to be "more quick, more decent, and more clean" than lengthy arguments.[62]

Beyond the walls of the college, students conspicuously spent weekends in the plazas of Mexico City, where they competed with civilian dandies for the attention of viewers.[63] They were also on display for numerous visitors invited into the college and given musical entertainment.[64] Interestingly, an American military visitor, Colonel H. T. Reed, despite his stodgy military background, saw nothing remiss in male cadets dancing with one another at these Thursday night soirées, perhaps because of the sexual distancing created by a uniform, or the cadets' youthfulness, or even an acceptance of homoerotic elements.[65] Reed's article appeared after the enormous scandal of the police raid on the 1901 transvestites' ball (the Famous 41 case), an event that has been described as a watershed in the sexualization of the homosocial in Mexico and the birth of modern homosexuality.[66] Given the extreme distress that the Famous 41 transvestites caused Mexicans, Reed's insouciance is surprising; perhaps, to him, dancing cadets were merely another curious Mexican custom.

In any case, these young men embodied a new class, and according to Alan Knight, theirs was a *"carrière ouverte aux talents*, especially middle-class talents."[67] Reed, who noted that the boys paid sixteen dollars a month, plus any expenses over and above room and board, to attend the college, indicates that, in spite of the egalitarian rhetoric of the college, the lads were at least middle class. Even though the fees were refunded after a successful four to seven years, few lower-class families could have afforded them. Reed further reported that they could earn weekend leave only through proper "deportment," and were served their meals by domestics.[68] As important as the curriculum in scientific warfare, trainers in the military college also taught, or reinforced, values appropriate to the *hombre de bien*. The young officer was ideally a national creature, not of any race or region, and an embodiment of the masculine nation and its values. Where the nation itself was gendered as male, the military man personified its best traditions and values; where the nation was portrayed as female, the military would present itself as guiding protector, dictating what it saw as moral and virtuous.

PERFORMING MASCULINITY

On the larger stage, the elite articulated ideas about the modern and masculine military in formalized ways. From a privileged seat at a 1905 Porfirian parade, Thomas H. Janvier, another American observer, saw a well-choreographed military:

> This force, splendidly armed and equipped, was paraded through
> the streets of the capital. The linen uniforms were replaced by
> suits of blue cloth, and the sandals by leather shoes, in which
> the men walked gingerly; the accoutrements and arms were in
> fine form; and the men, in broad columns, bore themselves in as

soldierly a fashion as the most rigid disciplinarian could desire. There was, moreover, a prompt, business-like air about the demonstration.[69]

This review, expensive, rehearsed, and enacted for a select audience, was one of many highly deliberate performances by the Porfirian army, a performance that was demonstration and proof of a particular vision of mexicanidad and masculinity. This passage is an indication of the kinds of choices that Díaz made regarding modernity in the military. Janvier himself acknowledges that the dress uniform and shoes were not practical for Mexican warfare. Nevertheless, the marchers were outfitted with full-dress uniforms and drilled for parade in order to send a clear message to the government's invited guests. It is also probable, given the reported figure of around 20,000 troops on parade, that the procession looped back on itself, or otherwise paraded in such a way that each man passed the reviewing stand two or three times, for there were fewer than 20,000 federal soldiers in all of Mexico at this time.[70] The discussion of the speed with which the soldiers marched confirms this, for it was "very unlike that of an ordinary parade or review . . . almost a double-quick." In order to maintain a constant flow of unfamiliar parading soldiers, the men had to pass the reviewing stand quickly to avoid recognition and reposition for the next pass. The painful and unfamiliar shoes may also have prompted the troops to hurry the whole process, which nevertheless lasted two full hours. In this way, the public male of the nation was repeatedly shown to the public, carefully choreographed and costumed, and this had the potential to frame ideas about male bodies and posture and to create connections between masculine identities and nationalist ideology.

Mexican efforts to convey a particular image to observers were concerted and deliberate. For example, the minister of war personally ordered handpicked soldiers of each regiment in the capital to present themselves to Janvier and to artist Frederic Remington to speak with and to sketch.[71] Foreigners saw soldiers and officers, both common occupants of Mexican city spaces, as dramatically different. Officers, as well as some higher-class men, appeared to these observers as somewhat ostentatious, cosmopolitan, and well armed. In many ways, the dandy and the officer struck similar chords in contemporary spectators. Bishop wrote of the riders on the wide avenues of Mexico City: "the Mexican dandy . . . wears not only his weighty spurs and silver-braided sombrero now, but a cutlass at his saddlebow, and a larger revolver than before."[72] This dandy, representative of a certain type of upper-class Mexican masculinity, was a highly troubling figure to many, representing what was seen as a dangerously feminine decadence.[73] While the military man tended to offer a direct contrast to this, some officers seeking to emulate the upper class adopted the conspicuous consumption patterns, use of make-up, and other behaviours that were seen with great suspicion and disdain by many in Porfirian society.

Bishop also spoke of the Paseo de la Reforma (Mexico City's showcase main avenue) "glittering with bayonets" during the frequent smaller military parades, where the soldiers were "mainly of Indian blood and small in stature…. The officers on the other hand are trimly uniformed and quite French in aspect."[74] This description highlights the racial division in the army, whether real or perceived; higher-class officers remained visually linked to cosmopolitan ideals of masculinity that were not shared with common soldiers. At this intersection of class and gender, the military efforts to deracinate troops through a homogenous appearance, to reduce them to simply men, seem to have fallen short. The appearance of indigenous soldiers conformed to a particular discourse of positivist racism, emphasized by viewers firmly convinced of the inferiority of the Mexican in the ranks. Uniform, posture, military spit-and-polish, and conspicuous wealth all spoke to, and for, a different sort of masculinity from the perceived roughness of the troops.

The military parade in Porfirian Mexico was an important and recurrent display of state rhetoric, projecting power, images and imaginings of what Mexico and mexicanidad might be. As a performance of masculinity, it differed from its antecedents, celebrating history and nation in new ways, emphasizing national citizens rather than regional communities, and drawing attention to modern accoutrements of cosmopolitanism and technology. For example, in performing the modern cosmopolitan nation as best they could, some indigenous Mexican soldiers carried the new "Porfirio Díaz" semiautomatic rifle, others carried Japanese, American, or German rifles, some wore spiked German helmets, and most had French-designed uniforms.[75] In exhibition, the cosmopolitan Mexican military had become quite proficient, and according to Prussian observers, the army "present[ed] itself very well in parades," being comparable to any in Europe.[76] Always an important part of Mexican public ceremony, especially in the form of the military band, the Porfirian military was on perpetual display in increasingly grand and impressive ways. Public anniversaries and commemorative events routinely featured military parades, honour guards were conspicuous at state funerals and foreign visits, important railways were visibly guarded, military and paramilitary units were exhibited abroad, and the president wore his own military uniform on most public occasions.[77] Reaching out to spectators in new and potent ways, early films also featured the military presence in state ceremonies and presidential tours.[78] This performance supported the goals of the regime by allaying the fears of investors and tourists, discouraging Guatemalan aggression, allowing increased inclusion into international military circles, and even providing mass entertainment. Equally important, nonetheless, the performative military offered an image of Mexico and the military man that was in keeping with the dreams and aspirations of cosmopolitan Porfirian nationalists.

CONCLUSION

Performance alone could not create concrete changes to the experience or ideal of masculinity; rather, it was a means for instructing behaviour, coaxing conformity, and suggesting agreement on one definition of acceptable masculinity. While not creative in an outright way, through repetition and reiteration it could silence alternative visions of masculinity, making cultural assumptions of masculinity seem natural. Some historians have argued that the most significant changes to personal identities came into being after the Porfiriato, especially through the impact of changing economic structures and mass media.[79] While it seems obvious that these developments had a significant influence on social and cultural understandings of identity, they did not occur in a vacuum, nor did they come into being *sui generis*. Instead, these changes tended to reuse and reinforce previously existing identities and images, including those of gender. The image and the spectacle of the military man were not entirely persuasive, like many of the Porfirian attempts to image the nation.[80] Although the regime made many unsuccessful attempts at instilling modern identities, these discourses and repeated spectacles inexorably created a visual and behavioural space for understanding the modern nation and gender. From this space came the basic templates and languages for the creation of new subjectivities in post-Porfirian Mexico.

The modern masculinity exemplified and performed by the Porfirian military given time, repetition, and narrative structure, had a major influence on basic cultural assumptions. The idea of the modern man and images of the soldier and officer all worked to enhance a sense of mexicanidad and masculinity that defied the image of Porfirian decadence or dandification. Defining and emphasizing heterosexuality and making clear articulations about racial preconceptions of male behaviour, the Porfiriato began the process of illustrating notions of what a Mexican man should be. These normative assumptions were further entrenched by the revolutionary state, which (thanks in part to the rupture of ten years of devastation) surreptitiously retained many of the Porfirian views of nation and citizen. The lapse of time merely lent a finish of natural inevitability and longevity to these perspectives, obscuring the memory of their origins.

Two alternative senses of the masculine generally emerged from this process: one that embraced cosmopolitan fashions, and assumed modernist conventions on male sexuality and manners, and another that was more concerned with physical ability, loyalty to traditions, and independence. While masculinity suitable to the tastes of the Porfirian elite was never successfully instilled in undisciplined recruits, whose masculinity had a much more vulgar edge, the officer classes were brought into ever-increasing accord with upper- and middle-class tastes and masculine ideals. Whereas the rank and file resisted infantilization and discipline by expressing an independent masculinity more comfortable with *pulque* and blood sports, officers were instructed in and seem to have adopted the diversions and formalized honour codes of higher society. The elite vision of the masculine was markedly cosmopolitan and strongly self-regulating, and was chiefly articulated through the performance of the military in public spaces, demonstrating the posture, dress, and obedient discipline of the officially national male body. From the Jockey Club to the rough tables of the pulquería, the ideal appearance of the manly nation set root within the Mexican national psyche during the Porfiriato.

NOTES TO CHAPTER 3

1 I thank William French, William Beezley, and the Contraversía crew for their valuable input into this paper; and more recently, Michael Matthews, Jennie Carlsten, and Jonathan Jucker. Thanks also to Social Sciences and Humanities Research Council (Canada) for ongoing financial support.

2 Claudio Lomnitz, *Deep Mexico, Silent Mexico: An Anthropology of Nationalism* (Minneapolis: University of Minnesota Press, 1996), 130.

3 Mauricio Tenorio Trillo, *Mexico at the Worlds' Fairs: Crafting a Modern Nation* (Berkeley: University of California Press, 1996), 1, 2.

4 William French, "Prostitutes and Guardian Angels," *Hispanic American Historical Review* 72:4 (Nov. 1992): 529–31.

5 Leo Braudy, *From Chivalry to Terrorism: War and the Changing Nature of Masculinity* (New York: Alfred A. Knopf, 2003), 336; George Mosse, *The Image of Man* (New York: Oxford University Press, 1996), 3–5.

6 Robert McKee Irwin, *Mexican Masculinities* (Minneapolis: University of Minnesota Press, 2003), 47.

7 Roderic Ai Camp, *Generals in the Palacio: The Military in Modern Mexico* (New York: Oxford University Press, 1992); Daniel Cosío Villegas et al., *Historia moderna de México*, 10 vols. (México: Editorial Hermes, 1984); Edwin Lieuwen, *Mexican Militarism: The Political Rise and Fall of the Revolutionary Army, 1910–1940* (Albuquerque: University of New Mexico Press, 1968).

8 Some notable examples include Frederick M. Nunn, *Yesterday's Soldiers: European Military Professionalism in South America, 1890–1940* (Lincoln: University of Nebraska Press, 1983); Celso Castro, Vitor Izecksohn, and Hendrik Kraay, eds., *Nova história militar brasileira* (Rio de Janeiro: Editora da Fundação Getúlio Vargas and Editora Bom Texto, 2004); Linda Alexander Rodríguez, *Rank and Privilege: The Military and Society in Latin America* (Wilmington: Scholarly Resources, 1994).

9 Judith Butler, *Gender Trouble: Feminism and the Subversion of Identity*, 2nd ed. (New York: Routledge, 1999), 33; Mosse, *Image of Man*, 29, 32, 33.

10 For an analysis of the "Porfirian Persuasion," see William Beezley, *Judas at the Jockey Club and Other Aspects of Porfirian Mexico* (Lincoln: University of Nebraska Press, 1987), 6.

11 Diane Taylor, *Disappearing Acts: Spectacles of Gender and Nationalism in Argentina's Dirty War* (Durham: Duke University Press, 1997).

12 W. H. Bishop, *Old Mexico and Her Lost Provinces* (New York: Harper's Brothers, 1883).

13 Ibid., 155.

14 Ibid., 190. Casualty figures are from Don M. Coerver, *The Porfirian Interregnum: The Presidency of Manuel Gonzalez of Mexico, 1880–1884* (Fort Worth: Texas Christian University Press, 1979), 204.

15 Austin C. Brady, "Mexico's Fighting Equipment," *Review of Reviews* (1906): 582.

16 Eduardo Paz, *A dónde debemos llegar: Estudio sociológico militar* (México: Tipografía Mercantil, 1910), 18, 19.

17 Juan S. Blake, "Uniformes en el Ejército," *Revista del Ejército y Marina* 2 (1906): 351.

18 Irwin, *Mexican Masculinities*, xxix, xxxi.

19 Marjorie Becker, "Torching la Purísima," in *Everyday Forms of State Formation*, ed. Gilbert Joseph and Daniel Nugent, 252 (Durham: Duke University Press, 1994); Michael Johns, *The City of Mexico in the Age of Díaz* (Austin: University of Texas Press, 1997), 77, 78.

20 Paz, *A dónde debemos llegar*, 85.

21 Gustavo Casasola, *Biografía ilustrada del General Porfirio Díaz, 1830–1965* (México: Ediciones Gustavo Casasola, 1970), 90.

22 Robert Martin Alexius, "The Army and Politics in Porfirian Mexico" (PhD diss., University of Texas at Austin, 1976), 34.

23 Ibid., 49. See also Manuel Balbás, *Recuerdos del Yaqui: Principales episodios durante la campaña de 1899 a 1901* (México: Sociedad de Edición y Librería Franco Americano, 1927).

24 Alexius, "Army and Politics," 68.

25 Mílada Bazant de Saldaña, "La modernización en la educación militar, 1876–1910," in *La evolución de la educación militar de México*, ed. Mílada Bazant de Saldaña et al., 197–98 (México: Secretaría de la Defensa Nacional, 1997)..

26 Vázquez Gómez cited in Paz, *A dónde debemos llegar*, 75.

27 Ibid., 76.

28 Victor E. Niemeyer, *El General Bernardo Reyes*, trans. Juan Antonio Ayala, 2nd ed. (Monterrey: Universidad de Nuevo León, 1966), 101.

29 Francisco L. Urquizo, *Tropa Vieja*, 2nd ed. (Mérida: Editorial Yucatanense "Club del Libro," 1950), 34–35, 42, 58.

30 Mariano Azuela, *The Underdogs: A Novel of the Mexican Revolution*, ed. and trans. Beth Ellen Jorgensen and Enrique Munguía (New York: Modern Library, 2002), 17.

31 Mexico, Secretaría de Guerra, "Article 1075," *Ordenanza general para el Ejército de la republica de México* (México: Imprenta de I. Cumplido, 1882), 46–47. For evidence that these rules were followed see Urquizo, *Tropa Vieja*, 54, 56–57.

32 John Keegan and Richard Holmes, eds., *Soldiers: A History of Men in Battle* (New York: Elisabeth Sifton, 1986); William McNeill, *Keeping Together in Time: Dance and Drill in Human History* (Cambridge: Harvard University Press, 1995).

33 See for examples see Thomas A. Janvier, "The Mexican Army," *Harper's New Monthly Magazine* (Nov. 1889): 813–27; H. T. Reed, "The Mexican Military Academy," *The Journal of the Military Service Institute* (1902–6): 817.

34 Bernardo Reyes, *El Ejército mexicano*, special ed. (México: J. Ballescá y Ca., 1901), 67.

35 Elizabeth Salas, *Soldaderas in the Mexican Military: Myth and History* (Austin: University of Texas Press, 1990); Andrés Reséndez Fuentes, "Battleground Women: Soldaderas and Female Soldiers in the Mexican Revolution," *The Americas* 51:4 (April 1995): 530.

36 Heriberto Frías, *Tomochic*, 5th ed. (Mexico: Librería de la Vda. de Ch. Bouret, 1911), 27–28; Janvier, "Mexican Army," 823–24.

37 Peter M. Beattie, *The Tribute of Blood: Army, Honor, Race, and Nation in Brazil, 1864–1945* (Durham: Duke University Press, 2001), 198–202; Robert Buffington, "Homophobia and the Mexican Working Class, 1900–1910," in *The Famous 41: Sexuality and Social Control in Mexico, 1901*, ed. Robert McKee Irwin, Edward J. McCaughan, and Michelle Rocío Nasser, 221 (New York: Palgrave MacMillan, 2003).

38 Mexico, Secretaría de Guerra, "Article 2440," *Ordenanza general*, 274.

39 For examples, see the character Pintada in Azuela, *Underdogs*; see also Salas, *Soldaderas*, 45–47.

40 Ana María Alonso, *Thread of Blood: Colonialism, Revolution, and Gender on Mexico's Northern Frontier* (Tucson: University of Arizona Press, 1995), 204.

41 Frederic Remington, "Mexican Major," *Harper's Weekly* (27 Sep. 1890): 755.

42 Buffington, "Homophobia," 210; Victor M. Macías-Gonzalez, "The Lagartijo at the High Life: Masculine Consumption, Race, Nation, and Homosexuality in Porfirian Nation," in *The Famous 41*, ed. Irwin, McCaughan, and Rocío Nasser, 228.

43 Daniel Nugent and Ana Maria Alonso, "Multiple Selective Traditions," in *Everyday Forms of State Formation*, ed. Gilbert Joseph and Daniel Nugent, 234 (Durham: Duke University Press, 1994).

44 Bishop, *Old Mexico*, 265.

45 Ibid., 268.

46 Beattie, *Tribute of Blood*, 178.

47 Alicia Hernández Chávez, "Origen y ocaso del Ejército porfiriano," *Historia Mexicana* 39:1 (July–Sep. 1989): 263.

48 Mexico, Secretaría de Guerra, "Articles 1427–40," *Ordenanza general*, 99.

49 Ibid.

50 Pablo Piccato, "Politics and the Technology of Honor: Duelling in Turn-of-the-Century Mexico," *Journal of Social History* 33:2 (Winter 1999): 331.

51 Angel Escudero, *El duelo en México* (México: Imprenta Mundial, 1936).

52 Federico Gamboa, *Santa*, 11th ed. (México: Ediciones Botas, 1938), 49.

53 Bishop, *Old Mexico*, 509.

54 Alonso, *Thread of Blood*, 182; Pablo Piccato, *City of Suspects: Crime in Mexico City, 1900–1931* (Durham: Duke University Press, 2001), 81.

55 Macías-González, "Lagartijo," 230.

56 Mexico, Secretaría de Guerra y Marina, "Article 17," *Reglamento del Colegio Militar* (México: M. Murguia y Co., 1854).

57 Mexico, Secretaría de Guerra y Marina, "Articles 12, 13, 27," *Reglamento provisional del Escuela Militar de Aspirantes* (México: I. Cumplido, 1905).

58 Mexico, Secretaría de Guerra, "Article 1432," *Ordenanza general*, 99.

59 Miguel Ruelas, "Los origenes del nuestro Ejército," *Revista del Ejército y Marina* 10 (1910): 252.

60 Alexius, "Army and Politics," 81.

61 Escudero, *Duelo en México*, 156–59.

62 Ibid., 158–59.

63 W. H. Bishop, "With the Vanguard in Mexico," *Harper's Monthly* (Jan. 1882): 226.

64 The frequency of public exercises is mentioned in *Revista del Ejército y Marina* 10 (1910): 610.

65 Reed, "Mexican Military Academy," 818.

66 Irwin et al., *Famous 41*, 2–5.

67 Alan Knight, *The Mexican Revolution*, vol. 1 (New York: Cambridge University Press, 1986), 18.

68 Reed, "Mexican Military Academy," 814, 818.

69 Janvier, "Mexican Army," 820.

70 For similar parades, see Captain F. H. Hardie, "The Mexican Army," *Journal of the Military Service Institution of the United States* 31:811 (1892): 1207; Frederick Remington, "General Mile's Review of the Mexican Army," *Harper's Weekly* (4 July 1891): 495. The more accurate estimate of army size is found in Hernández Chávez, "Origen y ocaso," 287.

71 Allen P. Splete and Marilyn D. Splete, eds., *Frederic Remington: Selected Letters* (New York: Abbeville Press, 1988), 63.

72 Bishop, "With the Vanguard," 225.

73 Mosse, *Image of Man*, 56–57; Macías-González, "Lagartijo," 230.

74 Bishop, *Old Mexico*, 127.

75 Warren Schiff, "German Military Penetration into Mexico During the Late Díaz Period," *Hispanic American Historical Review* 39:4 (Nov. 1959): 568–79; Gustavo Casasola, *Seis siglos de historia gráfica de México, 1325–1925*, 4th ed., vol. 3 (México: Editorial Gustavo Casasola, S.A., 1971), 1719, 1331, 1503.

76 Alexius, "Army and Politics," 10.

77 Casasola, *Biografía ilustrada*; Guy P. C. Thomson, "Bulwarks of Patriotic Liberalism: The National Guard, Philharmonic Corps and Patriotic Juntas in Mexico, 1847–88," *Journal of Latin American Studies* 22:1 (Feb. 1990): 31–68; Matthew D. Esposito, "Death and Disorder in Mexico City," in *Latin American Popular Culture: An Introduction*, ed. William Beezley and Linda Ann Curcio Nagy, 87–103 (Wilmington: Scholarly Resources, 2000).

78 Gustavo A. García, "In Quest of a National Cinema," in *Mexico's Cinema: A Century of Film and Filmmakers*, ed. Joanne Hirshfield and David Maciel, 5–8 (Wilmington: Scholarly Resources, 1999).

79 For one example, see Alan Knight, "Weapons and Arches in the Mexican Revolutionary Landscape," in *Everyday Forms of State Formation*, ed. Gilbert Joseph and Daniel Nugent, 58 (Durham: Duke University Press, 1994).

80 Tenorio Trillo, *Mexico at the Worlds' Fairs*, 1–2.

4 Playing with National Identity:

BRAZIL IN INTERNATIONAL FOOTBALL, 1900–1925

Gregg P. Bocketti

INTRODUCTION

International athletic competition in such venues as the Olympic Games offers participating countries the opportunity to display representations of their nations, often in idealized ways. Organizers carefully choose the nation's most accomplished representatives so that, for at least the duration of an event or match, the nation can be identified with a successful runner or a victorious rugby team. For Brazilians, who have taken great pride in the accomplishments of the tennis player Gustavo Kuerten and the late race car driver Ayrton Senna, the chief role in symbolizing the nation on athletic fields has for many decades been filled, not surprisingly, by the national association football (soccer) team. The team, known in Brazil as the *seleção*, or select team, with its distinctive yellow jerseys and even more distinctive "samba soccer" style of playing, seems to advertise an ideal Brazil: powerful, beautiful, richly diverse, and above all successful. Its famous victories, including an unrivalled five World Cup tournament victories, are but part of the story of the seleção. The team also seems to exemplify what some consider the best tradition of Brazil's heritage, bringing together players and drawing supporters from the length and breadth of a large country, with their different racial, ethnic, and class backgrounds. It is not surprising, then, that it has been suggested that Brazilians' sense of common national identity is most intense when the team is playing.[1] At its best, the seleção represents Brazil as many Brazilians would like it to be.

However, this is only an ideal. There are, it is true, Brazilians who are not football enthusiasts, and the team and its supporters are split by myriad off-field divisions only partially bridged by on-field successes. Race, class, and regional differences cause the identity of the seleção to be contested, as the preferences of organizers and other members of the football community sometimes clash in the constitution of the seleção. For example, many observers contend that the team represents the traditional centres of Rio de Janeiro and São Paulo more fully than other areas like Bahia in the northeast or Rio Grande do Sul in the south. And, in another instance, there is the striking circumstance of team members who play their professional football abroad, in places like Spain and Italy, being referred to as *estrangeiros*, foreigners, even as they represent Brazil on the national team.

Thus, the seleção, the nationally representative football side, can function as an expression of Brazilian national identity, but that identity is one contested by the different members of the nation's sporting community. The roots of this relationship between the sport and Brazilian national identity can be traced to the beginning of Brazil's experience with football. This chapter will trace those roots, concentrating on Brazilian football's formative years during the first decades of the twentieth century. It will demonstrate that, instead of the distinctively Brazilian seleção with which we are familiar today, elite and middle-sector organizers endeavoured to ensure that Brazil's first forays into international competition advertised a socially refined and culturally European version of Brazil. Eventually such preferences were undermined, but their defenders and their influences lingered, affecting the ways in which Brazilian sporting identity would be defined for many years to come.

Scholars have become increasingly sensitive to the importance of sport in recent years, especially in terms of its capacity to reflect and also influence notions of group and national identity. J. A. Mangan, for example, has detailed the "games ethic" developed by English public school masters during the nineteenth century. This ethic defined the physical and moral benefits that proponents expected participants to derive from playing team sports, and also advanced "muscular Christian" views of masculinity and Englishness among the nation's middle-class and elite boys and young men. Mangan has also explored the international career of the games ethic, as it was carried into the world when others began to take up British sports like football and cricket. Thus Mangan, along with other scholars, such as Joseph Arbena and Hilary McD. Beckles, has suggested that the adoption of British sports by people both within and outside the empire coloured developing constructions of nationality, often with the tincture of a fetishized Englishness.[2]

In the case of Brazil, many scholarly works have focused upon the relationship between the nation and football from a contemporary perspective. Among the most notable of such contributions have been those of Robert M. Levine and Janet Lever.[3] Recently, a small number of scholars have begun to consider the longer history of the sport, and its relationship to national identity, including the period of the late-nineteenth and early-twentieth centuries. Waldenyr Caldas and Leonardo Pereira have made significant contributions in this regard.[4] The present chapter draws on their work, as well as the work of Mangan and others, but there is still much work to be done, especially in terms of better understanding the transition from English *football* to Brazilian *futebol*.

During the early years of the twentieth century, Brazilians enthused about the prospect of football matches between native and foreign sportsmen for many reasons. Many viewed international competition simply as a good way to improve the local game. That is, Brazilians, whose football history dated only from the mid-1890s, could learn from more experienced opponents, such as Britons and other Europeans. Others viewed them as valuable to the nation's diplomatic efforts. Thus enthusiasts often described Brazil's international football representatives as "ambassadors," and prominent diplomats lent their support to the forging of sporting ties between Brazilian and foreign sportsmen. For example, the Baron of Rio Branco (1845–1912), Brazil's pre-eminent diplomat for many years, donated the Rio Branco Cup for competition between Brazilian and Uruguayan footballers. Likewise, Julio Roca, president of Argentina on two occasions (1880–86 and 1898–1904), donated a trophy for a similar competition between teams representing Argentina and Brazil.

But international sporting contests were about more than skill improvement and international friendship. Well into the 1920s, the Brazilian experience with international competition was dominated by urban, elite, white, Europhile sportsmen, the same men who constituted the first generations of footballers and sports organizers in Brazil. Having learned how to play during travels in Europe or through familiarity with European expatriates living in Brazil, they founded the country's first football clubs and leagues, and made early Brazilian football a preserve for themselves and their peers.

For such sportsmen, international sporting events were about individual, group and, ultimately, national identity. Modern sports, and international sporting contests, offered them an opportunity to define themselves, and their nation, according to ideal constructions of self-image. As organizers and managers of international matches and tournaments, they were able to control when and against whom Brazilians would play and which sportsmen would represent the group or nation. In control of the country's fledgling sports media, as owners, editors, and journalists, they were able to interpret according to their own lights the action and results of the playing field. In short, the international playing field offered a stage whereupon an ideal Brazil could be presented, without reference to realities with which sportsmen may not have been comfortable.

Not surprisingly, given what we know about the predilections of such men, the image of Brazil advertised during early experiences with international competition was racially, socially, and culturally circumscribed. That is, the period of the late-nineteenth and early-twentieth centuries was characterized by oligarchic rule in politics, vast ethnic and social inequalities, and by elite and middle-sector disdain for Brazilian cultural practices. As Jeffrey D. Needell has demonstrated, the period's dominant cultural discourse was that of well-bred urbanites who donned English frockcoats, read French-inspired poetry, and attended productions of Italian opera in an attempt to realize a Eurocentric "fantasy of civilization."[5]

For many of these Brazilians, European sports were as much a part of the cultural "fantasy" as were the correct clothes, literature, or music. They participated in the sporting community in great part because they took their cultural cues from Europe, and learned from Europeans that enthusiasm for modern sports was a mark of progressive modernity. Competition was for them a secondary concern; priority was instead given to cultivating the image of the ideal sportsman: a man who was wealthy, white, culturally European, and amateur. With few exceptions, Brazilians who did not meet this ideal, whether female, working class, nonwhite, or clearly parochial, were confined to roles only as spectators to the feats of acceptable and accepted representatives of the nation.

CORINTHIANS IN BRAZIL, 1910–14

One of the most important of Brazil's early experiences with international sporting competition was that with the Corinthian Football Club between 1910 and 1914. Brazilians had participated in a handful of "international" matches before 1910, but the experience with the British Corinthians proved crucial, especially as it helped define an ideal to which Brazilian organizers would aspire in the years to come. Indeed, it would be difficult to find, in that or in any other period, a group of athletes who more closely filled the sporting profile preferred by elite Brazilians and other

Latin American and Caribbean people than these English footballers. The most basic element in the Corinthian character was the devotion to the amateur practice of sports. Almost as important, for the Corinthians and for their Brazilian hosts, the club members were solid members of the English elite, as attendance at either Oxford or Cambridge universities was a usual qualification for team membership.

Despite these restrictions, the Corinthians were widely regarded as one of the best, most skilled football teams in the world in the period before World War One. However, after 1907, the club suffered for want of competition at home after relations between its Amateur Football Association and the rival Football Association were permanently broken. With this, the club began to look outside Britain for opponents and travelled to many foreign countries to find suitable opponents. The Corinthians' travels eventually took them to Brazil, where the club conducted tours in 1910 and 1913.[6]

On each trip to Brazil the Corinthians visited both Rio de Janeiro and São Paulo, staying two weeks and playing three matches in each city. The Corinthians' fame preceded them and the Brazilians extended them a warm welcome. According to one player, "We had a magnificent reception everywhere. No team could possibly have been treated better, and the people there couldn't do too much for us."[7] On the first tour, the Englishmen won all of their matches handily. They almost repeated the feat three years later, when they drew once and lost once, winning the balance of their matches.

Despite the relative lack of competitiveness, the matches of the Corinthians were extremely well attended, both in the media and in the stands. In Rio de Janeiro in 1910, "the ground at the Roso road was too small to hold the Carioca [resident of Rio de Janeiro] multitude, which wanted to witness the exploits of the famous English game."[8] Similarly large crowds greeted the Englishmen in São Paulo. Indeed, the popularity of the Englishmen on this occasion is amply illustrated by the story of the founding of Sport Club Corinthians Paulista. This football club, today one of the most popular and successful in Brazil, was founded in 1910, in the days following the visit of the English Corinthians. A group of young Paulistas, impressed by the abilities of the Corinthians, decided to found a club of their own, honouring their English heroes in the name of the club itself. As one founder stated, the club members settled on the name "in homage to the brave London students who, a few days before, were in São Paulo."[9] And the English Corinthians' popularity had not diminished in the three years between tours. In 1913 their matches drew between 6,000 and 10,000 spectators each, according to one estimate.[10]

The English Corinthians' fame and great football skill surely help explain their popularity in Brazil. Brazilians would have wanted to play against and witness the feats of these most skilled footballers. Many Brazilians looked on the Corinthians as a student does a master. But it is important to note that Brazilians' enthusiastic reception extended outside the stadiums of Rio de Janeiro and São Paulo. In both cities, team members enjoyed the entertainments of their hosts away from playing fields. In Rio de Janeiro in 1910, they were taken on a driving tour of the city, on a trip up Corcovado Mountain, and on a boating excursion in Guanabara Bay. Along with such tourist fare, their Brazilian hosts honoured them with a "soirée" as well as a farewell banquet including "Yorkshire ham" and "European fruits."[11] Similarly, in São Paulo, the young Englishmen received special treatment far from the football fields. As one writer has suggested of their reception in that city, "Had Edward VII visited São Paulo he would not have received a grander welcome."[12] Their farewell banquet in 1910 was a extravagant affair, the menu including even "Coeur de filet de boeuf à la Corinthian."[13] In 1913 they received tangible proof of the esteem in which they were held by their counterparts among Brazilian sportsmen, receiving "lavish presents, as mementos of their visit to S. Paulo." These included "ten pins with diamonds, rubies and pearls, for the necktie . . . and a gold and platinum watch chain." The presents were offered the Corinthians by the Associação Paulista de Sports Atléticos (Paulista Athletic Sports Association), their hosts in São Paulo, and the event received official sanction, as the English vice-consul in São Paulo, Charles Miller, himself the father of Brazilian football, distributed the gifts.[14]

The Paulistas, like the Cariocas, felt honoured by the Corinthians' visit. The Englishmen's tour was an important event in the life of the city, a highlight not only of the sporting season but also of the social life of the sportsmen and the women who entertained them. On the occasion of each visit a handful of Brazilian sportsmen had the opportunity to play against some of the best footballers in the world and thousands more witnessed their skills. Even more, Brazilian sportsmen responded enthusiastically to the social and cultural refinement of the Corinthians. Press accounts of their activities usually cited their connections to Britain's venerable universities, and emphasized their amateur status. In short, they were the "distinguished young Corinthians,"[15] and they dedicated themselves to the same amateur, patrician sporting ideal as did their elite Brazilian hosts. As one Corinthian noted with satisfaction, Brazilian sportsmen had "set their faces sternly against professionalism in any shape or form."[16]

The Corinthians' exclusivity had served to marginalize them in the world of English football. In Brazil, it helped make them not only respected opponents but honoured guests as well. After all, they had been invited to Brazil and hosted in Rio de Janeiro by the capital's most aristocratic and exclusive club, the Fluminense Football Club, whose members went to great lengths to impress their guests. Beyond honouring the Corinthians with parties and banquets, entertaining the tourists with sight-seeing trips, and hosting the matches in Rio de Janeiro, in 1910 the Fluminense club paid half the cost of the team's passage from Britain, and organized hotel accommodations for the travelling party.[17] In São Paulo, the team was hosted by the Liga Paulista de Foot-ball (Paulista Football League) in 1910 and by the Associação Paulista (Paulista Association) in 1913. The leading parts there were taken by the sportsmen of Club Atlético Paulistano and São Paulo Athletic Club, clubs much like Fluminense in their profile and in the deference with which they treated the English travelers.

Nonelite Brazilians attended the matches of the Corinthians as well, people like the young Afro-Brazilian spectator who ran onto the field and kicked one of the Englishmen "in the correct place with his bare foot" after a referee's decision had gone against the local team.[18] But many of the spectators at the matches of the Corinthians were quite well-heeled. Note the cosmopolitan use of English (in italics) in the following contemporary account:

> If anyone still doubted that *foot-ball* is the *sport* of fashion,
> the favourite *sport* of our fine and elegant society, yesterday
> afternoon would be enough to demonstrate this truth.
>   He who, curious, situated himself at Fluminense's main gate,
> at 3:30 in the afternoon, would have seen an intermittent parade
> of the most pretty *girls*, the most distinguished gentlemen,
> some wearing circumspect dress-coats and others, bright
> and cheerful suits; he would have seen parade by senators,
> deputies, diplomats, representatives of high commerce and high
> administration, [and] he would have seen the continual arrival of
> automobiles and coaches carrying the distinguished families of
> our society.[19]

The Brazilian representative footballers, almost exclusively white and wealthy, shared these spectators' social and cultural profile, as, of course, did the Corinthians themselves.

On the field, in the grandstand, in tuxedoed ballrooms, a visit by the Corinthians was an event for the Brazilian elite. In the international context of the tours, this elite portrayed Brazil nationalism as a projection of its own self-image, with a patrician, amateur sporting ethic and a culture of European refinement. The Corinthians were excellent judges to which Brazilian sportsmen could appeal for validation, for they epitomized the sporting profile preferred by the Brazilian elite. It is no coincidence that one English observer noticed that "the enthusiastic Brazilians made almost a national occasion of the first match."[20] To many Brazilians, it was exactly that: an opportunity to define the nation, in its choice of friends and in its own personality. Finally, the "national" importance attached to these occasions explains the horror of many Brazilians at the suggestion by the *Brazilian Review*, a local English-language newspaper, that some Paulista spectators had exhibited partisanship against the Corinthians. According to one editorialist, boos and hisses there may have been, but they could not be attributed to the society at large, much less to its "best elements." Instead, any such indiscretions were the fault of "a few tens of little-educated and perhaps illiterate individuals."[21] Thankfully, his newspaper was able to publish the Corinthians' letter of thanks to their Paulista hosts two days later, proving that Brazilians had indeed demonstrated themselves and their nation worthy of the Corinthians' friendship.[22]

RACE, CLASS, AND SPORTING VALUES

In the first decades of Brazil's participation in international sporting competition, then, the Corinthians experience can be viewed as a kind of preferred paradigm. The playing participants shared a social and cultural profile, as well as a dedication to amateur athletics. On and off the field, elite sportsmen used these international contests to demonstrate their mutual respect and their shared values. Brazilians hoped that their experiences against other foreign opponents would follow a similar profile. For their part, Brazilian organizers ensured that their representative footballers were, as far as possible, socially and culturally elite. Most often their opponents shared this elitist profile, exclusivity in sports during the period being certainly not limited to Brazil.

Moreover, it was expected that both sides in an international encounter would devote themselves to the most sportsmanlike behaviour on the field and in the grandstand, competitiveness secondary to gentlemanliness. Unfortunately, from the perspective of elite organizers and spokesmen, this was not always the case. Either way, the issue often drew the attention of Brazilian observers. For example, one writer lauded the "fidelity" of Argentine footballers to the sportsman's code during a match in 1914 in Buenos Aires between teams representing Argentina and Brazil. On that occasion, the Brazilian referee awarded a goal to the hosts, not having noticed an infraction by one of their players. However, the Argentine players insisted on the enforcement of the rules and refused to accept the goal. The Argentines went on to lose the match, but won the respect of their Brazilian guests, especially the patrician players, organizers, and journalists whom they were hosting.[23]

In another instance, when a Portuguese side visited Brazil, a Paulista crowd demonstrated its good manners when some of their number entered the playing field and carried off their victorious guests on their shoulders.[24] Finally, as with the Corinthians, off-field socialization encouraged camaraderie between competing sportsmen. Banquets and receptions may not usually have been quite as lavish as the events surrounding the visits of the Corinthians, but they were a constant feature of Brazilians' international contests. These events' importance in defining a specific sporting identity ought not be underestimated. Through them, sportsmen sought to diminish on-field rivalries and to emphasize the exclusivity of their sporting world, with its "Corinthianesque" elitism, refinement, and Europhilia.

This is not to say that all commentary on the Corinthians was complimentary. Some Brazilian observers were surprised at the English footballers' use of force in their play. Some asserted that, having shown their great abilities in all other facets of the game, the Corinthians wanted to show their hosts that they could also excel in its rougher aspects. Others suggested, perhaps facetiously, that the use of force was yet another area in which Brazilians could learn from their visitors. But it was pointed out that on at least one occasion players on both visiting and home sides employed rough tactics. Sportsmen would have preferred that the footballers rely on skill instead of force, but critics never suggested that the Corinthians were less than sportsmanlike.[25] After all, the Corinthians were still the "masters" of the game, and in the matches in which force became an issue they dominated the play. There was no diminution of Brazilians' respect for the Corinthians afterwards. The honourary banquets described above still took place. Significantly, the Corinthians were invited to return to Brazil not once, but twice.

The case was quite different when the Corinthians' countrymen representing the Exeter City Football Club visited Brazil in 1914. As with the Corinthians' tours, the visit of the professional footballers from Exeter was organized by the wealthy Europhiles of the capital's elite sporting organization, and it was met in Brazil by great interest and enthusiasm. Their games were well attended, and Brazilians were sure that they could learn from their guests' football. However, Brazilians were not only surprised but disappointed by the Exetermen's employment of rough tactics. One observer lamented: "The English '*team*' (it's a shame) seeing itself perturbed enough, made use of '*trucs*' [tricks] and even brutality. Thus it was that, attempting to avoid the '*goal*' that the Brazilians eventually marked, one of the Englishmen seriously injured the Brazilian '*centre-forward*' [Artur] Friedenreich."[26] In the view of many observers, here was a defining difference between the Corinthians and Exeter footballers. The Corinthians played roughly at times, but relied chiefly upon their skills. The team from Exeter used force, in the view of many Brazilians, in a quite unsportsmanlike and cynical manner, using rough tactics in lieu of skill, to avoid defeat. In reality there may or may not have been a great difference between the two teams' employment of force in their play. But Brazilian observers treated the episodes in different manners, criticizing the team from Exeter in much more forceful terms than they did the Corinthians. This difference in perspective, it seems clear, grew out of the difference in the social and cultural identity of the opponents. The Corinthians, patrician and amateur like their hosts, could be forgiven their missteps, for despite them they had "remained paragons of how the game should be played." The Exeter team, however, did not share these characteristics with their hosts, and this contrast, especially their professionalism, explains the difference in perspective. Competition between locals and the team from Exeter was assigned great significance in the definition of the proper profile of the sportsman. In the words of one author, for Brazilian observers, "it was important to assert the moral superiority of amateur over professional football."[27]

At the time, many Brazilian sportsmen attributed the Exeter footballers' unsportsmanlike behaviour to their professional status. Two years later, during the South American Championships of 1916, Brazilians discovered that amateur footballers too could conduct themselves in a less than gentlemanly manner on the playing field. This first edition of one of the world's oldest international tournaments featured representative teams from four countries: Brazil, Chile, Uruguay, and the hosts, Argentina. The Brazilians did not fare well, drawing once and losing twice in their three matches. However, according to one observer, they were "morally victorious in all the matches," because they had not resorted to the rough tactics of their opponents, namely the Chileans and Uruguayans, to whom they lost.[28] According to Brazilian observers, the Chileans were especially violent, employing "the most brutal methods" in securing their victory. In defeat, the Brazilians had preserved the proper demeanour and had thus identified Brazil with the highest sporting values:

Honour, then, to our compatriots! The *score* of matches does not always express the valour of the adversaries: victories can afterwards be discredited as defeats, but chivalry during the match, courtesy, the good, the true, calm, rational and intelligent game, without violence, with energy, the force of determination, with all of this together, finally, in the qualities which our compatriots implanted in Buenos Aires and which were rewarded with moral victory in all of the matches, this impressed because it is not the work of chance, this endures because it is not the fruit of materialism, this elevates, honours, dignifies and glorifies not only our *foot-ballers* but all of us, Brazilians, because it is the reflection of our culture, the expression of our character, the essence of our race.

"Ale goak! Hurrah"![29]

Brazilians had gone to Argentina to play three football matches. But by playing in an international arena, theirs was the responsibility of representing Brazil and asserting its national identity. In the elite-dominated sporting world of 1916, it was important that this identity reflect Brazilian elite sportsmen's self-image as refined, gentlemanly, Corinthian; victory was secondary.

The other South American teams, it seemed to Brazilian observers, were entirely too competitive and had sacrificed their dignity in search of victory, as had the professionals from Exeter. The reasoning in these cases may have been somewhat circular: the Exeter footballers had played roughly because they were not gentlemen but professionals; the Chileans and Uruguayans were not gentlemen because they played roughly. But the significant point is that in both cases the opponents had violated sporting behaviour deemed proper by Brazilian sportsmen. The Brazilians, on the other hand, had not. Brazilian sportsmen were proud that the national image projected by their players in these international matches had remained true to the elite amateur ethic.

Brazilian observers also criticized their own countrymen when they did not live up to that ethic, at least to a point. As has been mentioned, one writer noted that Corinthians and Brazilian footballers were alike guilty for the rough play of one match. And unsportsmanlike partisanship on the part of spectators drew the attention of Brazilian sportsmen on the occasion of the first visit by the Corinthians. Observers admitted that some were guilty, but did not allow that these were members of Brazil's better classes. Any such offender was deemed ignorant, perhaps illiterate, in the same class as the "horde of urchins" who disparaged a referee during a match against a visiting Italian team. Such activities were "absolutely condemnable," according to one writer, and had no place in Brazilian sporting circles, especially in the international context. Luckily, in his view, elite sportsmen were not to blame.[30]

A final violation of elite Brazilians' preferred sporting profile in the early years of international competition was highlighted during the South American Championships of 1919. One of the stars of this tournament was the Uruguayan Isabelino Gradin. He was one of its best, most skilled players, and he was black. Uruguay was the only South American country against which Brazilians played that consistently fielded black players during these early years. Gradin, for example, had played in the 1916 championship. However, in 1919, the championships were held in Rio de Janeiro. Thus the Brazilian sporting community had a closer look at the Uruguayan team, and many did not like what they saw. During this tournament, Brazilian newspapers criticized the presence of black Uruguayans on their playing fields, for example satirizing Gradin and his fellows in cartoons.[31] As historian Leonardo Pereira has pointed out, the Carioca media portrayed a homogenous Brazilian public opinion in which blacks and whites agreed that black players ought not participate in international contests, because, according to one newspaper, "the black man in Brazil does not want to be black."[32] Pereira notes that such a homogeneity did not in fact exist, and black Carioca spectators adopted Gradin as a favoured player, although he was a foreigner.[33]

But these sportsmen did not control the selection of representative teams nor the organization of international contests. This was the province of elite Brazilians like Epitácio Pessoa, the country's president (1919–22) and a member of the Confederação Brasileira de Desportos (Brazilian Sports Confederation, forerunner of the modern-day Confederação Brasileira de Futebol, the country's football governing body). Under Pessoa's direction, the federal government financed the participation of the Confederação team for the 1921 South American Championships, on the condition that Brazil's representatives be "rigorously white."[34] Like Pessoa, the elite Brazilians who directed the country's participation in international competitions sought, as far as possible, to ensure that representative players reflected their white, patrician vision of the nation.

During the first decades of Brazilian competition in international football, there was one consistent exception that proved this general rule. His name was Artur Friedenreich (Figure 4.1). Friedenreich was the son of a German father and Brazilian mother, a woman of colour. Despite the fact that he was not "rigorously white," Friedenreich regularly represented Brazil in international contests in the first decades of the

4.1. First Team of the Club Athletico Paulistano, *ca.* 1915
Note: Artur Friedenrich is seated front row, centre.
Source: Photo courtesy Centro Pró-Memória, Club Athletico Paulistano, São Paulo.

twentieth century, eventually becoming a fixture in the national seleção. This Paulista possessed an immense skill, and was without doubt one of the best Brazilian footballers of his era. But it is important to stress that it was not only Friedenrich's skill which made him acceptable to the elite sportsmen of the day. In many respects, he was one of their own. He was a member of the São Paulo social and cultural elite, a member first of Sport Club Germânia, the club of his paternal German roots, and later of Club Atlético Paulistano, one of the city's most aristocratic and exclusive institutions, expensive to join and exacting in its selection of members and players. Moreover, Friedenrich seems to have shared the elite sporting ethic which preferred educated, wealthy Europeans.[35] In the words of pioneering Brazilian sports journalist Mário Filho, Friedenrich "had a German father, [and] did not want to be mulatto." And elite administrators and organizers accepted his self-image; he was "neither white nor mulatto, colourless, above these things."[36]

Indeed, Friedenrich was exactly the type of nonwhite traditionally accepted by Brazilian elites. As Thomas E. Skidmore has demonstrated in his *Black into White*, the early twentieth century saw Brazilian intellectuals struggle with and ultimately reject European notions of the strict determinism of race. Instead, they championed the idea of racial and cultural whitening, and therefore improvement, both for individuals and for the nation. Race was presented as, at least in part, a social and cultural construct, not an inherited fact, and it could therefore be manipulated and negotiated.[37] For a man of colour like Friedenreich, this stance would have presented the possibility for social acceptance based on something other than physiognomy. He would have benefited from the view that, as Jerry Dávila has written, "individuals could escape the social category of blackness through improvement of their health, level of education and culture, or their social class."[38]

Thus, an exception could be made for Friedenreich. He was a man of colour, but possessed great football skill and supported the elite vision of Brazilian national identity. Moreover, given his success, his grace, and his cultural credentials as a "European," he may have seemed an exemplar of Brazilian elites' insistence upon the ameliorative possibilities of social and cultural whitening, the possibilities of the regeneration of the Brazilian "race." In these early years, Brazilian elite sportsmen were not prepared to go further. They instead sought to protect their preferred sporting profile. The closer the episodes of international competition came to this profile, the happier the experience, as with the Corinthians tours and the visit to "loyal" Argentina in 1914. When some aspect of the preferred sporting profile was violated, criticisms were levelled and controversies brewed. The rough play of Exeter's team, the catcalls of poorer Brazilian spectators, the presence of a black player in the Uruguayan side: these were out of place in football, especially in international contests. For Brazil's elite sportsmen, the organizers of such contests, international competition was an important arena for the assertion of their national ideal. Therefore, every particular should, as far as possible, express that ideal. In the early years, competitiveness and success were important in portraying a successful and progressive country; but they were secondary to the identification of Brazil with a specific national image: white, patrician, and culturally European.

Together, the organizers, administrators, coaches, players, journalists, and many supporters who embraced this image helped restrict the constitution of the seleção and the character of Brazil's experience with international football well into the 1920s. The first priority for these sportsmen was to use sport to identify Brazil as a modern, refined and, especially, European nation. After all, in the first decades of the twentieth century, to be elite, to be refined, to be modern for many upper-class Brazilians meant to be European. It is important to recognize that inherent in this project was a kind of nationalism, one in which Brazil itself was promoted, but in which the characteristics which distinguished it from a European culture and identity were obscured. Brazilian sportsmen were competitive, but they were more concerned with presenting a proper advertisement for their nation than they were with football victories. Thus there was nationalistic pride despite defeat in the South American Championships of 1916. While the Uruguayan and Chilean representative sides could be accused of rough, unsportsmanlike tactics, the Brazilian representatives could be lauded for their own demonstration of gentlemanly play even in defeat. Similarly, defeat against the famous, highly skilled English Corinthians was not cast as a national failure; instead, simply hosting such estimable guests was portrayed as a proof of national worth.

There were other, more overt expressions of nationalism in Brazil's international contests in the years before 1920, even in the elite-dominated episodes discussed above. When a young black boy ran onto the playing field and kicked a visiting English player, when sections of a Paulista crowd booed the victorious Corinthians, when a sports writer construed a club match between the Italian Torino Club and the Club Atlético Paulistano as "Itália vs. Brasil," Brazilian sportsmen were expressing nationalist pride through sport. Most commonly, nationalistic sentiments were expressed on the occasion of victories by representative sides. For example, many observers labelled a victory gained by a team representing Brazil over the professionals of Exeter City a "national victory."[39] And Friedenreich and his teammates were treated as national heroes due to their victory in the South American Championships in 1919, feted by the sporting public and lionized by the sporting media. In these and other instances, sportsmen demonstrated that nationalism and competitiveness could exist even within the generally elitist, amateur, and Europhile environment of these early sporting events.

CONCLUSION

When change finally came during the 1920s and 1930s, it was in great part due to success itself. During those years, Brazilian victories in international football became more and more commonplace, and with it came the nationalistic sentiments that success elicited. Brazilians gained more experience with the game and more frequently played against foreign opponents, yielding such achievements as the successful European tour conducted by São Paulo's Paulistano club in 1925, in which the team lost only one match in ten against continental opponents; the 1932 seleção victory over world-champions Uruguay in the Rio Branco Cup; and the strong performance of the seleção in the 1938 World Cup, where the team lost to eventual champions Italy at the semifinal stage.

Building upon past victories, such successes demonstrated to Brazilian sportsmen the emerging football excellence of their countrymen. Moreover, they fired the imagination and the competitive instincts of players, organizers, and public alike, helping to break down the elitist paradigm discussed in this chapter. That is, victory presented the possibility that on-field success, and not simply gentlemanly participation, could become a means to promote Brazil in the context of international sports. It presented the possibility of Brazilians replacing their erstwhile European teachers as the masters of the sport. With victory on the playing field, the nation could be portrayed as powerful and important, notwithstanding its diplomatic or economic significance, despite the racial and cultural backwardness that many foreigners and not a few Brazilians detected in the national character.

And so, in search of victories, organizers slowly opened up the field to the most skilled footballers, regardless of their backgrounds. White elite and middle-sector sportsmen made sure to retain for themselves control over sports administration and sports media, but they increasingly turned to talented nonwhite and working-class players, men such as the "Black Marvel," Fausto dos Santos, and the "Marshal of Victory," former soldier Floriano Peixoto Corrêa, to represent Brazil in the international arena. In their desire to achieve good results, and recognizing that such results had by the 1920s become a realistic possibility, organizers deconstructed some of the old limitations which they had placed on Brazil's participation in international football. They retained their faith in the importance of sports as a means to advertise an idealized vision of Brazil, but expanded their vision to include those who could bring glory to the homeland. In the process, the seleção, Brazil's nationally representative team, became more truly representative of Brazilian reality.

Something similar occurred in domestic Brazilian football as well during this period. Among the more important changes in the world of football which occurred during the 1920s and 1930s were the geographic and numerical expansion of the football community, the increasing acceptance of nonwhite, nonelite players in first-class competition, and, finally, the professionalization of leagues in São Paulo and Rio de Janeiro in 1933. As in the international case described above, these changes owed much to organizers' and administrators' search for competitive advantages. That is, they discarded old notions of exclusivity in their search for victories and championship titles.[40]

Of course, such changes within football did not take place in a vacuum. They were in part reflective of larger cultural trends occurring in Brazil during the 1920s and 1930s. Just as the earlier Eurocentric construct of Brazilian football was an expression of Brazilian elite and middle sectors' predilection for all things European, so too was the shift towards a more Brazilian football reflective of a more general re-evaluation of influence of European traditions on Brazilian culture. The devastation of the 1914–18 war shook many elite Brazilians' confidence in the superiority of Western civilization, and the "culture wars" of the 1920s and 1930s yielded a new appreciation for Brazil's distinctive, non-European traditions.[41] Moreover, this period saw the growth of new ideas about race in Brazil, and "a new confidence that the variable of race did not necessarily preclude Brazil's future as a great nation,"[42] as intellectuals such as Gilberto Freyre and Mário de Andrade began to insist upon the contributions that nonwhites had made to Brazilian culture and nationality.[43] Such developments could not but influence the football community and the image of the nation that sports organizers sought to cultivate abroad.

This is not to say, however, that the evolution of international football in Brazil was dependent upon "high culture" or larger political and social events. Football may have been influenced by changes in such areas, but it possessed its own history and its own logic. Just as important as the world war to Brazilian sportsmen's disillusionment with European cultural leadership was the behaviour of the footballers from the Exeter City club and the successes of Brazilians against European opponents. Just as important as the writings of social scientists in establishing respect among sporting Brazilians for Afro-Brazilians was the patent ability and accomplishments of footballers like Fausto dos Santos, especially when they represented Brazil in the seleção. Indeed, given football's historic and continuing importance in Brazilian culture and society, it would perhaps not be inappropriate to suggest that, as football enthusiasts played with national identity during the early decades of the twentieth century, they influenced Brazilian nationalism as much as any Brazilian litterateur, academician, or politician.

1 For example, journalist Mário Filho noticed that during the World Cup championship of 1938, on the occasion of a match between the representative teams of Italy and Brazil, Italo-Brazilian newsstand owners displayed not the Italian flags that they traditionally exhibited, but Brazilian flags and posters of Brazil's best player, Leônidas da Silva. See Mário Filho, *O negro no futebol brasileiro*, 2nd ed. (Rio de Janeiro: Civilização Brasileira, 1964), 245.

2 See J. A. Mangan, *Athleticism in the Victorian and Edwardian Public School: The Emergence and Consolidation of an Educational Ideology* (New York: Cambridge University Press, 1981), and *The Games Ethic and Imperialism: Aspects of the Diffusion of an Ideal* (New York: Viking Press, 1986). See also Joseph Arbena, ed., *Sport and Society in Latin America: Diffusion, Dependency, and the Rise of Mass Culture* (New York: Greenwood Press, 1988), and Hilary McD Beckles, *The Development of West Indies Cricket*, 2 vols. (Kingston: The University of the West Indies Press, 1998).

3 Robert M. Levine, "Sport and Society: The Case of Brazilian Futebol," *Luso-Brazilian Review* 17:2 (Winter 1980): 233–52, and Janet Lever, *Soccer Madness* (Chicago: University of Chicago Press, 1983).

4 See Waldenyr Caldas, *O pontapé inicial: Memória do futebol brasileiro (1894–1933)* (São Paulo: Instituição Brasileira de Difusão Cultural, 1990), and Leonardo Affonso de Miranda Pereira, *Footballmania: Uma história social do futebol no Rio de Janeiro, 1902–1938* (Rio de Janeiro: Nova Fronteira, 2000). One brief English-language consideration of the era is Darién J. Davis, "British Football with a Brazilian Beat: The Early History of a National Pastime (1894–1933)," in *English-Speaking Communities in Latin America*, ed. Oliver Marshall, 261–84 (New York: St. Martin's Press, 2000).

5 Jeffrey D. Needell, *A Tropical Belle Epoque: Elite Culture and Society in Turn-of-the-Century Rio de Janeiro* (Cambridge: Cambridge University Press, 1987).

6 The Corinthian Football Club began another tour of Brazil in 1914, but war intervened immediately after the club's representatives reached Brazil, and the travelers returned to Britain without playing a single match.

7 "The Corinthians' Return," *Sporting Opinion* (Port-of-Spain, Trinidad), 12 June 1910.

8 A. Ford, "Sports," *A Leitura Para Todos* (Rio de Janeiro), Aug. 1910.

9 For the founders' story of their club's beginnings, see Leop, "Reconstituindo a historia corinthiana," *A Gazeta Esportiva* (São Paulo), 7 Sep. 1930.

10 F. N. S. Creek, *A History of the Corinthian Football Club* (London: Longmans, Green, 1933), 88.

11 Pamphlets, "Programme of Entertainments, etc. Organized by The Fluminense F. C. during the Stay of the Corinthian Team in Rio de Janeiro, August 1910," and "Banquet [sic] em honra dos Corinthians offerecido pelo Fluminense Football Club, Rio de Janeiro, 28 de Agosto de 1910," Archive of the Fluminense Football Club, Rio de Janeiro (AFFC).

12 Aidan Hamilton, *An Entirely Different Game: The British Influence on Brazilian Football* (Edinburgh: Mainstream Publishing, 1998), 71.

13 Ibid., 76.

14 "Banquete aos Corinthians," *Sportman: Revista Quinzenal de Sport e Variedades* (São Paulo), 4 Sep. 1913. Tradition credits Charles Miller with the introduction of football to the country when, after ten years of schooling in England, he returned to Brazil in 1894 with two footballs and a copy of the official game rules.

15 "Foot-Ball: grandes matchs [sic] internacionaes S. Paulo versus Campeões de amadores inglezes," *A Vida Moderna* (São Paulo), 15 Sep. 1910.

16 "Corinthians' Return."

17 Minutes, 17 Aug. 1910, *Actas da Directoria: 5 de Maio 1905 a 23 de Maio 1911*, AFFC.

18 According to Creek, the incident occurred during one of the matches on the occasion of the first visit to São Paulo in 1910. See his *History*, 84.

19 "Os Corinthians," *A Noticia* (Rio de Janeiro), 25 Aug. 1910, Yearly Album, 1910, AFFC.

20 Ernest Hambloch, *British Consul: Memories of Thirty Years' Service in Europe and Brazil* (London: George G. Harrap, 1938), 120.

21 "Foot-Ball," *Jornal do Commercio* (Rio de Janeiro), 17 Sept. 1910, Yearly Album, 1910, AFFC; Hamilton, *Entirely Different Game*, 77–78.

22 "Foot-Ball," *Jornal do Commercio*, 19 Sep. 1910, *Yearly Album*, 1910, AFFC. In this article, the *Brazilian Review* was called an example of "yellow press" (English in original). In fact, the Corinthians themselves noticed the alleged partisanship, although they seem to have been unoffended. See "Corinthians' Return."

23 "Foot-ball," *A Leitura Para Todos*, Oct. 1914.

24 "Matches Internacionaes: Portuguezes vs. Paulistano," *O Estado de São Paulo*, 28 July 1913, *Yearly Album*, 1913, Archive of the Club Atlético Paulistano, São Paulo (ACAP).

25 For example, "O Team Corinthians em S. Paulo," *O Estado de São Paulo*, 3 Sep. 1910, *Yearly Album*, 1910, ACAP.

26 "Foot-ball," *A Leitura Para Todos*, July 1914. The French word, *trucs*, and the English words appear in quotation marks in the original.

27 Hamilton, *Entirely Different Game*, 112.

28 Francisco Pereira Lima Filho, *O Campeonato Sul-Americano de Foot-Ball* (n.p., 1916), AFFC.

29 Ibid. I have been unable to identify the exact meaning of the phrase, "Ale goak." Apparently it was some sort of cheer.

30 "Foot-ball," *A Leitura Para Todos*, Sep. 1914.

31 See, for example, the cartoon "Uma torcida negra," *O Imparcial* (Rio de Janeiro), 7 May 1919, *Yearly Album*, 1919, AFFC.

32 *O Imparcial*, 14 May 1919, quoted in Pereira, *Footballmania*, 171.

33 Pereira, *Footballmania*, 174.

34 Epitácio Pessoa quoted in ibid., 176. The government awarded the Confederação Brasileira de Desportos Rs. 50:000$000 (approximately US$6,500) in 1921.

35 Friedenreich later played football professionally. He joined the São Paulo Futebol Club in the early years of Brazilian professional football, after Club Atlético Paulistano had closed its football section, largely due to the democratization of football, of which professionalism was a part.

36 Mário Filho, *Negro no futebol brasileiro*, 119.

37 Thomas E. Skidmore, *Black into White: Race and Nationality in Brazilian Thought* (Durham: Duke University Press, 1993).

38 Jerry Dávila, *Diploma of Whiteness: Race and Social Policy in Brazil, 1917–1945* (Durham: Duke University Press, 2003), 6. See also Dain Borges, "'Puffy, Ugly, Slothful and Inert': Degeneration in Brazilian Social Thought, 1880–1940," *Journal of Latin American Studies*, 25:2 (May 1993): 235–56.

39 For example see "Foot-ball," *A Leitura Para Todos*, July 1914.

40 On these developments see Pereira, *Footballmania*, and Caldas, *Pontapé inicial*.

41 See Needell, *Tropical Belle Epoque*, and Daryle Williams, *Culture Wars in Brazil: The First Vargas Regime, 1930–1945* (Durham: Duke University Press, 2001).

42 Skidmore, *Black into White*, 176.

43 See for example Borges, "'Puffy, Ugly, Slothful and Inert,'" 251–55.

Part II: Foreigners in Latin America

5 Merchants, Abolitionists, and Slave Traders:

BRAZILIAN PERCEPTIONS OF
THE BRITISH IN BAHIA, 1808–1850

Louise H. Guenther[1]

> *The presence of British culture in the development of*
> *Brazil, in the space, the scenery, the collective whole of*
> *Brazilian civilization, cannot be – or should not be? –*
> *ignored by any Brazilian interested in comprehending*
> *and interpreting Brazil.*
>
> —GILBERTO FREYRE[2]

INTRODUCTION

When the ports of Brazil were opened to international trade for the first time in 1808, an intense change came about in the outlook of Brazilian-born elites. After having been a closed colony for most of its history, Brazil underwent the experience – unique in the New World – of being the seat of its own imperial metropolis between 1808 and 1822.[3] The very birth of Brazil as an independent nation was watched over by a British midwife, in the form of the naval escort for the flight of the Portuguese court to Rio de Janeiro in 1807–8, and then in negotiating diplomatic recognition of Brazilian independence in return for favourable commercial treatment and anti-slave trade concessions. The rapid influx of British merchants into Brazil's ports was part and parcel of this change. By the 1820s, British merchant communities had become established in all of the main port cities of Brazil. As society changed in response to political independence, the abolition of the slave trade and eventually of slavery, efforts at modernization, and increased European immigration, the status of British merchants gradually improved. From being viewed as odd itinerant traders and objects of Brazilians' curiosity, they

93

developed a community presence within urban centres. They were alternately harassed for British anti-slaving activities and praised for their cultural virtues, but by the turn of the twentieth century the British had become, in Brazilian eyes, an elite to be imitated in manners, clothing, and customs.[4] This study encourages a broader historical redefinition of how Latin America's relationships to Europe were formed, defined, contested, and negotiated over the half-century during which some of the first postcolonial nations developed their independent identities in relation to the rest of the world – a world unquestionably dominated by the commercial and political networks of Great Britain.

Many twentieth-century Brazilian historians have expressed the need for their national histories to reflect a deeper understanding of the British presence in their midst, particularly during the nineteenth century. In 1965, Olga Pantaleão stated unequivocally that the nineteenth century was "the British century in Brazil," especially its first half.[5] In 1948, sociologist Gilberto Freyre published a social history of the British residents of nineteenth-century Brazilian cities. Freyre agreed with Pantaleão in stating that the most influential period of the British presence was the first half of the nineteenth century.[6] Historian José Honório Rodrigues argues that the "clash between national needs and English demands was the very essence of our history in the first fifty years of the nineteenth century."[7]

The history of Brazil in the eighteenth and nineteenth centuries is broadly understood as a gradual, more or less linear transition from a colonial, slave-based, northeastern-centred sugar colony to an independent, southeastern-centred, "modernized" nation. Initially this started through the expansion of precious minerals extraction, then coffee exports, and ultimately by financial modernization and industrial development.[8] Thus, existing studies of British influence in Brazil have tended to focus on the ways in which British capital and political pressure helped to advance the process of economic development or to intensify dependency, and have primarily been concerned with São Paulo, Rio de Janeiro, and Minas Gerais.[9]

However, during the early decades of the nineteenth century, precisely the years when Brazil was negotiating its independent status with respect to Portugal, Bahia had temporarily regained its economic pre-eminence due to the exhaustion of the richest gold deposits of Minas Gerais and the rise in sugar prices stimulated by the Haitian Revolution. Southeastern coffee did not become centrally important to the Brazilian economy until the 1840s, and the transatlantic slave trade – Bahia's lifeline – would not be fully abolished until the 1850s.[10] The British were well aware of the economic importance of Bahia to the Portuguese empire, and it is no surprise that many British merchants chose to settle there rather than in Rio de Janeiro or Pernambuco, for Bahia offered them many economic, material, and social advantages to offset the hardships of expatriate living.

British merchants arrived on the scene at Bahia just after the Portuguese prince-regent João (later King João VI) and his entire court had narrowly escaped from the Napoleonic invasion under the protection of a British naval escort. Immediately after arriving at Salvador in 1808, on his way to Rio de Janeiro where he would establish his court and capital, João opened the ports of Brazil to trade with all friendly nations, which in practice meant primarily Great Britain. Negotiating from a position of political strength, the British government obtained a favourable commercial treaty in 1810. Destined to become a point of contention between Portuguese and British merchants throughout Brazil, the treaty allowed British manufactured goods to enter Brazil at a tariff of 15 per cent. This was one percentage point lower than that allotted to Portuguese imports, and nearly half the 28 per cent tariff rate for imports from all other foreign nations.[11] British manufactures, mostly textiles, flooded into the main ports of Brazil as merchants became established in wholesale trade all along the Brazilian coast. The continental blockade combined with the rapid saturation of the limited Latin American markets to create downward pressure on the prices of British goods in Brazil, which reached rock-bottom levels before British trade with Europe resumed in the mid-1810s.

Brazilian independence strengthened the position of British merchants. In Bahia, this process took the form of a bitterly fought, year-long war between patriot forces in the interior and a substantial Portuguese garrison in the city of Salvador (1822–23). Despite the British government's official policy of neutrality, individual merchants sided with the rebels and sold arms to them openly enough to alarm the consul. Tensions between the British community and Portuguese loyalists escalated as British merchants were attacked in the pro-Lisbon newspapers for trading with the rebels. Loyalists began refusing to pay debts owed to the British and urged the Portuguese government to revoke the group's privileges.[12] In late 1821, the Portuguese government at Lisbon alienated British merchants all over Brazil by suddenly doubling import duties on British woollens,[13] and by August 1822 even the British consul in Salvador, William Pennell, admitted that the merchant community strongly favoured Brazilian independence, although he hoped that their partisanship would not "become sufficiently notorious to excite corresponding sentiments in the two parties."[14] Individual Britons thus appear to have suffered an alteration to a particular identity marker – that of the rationally calculating, responsibly neutral British merchant – in favour of a Byronic enthusiasm to become active participants in the tumultuous political events of their time, gambling for advantage in the fortunes of war. This change in disposition also changed the community's overall image in Brazilian eyes, which in turn helped to intensify the sense of legitimate cause on the part of Brazilians who desired political independence. In a word, British merchants and Brazilian patriots seemed to be identifying with one another, across all of the cultural barriers.

Taking advantage of the increasing tensions between the Portuguese and the British, the Conselho Interino (the patriot government) did much to encourage and reward British support. Not only did the province eagerly continue to purchase British manufactures throughout the struggles, but as the conflict came to a head, the Conselho Interino invited British merchants and their families to move temporarily to Cachoeira in advance of a planned assault on Salvador, to prevent any injury or loss that might result from the attack.[15] When the Portuguese loyalists finally evacuated the city in mid-1823, the Conselho Interino immediately began to meet British claims on property confiscated from the fleeing Portuguese.[16] The merchants had won their gamble, and gained not only fortune, but also the gratitude and respect of their Brazilian hosts (and customers).

By the 1820s, British merchant communities were well established in all of the main port cities of Brazil. Bahia's British expatriates numbered about 120 by the mid-1840s,[17] but wielded an influence disproportionate to their numbers. Certain British institutions gained sanction in the commercial treaty of 1810. These included a local consulate, a special Judge Conservator with extraterritorial jurisdiction, a private hospital, and an Anglican place of worship, all financed by a tax levied on British commercial activity and administered by the consulate in each city. As their prospects in Brazil grew more promising, British merchants buttressed their sense of themselves in the unfamiliar tropical setting by keeping these cultural markers close to hand, and making them increasingly visible to outsiders. Such markers not incidentally functioned to partition the British from the local Brazilians, and this ultimately had an ambiguous effect on the developing relationship between the two communities.

BUILDING BRITISH COMMUNITY INSTITUTIONS

The British at first had to bury their dead in unconsecrated ground, until royal permission was granted in 1813 for a small Protestant cemetery to be built off the Ladeira da Barra, on a scenic site overlooking the bay, just beyond the modern-day Corredor da Vitória, where most of the British had their residences. The British hospital was opened in 1815, housed under the same roof as the Protestant chapel at the cemetery. As was mandated by the later 1824 constitution, official permission for non-Catholic services included certain conditions: the building had to resemble a normal house and no form of proselytizing was allowed. In 1821, Maria Dundas Graham found the community's institutions firmly in place. She was pleased with the service that she attended at the English chapel, "surprised, perhaps unreasonably, to hear [Reverend] Synge pray for 'Don John of Portugal, Sovereign of these realms, by whose gracious permission we are enabled to meet and worship God according to our conscience,'" and wryly added that the British were not so polite in Rome as to pray for the pope.[18] However, Synge's expression of gratitude to João VI could be seen to express the British merchants' keen awareness, at that time, of their dependence upon the goodwill of Brazilian authorities for their political and social security – which underpinned their economic survival – in Brazil.

By 1845, roughly half of the British community regularly attended Anglican services in a building large enough to accommodate a hundred.[19] A yellow fever epidemic in 1853 forced the British hospital to relocate to the peninsula of Bonfim, on the opposite side of town. At about the same time, the Anglican church came to be housed in a handsome neoclassical building on Campo Grande (Figure 5.1), which was then a large military practice field where the Vitória road met the Fort of São Pedro on the edge of the old town. The church and the cemetery thus marked the informal geographical boundaries of the British space, which was visibly away from the Brazilians, but not so far as to be out of sight.

Despite these appearances, there was no inherent cohesion among the British subjects in Bahia who lived in the city during the first half of the nineteenth century. Once the first hectic phase of market entry had passed, the merchants had proceeded to use their treaty privileges to set themselves up as a proper social community, with the conscious objective of rendering their presence more respectable to Brazilian eyes. This was meant to improve the merchants' chances for successful commercial relations with the Brazilians, even as it created a safer emotional environment for themselves. The main task was to establish the respectability and the trustworthiness, in the eyes of a fervently Catholic population, of a foreign group made up mostly of Protestants. Paradoxically, the insistent performance of cultural practices associated with private life, which often jarred with the physical and social climate of Bahia, enabled the British businessman to appear more respectable to Bahians than he would as a random foreigner. With somewhere to belong and rules of his own to follow, his foreignness did not render him as vulnerable to the risk of judgement or rejection. The situation carried the added benefit for the community of making it more difficult for the individual Briton to "go native," as he would then lose the full emotional protection of the enclave (although the cultural notion of eccentric individualism might have been available to save him even then, or to facilitate his eventual re-entry into the community). Nevertheless, the line was drawn and the cross-cultural camaraderie of the earlier years was thus discouraged.[20]

Possibly as a result of this self-segregation, with the passing of decades and the advent of ideas about modernization, it became increasingly fashionable for Brazilian elites to construct, and later to revere, the cultural superiority of the *ingleses* (the English). In 1993, the prominent Bahian historian Thales de Azevedo wrote a piece for the city newspaper in which he supported efforts to establish the historical monument status of Bahia's British cemetery, belatedly lamenting the 1975 demolition of the English chapel in Campo Grande (Figure 5.1). The fact that the destruction of such a significant historical structure had not brought any sort of protest from the local community suggested to him that the importance of the British presence in Bahia was insufficiently appreciated.[21] This may be further evidence that their project of self-isolation, while making the community as a whole more imposing within the local landscape of the time, succeeded only too well at making their memory irrelevant to Bahians in the long term. Most recently, however, the well-funded and successful restoration of Bahia's British cemetery has led to significant media coverage and public interest. The recovery of the cemetery and the creation of historical displays associated with the British presence allude to a long-overdue reintegration of these important actors into the historical self-awareness of Bahia, hopefully casting some light upon the deep roots of economic globalization which has become the catchword of our own time. Thus, the line drawn long ago to separate the memory of the British community from that of Bahia itself appears to be dissolving at last, even as the high wall that symbolized it is restored to its former might.

But how true was the image expressed by Azevedo and others? Were the British viewed by nineteenth-century Brazilians primarily as hard-working, useful vectors of European culture and Anglo-Saxon industry? Relations between the British and Brazilians were unstable throughout the early nineteenth century, changing rapidly as the British government regularly intervened in Brazilian affairs. The British merchants of Bahia

5.1. Church of England Chapel in Bahia, *ca*.1859
Source: Charles Ribeyrolles, *Brasil pittoresco: história – descripções – viagens – instituições
– colonisação* ..., 4 vols. (Rio de Janeiro: Typ. Nacional, 1859-61), vol. 4, plate 45.

were frequently caught in the middle. They were often unable to identify internally with their government, when its actions directly interfered with their local interests; yet it was just at such times that the Brazilian public would object most stridently to the merchants' presence in their midst, perceiving no difference between what they and their government were doing to Brazil. In particular, the role of the British in ending the Brazilian slave trade contributed strongly to these oscillations.

This lack of public understanding was not really surprising. Many early British visitors remarked on the Brazilians' overwhelming ignorance of their country. Charles Fraser, an adventurous English gentleman who lived in Bahia in 1812, provided an illuminating picture of Luso-Brazilian views of the British at the time. Fraser came to Brazil in 1808 and made his way overland from Rio de Janeiro to Porto Seguro, on the coast of the province of Bahia, hundreds of miles south of Salvador. There he purchased property in the most isolated place that he could find, boasting that he was "the only settler in the extent of 20 leagues of seacoast,"[22] and began a one-man effort to civilize the local Patachó Indians. Fraser wrote to Viscount Castlereagh concerning the alarming "extreme ignorance" about the British entertained by the Brazilians whom he had met: "The old [isolationist] policy of their respective governments, together with their awe of the Church and belief in its infallibility, had succeeded so well that 90 parts of 100 of the inhabitants of Brazil are ignorant at this day that there is even a parliament in Great Britain." Moreover, "finding their interests suffering severely from the restraints and interruptions of a trade [the slave trade] which was originally encouraged as humane and meritorious by the Church ... proceed[ing] from a nation of foreigners and heretics whom the same infallible Mother Church had uniformly taught them to regard with that peculiar degree of horror and detestation with which we contemplate the inhabitants of the infernal regions"; they clearly held a dim view of the newcomers.[23] Fraser suggested that Brazil's relations with Great Britain could be improved if the British government ceased the anti-slave-trade crusade, instead directing resources to persuade the local Indian populations to provide the labour needed to develop Brazil, as the Jesuits had been trying to do until their expulsion by the Marquis of Pombal in 1759.

Another expatriate visitor, Henry Koster, who was raised in Portugal and probably was the only British merchant to become a sugar planter in northeastern Brazil, noticed similar problems in Recife during the early 1810s. More so than most travellers, he was interested in the Brazilian point of view. Before Recife had a British chapel or cemetery, Koster offered an extensive and perceptive analysis of attitudes toward the resident British merchants:

> Although they are now aware that at any rate we have the forms
> of human beings, that we have the power of speech, and that we
> have our share of intellect in all the common transactions of the
> world, still how are we to look for respect from them towards
> a set of men, who have no appearance at least, of possessing
> any religious feelings? [Their] devotedness to their church
> establishment surpasses every other feeling.... Without any
> outward appearance of religion, how are we to expect that the
> people of Brazil are to regard us as anything better than what we
> were represented to them as being in former times? – as pagans,
> animals, and horses.[24]

For Koster, the appearance of religiosity, especially its visible, physical structures, would be sufficient to generate a basic respect from the Brazilians. Azevedo's 1993 lament over the destruction of the British temple, together with the protectiveness of present-day authorities toward the cemetery as a final surviving legacy of the history of British civilization in Bahia, would suggest that Koster's assessment had been correct.

While Fraser differed from the more respectful Koster in his attitude toward Brazilian Catholicism, he too suggested that Brazilians largely perceived the new British arrivals as alien, odd, spiritually (and thus morally) inferior to themselves. Within a few decades this impression would change, as the British set up social and physical markers of status and difference that asserted their equality to Brazilians, and eventually came to proclaim their superiority. Koster, perceptive about the Brazilian point of view and sympathetic to it, expressed alarm at the lack of unity among British expatriates in Recife, which made it difficult for them to achieve a positive status in Brazilian eyes. His comment is worth quoting at length:

> It is not thus that the British nation is to become respectable;
> we may have relations of trade with these people, but we must
> be content to be merely regarded according to our utility; there
> can be no respect for our general character as a body of men,
> none of that regard which would make us listened to in any great
> question, which would make our opinions and our assertions
> depended upon as coming from men of steadiness – of religious
> habits. Nor can we be accounted as more than residents for a
> time, we cannot be considered as an established community,
> who are thus without any common bond of union, who have not
> any one point to which all are directed; we have no appearance
> of belonging to one nation, as if we were brethren meeting in a
> foreign land.[25]

Perhaps equally important to British self-identity and to Brazilian perceptions of these foreigners were the informal community institutions. These men, women, and children appear, at least on the surface, to have led the lives of characters from contemporary author Jane Austen's novels, transposed to the tropics. The British society of Bahia was said to be more congenial and welcoming than that of most places in Brazil. James Henderson, an Englishman who made an unsuccessful bid for a diplomatic position at Rio de Janeiro and later became British consul general in Bogotá, Colombia, noted in 1821 that "Bahia is considered by the English merchants a more agreeable place of residence than any of the maritime towns of the Brazil, and a more social intercourse has existed among themselves than at some of the other places."[26] Besides the daily promenades, social visits often took place in the evenings.[27] British travellers gave descriptions of rounds of social dinners given in honour of their visits. In addition to entertainment in private homes, opera and theatre performances were available to the British when touring European companies stopped at the São João Theatre.[28] Cricket matches on the Campo Grande military practice field probably helped to serve the need of the community to congregate in a culturally specific social activity, incidentally in the public eye. In the affirmation of a group identity, an audience of Others is essential, and in an illustration of one such cricket match, an Afro-Brazilian woman in traditional costume is prominently placed in the foreground, directly beneath an improbably large Union Jack waving from a flagpole in the background.[29]

By the early 1820s, the British had erected deliberate representations of themselves as a unified, respectable, and civilized group of foreigners. The resulting image has remained, as a historical legacy, in the minds of historians in Bahia and throughout Brazil.

BRITISH EXPATRIATES AND THE CAMPAIGN AGAINST THE SLAVE TRADE

Yet the Brazilian image of the British in the early nineteenth century was contradictory. As their elegant temple was being built in Campo Grande, waves of violence erupted against the merchants and their families in the streets and even inside their homes. Although the image of the dangerous Protestant heretic had given way to the more positive one of a scrupulous, eccentric, and reclusive businessman, new images of a threatening Britain loomed as British pressure against the slave trade increased after Brazil's independence. Ordinary Bahians experienced much distress due to British abolitionist activity, and many of them held the British merchants personally responsible for the problems caused by this activity. Only after the ending of the slave trade and the resolution of other Anglo-Brazilian diplomatic incidents would the generally positive perception of a homogeneous, hardworking, civilized group take full root.

British efforts to suppress the illegal Brazilian slave trade during the 1830s and 1840s led to clashes and conflicts of identities and perceptions between the British merchants on the one hand, and different groups of Brazilians on the other. The abolition of the international slave trade over the course of the nineteenth century was driven largely by British policies and actions. Brazil was the largest slave market in the Americas, and Bahia accounted for a significant proportion of that demand, receiving 18.4 per cent of slave imports between 1800 and 1850. Almost one-third of the 316,300 Africans landed in Bahia during this period arrived after 1830, when the trade was declared illegal.[30] However, Brazil was also Great Britain's third-largest foreign market, and the British government desired to remain on good terms with Brazil as well as with Portugal.[31] Treaties were signed guaranteeing an end to the trade by 1831, but it still continued for another twenty years due to the great demand for slaves; profits of up to 500 per cent were available to those who successfully smuggled the human cargo into Brazil.[32] As early as 1812, Charles Fraser reported that while the importation of British goods had disturbed the Brazilian urban merchant elites, the landed elites had still remained favourable to British interests; however, the aggressive abolitionist activities of the British government finally alienated them entirely.[33] This evolving situation, unprecedented in the country's history, gradually created a deep rift in mutual perceptions, as well as a serious conflict of interest for British merchants in Bahia. As the change took place only a decade or two after the merchants had made themselves heroes in the cause of independence, it may have also involved conflicts of identity on both sides.

Diplomatic correspondence links the international incidents of slave ships captured by British naval forces to the increasing animosity and scapegoating episodes involving ordinary Brazilians and individual Britons in Bahia. As early as 1821, Consul Pennell reported that the arrival of a captured Portuguese ship loaded with four hundred slaves, escorted into the harbour by the *Morgiana*, a Royal Navy sloop, "tended to revive prejudices and irritations connected with former captures of Portuguese ships." He recommended that the British sailors should avoid "discussions under the influence of irritated feelings calculated to disturb the harmony of existing friendly relations."[34]

This pattern intensified as the century wore on, with increasing incidents of violence between British sailors and merchants on the one hand, and angry Brazilians on the other. In the mid-1820s, a wave of crimes against the merchants took place in Bahia, serious enough for the community to write a collective complaint to the president of the province.[35] By 1829, the consul was directly linking the street violence – and its implicit official condonation – to the general prevalence of openly anti-British sentiment. A "most atrocious attempt" to murder "Mr. Richard Nicholson, a very respectable British merchant established in this city," and two of his nephews had left them "most severely wounded." The perpetrators were known to be soldiers, and it was "not for the first time that complaints have been made to me on the insolence with which the soldiers of this garrison behave to foreigners and to British subjects in particular in the streets without the slightest provocation."[36] The Brazilian soldiers and sailors may have been acting out of a sense of outraged sovereignty. British anti-slave-trade pressures were increasing, but the British manufactured goods still enjoyed their preferential import tariffs. Furthermore, the institution of the Judge Conservator, a special court allowing extraterritorial rights to all British subjects, was still in place. The popular perception of the British as pushy, privileged, and insolent representatives of their government was a counterpoint to the more positive view of scrupulous good character, which was more based on personal acquaintance. Between these extremes of public and private opinion, the lives of individual merchants were affected in ways that probably caused them to draw together even more strongly.

Ironically, the health of British commerce in Bahia itself depended in no small part upon the continuation of the illegal trade. Since the British catered mostly to Brazilian elites, that is to say the slave-holding classes, they had a high financial stake in the illicit trade. Evidence suggests that British merchants were actually heavily involved in financing the trade, directly or indirectly. The credit system used by the merchants was timed to the expected flow of illicit profits from slave shipments; goods used in the trade itself, along with the paraphernalia of slave ships, were manufactured in the United Kingdom. This implied collusion was not news to Brazilian elites. Daniel Kidder, an American observer, remarked in 1845: "It has not been generally known that, notwithstanding the opposition of the English nation to the slave trade, and her vigorous efforts to suppress it ... the strong bulwark of that traffic has been the English capital, by aid of which it has been carried on." Still, he observed, the clash between "English philanthropy and English cupidity" was rapidly resolving in favour of the former.[37] A persuasive case for the participation of British merchants in the slave trade – a trade declared illegal by Brazil only under the tremendous pressure of the British government – has been made by historian Luis Henrique Dias Tavares.[38] Elite groups in Brazil clearly understood that British merchants had an interest in supporting the slave trade. It was the non-elite Brazilians who associated official British abolitionism with the privileged status of British merchants, expressing their outrage in personal attacks against the nearest available merchant. Consul Pennell recognized this in 1821 when he complained to the provincial government about the behaviour of "the lower ranks of society," whose hostility against the *Morgiana*'s crew had failed to reflect the spirit "which ought to exist between friendly, and allied nations."[39]

The issue of negotiated identity is complicated further by the fact that all of the British merchants were almost certainly using slaves in their households throughout the first half of the nineteenth century, and probably beyond. Slave labour was a fact of life in nineteenth-century Bahia, where even the city's water supply had to be carried up to the houses on the heads of slaves. The evidence for the practice is abundant. Maria

Graham commented sarcastically on it in the early 1820s, and George Pilkington wrote a treatise in 1841 describing and condemning it in considerable detail.[40] At the time of his death in 1862, George Mumford, a prominent British merchant in Bahia, owned ten slaves.[41] Yet the fact of slave ownership and use is hardly mentioned in the published British travel narratives of Brazil; Maria Graham is the exception. This seems to support the argument that the British as a community were invested in sustaining an identity that assumed their social and moral superiority to the host society, even as they were privately engaging in practices that were contemptible by their own moral standards.[42]

A complex interplay of factors thus shaped the Brazilian-British relationship, each with its own implications for the question of identity. The British government's interest in abolishing the trade on the one hand, and the British merchants' interest in keeping it alive on the other; the implicit condonation of slavery through private household practices versus the complicity of Brazilian elites with the merchants' financial interests; and throughout, the ordinary Brazilians' likely perception of the British as alien, meddlesome, privileged, and threatening to the best interests of their country. It should come as no surprise that conflicts erupted around this complex problem. The most damaging of these was probably the urban slave rebellion of January 1835, known as the Revolt of the Malês, which, although betrayed at the last moment, was nevertheless the greatest urban slave revolt of the century. The subsequent trial revealed that a disproportionate number of its leaders were slaves owned by the British merchants, which did nothing to improve the image of the community in Brazilian eyes.[43]

The Aberdeen Act of 1845 declared the slave trade to be piracy and unilaterally empowered the British navy to search and seize Brazilian and Portuguese ships on an unprecedented scale. Together with a renewed commitment by the Brazilian government to end the slave trade, the number of slaves imported into Brazil had been dramatically reduced by 1851. The image of the British in popular eyes, of course, only grew worse. British traveler Edward Wilberforce wrote of his encounter with a tavern-keeper in Braganza, near Rio de Janeiro, in 1850. When their conversation had turned to the slave trade, the Brazilian "grew vehement, and, taking up the last number of a Brazilian paper, showed us an article wherein the English were stigmatized as robbers, pirates, cut-throats, and whatnot, because the *Harpy* had taken a vessel which the Brazilians obstinately chose to consider a legal trader. The hotel-keeper shouted out 'Pirates, Pirates, *Ingleses!*'" Wilberforce chose to humour the man, but was clearly disturbed by the incident.[44]

A decade later, a diplomatic incident known as the Christie Affair involved a British diplomat who refused to apologize for the seizure of a legitimate Brazilian vessel. The incident added to the litany of British outrages against Brazilian sovereignty, and so incensed the public that the poet Fagundes Varella published an entire volume of verses critical of the British. It expressed his outrage at what he viewed as their disrespect and rapaciousness towards the hospitable Brazilians.

Pisaste uma nação, – nação tão grande
Que a loucura perdoa-te! – Cuspiste
Na face dessa que afogára em vagas,
Em rios de ouro teu país ingrato!
Procuraste lançar um veu de sombras
Sobre essa terra que fascina o globo
Ao clarão dos diamantes, e piedosa
Teus irmãos agasalha junto ao peito![45]

You have trod on a nation—a nation so great
That [only] insanity may pardon you!—You have spat
In the face of this [nation] which flooded with waves,
With rivers of gold, your ungrateful country!
You have tried to darken in shame
This land that dazzles the world
In her sparkling diamonds, and gently
Your brothers yet hold to her breast!

British merchants could only have dealt with such perceptions by glossing over the issues, remembering that they were in Bahia primarily to make a profit. The most profitable enterprise available to investors there was the slave trade; and so, in the short run, it made sense that British capital would go to support the slave trade, legally or not. This compromise cost the British community much of its perceived sense of moral superiority, however, as judged by its own cultural standards; and with this it also lost the respect of the local population, as well as some local political influence, if the diplomatic correspondence is any guide.

BRAZILIAN IMAGES OF THE BRITISH

Although respectable community institutions existed by the 1820s, and Brazilians eventually would move beyond the hostility of the abolitionist years and come to accept the British as equals, they were constantly struck by the visible cultural difference of the group. Gilberto Freyre devoted most of his four-hundred-page 1948 study of the British in Brazil to exploring the stereotypes associated with the image of the *inglês* – the Englishman. This he often did uncritically, though with an assurance that probably stemmed from his own understanding of Brazilian cultural stereotypes. According to Freyre, nineteenth-century British residents of Brazil were generally viewed as scrupulously honest, eminently practical, and careful with money, but also overly concerned with material things, to the detriment of their private relationships, particularly with their wives.[46] This layered image in Brazilian eyes may have been a way of using humour as a means of resistance by ridicule, which may be a Brazilian cultural trait. The still-current practice of jokes about the Portuguese apparently began at this time also, probably as an effort to come to terms with the perceived thrift and industry of Portuguese merchants and shopkeepers.[47]

The British reputation for honesty in business was so strong that the expression *palavra de inglês* (the word of an Englishman) was used among Brazilians as an oath. The still current expression *para inglês ver* (for Englishmen to see), meaning something that is being done mostly to keep up an appearance of legitimacy, provides further evidence of the stereotype. Brazilians frequently demonstrated fascination with British practicality in technological innovation and with their business acumen. Robert Walsh encountered it throughout his travels in the interior of Minas Gerais during the early 1820s, where "the people entertained some such ideas, of the summary and almost magical processes the English were to apply, to bring to light treasures which the Brazilians could not reach. Machines, they thought, would convey a river from a plain to the top of a mountain, and perform other wonders of a like miraculous nature."[48] The greatest British technological contributions to Brazil were made in the engineering of public works. However, most of these did not take place until the second half of the century. The Bahia & São Francisco Railway, for example, began construction in 1852, and opened its first section in 1860.[49] Furthermore, although the Brazilians still associate the British presence generally with the construction of railroads and public works, the merchants may not have concurred. After a yellow fever crisis in Bahia at mid-century claimed the lives of many British engineers and workmen, the merchant community commemorated the event by installing a single plaque on the wall of its cemetery, presumably identifying them as a group of Britons separate from themselves.

The British were viewed as scrupulous businessmen, and this trait appears to have been entrenched enough in their self-image to be worth a loss of profit, at least in the short run. Freyre cites the case of a British merchant, Charles Cannell, who advertised in Rio de Janeiro's *Jornal do Comércio* in 1827 an auction of "various fabrics, slightly imperfect," and "biscuits of inferior quality." Freyre observed that this happened at a time when any European goods, even those that were outdated or second-hand, would usually be advertised as new and flawless. He asserts that "with few exceptions, [the ads] are a lesson in good taste, sobriety, and professional ethics, and contrasted to the over-emphasis, exaggeration, and occasional charlatanism of many other advertisements placed by other Europeans."[50]

Despite these positive attributes, or perhaps because of them, a myth gradually arose among Brazilians about the private life of these amazingly skilled, wealthy, and eccentric foreigners. Nicknamed *missa-seca* (dry mass – a reference to Protestantism), *mister*, and *godeme* (goddammit), the stereotypical *inglês* was "unattractive and arrogant, with a pronounced overbite, blond sideburns, a pipe in the corner of his mouth, plaid clothing and thick-soled walking shoes."[51] Such a caricature playfully emphasized social crassness and lack of style, without denying the professional competence for which the British were so well known. British engineers, railroad officials, and sailors were eventually subsumed into the stereotype, which often appeared in Brazilian jokes about the *ingleses* and in popular comedies such as Martins Pena's *Os dous ou o inglês maquinista* (1842), performed in Bahia in October of 1849.[52] This one-act farce displayed the stereotype to strong effect, albeit good-naturedly. The story played on the merchant character's excitement about newfangled machines, his readiness to get into fistfights, and a marked tendency to be constantly calculating profitability, all expressed in comically (and confidently) misused Portuguese. The general stereotype became a staple of café conversation, caricatures, magazines, carnival costumes, folklore, and racy jokes among Brazilians of all classes in the nineteenth century and beyond. According to Freyre, the British merchant's single-minded pursuit of worldly success, machines, drinking and sports, which meant that he had little time or interest for sexual pursuits, always drew a smile from the Latin audience. The suggestion of British men's sexual impotence was thus contrasted in imagination to their potency in so many public areas.[53]

Unfortunately, little documentation is available about the lives of real British women in Brazil. It appears that British women's lives were generally limited to the British community enclave. One historian reports that white women who attempted to walk in public streets were jeered at and otherwise harassed.[54] In all likelihood, due to British women's detachment from all aspects of their husbands' and fathers' businesses,

Brazilians would have viewed them as more admirable, more refined, and more cultured than their menfolk. Bahian historian Wanderley Pinho notes that the increasing orientation of Bahian society toward northern European cultural ideals was reflected in the growing demand for European tutors and governesses, especially Englishwomen.[55] Elsewhere in nineteenth-century travel narratives, occasional references were also made to elite Brazilian families who sent their daughters to be educated in London, in preparation for lives as brilliant society wives after their return to Brazil. This desire of some elite Brazilian women to take on identity markers associated with British women of good background stood in contrast to the sharp division between Brazilian and British men.

In that context, marriage to an attractive British woman who could perform the requisite rituals of upper-class identity would have been a desirable move for Brazilians intent on gaining social status. But male British writers did not discuss Brazilian men's feelings for British women, perhaps understandably. Freyre hinted at desire, when his unflattering physical description of the stereotypical "mister" (blond sideburns and all) was followed by a short passage about the respective "madame"; "blond, elegant, erotic, and refined," whose influence upon Brazilian life in the nineteenth century merited further study.[56] Keeping in mind the virility aspects of the Brazilian stereotype, it would not be surprising if it connected to a sense of sexual attraction toward the Englishman's wife. Possibly her up-to-date European fashions, refined taste and manners, and her effective seclusion within the British enclave would have helped a mystique of desirable femininity to emerge.

The British, too, had their stereotypes of Brazilians. The circular reasoning typical of prejudiced thinking is a key to the perpetuation of stereotypes that appear to offer a predictable reality in a complex, foreign world. For example, although there was abundant evidence that the more socially aspirant Brazilians looked down on most kinds of manual and commercial work, neither British nor American observers seemed to recognize that the Brazilians probably looked down on them for being merchants, regardless of their care to maintain a distinction between wholesalers and retailers. Pinho's study of gentlewomen's salons in nineteenth-century Brazil provides some evidence of this.[57] Writing in 1944, Pinho was piqued at Maria Graham's snobbish dismissal of Bahia's upper-crust society more than a century earlier, when she declared its level of social awareness to be well below that of Bahia's British residents.[58] Pinho retorted that Graham's host, Consul Pennell, obviously did not mix with the best circles, as there were no military personnel, government officials, or sugar planters at the consul's ball. These were the people who, as anyone ought to know, made up the real elite of Bahian society.[59] Furthermore, while Graham imputed the orchestra's early departure from the ball to its lack of professionalism, Pinho asserted that the consul ought never to have allowed his guests to be left without an orchestra.[60] Pinho's conclusion may simply attest more to his own view of the British merchants than to that of early nineteenth-century Bahian elites, but it is still apparent that the British in 1821 did not quite have the access to local society that they seemed to take for granted. British travellers who judged their merchant compatriots "the aristocracy of [Brazil's] cities" exaggerated, to say the least.[61]

CONCLUSION

The British merchant community was accepted by Brazilians on the basis of their European status, considerable wealth, and perhaps even their eccentric tendency to keep to themselves. Because they never wielded personal political power over the Brazilians, the imperial dynamics of racist self-legitimation evident in many parts of the mature British Empire did not take hold in Brazil, regardless of whether the merchants themselves shared such a mentality. Neither, then, did strategies of resistance on the part of the locals come to play a significant role in the process, apart from the relatively mild forms of satire. Because of the relatively benign setting, the identity negotiations that were played out between Britons and Brazilians in early nineteenth-century Bahia were in a sense more gentle, human, and gradual. These were merchants with ideas of grandeur that had been acquired at home, usually at second hand, who were attempting to live them out in Bahia as well as they could. Inside the enclave, the artificiality of the identity situation led to the development of private difficulties and even pathologies, and these have been discussed elsewhere.[62] But at the boundary between the two communities, the situation appears generally to have been handled with considerable gentility on both sides as the larger relationship developed from day to day, with the significant exception of certain violent episodes associated with the ending of the slave trade.

Compared to the effect of the British presence in, say, Africa or South Asia during the latter part of the nineteenth century, the presence of these merchants did not have much impact on the daily lives of Brazilians. Nevertheless, their imported manufactures greatly expanded the range of products available to the public, their unusual religious practices counted on the continuing awareness and tolerance of the local community, and their self-conscious performance of Britishness excited curiosity, creativity, imitation, and perhaps even the sense of benevolent cultural hospitality on the part of Bahians. By the turn of the twentieth century, when Brazilians resolved to modernize their cities according to European norms and the British Empire was reaching its height, the self-assured cultural superiority of a bona fide British identity would come to be fully accepted by many elite Brazilians, who by then were keen to whiten the image of their own country in European eyes.

The British men and women who lived part or all of their lives in Bahia and the rest of Brazil changed the landscape around them, in physical as well as nonphysical ways. They built houses, gardens, social circles, and codes of conduct that were self-consciously separate from Brazilians. But they did not live in enclaves entirely separate from local society, as did so many later nineteenth- and early twentieth-century Americans and Europeans in Latin America.[63] Indeed, the British community of Bahia could not have really existed without the constant audience that was the Bahian population, which the British provided with much amusement and perplexity in the process. In erecting the walls that kept them apart, the British left a mark upon the place and upon its history.

NOTES TO CHAPTER 5

1 I thank the Centre for Brazilian Studies at the University of Oxford, the Fulbright Commission, and the MacArthur Program on Global Change, Sustainability, and Justice at the University of Minnesota for their support.

2 Gilberto Freyre, Ingleses no Brasil: Aspectos da influência britânica sobre a vida, a paisagem e a cultura do Brasil (Rio de Janeiro: José Olympio, 1948), 35.

3 Leslie Bethell, "The Independence of Brazil," in The Cambridge History of Latin America, vol. 3, The Independence of Latin America, ed. Bethell (Cambridge: Cambridge University Press, 1987), 157–96.

4 Jeffrey Needell, A Tropical Belle Epoque: Elite Culture and Society in Turn-of-the-Century Rio de Janeiro (Cambridge: Cambridge University Press, 1987), 28, 231.

5 Olga Pantaleão, "A presença inglesa," História Geral da Civilização Brasileira, tomo 2, vol. 1, ed. Sérgio Buarque de Holanda (São Paulo: Difusão Européia do Livro, 1965), 65.

6 Freyre, Ingleses no Brasil, 33.

7 José Honório Rodrigues, Brazil and Africa, trans. Richard A. Mazzara and Sam Hileman (Berkeley: University of California Press, 1965), 115.

8 See especially E. Bradford Burns, A History of Brazil, 3rd ed. (New York: Columbia University Press, 1993); Richard Graham, Britain and the Onset of Modernization in Brazil, 1850–1914 (Cambridge: Cambridge University Press, 1968); Alan K. Manchester, British Pre-Eminence in Brazil, Its Rise and Decline: A Study in European Expansion (New York: Octagon Books, 1973); and J. F. Rippy, British Investments in Latin America: A Case Study in the Operations of Private Enterprise in Retarded Regions (New York: Arno Press, 1959).

9 Graham, *Britain*; Manchester, *British Pre-Eminence*; Rippy, *British Investments*; Marshall C. Eakin, *British Enterprise in Brazil: The St. John d'El Rey Mining Company and the Morro Velho Gold Mine, 1830–1960* (Durham: Duke University Press, 1989).

10 Leslie Bethell, *The Abolition of the Brazilian Slave Trade: Britain, Brazil and the Slave Trade Question, 1807–1869* (Cambridge: Cambridge University Press, 1970); Kátia M. de Queirós Mattoso, *Bahia, século XIX: Uma província no Império* (Rio de Janeiro: Editora Nova Fronteira, 1992); Luís Henrique Dias Tavares, *Comércio proibido de escravos* (São Paulo: Ática, 1988).

11 Leslie Bethell and José Murilo de Carvalho, "Brazil from Independence to the Middle of the Nineteenth Century," in *The Cambridge History of Latin America*, vol. 3, *The Independence of Latin America*, ed. Bethell (Cambridge: Cambridge University Press, 1987), 723–24; Bethell, "Independence," 173.

12 William Pennell to Lord Bathurst, Salvador, 29 Oct. 1822, Public Record Office, Foreign Office (PRO/FO) 63, vol. 249.

13 Pennell to Francisco José Pereira, Salvador, 30 Oct. 1821, PRO/FO 63, vol. 240.

14 Pennell to Marquis of Londonderry, Salvador, 28 Aug. 1822, PRO/FO 63, vol. 249 (emphasis in original).

15 Pierre Labatut to Pennell, Quartel General no Engenho Novo, 26 Nov. 1822, PRO/FO 63, vol. 249.

16 Governo Provisório to William Follett, Salvador, 10 Nov. 1823, PRO/FO 268, vol. 1.

17 Daniel P. Kidder, *Sketches of Residence and Travels in Brazil, Embracing Historical and Geographical Notices of the Empire and Its Several Provinces*, vol. 2 (Philadelphia: Sorin and Ball, 1845), 25–26.

18 Maria Dundas Graham, *Journal of a Voyage to Brazil, and Residence There during Part of the Years 1821, 1822, 1823* (London: Longman, Hurst, Rees, Orme, Brown, and Green, 1824), 141.

19 Kidder, *Sketches of Residence*, 25.

20 In examining the identity negotiations of this British expatriate community, I have attempted an original interdisciplinary approach by making use of seminal theories from various sources. Chief among these are Benedict Anderson, *Imagined Communities: Reflections on the Origin and Spread of Nationalism*, 2nd ed. (London: Verso, 1991); Gregory Bateson, *Steps to an Ecology of Mind: Collected Essays on Anthropology, Psychiatry, Evolution, and Epistemology* (London: Paladin, 1973); Erving Goffman, *The Presentation of the Self in Everyday Life* (Garden City: Doubleday, 1959). Finally, Keith Johnstone, *Impro: Improvisation and the Theatre* (New York: Routledge, 1981), offers a practical model for actors imitating the specific ways in which people constantly adjust their social identities in any given situation so as to secure a desired status, high or low, usually expressing a closely held self-image.

21 Thales de Azevedo, "Ingleses, Árabes na Bahia," *A Tarde* (Salvador), 4 June 1993.

22 Charles Fraser to Foreign Secretary Viscount Castlereagh, n.p., 1 Dec. 1812, PRO/FO 63, vol. 149.

23 Fraser to Castlereagh, Porto Seguro, 14 April 1812, PRO/FO 63, vol. 149.

24 Henry Koster, *Travels in Brazil* (London: Longman, Hurst, Rees, Orme, and Brown, 1816), 400 (emphasis in original).

25 Ibid., 401.

26 James Henderson, *A History of Brazil Comprising Its Geography, Commerce, Colonisation, Aboriginal Inhabitants, etc. etc. etc.* (London: Longman, Hurst, Rees, Orme and Brown, 1821), 346.

27 John Candler and Wilson Burgess, *Narrative of a Recent Visit to Brazil; to Present an Address on the Slave-Trade and Slavery, Issued by the Religious Society of Friends* (London: Edward March, Friends' Book and Tract Depository, 1853), 78.

28 Although the building was elegant, the performances held there were nearly always declared to be dreadful. See for example Pedro II, *Diário da viagem ao norte do Brasil* (Salvador, Bahia: Universidade da Bahia, 1959), entry of 10 Oct. 1859; Graham, *Journal of a Voyage*, 140; James Wetherell, *Brazil: Stray Notes from Bahia: Being Extracts from Letters, &c., during a Residence of Fifteen Years* (Liverpool: Webb and Hunt, 1860), 72.

29 John James Wild, *At Anchor: A Narrative of Experiences Afloat and Ashore during the Voyage of H.M.S. "Challenger," from 1872 to 1876* (London: M. Ward, 1878), 46.

30 David Eltis, *Economic Growth and the Ending of the Transatlantic Slave Trade* (New York: Oxford University Press, 1987), 243.

31 Joseph C. Miller, *Way of Death: Merchant Capitalism and the Angolan Slave Trade 1730–1830* (Madison: University of Wisconsin Press, 1988), 505–31.

32 Jane Elizabeth Adams, "The Abolition of The Brazilian Slave-Trade," *The Journal of Negro History* 10:4 (Oct. 1925): 620.

33 Fraser to Castlereagh, 14 April 1812, PRO/FO 63, vol. 149.

34 Pennell to Castlereagh, Salvador, 21 June 1821, PRO/FO 63, vol. 240.

35 British Merchants of Bahia to President of Bahia, Salvador, 14 Aug. 1824, Arquivo Público do Estado da Bahia, Seção de Arquivo Colonial e Provincial (APEB/SACP), box 1186.

36 Acting Consul Charles Weiss to the President of Bahia, Salvador, 27 Nov. 1829, APEB/SACP, box 1189.

37 Kidder, *Sketches of Residence*, 86–87.

38 Tavares, *Comércio proibido*. As early as 1925, the use of British capital in the Brazilian slave trade was well known to Anglophone historians, yet it has not always received sufficient attention, Adams, "Abolition of the Brazilian Slave-Trade," 631.

39 Pennell to Secretary to the Provincial Junta of the Department for Foreign Affairs, 8 Nov. 1821, APEB/SACP, box 1191.

40 Graham, *Journal of a Voyage*, 148; George Pilkington, *An Address to the English Residents in the Brazilian Empire* (Rio de Janeiro: Laemmert, 1841).

41 Inventário, George Mumford, 29 Mar. 1862, APEB, Seção Judiciária, 01/199/352/02.

42 Concubinage with the local women was another such practice, although it was not quite so problematic for the community in political terms; see Louise Guenther, *British Merchants in Nineteenth-Century Brazil: Business, Culture, and Identity in Bahia, 1808–50* (Oxford: Centre for Brazilian Studies, 2004), 150–56.

43 Guenther, *British Merchants*, 54–56; João José Reis, "Slave Resistance in Brazil: Bahia, 1807–1835," *Luso-Brazilian Review* 25:1 (1988): 111–44.

44 Edward Wilberforce, *Brazil Viewed Through a Naval Glass, with Notes on Slavery and the Slave Trade* (London: Longman, Brown, Green, and Longmans, 1856), 69.

45 Fagundes Varella, *O estandarte auri-verde: Cantos sobre a questão anglo-brasileira* (São Paulo: Typografia Imparcial, 1863), 10–11.

46 Freyre, *Ingleses no Brazil*.

47 Thomas Ewbank, *Life in Brazil: Or, a Journal of a Visit to the Land of the Cocoa and the Palm* (New York: Harper & Brothers, 1856), 185.

48 Robert Walsh, *Notices of Brazil in 1828 and 1829*, vol. 1 (Boston: Richardson, Lord & Holbrook, William Hyde, Crocker & Brewster, and Carter, Hendee & Babcock, 1831), 78.

49 Graham, *Britain and the Onset of Modernization*, 70.

50 Freyre, *Ingleses no Brazil*, 52, 179, 257.

51 Ibid., 56.

52 *A Tolerancia* (Salvador), 11 October 1849; Luis Carlos Martins Pena, "Os dous ou o inglês maquinista," in *Comédias de Martins Pena*, ed. Darcy Damasceno, 106–35 (São Paulo: Ediçoes de Ouro, 1966). On this play, see Ross Forman, "Imperial Intersections: Imperial Visions in Collision and Collapse in the Late Nineteenth and Early Twentieth Centuries" (PhD diss., Stanford University, 1998), chap. 6.

53 Freyre, *Ingleses no Brazil*, 53.

54 Moema Parente Augel, *Visitantes estrangeiros na Bahia oitocentista* (São Paulo: Editora Cultrix, 1980), 219.

55 José Wanderley Pinho, "A Bahia, 1808–1856," in *História Geral da Civilização Brasileira*, tomo 2, vol. 1, ed. Sérgio Buarque de Holanda, 291 (São Paulo: Difusão Européia do Livro, 1967).

56 Freyre, *Ingleses no Brazil*, 56.

57 José Wanderley de Araújo Pinho, *Salões e damas do Segundo Reinado* (São Paulo: Martins, 1944).

58 Graham, *Journal of a Voyage*, 142.
59 Pinho, *Salões e damas*, 39–40.
60 Graham, *Journal of a Voyage*, 143; Pinho, *Salões e damas*, 40. The details of Pennell's reception were probably planned by his daughters, who had only recently arrived in Bahia, so Pinho's judgment was probably correct on this count.
61 Candler and Burgess, *Narrative of a Recent Visit*, 78.
62 Guenther, *British Merchants*, 84–109.
63 See Ronald Harpelle's chapter in this volume.

6 Cooking Class:

ORDER AND THE OTHER IN THE CORPORATE KITCHENS OF LATIN AMERICA

Ronald N. Harpelle[1]

> *We may live without friends; we may live without books;*
> *But civilized man cannot live without cooks.*
>
> — EDWARD GEORGE BULWER-LYTTON

INTRODUCTION

"We are what we eat" because food preparation and consumption are among the most intimate rituals of daily life. Of course dietary preferences are a function of factors like the availability of food items, climate, and geography, but preparation methods are cultural signatures.[2] Like sacred texts, recipes are keys to a community's identity because some of our most carefully guarded secrets are culinary. Identities are, therefore, transmitted through the standardization of food preparation and recipes serve as markers that delineate the boundaries that exist between one group and another. Consequently, the foods with which we identify define ethnic, regional, religious, national, class and cultural boundaries, and the choices that we make in selecting ingredients, readying them for consumption, and choreographing their consumption impose order on the kitchen and, by extension, on the household and the community itself.

Traditionally, families and the communities to which they belong have handed their culinary heritage down orally, from generation to generation, through a system of apprenticeship. Although recipes have been recorded for hundreds of years, only in the last century did the cookbook

115

emerge as a fixture in most modern households. Urbanization, better communication, modern appliances, supermarkets, and other innovations have revolutionized kitchens everywhere in the modern world. By introducing new food ideas and techniques, cookbooks dictate social etiquette and have changed many aspects of home management. Cooks are no longer bound by seasons, the availability of food items, or the dietary norms imposed by the communities in which they live. The only significant obstacle to success in a modern kitchen is the knowledge required to deal with all of the new possibilities that advances in technology and the presence of exotic food items provide. Not surprisingly, the cookbook has emerged as an essential kitchen tool and it has become the most common means of disseminating culinary information. Cookbooks, like the ancestral recipes of old, are handed down from generation to generation. They therefore exist, according to Colleen Cotter, as a "connection of purpose and text to context and audience," and they can offer insights into the past.[3]

One example of a cookbook functioning as both an expression of and a contributing factor to changing lifestyles is the *Good Housekeeping Cook Book: Recipes and Methods For Every Day and Every Occasion.*[4] The cookbook was produced by the Good Housekeeping Institute, which was founded in 1900 for the purpose of "improving the lives of consumers and their families through education and product evaluation." In addition to providing recipes, the *Good Housekeeping Cook Book* was a manual for a middle-class lifestyle. The cookbook was only available to subscribers of *Good Housekeeping* magazine, which meant women with means. In 1911, the institute became a part of the Hearst Corporation and it continued to provide women with information on "housekeeping" and the "management" of the home. One of the institute's key functions was to provide reports on foods, recipes, and household appliances tested in its laboratories. Readers were assured that all of the recipes contained in the book were tested, tasted, and given a "Seal of Approval" by the staff at the Good Housekeeping Institute.

The *Good Housekeeping Cook Book* was only one of myriad pamphlets, magazines, and other publications from the period that espoused "true womanhood" and "scientific housekeeping" as the foundation for ideas about the place of women in modern society.[5] According to the doctrine of "true womanhood," women's nature was expected to be pure, pious, submissive, and nurturing because they were the custodians of virtue and the guardians of morality. "Scientific housekeeping" was a means to an end; modern methods were to be used to achieve and uphold traditional roles and values. Although the obvious subtext to the *Good Housekeeping*

Cook Book and similar publications was gender, the boundaries of class and race also permeate the publication. Those who adhered to the ideals of true womanhood, "Good Housekeepers" all, served as role models in a rapidly changing society. Manuals like the *Good Housekeeping Cook Book* were intended to shape society, and the middle-class women who used them set the pace for others.

Another example of social construction as the subtext of cooking can be found in the ubiquitous community cookbooks that began making their appearance in the first half of the twentieth century.[6] Communities, like individuals, are what they eat, and community cookbooks are one of the ways that members of a self-defined group express themselves. Community cookbooks are edited compilations of recipes submitted by enfranchised members of a particular social, religious, or ethnic group. As such, they are elaborate membership lists that put a community "Seal of Approval" on the members of the group, their kitchens, and their households. Although community cookbooks can be purchased by outsiders, the purpose of the publication is to reinforce boundaries by establishing the difference between those who contributed and are, by their inclusion, full members of the collective, and everyone else. Those who wish to replicate the community-sanctioned formulas operate within what are considered to be the "acceptable" limits established by the contributors and editors. As a result, community cookbooks tell us about the people who participated in the publication and where they construct their boundaries.

One community cookbook that demonstrates how ideas about food formed both a bond and a barrier is a publication produced by women who followed their husbands to the multinational enclaves in Latin America in the early-to-mid twentieth century. In 1942, the "ladies resident in the oilfields" of Peru produced the first edition of *The International Cook Book/Recetario Internacional*, a bilingual cookbook similar to those commonly associated with fundraising for community organizations.[7] The contents and general structure of *The International Cook Book* are familiar to anyone who has ever read or purchased a community cookbook. It contains a total of 321 contributions by 106 individuals whose names appear at the bottom of each recipe. The cookbook is divided into sections that cover a full range of recipes that are common fare in many North American households. Profits from the first edition's sale were donated to the Red Cross Fund, while the second edition, published in 1948, helped pay for the Church of the Good Shepherd in San Isidro, Peru. Local individuals, merchants, and corporations purchased advertising space in the book, which was distributed within the community.

The most remarkable feature of *The International Cook Book* is the near total absence of non-Euro-American dishes in the compilation.[8] Donna Gabaccia argues that American food is immigrant food and, therefore, international; however, aside from Chicken à la King and a handful of other recipes, *The International Cook Book* does not have an international dimension to it.[9]

To understand *The International Cook Book* as historical evidence, it is necessary to situate it within the context of the lives of the people who provided the recipes. At the time of publication the contributors were living in a company town in the oilfields of Talara and Negritos, Peru, and they were almost exclusively English-speaking women of European descent. The contributors belonged to an artificial community that was a functional extension of the operations of a multinational corporation in Latin America. Their community was corporate before it was social and the cookbook that they produced was a class-specific aid for surviving long sojourns in Latin America.[10] Therefore, *The International Cook Book* can be read as an expression of the culture and values of the people who were commanders in a campaign of corporate conquest in Latin America.[11] A more appropriate title for the publication might be "The Multinational Cook Book," because it reflects the interests of large corporations like Standard Oil in countries like Peru.

The women who contributed to *The International Cook Book* were among the many thousands of women from the United States, Canada, and Europe who ventured to Latin America in the early twentieth century to live in communities built for the managerial elite by the multinational corporations they worked for. In doing so, they entered a world engineered in corporate boardrooms and they became company wives, adjuncts to American enterprise. The "ladies of the oilfields of Peru," like their counterparts throughout Latin America, were elite women assigned a rearguard role in justifying and maintaining the hegemony of American corporations over the people and countries of the region. The incentive and reward for loyalty was a lifestyle befitting specialists working in the adverse conditions of the remote base camps that served as company headquarters in Latin America. *The International Cook Book* was conceived as a means to help ensure that the families of the Euro-American oilfield workers enjoyed a home environment that reinforced their identity as leaders of a corporate campaign. Therefore, the subtext of *The International Cook Book* is best appreciated when cast against a backdrop of the planned corporate compounds that sprung up wherever multinational enclaves were established in Latin America.

Talara's history is typical of enclaves in that it was "new" by Latin American standards, but seen as an "artificial" settlement by those who visited it.[12] It is located in an isolated region of the country, approximately 1,800 kilometres from Lima, near the border with Ecuador. The London and Pacific Petroleum Company began building a corporate town site near a small fishing village in 1889 and, in 1914, the property was transferred to the International Petroleum Company, a Canadian subsidiary of Standard Oil.[13] By 1940, the company had over 1,700 wells in the Talara district and "23,000 men, women and children under its jurisdiction."[14] As a company town, Talara contained a sizeable section reserved for the Euro-American "staff."[15] The houses built for the staff were fully equipped with electricity, modern appliances, and suitable space for an entire family. Staff houses also came with "little green gardens irrigated on sand," and Talara had "one of the best equipped hospitals in Peru."[16] According to one source, the staff quarters was where, "in amicable work and play, live[d] the Americans, English, Canadian, Irish, Scotch, and French" employees of the company.[17] In addition to modern housing, the company elite became members of the "English Club," an exclusive social club for managers and their families. Male residents could also frequent the "Bachelor Club," also known as the "Casa de Locos," where single oilmen went to unwind. The influence of "gringos" in Talara was evidenced by the celebration of American Independence on 4 July and Halloween in October. While "tennis, basketball, bowling, and baseball" were played by all in the enclave, "golf and especially polo" were the preserve of the Euro-Americans.[18] In short, from its inception, Talara was a company town run by and in the interests of the petroleum industry.

Like corporate enclave communities everywhere, the homes of the Euro-American managers were shielded from the rest of the community by barriers, both natural and unnatural. The staff quarters were located in Punta Arenas, a separate section of town surrounded by barbed wire, to which access was restricted. Similarly, the company maintained a private beach called "Acapulco" adjacent to Punta Arenas. Like the "English Club," Acapulco beach was for the exclusive use of the "staff" and their families.[19] Staff quarters were, therefore, bordered by corporate headquarters and the refinery to the south and west, the Pacific Ocean to the north, and rings of class-specific housing to the east. As might be expected, the nearest residential neighbourhood to Punta Arenas was reserved for Peruvian engineers and other "native" professionals, and the farthest, Barrio Chorrillos, was where the common labourers and their families lived. The staff quarters were the domestic sphere of the corporation's operations and within its walls company wives reigned supreme.[20]

Although the term "company wife" simplifies the complex identity of women from different social and economic backgrounds who joined their husbands in Latin America, it locates them within the context of privileged members of an enclave society. The wives of administrators, skilled workers, missionaries, and others who grasped at the opportunities afforded by multinational corporations were individuals who brought with them their particular class, ethnic, and social backgrounds. Upon arrival, company wives became conscious of the rank extended to them as the spouses of specific individuals, and of their apparent superiority over those who lived outside the compound walls. Living in the Euro-American enclave meant conforming to its self-identity and accepting the predetermined role of a company wife. Many of these women were confronted with the exigency of reconstructing and reorienting class barriers to conform with the identity imposed upon them by the Euro-American, English-speaking, and segregated communities of which they became a part. Gender and class interests diverged within the company compounds, but as members of the corporate elite, they enjoyed a higher status than most save the wealthiest people in the countries in which they found themselves.

Although women like those connected to the oil fields of Peru seldom worked outside of the home, they were not merely housewives. Corporations offered superior housing and other privileges to the people who were posted to the frontiers of the American Empire, but along with status came an obligation to maintain and defend the distinctions between the leaders and the led. Euro-American managers, and by extension their wives, were a cadre of trustworthy employees who were selected because they shared the values, cultural attitudes, and racial identity of the corporation's directors. The men who went to Latin America were entrusted with the profitability of operations abroad, and their families played a functional role in ensuring corporate interests. The realm of the company wife was in the home where cultural identity and common values were maintained as a safeguard against the moral degradation of the men who were leading the campaign.[21]

The issue, as described by A. Grenfell Price in a 1939 "scientific" study of European settlements in the tropics, was that the presence of women had a civilizing influence that "prevented some of the worst evils of tropi-

cal white settlement" and "contributed greatly" to the success of enterprises abroad. One of Price's main concerns was the biological "threat"
posed by the cohabitation of "Whites" and "non-Whites" in a tropical
environment. His research showed that northern Europeans could "survive and breed" in the tropics despite "racial competition and tropical
disease," and that they were "making definite and encouraging progress"
in warmer climates. However, Price believed that "[d]egenerate members of the more advanced people will always mingle with their belated
neighbors," and that this was a serious drawback to having white people
live in the tropics.[22] An important role for company wives was, therefore,
to maintain the social barriers that surrounded their community and
protected their way of life.

Unfortunately, little is known about the lives of the people who pushed
expansion in Latin America, and women, when they do appear, are usually a footnote in a male-centred story of conquest. When scholars have
looked at women in multinational enclaves they have encountered the
silence of the official record, and few alternative sources of information
exist. If women are mentioned, they tend to appear in the society pages of
local newspapers or as characters in travelogues or autobiographies, but
never as the central focus of government, industry, or general historical
records.[23] The only developed literature on white women in the tropics
focuses on the European colonial experience of the nineteenth and twentieth centuries. Therefore, the place of company wives in Latin American
history is best appreciated if they are cast in the light of the women who
participated in Europe's colonization of Asia and Africa. Although the
differences between European imperialism and its modern American
equivalent are significant, the structure of power-relations in both situations are very similar. Studies of European women in imperial settings
thus offer a foundation upon which to build a study of Euro-American
women in the American tropics, and one of the most enduring female
figures in the history of colonialism was the memsahib, or "madame boss,"
as she was known in British India.[24]

The memsahib was the product of a nineteenth-century colonial culture and society. She was both feminine and imperial in her presence and
she was the female expression of European superiority. Men were the
explorers, the soldiers, and the commanders of the colonial campaign,
while women remained in compounds established for Europeans. Here
they were engaged in a struggle on a domestic level that was every bit as
important as that of their male counterparts. As Rosemary Marangoly
George argues, in colonial discourse "management of the Empire" is represented as "'home management' on a larger scale," and "housekeeping in

the colonies [was] often represented as a military/imperial campaign."[25] Women played a complementary role by ensuring that the domestic sphere, which was reserved for the family, was free of the debauchery and corruption that men were obliged to face in their daily lives. As a result, memsahibs carried the weight of the Empire on their shoulders and took seriously their responsibilities for domesticating the conquered. Their homes were sanctuaries of evangelical Christian family values and they were entrusted with the defence of their realm against the social threat posed by the presence of servants and other non-Europeans in their midst.[26] The homes of the European elite, with servants working in them, were cultural battlegrounds where European and non-European identities clashed.

However, the memsahib, like the company wife, was a contradiction, because in colonial settings European women enjoyed power and prestige that most were denied in their home societies.[27] Despite being both "subordinates in colonial hierarchies and ... active agents of imperial culture," they could not see the obvious parallels between their position in European society and that of colonized peoples.[28] The memsahib's home was a surreal representation of the European home reproduced in a tropical setting and decorated with a combination of local and imported furnishings. Within its confines, different standards and rules were applied to domestic tasks. Male servants took orders from European women and children, uniforms were worn and the rituals of daily life followed a European design. Fortunately, British women in the Raj were assisted in their duties by F. A. Steel and G. Gardiner's *The Complete Indian Housekeeper and Cook*, a compendium of recipes, as well as tips on the general management of the home and explanations of the duties of servants.[29] Company wives in Latin America were not so lucky as to have a comparable guide to household management despite facing the same challenges as memsahibs.

Like their counterparts in other colonial settings, the Euro-American "memsahibs" whose lives intersected with the creation of corporate enclaves in Latin America lived in the exclusive world of the foreign elite. As one author argues, the "white woman's status in society was the norm, the yardstick by which, 'native' lack [of status] was measured."[30] They were immediately recognizable as members of an elite group of foreigners because their lives were stamped with the corporation's "Seal of Approval." Euro-Americans lived in enclosed compounds, sometimes called "White Zones," where middle-class America, with its social life, household accoutrements, and dietary preferences were recreated. Their community, the houses in which they lived, the furniture, the decorations, and everything else in the enclave was based on a model developed by the architects of multinational corporations.[31] Corporate managers believed that "an adequate standard of living was almost as vital to the employee in the low tropics as the work of the medical scientist and the sanitarian in safeguarding health."[32] Therefore, the communities built for Euro-American workers were more than mere housing compounds – they were an instrument engineered with precision to maximize production. Corporate communities were designed with profits in mind and company wives were expected to play the role of the "Good Housekeeper" in order to maintain the viability of enterprise abroad. In this respect, company wives were "homemakers" in every sense of the word.

As part of the business plan, Euro-American women were given management positions in the home, where they had control over human and financial resources to ensure that social and cultural prerequisites of the corporate enclave were maintained. Upon arrival in the company compound, women found that their duties included the management of household finances, and the supervision of cooks, laundresses, house-boys, and other servants. For most, this was the first time they found themselves managing what was in essence the staff of a small business within their homes. Company wives tended to be working-class or lower middle-class women who would one day return home to a life without the benefit of domestic labourers. In addition, they were expected to fulfill the moral and social expectations the corporation had of its Euro-American employees. "Whiteness" and "American-ness" afforded company wives a status that they did not necessarily enjoy at home, and most were unaccustomed to the responsibilities that came with being a part of an elite community in a foreign land.[33] The Euro-American women living in Talara were not exceptions in that they did not hail from the servant-keeping classes of North America and, therefore, had to learn how to deal with the challenges of home management in a foreign land.

One of the biggest challenges for women who were not accustomed to an elite lifestyle was the management of domestic servants in the home.[34] The greatest obstacle to finding domestic labour was the general shortage of workers considered acceptable by the company wives. The enclaves were usually located in remote regions where the existing communities were often too small to supply the demand for female workers. Company wives also had to compete among themselves and at times against the company itself for domestic labour. In addition to working in the homes of the Euro-American elite, local women were hired by the company to cook and clean for the single men housed in "Bachelor's Quarters." Similarly, the labour camps often consisted of company barracks housing hundreds of single males whose basic domestic needs were provided by their employers. Nearby communities also provided employment for local women, including serving in wealthier households, along with other opportunities like operating a market stall or a commercial establishment, taking in boarders, or doing laundry. The result was that company wives were forced to compete for labour, which meant that there were limits to what could be expected from domestic servants.

Corporations provided an allowance to employees of rank to cover the cost of domestic servants. In the home, company wives determined wage scales, job descriptions, and working hours.[35] They also supervised all tasks, dictated what needed to be done, and the ways in which labour was performed. Even when the company did not pay for domestic service, status-conscious members of the Euro-American elite were quick to take advantage of what was for most a "once-in-a-lifetime" opportunity of having a domestic servant. The result was that company wives, like their husbands, managed a sector of the local labour supply, and they shared many of the corporation's concerns. Domestic servants were unorganized, which meant that working conditions, pay raises, and fringe benefits were set on an individual basis, and all decisions were made by the company wife. Company wives brought with them notions of proper work ethic, cleanliness, morality, and a determination to instruct their charges about the "American way" of doing things. The importance of reliable, efficient, and deferential domestic workers meant that finding and retaining suitable domestic labour was a challenge that preoccupied company wives. Yet, despite the difficulties of finding and keeping good domestic servants, they were considered an indispensable part of life in a corporate enclave.

Another major stumbling block was the double barrier of language and culture. Reports by the women who went to Latin America are filled with stories illustrating the enormous cultural gap that existed between the memsahib and the hired help. Since company wives were often unwilling to socialize with Hispanics of any social class, and because their communities were islands of Anglo-Saxon solidarity, few women learned Spanish well enough to be able to fully communicate their desires to the women working for them. Therefore, domestic servants who could speak English were a hot commodity. English-speaking servants were more familiar with the culture of their corporate masters, and they could be expected to understand and follow instructions. The problem was that English-speaking servants were a rarity outside of the circum-Caribbean region, and in remote locations it was even difficult to find women who could speak any European language, including Spanish.

Language barriers were a major problem, but they did not keep Euro-American women from hiring domestic servants because freedom from the drudgery of domestic labour was one of the attractions of living as a company wife in Latin America. Alicia O'Reardon Overbeck, a woman who ventured to the Bolivian Andes as the wife of a mining engineer, saw the chance at having a domestic servant as a reason for giving up life in Long Beach, California. In her own words, Overbeck left behind what she considered to be a "settled and ordered existence," living "as ninety-nine and nine-tenths of the civilized inhabitants of the world regularly live." By this she meant living in the United States with her young family in a quiet neighbourhood with parks, schools, and other services nearby. She also recognized that her life in the United States was not ideal and had "certain drawbacks for a woman with two small children and no real flair for housework." As a consequence of her yearning for adventure and her distaste for the "checkered apron," she jumped at the chance to get away when her husband was offered a job as manager of a mine in Bolivia. In her own words, Overbeck gave up "living like other people" and left for Latin America where she set up a new household that included servants.[36]

Overbeck's chronicle of her experiences in Latin America offer some of the clearest insight into the challenges faced by Euro-American mem-sahibs. For example, like most other company wives, she discovered that it was one thing to be able to afford servants, but quite another to find reliable women to work in her home. The first servants whom she hired, María Emma, Juana, Lucia, and Felicia, were, according to Overbeck, "hopelessly incompetent," untrustworthy, and even dirty. Euro-American concerns about personal hygiene were rooted in the perception that Latin American women were dirty and disease-ridden. Personal hygiene extended to the kitchen, where culinary hygiene was of utmost importance. For women like Overbeck, Latin Americans could never be too clean, and they could never be completely trusted in the preparation of food.

Eventually, with the help of a more experienced company wife, Overbeck found a "small Chola" named Teresa who proved to be a godsend. Teresa impressed her mistress with her honesty, her ability to get the best price from local merchants, and her stern stewardship of the family home. She was a good cook, kept the house clean, and managed the rest of the staff well. However, Teresa was only willing to go so far in accommodating her employer's vision of a domestic servant. When Overbeck presented her with a white-trimmed black uniform, Teresa refused to give up her traditional dress, much to her mistress' displeasure. Despite standing firm on the question of traditional identity, Teresa offered what Overbeck saw as four advantages over the other women who had come into her home to work as domestic servants: she could read, write, tell time and, a bit later, she was married.[37]

The question of marital status was an important consideration for Overbeck and other company wives because they were suspicious of single women. According to Sidonie Smith, in the imperial setting, the "natives" were considered to have an "abnormal sexual appetite," which was also a "'dark' force lurking inside 'civilized man'" and a threat to Western culture.[38] They worried about having single women in their homes because, in their eyes, the morality of the local population was always suspect. To someone like Overbeck, marital status was important because, by definition, company wives were married women and, since they were the corporate standard by which all others were measured, relationships without legal sanction were evidence of inferiority. A Euro-American woman's role was to get married, become a good housekeeper, and protect her husband from himself, and from other women.

Although there were many problems associated with finding, keeping and managing servants, domestic labour, servants were considered essential. According to a company wife who spent time in Guatemala, the "extreme heat" made it impossible for the foreign woman to do any but the lightest housework. In fact, housework in the tropics was so arduous that some women would hire "a cook, a laundress and a house boy." Others, whose husbands occupied lower ranks within the corporation, were obliged to settle for the paid services of one all-round domestic labourer.[39] However, the fact that a family was only entitled to one domestic servant did not mean that the company wife performed the tasks that were left undone. As the lone employee hired to cook for a Euro-American household, Inez McNabb stated that her job was not limited to the kitchen; "I did everything, I did laundry, I cooked, I cleaned, I took care of kids."[40] Euro-American women often exploited their servants as much as possible and, according to one study, to the detriment of their own health. Grenfell Price found that with "coloured servants and fair financial resources it [was] probable that American women [were doing] insufficient housework" for their own good.[41] Too much of a good thing was not good for the health of the company wife.

COMPANY WIVES AND DOMESTIC SERVANTS IN THE KITCHEN

While lack of exercise was a concern to some, company wives had far more pressing issues to deal with because they had households to run and corporate images to maintain. One of the biggest problems with hiring women in Latin America was their inexperience with modern appliances or the kinds of foods that they were expected to prepare. To most servants, the memsahib's modern kitchen resembled less a kitchen than a scientific laboratory with all its modern appliances and foreign foods, imported, duty-free no less, from abroad.[42] As a result, the task of managing a household included training domestic labour to work in a modern environment and to perform at a level befitting the position and lifestyle of the Euro-American elite. Accounts by women who managed domestic servants often refer to disastrous meals prepared by a cook who had no idea how to produce meals within the realm of their employers' experience. Frances Emery-Waterhouse recounts her experiences of being served "calves' brains," and her disgust at lifting the cover on a kettle to find turkey feet, "the more unseemly appendages of fowl," protruding from the broth.[43] Euro-American notions of hygiene in the kitchen extended to ingredients and the procedures used to prepare food. These anxieties were amplified by the general health risks associated with life in the tropics, and consequently the cook often became the focus of obsessive vigilance. Therefore, the only option for a Euro-American woman who did not wish to have her family served "unseemly" bits of domestic animals or combinations of ingredients that she had never seen before was to train her cook in the finer arts of "American" cooking.

Training by example, whereby the company wife donned an apron, rolled up her sleeves, and demonstrated the means of obtaining "acceptable" results in the kitchen, was the only real option open to most women. However, training was fraught with difficulties because, in addition to being time-consuming and stretching the limits of a white woman's ability to work in the tropics, it involved intimate contact with the hired help. Company wives employed women whom they often considered to be inferior to themselves, and in such cases they consciously minimized their social contact with them. Although Susan Leonardi argues that sharing kitchen secrets might permit women to cross the "social barriers of class, race, and generation," this was rarely the case in the corporate enclaves of Latin America.[44] Working with someone in a kitchen and sharing recipes across the table is intimate because it involves divulging details that might be considered personal. As Anne E. Goldman argues, in the kitchen, women of different races and classes do not "easily fall into sisterhood."[45] In the corporate enclaves, the distance between the colonizer and the colonized had to be maintained, and familiarity breeds even more contempt when the exploited finds out just how artificial the divide is. The diesel mechanic's wife was not the wife of the superintendent, and domestics could see – and even smell – the difference.

Even if a company wife spoke Spanish and was not opposed to fraternizing with the locals, the next great hurdle, after teaching the cook to cook, was to get her to remember how to make things in the way that she was first taught. Another problem was the need to train every new kitchen recruit. This was time-consuming and even established cooks required constant upgrading. Experience in the culinary world of the Euro-Americans also meant that a good cook soon understood the value of her skills on the open market. The truth of H. H. Munro's aphorism, "the cook was a good cook, as good cooks go; and as good cooks go, she went," played itself out in Latin America. Cooks developed talents in the corporate kitchens of the "White Zones" and company wives worried constantly about losing their most highly-skilled labourers. The demand for good cooks was high and company wives sought ways of facilitating their training, so that any local woman could become a good cook.

One solution for a company wife was to hire servants who could read and then translate the family's favourite recipes for the cook to follow. Finding women who could read was not necessarily easy, but a bigger problem was to provide the cook with sufficient recipes suitable for the Euro-American palate. An entire cookbook was necessary and it had to be a cookbook that both the company wife and the cook could understand. A cookbook in the hands of a servant meant that orders could be given, the task of cooking could go on without supervision, and the results could be predicted. A cookbook could make a better cook out of anyone and it made it easier to replace cooks who left. While English-speaking cooks could rely on recipes supplied by the boss, non-English-speaking women, the vast majority of household servants in Latin American enclaves, could not make use of any existing cookbooks because they were either in English or did not contain the recipes demanded by people living in the artificial confines of a "White Zone." Moreover, cookbooks in Spanish did not permit the English-speaking boss to maintain control over the kitchen or ensure that the ingredients being used were acceptable. This very dilemma led the "ladies resident" in Peru to develop a training manual that allowed them to share culinary secrets while maintaining the distance that separated Euro-American women from the women they employed.

The International Cookbook is, therefore, a discourse of empowerment and not a cross-cultural exchange – the kitchens of the management elite in multinational enclaves were a domestic extension of the industries that they served. The book is bilingual, with recipes in English appearing on the even numbered pages and the translated version appearing on the facing page, but it was never intended to serve as a means

THE INTERNATIONAL
COOK BOOK

RECETARIO
INTERNACIONAL

6.1. Cover of The International Cookbook/Recetario Internacional, 1942
Source: Collection of Ronald N. Harpelle.

of exchange, and the cultural and social biases of the authors is evident throughout. The "ladies of the oilfields" were not attempting to bridge the social gap between themselves and their Peruvian counterparts; rather, *The International Cook Book* served to reinforce divisions by casting the company wife as the teacher, and the domestic servant as the student.[46] In the case of *The International Cook Book*, it is possible to tell a book by its cover. It depicts a shapely blond woman in a colourful, frilly dress holding a cookbook open for a dark haired, heavy set woman wearing a maid's uniform and apron. The cook is shown reading the cookbook and, under the watchful eye of the "mistress," the "cook" is about to attempt to prepare a recipe (Figure 6.1).

The International Cook Book is laden with imperial discourse because it draws a sharp line between the women who decide what is to be cooked and those who have to prepare it. The ingredients used in the recipes also serve to highlight the differences between women from the industrialized world and those from developing countries. The Peruvian diet had developed over the course of thousands of years and was reliant on foodstuffs available locally. By contrast, the "haute cuisine" demanded by Euro-American families was a modern construct imposed upon the women who became cooks in American households. Peruvian women learned that the "best" meals, things like "Tinned Corn Fritters," "Salmon and Hominy," and "Tuna Fish Delight," required the use of processed foods imported from abroad.[47] They also learned that Euro-American families did not eat food common among Peruvians. Model communities, based on modern designs and built for an idealized white American middle-class, were fuelled by exotic foods prepared in ways that were as foreign as the people who ate them.

The ingredients for many recipes were not readily available elsewhere in the country, but people with money in Talara had access to the company-run commissary, which was a standard part of every major corporate enclave in Latin America. In a typical enclave, the company commissary had "a large stock of canned goods and bottled drinks" with everything arriving "from the United States and Britain . . . nearly duty free, so the prices charged [were] nominal."[48] Consequently, among the few things truly international about *The International Cook Book* were the ingredients of the recipes that relied on processed foods imported from abroad. While local substitutes may have been available, *The International Cook Book* made no provision for their use because processed foods were readily available at the company store.[49] *The International Cook Book* was designed to restrict creativity by requiring the cook to follow a preset formula to reproduce an invariant product to the exacting standards of their Euro-American bosses.[50]

A survey of the recipes in the book offers hints about the lives of some of the people who ventured into the wilds of Latin America. For example, among the more than three hundred favourite recipes provided by company wives are three different recipes for "Meatloaf," and one, the only recipe for food submitted by a man, for hamburgers. These recipes say something of the working-class origins of the contributors and the relationship of their men to cooking. Another aspect of the cookbook that merits mention is the fact that more than half of the recipes are devoted to desserts, sweets, and drinks suitable for entertaining guests in the home.[51] The emphasis on entertainment food while living in a country where the basic dietary needs of the majority of its citizens were often barely met highlights the distinctions between the women who produced the book and the women who would be expected to use it. Cooks did enjoy days off during which they might entertain their own guests, but for company wives and their families, leisure time was one of the perks of life in the tropics. Consequently, the entire final section contains recipes for cocktails so that the cook could also function as a bartender. *The International Cook Book* is a manual that gave cooks the formulas necessary to fulfill almost every culinary function within the middle-class home.

The social and ethnic divide cultivated by the town planners in Talara is echoed in *The International Cook Book* by the fact that, with the exception of a few contributions by Señora Blanquita de Pflucker and by Señora Ana María de Pérez, all of the recipes were provided by people with non-Hispanic names. Obviously, these women, the only two of the one-hundred and six contributors who appear not to be Euro-American, met with community's "Seal of Approval." The inclusion of only two "Peruvian" recipes, "Arroz con Pato" (Rice with Duck) and "Papas a la Huancaína" (Huancaína-Style Potatoes), reveals the overall homogeneity of the community that produced the cookbook. Thus the Euro-American home in Talara was a site of interaction with Peruvians, but not of exchange. This is in marked contrast to other imperial settings. For example, Mary Procida argues that the "voracious appetite of the British empire was nourished not just by the roast beef of old England, but also by the chutney and curry of India."[52] To be sure, *cuy* (roast Guinea pig), a Peruvian delicacy, would have been a risky gastronomic inclusion, but many foods commonly consumed in Peru are compatible with the recipes in the cookbook and could have been included.[53] Unlike the British in India, Euro-Americans did not embrace the foods of the lands that they conquered. It may be true that taste in food is acquired and company wives cannot be blamed for their lack of experience with non-American cuisine, but the cookbook is not just about eating, it is also an expression of the memsahib's distrust of her domestic servants.

The attitude of the "ladies of the oilfields of Peru" toward the women who laboured in their kitchens is expressed most clearly in the existence of two formulas that were deliberately kept out of the hands of domestic servants. Out of 321 inclusions for everything from "Meat Puffs with Mushroom Sauce" to "Tom Thumb Cookie Bars," only two recipes were not translated into Spanish, and they represent the exclusive preserve of the company wives.[54] At the very end of the book, wedged in as an unindexed attachment, are the formulas for idyllic American middle-class family life.[55] Although written tongue-in-cheek, they are confidential and only for women who could read English. The hidden secrets are the keys that make all of the other formulas in the book work, and they speak to the fundamental divisions between the company wives and the Peruvian women whom they employed.

The first secret recipe is entitled "How to Cook a Husband," and it instructs the reader on how best to manage the relationship with a spouse.[56] The objective is simple; please him in order to control him. The recipe begins with the caution that husbands are "utterly spoiled by mismanagement . . . and so, are not tender and good." In order to prepare a man, the cook is instructed to make a fire "out of love, neatness and cheerfulness," and to include kisses, "but no vinegar or pepper on any account." In addition to duty and devotion, the cook is told that a "little spice improves [a man], but it must be used with great judgment." Carnal pleasures may, therefore, be indulged in, but with a judicious amount of restraint to uphold notions of Christian morality. These secrets of marital bliss are said to ensure that a husband, "thus heated," will be "digestible, agreeing perfectly with [the cook] and he will keep" for a long time, unless the woman should become "careless and set him in too cold a place." This recipe for a successful married life was printed in English because it was to be kept only within the group.

In a similar fashion, the second hidden recipe delves into the issues of family life. "To Preserve Children," like many of the other concoctions in the book, required ingredients that were beyond the means of the women in the employ of company wives. In addition to requiring the leisure time to enjoy a family outing, the recipe calls for access to a "large grassy field," leisure time for "half-dozen children," "two or three small dogs," and a "pinch of brook and pebbles." Again, the recipe paints an idyllic picture of family life for those who can afford the ingredients. For the servants from a poor country, access to a large grassy field was an invitation to graze domesticated animals; children would be obliged to help care for the animals and dogs would not be pampered pets. Moreover, the fact that the recipe calls for children who would "brown in the sun," and not those of permanently brown complexions, means that domestic servants in Latin America could not provide the key ingredient for this mixture. The women who entered the home to do the cooking and cleaning were, by their exclusion, judged to be unworthy of this lifestyle, and incapable of benefiting from advice shared among the company wives. Once again, notions of superiority prevented Euro-American women from opening their world to women whom they judged to be inferior.

The International Cook Book was intended to demonstrate the extension of Euro-American superiority to the domestic sphere of the empire. Although the company wife's kitchen was a scene of interaction, these two recipes, guarded like family secrets, were too intimate to share with outsiders. The decision to exclude Peruvian women from one part of the cookbook illustrates a key point at which the sharing of experiences with Peruvian women ended, and where exclusion began. Consequently, the barriers that prevented domestic servants from enjoying a success-ful middle-class existence were reinforced by the fact that the company wives were often the only exposure that servants had to non-Peruvian society. With no other reference points, they were obliged to rely on the world inside the homes of foreigners in order to develop a greater un-derstanding of the world beyond their community. Every company wife knew that it was one thing to teach servants how to prepare meals that they could not afford, and to clean a house of the sort they would never live in, but it was quite another thing to give away all the secrets to being a successful company wife.

CONCLUSION

Historians of imperialism agree the that domestic realm of the empire reflected the cultural, gender, and racial divisions required to maintain control, but Euro-American company wives were not merely engaged in a rearguard action. The homes that they established and managed within the corporate compounds of Latin America were unique sites of imperial dominance. *The International Cook Book* is one example from Peru of the technology of rule that facilitated and helped to maintain Euro-American dominance in Latin America. It served many imperial purposes beyond the functions of a cookbook because it was class- and race-specific. As one facet of the presence of multinational corporations in Latin America, Euro-American memsahibs contributed to the creation, collection, and dissemination of imperial knowledge by producing the cookbook. *The International Cook Book* served to shape ideas about Euro-American superiority among Peruvian women while at the same time restricting access to the means by which power was obtained.

In the corporate enclaves of Peru, company wives served as the defend-ers of the status quo and *The International Cook Book* is an expression of their interests. The kitchens managed by company wives were extensions of corporate power relations; therefore, the relations in the kitchen were functional, not social or personal. The connection of purpose and context to text and audience is made as clear by what the authors of the cookbook share and do not share with their Hispanic counterparts. Recipes for a successful marriage, a happy family life, and middle-class bliss were kept out of the hands of Peruvian women. In this way, company wives guarded their community's monopoly on power and maintained the self-percep-tion of its moral superiority. Like the *Good Housekeeping Cook Book*, *The International Cook Book* is a manual for a middle-class lifestyle, and some of the information that it contains was for subscribers only.

1 I thank Kelly Saxberg, T. E. Vadney, Lori Chambers, Michael Conniff, and Geoffrey McCafferty for their comments on drafts of this chapter.

2 Margaret Visser, *Much Depends on Dinner* (Toronto: Harper Collins Publishers Ltd., 1992), 12.

3 Colleen Cotter, "Claiming a Piece of the Pie: How the Language of Recipes Defines Community," in *Recipes for Reading: Community Cookbooks, Stories, Histories*, ed. Anne L. Bower, 70 (Amherst: University of Massachusetts Press, 1997).

4 *Good Housekeeping Cook Book: Recipes and Methods for Every Day and Every Occasion*, tested, tasted and approved by Dorothy B. Marsh, Katherine Norris, and Adeline Mansfield (New York: International Magazine Company, Inc., 1933).

5 Other cookbooks had their origins in this period. Fannie Farmer's *Boston Cooking-School Cook Book* (Boston: Little Brown and Company, 1896) is considered the first modern American cookbook because it contained ingredient lists, exact measurements, and was written in authoritative style. A later example is Irma Rombauer's self-published, *The Joy of Cooking: A Compilation of Reliable Recipes with a Casual Culinary Chat* (St. Louis, 1931). Earlier cookbooks, like Isabella Beeton's *Book of Household Management* (London, 1861) were aimed at the expanding middle class, containing, in addition to recipes, suggestions on how to deal with servants and other information on managing a household. For a full discussion of the modern cookbook's evolution, see Anne Mendelson, *Stand Facing the Stove: The Story of the Women Who Gave America the Joy of Cooking* (New York: Scribner, 1996). In Canada, Nellie Lyle Pattinson's *Canadian Cook Book* (Toronto: Ryerson Press, 1923), set the standard for culinary arts outside of Québec.

6 One of the early "community cookbooks" produced in the United States was *Lord Fairfax's Kitchen: A Collection of Tried Recipes from Winchester Housekeepers* (n.p., 1892). The cookbook was compiled by the women who taught cooking at the Winchester, Virginia, "Colored Public School" to raise money to help pay for the program.

7 *The International Cook Book/Recetario Internacional* (Lima: Imprenta del Ministerio de Guerra, 1941). On community cookbooks, see Bower, ed., *Recipes for Reading*.

8 A comparison of *The International Cookbook* to the *Canadian Favourites Cook Book* (1944) produced by a committee of women belonging to the Co-operative Commonwealth Federation (CCF), a Canadian social democratic political party, makes evident the working-class origins of the women in Peru. The CCF cookbook was compiled and sold as a fundraiser for the party. Although it reflects the diversity of the Canadian population in the 1940s, the recipes tend to be basic and nonornamental, just like those found in *The International Cookbook*. For example, the wife of the party's founder and an elite member of the organization, Mrs. J. S. (Lucy L.) Woodsworth's contribution is a recipe for Marshmallow Salad, Scalloped Potatoes, and Velvet Cream.

9 Donna R. Gabaccia, *We Are What We Eat: Ethnic Food and the Making of Americans* (Cambridge: Harvard University Press, 1998). The author uses the idea of the United States as a melting pot in her examination of the country's stewing pots and the book celebrates diversity and democracy.

10 Anne E. Goldman, "'I Yam What I Yam': Cooking, Culture, and Colonialism," in *De/Colonizing the Subject: The Politics of Gender in Women's Autobiography*, ed. Sidonie Smith and Julia Watson, 187 (Minneapolis: University of Minnesota Press, 1992).

11 For an elaboration of concept of colonialism and cultural control see Nicholas B. Dirks et al., "Introduction," *Colonialism and Culture*, ed. Nicolas B. Dirks, Geoff Eley, and Sherry B. Ortner, 3–5 (Ann Arbor: The University of Michigan Press, 1992).

12 Agnes Rothery, *South America: The West Coast and the East* (Boston: Houghton Mifflin, 1930), 5.

13 Edit Aranda Dioses, *Del proyecto urbano moderno a la imagen trizada: Talara, 1950–1990* (Lima: Pontificia Universidad Católica del Perú, Fondo Editorial, 1998), 44–47.

14 Edward Tomlinson, *New Roads to Riches: In the Other Americas* (New York: Charles Scribner's Sons, 1940), 259.

15 Talara was redesigned in the 1950s after a church fire in 1947 exposed the potential threat to the company's interests of having so many wooden buildings near the oil refinery.

16 For a biting description of Talara, see Christopher Morley, *Hasta La Vista: Or, a Postcard from Peru* (Garden City: Doubleday, 1935), 152–60.

17 Rothery, *South America*, 3.

18 Ibid. 56–57.

19 Harris-Clichy Peterson and Tomás Unger, *Petróleo: Hora certa* (Lima, 1964).

20 For another view of life behind bars see Setha Low, *Behind the Gates: Life, Security, and the Pursuit of Happiness in Fortress America* (New York: Routledge, 2003).

21 A classic example of the literature on the development of a multinational corporation is Frederik Upham Adams, *Conquest of the Tropics: The Story of the Creative Enterprises Conducted by the United Fruit Company* (New York: Doubleday, 1914). For an analysis of an American expatriate community, see Herbert and Mary Knapp, *Red, White and Blue Paradise: The American Canal Zone in Panama* (San Diego: Harcourt Brace Jovanovich, 1984).

22 A. Grenfell Price, *White Settlers in the Tropics* (New York: American Geographical Society, 1939), 177–178.

23 For first-hand accounts by women, see Winifred Lewellin James, *A Woman in the Wilderness* (London: Chapman & Hall, 1915); Jane Harvey Houlson, *Blue Blaze: Danger and Delight in Strange Islands of Honduras* (Indianapolis: Bobbs-Merrill, 1934); Cecile Hulse Matschat, *Seven Grass Huts: An Engineer's Wife in Central and South America* (New York: Literary Guild of America, 1939); and Karena Sheilds, *The Changing Wind* (London: John Murray, 1960). For a somewhat different account see Charlotte Cameron, *A Woman's Winter in South America* (London: Stanley Paul, 1911).

24 See for example Penny Tinkler, "Introduction to Special Issue: Women, Imperialism and Identity," *Women's Studies International Forum* 21:3 (Winter 1998): 217–22; Frederick Cooper and Ann Laura Stoler, *Tensions of Empire: Colonial Cultures in a Bourgeois World* (Los Angeles: University of California Press, 1997); Francis Gouda, "Nyonyas on the Colonial Divide: White Women in the Dutch East Indies, 1900–1942," *Gender and History* 5:3 (Autumn 1993): 318–42; James A. Boutiler, "European Women in the Soloman Islands, 1900–1942: Accommodation and Change on the Pacific Frontier," in *Rethinking Women's Roles: Perspectives on the Pacific* (Los Angeles: University of California Press, 1984), 173–200. For a less critical but revealing survey of the lives of the foreign elite, see Katie Hickman, *Daughters of Britannia: The Lives & Times of Diplomatic Wives* (London: Harper Collins Publishers, 2001).

25 Rosemary Marangoly George, "Homes in the Empire, Empires in the Home," *Cultural Critique* 26 (Winter 1994): 108–9. See also Anne McClintock's discussion of the exotic and erotic images of empire in *Imperial Leather: Race, Gender and Sexuality in the Colonial Contest* (London: Routledge, 1995).

26 For a discussion of the boundaries of elite culture in the colonial context, refer to Ann Laura Stoler, "Carnal Knowledge and Imperial Power: Gender, Race, and Morality in Colonial Asia," in *Gender at the Crossroads of Knowledge: Feminist Anthropology in the Postmodern Era*, ed. Micaela de Leonardo, 73 (Berkeley: University of California Press, 1991).

27 For examples of the literature on how women projected imperial power abroad while at the same time struggling for political rights at home, see Lora Wildenthal, "'When Men Are Weak': The Imperial Feminism of Frieda von Bülow," *Gender & History* 10:1 (April 1998): 53–77; Antoinette Burton, *Burdens of History: British Feminists, Indian Women, and Imperial Culture, 1865–1915* (Chapel Hill: University of North Carolina Press, 1994); Vron Ware, *Beyond the Pale: White Women, Racism and History* (London: Verso, 1992); and Pratibha Parmar, "Challenging Imperial Feminism," *Feminist Review*, 17 (1984): 3–19. Also of interest is the impact of imperialism on women in Europe. Anna Davin, "Imperialism and Motherhood," *History Workshop Journal: A Journal of Socialist Historians* 5 (1978): 9–65, raises questions about the emphasis that came to be placed on motherhood as part of the imperial project.

28 For an excellent discussion of contradictions of European women's roles as extensions of empire, see Stoler, "Carnal Knowledge," 51.

29 F. A. Steel and G. Gardiner's *The Complete Indian Housekeeper and Cook*, 7th ed. (London: William Heinemann, 1909).

30 George, "Homes in the Empire," 116.

31 Stacey May and Galo Plaza, *The United Fruit Company in Latin America* (Washington: National Planning Association, 1958), 187.

32 Price, *White Settlers*, 134–35.

33 See George, "Homes in the Empire," for a full discussion of race and class in the discourse of empire. See also Ann Laura Stoler, "Rethinking Colonial Categories: European Communities and the Boundaries of Rule," *Comparative Studies in Society and History* 31:1 (Jan. 1989): 134–61; Jenny Sharpe, *Allegories of Empire: The Figure of Woman in the Colonial Text* (Minneapolis: University of Minnesota Press, 1993); and Gouda, "Nyonyas on the Colonial Divide." See also Mary Procida, "Feeding the Imperial Appetite: Imperial Knowledge and Anglo-Indian Domesticity," *Journal of Women's History* 15:2 (2003): 123–49.

34 For a revealing account of the "difficulties" encountered by "White" women in dealing with domestic labour see Hickman, *Daughters of Britannia*, 69–89.

35 See May and Plaza, *United Fruit Company*, 187, and Frances Emery-Waterhouse, *Banana Paradise* (New York: Stephen-Paul Publishers, 1947), 93.

36 Alicia O'Reardon Overbeck, *Living High or at Home in the Far Andes* (London: Lovat Dickson & Thomson, 1935), 2.

37 Ibid., 60, 62.

38 Sidonie Smith, "The Other Woman and Racial Politics of Gender: Isak Dinesen and Beryl Markham in Kenya," in *De/Colonizing the Subject: The Politics of Gender in Women's Autobiography*, ed. Sidonie Smith and Julia Watson, 411 (Minneapolis: University of Minnesota Press, 1992).

39 Emery-Waterhouse, *Banana Paradise*, 92

40 Inez McNabb, interview with the author, 16 Jan. 2000, Tela, Honduras.

41 Price, *White Setters*, 160.

42 Modern appliances, sometimes referred to in hardware circles as "wife savers," were the exclusive preserve of the households of the enclave elite because the corporations provided all of the furnishings. Some appliances may not even have been found in the homes that they left in the Unites States. All of the homes in the "White Zones" were electrified, but in 1930 in the United States, 90 per cent of rural homes were not connected to the electric power grid.

43 Emery-Waterhouse, *Banana Paradise*, 175.

44 Susan J. Leonardi, "Recipes for Reading: Summer Pasta, Lobster à la Riseholme, and Key Lime Pie," *Proceedings of the Modern Languages Association* 3 (May 1989): 342.

45 Goldman, "'I Yam,'" 172.

46 On the politics gender and race in the kitchen, see Leonardi, "Recipes for Reading"; she presents the kitchen as a space where the interests of all women converge and where men intrude. In contrast, Goldman, "'I Yam,'" 171–72, argues that because recipes are written and cooking takes place "within a specific social context, it encodes a political problematic."

47 Tuna Fish Delight, submitted by Mrs. G. W. Merrill, calls for one can of tuna fish, one can of mushrooms, half a can of pecans, and a cream sauce.

48 Emery-Waterhouse, *Banana Paradise*, 96–97.

49 Canned foods started appearing on grocery store shelves in large numbers in the 1920s and were typical of the foods that were shipped to company commissaries in Latin America.

50 For a discussion of this topic refer to Elizabeth J. McDougall, "Voices, Stories, and Recipes in Selected Canadian Community Cookbooks," in *Recipes for Reading*, ed. Anne E. Bower, 39-65 (Amherst: University of Massachusetts Press, 1997).

51 The proportion of main course to dessert recipes in *The International Cook Book* is roughly equivalent to that of other community cookbooks such as St. Michael's Anglican Church Women (Deer Lake, Newfoundland), *Out of Deer Lake Kitchens* (Winnipeg: Gateway Publishing Co. Ltd., n.d.). For noncommunity cookbooks refer to Collette Hanicotte, ed., *Le Petit Larousse de la cuisine* (Paris: Larousse-Bordas, 1998), which devotes approximately 30 per cent of its pages to similar entertainment foods.

52 Mary Procida, "Feeding the Imperial Appetite," 143.

53 For example, despite the common appearance of *lomo saltado* (a Peruvian stir fry) and *aji de gallina* (chicken in a pepper sauce) on dinner tables in Peru, neither is included in the cookbook, but "Chop Suey" and "New Orleans Creole Chicken Gumbo" are.

54 Of note is the translation of "Love Knots" into "Pastelitos de Nuez Moscada" (Brown Sugar and Nut Cookies), in which the emphasis is on the ingredients and not on the cookies' seductive potential.

55 Refer to Jessamyn Neuhaus, "The Way to a Man's Heart: Gender Roles, Domestic Ideology, and Cookbooks in the 1950s," *Journal of Social History* 32:3 (Spring 1999): 529–55.

56 This recipe can be found in several community cookbooks of the period. "How to Cook a Husband" also appears in the St. Paul's United Church Women's Federation Cook Book from Schefferville, Québec (1961). Of interest is the fact that the women who reproduced the recipe in Schefferville were company wives whose husbands worked for the Iron Ore Company of Canada. They too lived in a community that was designed in a boardroom and constructed in a remote region. See also Lynne Ireland, "The Compiled Cookbook as Foodways Autobiography," in *The Taste of American Place: A Reader on Regional and Ethnic Foods*, ed. Barbara G. Shortridge and James R. Shortridge 111–17 (Lanham: Rowman and Littlefield, 1998).

7 (Re)turning Home:

NARRATIVES OF BOLIVIAN TRANSNATIONAL MIGRANTS

María Eugenia Brockmann Dannenmaier[1]

INTRODUCTION

Don Pedro lives in Cochabamba, Bolivia. He has lived there since he was born fifty-five years ago, except (we may suppose) for a few months every year when he worked in Buenos Aires, Argentina. Don Pedro first went to Buenos Aires in the late 1960s; he went to work in the construction sector, an area, as he was told by friends, which was "in need" of Bolivian workers. Because he was a trained marble worker and stonemason, he decided to go. After working for a year or so, don Pedro returned "home" to Cochabamba where his wife and young children were expecting him. As he liked Buenos Aires and his work was much appreciated by Argentine bosses, he decided to go back there after three months. This time he spent only eight months in Buenos Aires before returning to Bolivia. He does not remember how many times he repeated this pattern, how many times he travelled back and forth between Bolivia and Argentina, but he remembers the first time that he took his oldest son with him; it was during the first presidency of Carlos Menem in Argentina, around 1992–93. During that time the pay was good and both could save since they shared a rented room and other expenses. In the years that followed, each time that he returned to Buenos Aires, he was accompanied by one of his sons or daughters. Five of them live there now, all of them married to a Bolivian partner, and all of them have Argentine-born children. At one point, seven of his eleven children lived in Buenos Aires, but the youngest ones returned to Bolivia in January 2002 because of the bad economic situation. Two other daughters were planning their return to Bolivia in December 2002. Don Pedro "returned definitively" in 1999; that is, he is not planning to travel again to Buenos Aires (at least not for the purpose of working), because he has young children who need a father by their side. His two teenage daughters, Roxana and Zulma, along with a growing number of other Bolivians, are planning to travel to Spain next year to investigate work prospects there.

Don Pedro's experience poses several important questions to migration theorists: What kind of migrant is he? Is he a migrant or an immigrant? Is he engaged in a seasonal, temporal, or cyclical migration? How can we understand the fact that he has been working in Argentina for more than twenty years, but he still says that he has "lived" all his life in Bolivia? Has he "returned" definitively "home"? Have his teenage daughters returned? What is the significance of home for him? What does it mean for him that five of his eleven children are in Argentina? What are the meanings that he gives to his migratory experience? Is migration just an experience, or is it a state of being, as some theorists argue?[2] As these questions suggest, don Pedro's situation is ambiguous, yet his experience is not unique.

Tomás, Julieta, Enrique, and Rita are Bolivian men and women whom I met in the summer of 2002 in Cochabamba and who, like don Pedro, migrated to Buenos Aires during the 1970s, 1980s, and 1990s. They are among the more than 400,000 Bolivians estimated to have migrated to Argentina in the last thirty years, but they are also part of the unknown number of Bolivians who have returned to Bolivia since 2001, when the Argentine economy collapsed. The multiple linkages and networks developed by these Bolivian migrants, in both Bolivia and Argentina, and their continuous comings and goings, raise our awareness of the transnational character of their movement and prompt us to question their particular experiences insofar as they manage to live *simultaneously* in two countries, challenging the notion that migration is a linear or permanent move between bounded communities.[3]

A transnational analytical framework raises important questions about conceptualizations of immigrants as people who move from one place to another to stay and to make a new home, and of migrants as people who move only on a temporary basis in order to work. Instead, transnational analysis emphasizes that migrants abroad maintain multiple economic, cultural, social, and political ties to their communities of origin. They move freely back and forth across international borders and between cultures, and often build homes in more than one country.

Other analytical approaches, stemming mainly from modernization, dependency, and world-systems theories, have variously conceptualized migration as seasonal, temporary, continuous, returning, transient, or permanent moves between two or more bounded communities. Yet, the experience of the Bolivians described in this chapter fails to fall into any such categories. Their migratory movement appears to be continuous and fluid. In essence, they repeatedly leave, return, and remain at the same time, making it difficult to "pinpoint clear, time- or space-bounded migrant categories, which become, instead, part of a complex, and often ambivalent, process of negotiation and representation among various contexts."[4]

This chapter is an exploration of how particular Bolivian men and women who have migrated from Bolivia to Argentina, and have recently "returned" to Bolivia, define, negotiate, and (re)create their identities in the migration experience. By using a transnational analytical framework, I examine some of the concrete practices through which cross-border links are developed and maintained by Bolivian transmigrants, and how in that process, migrants (re)shape multiple identities that challenge the hegemonic constructions that define them as marginal Others in both Bolivia and Argentina. Both the narratives and the experiences of transnational migration for these people vary according to gender, age, economic possibilities, and legal circumstances.

While many transnational studies of migration focus on migrants' participation in nation-building processes across countries,[5] my analysis privileges the voices and the reflections of Bolivian women and men who have returned to Bolivia after an experience of migration to Argentina. By using a conceptualization of migration in transnational terms, my work centres on how these migrants conceive of the social conditions in which they live and how they actively search for ways to improve their living conditions in both Bolivia and Argentina. In this sense, the meaning of home is critically explored in order to grasp the complex narratives of belonging and displacement in both places.

SITUATING THE MIGRATION OF BOLIVIANS IN ARGENTINE HISTORY

Los mexicanos descendemos de los aztecas, los peruanos de los incas y los argentinos descienden de los barcos.

[*We Mexicans descend from the Aztecs, Peruvians from the Incas, and Argentines descended {disembarked} from ships.*]

— Popular saying, origin unknown

The migration of Bolivians to Argentina has a long history, dating back to at least 1869, when the census first recorded the presence of Bolivians in Argentina; at that time, there were about six thousand, representing 2.9 per cent of the total foreign population. This Bolivian population, whose origin was the impoverished areas of the *altiplano* (highlands) of Potosí and the valleys of Tarija, settled mostly in the northwestern provinces of Jujuy and Salta in response to the demand for temporary and unskilled labour for agriculture production, mainly on sugar cane and tobacco plantations.

In 1876, under the presidency of Nicolás Avellaneda, the Argentine congress approved the first Law of Immigration and Colonization, a law that defined the composition and characteristics of the Argentine nation-state. This law reflected the aspiration of the elites to promote a modern nation-state in which the European immigrant was seen as a fundamental protagonist. Considered civilized and rational actors (in contrast to "barbaric" indigenous peoples), European immigrants had the mission not only of increasing the population, but also of modernizing and civilizing the country. The intellectual author of this dichotomy – "civilization and barbarism" – was Domingo Faustino Sarmiento, one of Argentina's founding fathers, who posited that the infusion of a superior racial stock would correct once and for all the rural barbarism of mestizos and indigenous peoples.[6] According to Alejandro Grimson and others, Argentine leaders instituted European immigration in order to remake (and "improve") their country's national identity.[7] The "national culture" was based on the aspiration that, through transculturation and acculturation, the diverse cultural groups would fuse in a type of a creole melting pot. Between 1871 and 1914, 5.9 million European immigrants arrived in Argentina (mostly Italians, Spanish, French, and Portuguese) of whom 3.1 million became permanent residents.[8]

Compared to this massive flow of people from Europe, non-European Bolivian migration and that of other neighbouring countries did not represent a menace, in quantitative terms at least, to the Argentine elite's project of forging a modern European-style nation-state. Bolivians were in demand as workers in industries that needed unskilled and cheap labour that the native population could not supply; therefore the Bolivians' ethnic identity mattered little.[9] Besides, their presence in Argentine territory was regarded as temporary or seasonal; once the job was done, the workers returned to their homeland.

After the Great Depression of 1929, the Argentine government began to develop a new mode of accumulation and growth based on a state-led model of import substitution industrialization. As a result, the industrial sector grew rapidly, especially in Buenos Aires, where labour was in high demand. Internal rural-to-urban migration of Argentines supplied most of the industrial work force, but migration from neighbouring countries – Bolivia, Chile, Paraguay, and to a lesser extent Brazil and Uruguay – also contributed; migration from these countries was initially a response to regional labour scarcity in the primary sector of Argentina's border areas.[10] In the cities, a xenophobic response emerged in response to this internal migration; metropolitans called such migrants *"cabecitas negras"* (little black heads) because of the dark colour of their hair.

In the middle of the twentieth century, Bolivia underwent several changes that help explain the movement of its population. It was one of the few Latin American countries to experience a revolution in the true political sense of the word – that is, a complete collapse of the oligarchic system of government that had characterized it since the Conquest. The Revolution of 1952 was the consequence of an unstable economic, social, and political situation that could no longer be tolerated by Bolivians. The revolution brought major changes, including the nationalization of the mines and major industries, the legalization of peasant and miner unions, and the granting of full citizenship to the Indian population. Voting rights were also extended to women and illiterates, who (like Indians) had been barred from political participation. The growing mobilization and organization of the Indian peasantry forced the newly-installed government to enact a sweeping land reform. Land was redistributed on the basis of the principle that land belongs to those who work it; thus the system of haciendas (large estates) was destroyed, and Indian peasant forced labour eliminated.[11] Scholars agree that the land reform was one of the factors that triggered urbanization in Bolivia through rural to urban migration, not only because many Indians were left with no land, but also because they could now move freely throughout the country.[12] In this period, Bolivian emigration to Buenos Aires also increased, although not substantially.[13]

In the 1980s, the number of Bolivian immigrants who settled in Buenos Aires grew and, according to census data, it reached or surpassed in size the population that lived in the border cities of Jujuy and Salta. The 2001 census counted 233,464 Bolivians in Argentina. Other sources of information suggest that the number of Bolivians is higher than the census figures. Between 1974 and 2002, the *Dirección Nacional de Migraciones de Argentina* (National Migration Office of Argentina or DNM) granted a total of 188,118 *radicatoría* documents to Bolivians, thereby giving them the right of permanent residence in Argentina. Bolivians requested these documents directly from the DNM, or received them through the nine amnesties decreed by the Argentine government between 1949 and 1998 in order to regularize the status of illegal immigrants from neighbouring

Table 7.1: Number of Bolivians Receiving Radicatoría Documents, 1974–99

Year	Number
1974[a]	22,596
1980	14,314
1984[a]	18,739
1990	1,528
1992	2,218
1993–94[a]	10,253
1995–2002	18,470

Notes: a. By amnesty decree.
Sources: Enrique Otieza, Susana Novick, and Roberto Aruj, *Inmigración y discriminación: Políticas y discursos* (Buenos Aires: Grupo Editor Universitario, 1997); data for 1995–2002 drawn from INDEC's web page, *www.indec.mecon.gov.ar* (31 May 2005).

countries.[14] The fact that most radicatoría documents were granted through amnesties reveals the difficulty of keeping track of undocumented migrants. It also suggests that, were it not for the amnesties, many Bolivian migrants would have remained undocumented immigrants, in many cases working without official permits (Table 7.1).

Some studies indicate that, over the past twenty-five years, the migration of Bolivians to Argentina has intensified to the point that there are now about 1.5 to 2 million Bolivians in Argentina, of whom almost half are undocumented. This means that one out of five Bolivians now live in Argentina, with Buenos Aires having the third largest urban Bolivian population, after the cities of La Paz and Santa Cruz.[15] The increase in the migration of Bolivians to Argentina in the last two decades is explained by political and economic factors. According to Alberto Zalles, migration since the 1980s has been propelled by the economic crisis in Bolivia and the structural reforms applied since 1985, which included the privatization of government-owned mines and other enterprises, which left more than 30,000 people unemployed (Figure 7.1).[16] On the other side of the border, following the implementation of neo-liberal reforms under the presidency of Carlos Menem, Argentina managed to recover from decades of instability and stagnation, achieving high rates of economic growth, especially from 1991 to 1997 when GDP grew more than 40 per cent and exports increased by more than half. Menem also launched a "Convertibility Plan" that stipulated the exchange rate of one peso per U.S. dollar, which prevented a relapse into hyperinflation; the Argentine

7.1. Casual Labor Market in La Paz, Bolivia, *ca.* 2000
Source: Photo by Eric Dannenmaier.

government also opened the economy to imports, which damaged the already weakened local manufacturing sector.[17] This economic growth had an attraction or "pulling" effect on unemployed and impoverished Bolivian migrants.

Discussion of the pull-push factors that have caused a massive migration of Bolivians to Argentina is not limited to academic circles. Large-scale migration is also discussed in newspapers from both countries and it figures in the discourses of government leaders. Members of the Bolivian community in Argentina discuss it extensively and the web page of *La Comunidad Boliviana en Argentina* (The Bolivian Community in Argentina), created by members of several Bolivian social organizations in Argentina, claims that there are two million Bolivians in Argentina.[18] This number likely includes the sons and daughters of Bolivians born in Argentina, who are considered Bolivians by the community, although they have Argentine citizenship; place of birth does not necessarily have a fundamental role in how Bolivians define themselves.[19]

Nevertheless, this evidence of a "massive" migration of Bolivians to Argentina in the last decade contradicts the statistical and census data of both countries. Even if we recognize that census data might hide the real number of Bolivians in Argentina, or undercount them due to their illegal status, the number of two million migrants seems inflated. A 2002 Bolivian demographic study suggests that there can be no more than 400,000 Bolivians in Argentina, because this number does not match the Bolivian government estimates of population growth for the past decades. In addition, in 1996, 25,112 Bolivians travelled to Argentina, and 17,510 returned, a net emigration of only 7,602 Bolivians.[20]

A number of questions arise from these data. What explains the huge discrepancy among official data, academic studies, and informal numbers that appear in news accounts? Has not the presence of Bolivians in Argentina been historically continuous? Why does the number of Bolivian migrants in Argentina matter? To whom does it matter? If there are so many Bolivians in Argentina, why have they not taken advantage of the numerous amnesties issued by the government? What leads Argentine and Bolivian newspaper accounts to talk about a "massive invasion" and "flows" of Bolivian migrants?

Grimson is right to suggest that the increased "social visibility" of Bolivian migrants is a response to socio-cultural motives and not quantitative ones. Furthermore, both in the study of migration of Bolivians in Argentina and in the experience of Argentines and Bolivians, there is much fear of the Other regularly expressed in government leaders' public discourse and in that of both countries' inhabitants, fear that is also replicated in newspapers and expressed by the Bolivian migrants with whom I spoke.

Buenos Aires? In Buenos Aires everything is big.
There are almost no small buildings. Everything was
*   huge, immense.*
People were also immense, tall and white, very white,
*   like their buildings.*

— MÓNICA

The Bolivian men and women who narrated their stories of migration to me in Cochabamba had recently returned from Buenos Aires. Each narrative reflects multiple adventures and dramas, multiple encounters with multiple Others located at different points of the transnational circuit: Bolivians at home, Bolivians who migrated to Argentina between the 1960s and the 1980s who are now *bien ubicados* (well-established), Argentine *porteños* (natives or residents of Buenos Aires city), and Argentines of the provinces, Koreans, and other Latin American migrants. But each narrative also revealed that this particular return trip to Cochabamba was different from others that they had made in previous years. This time, the return was very much influenced by the critical economic and political situation that Argentina was experiencing in 2002.

By the end of 2001, economic growth in Argentina had reversed and in November a political and economic crisis exploded. President Fernando de la Rúa implemented drastic economic measures such as the *corralito* or the freezing of bank deposits, the devaluation of the peso, increasing tax rates, and the forced conversion of dollar bank deposits and contracts into pesos (the so-called *pesoficación*), which had dramatic consequences in the lives of millions of Argentines and non-Argentines. Bolivians were not immune to the economic and political crisis. The men and women with whom I spoke explained the Argentine economic and political crisis in complex terms. They were well aware of the policies and measures implemented by the Argentine government, and the restrictions and conditions imposed by the International Monetary Fund. But most of all, they had personally lived the impact of the corralito, the pesoficación, and the devaluation of the peso on their salaries and savings.

Until that year, when Bolivian migrants received their salaries, they would immediately exchange them for United States dollars in order to save or to send to Bolivia. Since convertibility had been established in 1991, the peso had been worth one dollar. This equivalency in the exchange rate was extremely attractive to Bolivian migrants, for most of them were earning more than US$500 per month in Argentina. Compared to the average wage of US$80 that they could make at home, Argentina seemed the place where they "had to be." Nevertheless, when the Argentine peso was devalued, Bolivians saw their money literally disappear. For example, Rodrigo's salary of 300 pesos was reduced to almost US$100, and the same thing happened with the salaries of all the migrants whom I interviewed. Adela and her husband could not take their savings out of the bank, and they were afraid of losing years of savings due to the pesoficación. In addition, the prices of consumer goods fluctuated hourly, making it impossible to plan, in the words of Gabriela, even "what we would eat and buy the next day."

In response to this critical situation, most of the Bolivian transmigrants that I spoke to decided to return home to Bolivia. For these men and women, home is constituted in the relationship and awareness of two places that supply different yet complementary resources that are fundamental for their lives. Cochabamba is seen as the place where freedom, safety, and tranquility are lived, where one has a better time (*se la pasa mejor*), where "you can do things" outside the house. In that sense, Cochabamba is conceived as a place where actions can take place with freedom. But Cochabamba is also constructed in emotional terms. Not only do family members live there; it is also where "people like oneself" (*gente como uno*) live. It is a place of familiarity. Nevertheless, this familiarity can now, after an experience of migrating, be put into question. In this questioning that what was familiar becomes strange.

Adela's perception of "returning home" expresses this idea:

> "[H]ere" [Bolivia], you see things that you don't see "there"
> [Buenos Aires] or anywhere else. You see children working, and
> working in terrible conditions, children without shoes. In my
> neighbourhood you see naked children peeing in the street, and
> even if you don't want to look you see it and you think to yourself
> there's another way of living. Before I travelled I didn't notice
> those things, that's why sometimes it's not good to learn other
> things; if you don't know the difference and that there are better
> places, if you don't know, then you don't suffer.

For Adela, the return home has a meaning that resonates with what Stuart Hall refers to as the impossibility of homecoming.[21] In Adela's case, this impossibility takes on a metaphorical sense, migration as a one-way trip. Home has changed because the meaning given to it has been transformed; that is, because Adela herself has changed. Poverty is now visible, she has learned, and she finds it difficult to acknowledge.

If, as Iain Chambers argues, the difference between migration and travel is that travel "implies an itinerary from a fixed point of departure to an equally stable point of arrival ... and migrancy involves a movement in which neither the points of departure nor arrival are immutable or certain," then Adela will never quite be back home.[22] It is not surprising then, that Adela and her husband were planning to migrate to Spain in the near future.

Paradoxically, other Bolivian men and women whom I interviewed perceived their Bolivian home in a more positive way now than when they first migrated to Buenos Aires. Pablo was one of those who told me that his motivation to go to Buenos Aires was to be in a "culture that was more advanced than ours." In a way, for Pablo, and others like him, Buenos Aires represented "progress." Progress was spatially located in Buenos Aires because there were jobs there, the city had tall buildings, and there were many people. But a sense of belonging to Buenos Aires was never achieved by Pablo or by others whom I interviewed. The paradox lies in that, through the experience of displacement, of strangeness abroad, the migrants whom I interviewed learned the value of their place of origin, a home "where one should be, where one is free," as Mónica put it.

The concept of home can be described and explained by multiple meanings, often contradictory and yet complementary. For these migrants, home was expressed in abstract terms as a feeling of belonging, as a memory, as a desire of what is longed for and not achieved, as a dream, as a future. Ultimately it was conceptualized – in contrast to the place where they actually resided – as a place where a person and his or her family can live freely.

In contrast, Buenos Aires is the place where jobs can be found (at least before 2001), but no sense of belonging is achieved there. Yet Buenos Aires provides the means and the resources to build a home in Cochabamba, both materially and symbolically. This resonates with what the author bell hooks says about home: it is no longer just a singular place. Rather, home is the place "which enables and promotes varied and ever changing perspectives, a place where one discovers new ways of seeing reality."[23]

The particular vulnerability of Bolivia in the global economic system, the lack of job opportunities in the country, and the process of migration reproduce the vulnerable place that Bolivia has in the world system. Only this can explain why Gabriela, a school teacher with a university degree in Bolivia, worked as a housemaid in Argentina, or the case of Juan, also a high school teacher, who told me that his students now talk about migrating to Spain rather than continuing their university studies in Bolivia.

All of the Bolivian men and women with whom I spoke knew someone who was either in Spain or someone who was preparing to go there. Spain and Buenos Aires are the places where money can be earned and saved to build a home back in Bolivia. As Nancy puts it: "I might go to Spain, I have a sister there. I have learned in Buenos Aires, now I can go anywhere. I know what it's like to be outside of the country ... besides, now that I have built the first floor [of the house] with [savings from] Buenos Aires, maybe I can build the second with Spain." (In the near future scholars may well begin to ask how Bolivians organize themselves in Madrid, Barcelona, or Bergamo; or about the type of relations Bolivians establish in these new places from which a return migration is much more difficult, and how they change their conceptualizations of home in that process.)

Being in Buenos Aires made sense for them while they could earn enough money to save and send to Bolivia. However, once this situation changed, the meaning of Buenos Aires changed and the most negative aspects of their lives in the city became apparent and intolerable. Discrimination, strenuous work schedules, insecurity, and the uncertainty associated with an undocumented status became unbearable to the point that, as Rodrigo put it, "there was no life there . . . life was terrible."

The workplace is a key space in the construction of identities since it represents a space of encounter and relationship among workers of different nationalities and from different Argentine provinces. All of the men whom I interviewed had worked at some point as masons in construction sites where most of their coworkers were Argentines, Paraguayans, and Peruvians. The Bolivian men distinguished among Argentines, between porteños and Argentines from the interior provinces. As Diego said:

> Porteños are kind people, they know how to speak to you, they
> teach you things and the bosses keep their word. Argentine
> bosses always search for Bolivian workers because their money
> is worth the work we do ... what I've seen is that we go to work
> at six in the morning and the Argentines arrive at eight, and
> they *matean* [drink a type of herb tea], so they begin to work at
> nine or nine thirty; and then again they are taking *mate* [tea] at
> eleven.... As the shift ends at six, ten minutes before that time,
> they are ready to leave. Bolivians don't leave; we stay until we're
> finished with the job.

Gervacio adds: "I liked the job, and the Argentine bosses liked me, but other fellow workers told me 'you are doing too much'; so the boss, seeing that I worked [hard] he liked me. But others called me names ... they called me *bolita, forro.*"

The porteños are seen as being well educated, kind, respectful, and sociable; but most of all they are viewed as the middle- or upper-class Argentine who is the preferred *patrón* (boss). Argentines from the interior are depicted as lazy and relaxed individuals who drink mate and leave when the shift is over, not when the work is done. This image reinforces the self-definition of Bolivians as hard-working people and as the ones who are preferred by Argentine bosses. But at the same time, because of these same characteristics, Bolivian men are criticized as doing too much (thus threatening Argentine jobs), and insulted as bolitas.

Indeed, Argentine society has built a stereotype of Bolivian migrants, one that labels them as bolitas, which could translate to English as "small people." When I asked my informants why they were called bolitas most of them answered: "because they say we are small, round, and black." According to Grimson, there is a hegemonic construction in Argentine society that homogenizes migrants from Bolivia, Peru, Paraguay, and the Argentine interior based on such phenotypic characteristics.[24]

If this is so, the Bolivian narratives that I have gathered show an active discourse, one that constantly defies the homogenizing construction made by members of Argentine society. Bolivian migrants do not want to be recognized by the host society as marginal cabecitas negras or bolitas. Rather, Bolivians differentiate themselves from Others by emphasizing attitudes and behaviours which they believe to be distinct from others: in that sense, Bolivians identify themselves as hard-working and trustworthy people, different from other foreign and Argentine migrants.

This reputation as hard-working people often makes Bolivians victims of assault and robbery. Of the twenty-three interviewees, only one man had not been a victim of a major robbery or assault carried out by *choros* or other common criminals.[25] It may not be a coincidence that, compared to the people I interviewed, the one not assaulted, don Pedro, is the tallest and has fair skin. As one woman said, "they knew I was Bolivian, they always know"; and the way that they know is by phenotypic characteristics that recognize Bolivians as bolitas, "round, small, and black."

What for me was clearly an issue of racial discrimination was not for the Bolivian men whom I interviewed. When I asked them whether they had ever felt discriminated against by Argentines, they commonly responded no. I was puzzled. Had they not just a moment before told me that, because they were Bolivian, they were being robbed? Maybe I was not asking the right question. Or maybe they were not saying what I wanted to hear. Or perhaps there was simply no straightforward answer. Complicating matters further was the fact that the Bolivian women whom I interviewed all considered themselves victims of racial discrimination. Why did Bolivian women feel racially discriminated against in Buenos Aires while the men did not?

While most Bolivian men worked in construction at some point of their lives in Buenos Aires, most Bolivian women worked as housemaids for Argentine families. Alicia explained:

> They don't eat as we do. They eat a steak, or a sandwich with a leaf of lettuce, and that's it!! At night, they drink tea ... those people don't eat ... my boss only ate salads and on weekends he ate meat. They don't make desserts. They like the pasta only with cheese, but for me, I prepared it like we do here, with *aji* [chili] and vegetables, so I had to eat when they didn't see me.

Gabriela also told me:

> The lady of the house, the wife [of the boss] ate a cookie for lunch. They don't eat a thing! At night, to join her husband, she ate a salad. She did a lot of exercise and a masseuse even came weekly to give her massage. She told us "don't be fat." ... There, I was fat, because Argentine women are thin as sticks, as brooms ... at the beginning I thought she was too thin, but as time went by, I too wanted to lose weight.

Alicia's and Gabriela's statements echo other opinions that I heard from Bolivian women who had returned recently from Argentina. Alicia, Marcia, Valeria, Julieta, Rita, and Adela all told me that they had to cook for themselves when no one was home. Argentine bosses, they explained, do not like the smell of onions or aji. What seemed to bother the bosses was not only the smell of the food, but also the amount of food that they ate. As Gabriela expressed, her boss was always telling her to watch her weight – "don't be fat" – something that Gabriela never cared about before she travelled to Buenos Aires. As she explained to me, she never thought of fat or thin bodies until she went to Buenos Aires, or how her hair was done, or whether she used lotion on her skin or not. There are issues of power involved in these statements. Food is not just food and it is clear that its significance is not solely nutritional; it is intimately bound up with relations of power, inclusion, and otherness. By cooking their own food, these Bolivian women constructed meaning around the food that they consumed, and identified themselves as social actors different from the Argentines for whom they worked. But they were also actors in the sense that they maintained food habits that they had learned in Bolivia. For them, food was a symbol of ethnicity, essential to the creation of a stable and familiar environment in a place in which migrants do not feel fully comfortable, such as the boss's house.

One of the questions that I posed to Bolivian transmigrants was whether they missed something in Argentina; curiously, most of the men said that they missed "the meat." As José and Enrique recall, at the construction site, "there was always a small grill and we ate meat. I miss that meat, we [Bolivians] will never have that meat." The fact that "there was always a small grill" suggests that this was a shared activity among workers, a space for encountering each other and for the formulation of shared identity through sociality. Eating "almost the same things," as one of the man explained, was the first step to diminishing the distance between him and his boss. Food is fundamental here, because it is here used as a symbol that can break the differences between classes and nationalities at the same time that can also express group membership and relationship.

How does the experience of migration for both Bolivian men and women produce and reproduce unequal gender relations in both home and host societies? The difference in what is eaten offers clues as to why the Bolivian women whom I interviewed felt racially discriminated against, while the men did not. Anthropological and sociological studies of gender and food reveal that there are particular foods that are associated with one gender rather than the other.[26] This is particularly notable in the case of the consumption of meat, which is usually linked with masculinity. For Bolivian men, eating meat was a shared and public activity, something that was done in the workplace. Thus eating meat linked them to Argentines, and created a sense of integration, sameness and, arguably, of masculinity. As Bolivian men ate the same food that Argentine men ate, they understood their relationship as one between equals; therefore, they did not feel discriminated against by Argentines, or at least they felt that the sharing of meat was a significant gesture that overrode any discrimination that they did sense.

For Bolivian women the situation was different. Eating for them was largely a private and hidden activity; not only did they not eat the same food as their Argentine bosses, they also ate different quantities. Thus, the contradictions of power relations are embodied; while they ate and cooked their own food – thus manifesting their difference from Argentines and their own agency – Bolivian women also were more vulnerable to power relations and racial discrimination. They were constructed as bolitas, as "round, black, and small," in the private domestic space of the household. Only thus can we understand why her boss constantly told Gabriela that she should not be fat. Gabriela does not see herself as fat now that she is in Bolivia, but she did so in Argentina, especially when she compared herself to Argentine women. For Bolivian women, food marks cultural identities in a distinction between "what we eat" and "what they eat." For men, eating was a statement of inclusion, of sameness: "here we eat," linked Bolivian men with their *patrones*.

The Bolivian men and women whom I interviewed travelled back and forth numerous times between Cochabamba and Buenos Aires. Don Pedro and Rita, who were among the older interviewees, emphasized this; but even Roxana and Zulma, who were only thirteen and fifteen years old the first time that they migrated, moved back and forth between these two cities. In that sense, their experience challenges conceptual categories utilized in migration literature, which see migration as exclusively seasonal, temporary, recurrent, continuous, or permanent.[27] In fact, these categories are fluid, changing, and overlapping, since the movement of Bolivians from one city to the other involves different forms of migration which include temporary, permanent, and return migration, but which cannot be reduced to any one category.

All the transmigrants whom I interviewed also had family members, friends, or *compadres* who gave them shelter and advice, and connected them to job opportunities in Buenos Aires. These were Bolivians who migrated during the 1960s, 1970s, and 1980s. Therefore, they were well established in Argentina. But the narratives of the Bolivians with whom I spoke cast into doubt the so-called "Bolivian community in Argentina." As Severino recalls,

> Bolivians in Buenos Aires are very bad people. They try to exploit those who arrive after them because they are well established. They have their sewing-shops, or grocery stores, or stands at the market ... so the Bolivians that are there from before, twenty or more years, that have machines, or cars, or are patrones, they come to Bolivia to take workers and they tell us that they'll pay us a good salary. But once you're there [Buenos Aires], they exploit you, and they don't pay you what they said.

Valeria's statement complements the perspective of others whom I interviewed:

> I started working for other Bolivians in a grocery store, but even though they are Bolivians, they treated us [Valeria and her friend Julieta] bad. They threatened to report us to the *migración* [immigration officers] and tell them that we were illegal, so we had to work quietly and not complain ... they also took our passports, so we could not leave without them knowing.

In the narratives of the people whom I interviewed, there appeared to be a contradiction regarding the opinions and feelings they had towards Bolivians who had earlier migrated to Argentina as opposed to the present generation of migrants. While this older generation of Bolivian migrants often helped more recent arrivals in different ways, by offering a place to stay in Buenos Aires, by getting them jobs or offering to hire them, and even convincing them to travel to Argentina, they also exploited the new migrants by not paying them promised salaries, by taking away their passports, by threatening to denounce them to Argentine immigration officers, or by betraying their trust as members of a Bolivian community. As Miriam told me,

> Family members told us that "there" [Buenos Aires] work was good, and they offered us help, and they told us that they would give us this and that. But once the moment came for them to give us what they offered, they turned their backs on us. I don't know if it's envy or shame, but I am disappointed with my family. I don't know what happens to Bolivians in Buenos Aires, maybe it's because they've lived there for years and they earn a lot [of money] ... at least at that time they earned good money, they had cars and houses, and they want to make you feel down.

The general opinion of the transmigrants whom I interviewed was that Bolivians who went before them were mean and took advantage of the newcomers. This puzzled me due to the theoretical constructions I had previously read regarding "Bolivians" in Buenos Aires. For example, Dandler and Medeiros give central importance to the existence of networks that connect Cochabambinos in Buenos Aires.[28] According to them, because Cochabambinos share a common root and a common recognition of belonging to the same place of origin (the city of Cochabamba), they consider it a moral obligation to help the arriving migrant; in this way, family and community links and networks are maintained and re-produced in both cities. Grimson also studied how Bolivians in Argentina organize and build a discourse whereby a new *Bolivianidad* ("Bolivian-ness") is created.[29] This "new Bolivianidad," according to Grimson, serves to promote solidarity and strengthen political and social organization of Bolivians in Buenos Aires, and thus operates to blur class, ethnic, and regional identities among migrants. Instead of using the Bolivian state as its major referent, this Bolivianidad is built upon a process of "ethniciza-tion" that allows Bolivians to present themselves as members of a com-munity who can dialogue, resist, accept, and accommodate themselves within the larger Argentine society. While Grimson's fascinating study offers an understanding of how different social, cultural, and political organizations of Bolivians create a politics of identity in Buenos Aires, it does not explain why Bolivian migrants talk of a rather fragmented community of Bolivians.

Indeed, the narratives that I gathered on the whole reflect a disap-pointment with Bolivian family members, friends, neighbours, *compa-dres* and *comadres*, and other Bolivians in Buenos Aires. If, as identity theorists suggest, identities are based on contrasting oneself with a con-structed Other, the self-representations and narratives of the Bolivians whom I interviewed reveal that the Bolivian men and women who migrated to Argentina in previous decades are constructed as Others with whom bonds of sameness and bases of differentiation intertwine.[30] Rodrigo's and Monica's statements clarify this ambivalence: "Bolivians in Argentina think that they are Argentine, but they are Bolivian. Bolivians in Argentina are too Argentine [*son demasiado Argentinos*]. They behave like Argentines, they talk like Argentines. Being Bolivian, they are more Argentine than the Argentines."

Here "too Argentine" refers to embodied practices that older genera-tions of Bolivians have acquired in Argentina. That is, "they behave like Argentines, they talk like Argentines." Argentines have a particular accent that is not appreciated by Bolivians. Nancy echoes the opinions that I heard regarding this: "I do not like how they speak, I don't understand them." But it is not only the accent that they dislike; they also dislike the high volume that the Argentines customarily use to speak. Many Bolivian migrants commented that Argentines "spoke too loud." Speech may thus function as another signifier of ethnicity. While the Bolivians whom I interviewed differentiated themselves from Argentines by their way of speaking, by their accent, it seems that the older generation of Bolivian migrants seek to be recognized as "legitimate" Others who speak the same way that Argentines do.

For the Bolivian men and women whom I spoke to, home is constituted in the relationship and awareness of two places that supply different and complementary resources that are fundamental for the development of their lives.[31] Bolivia is the place where one is free, where family and others like oneself live. But it is also the place where there are few jobs and political instability, and thus limited resources to build a home. Therefore, home has to be sought in another place. Buenos Aires is the place where jobs can be found, but no sense of belonging is achieved there. Nevertheless, Buenos Aires provides the means and the resources to build a home in Cochabamba, both materially and symbolically.

Thus, we encounter a contradiction: while concepts such as "deterritorialization" have emerged in order to explain how identities are detached from local places, the Bolivian migrants whom I spoke with still give a central importance to their place of origin as a reference point with which they identify and in which they long to be.[32] However, the belief that some migrants express that they cannot build a home in Bolivia because of the depressed economic and political situation opens the possibility for migrating again, this time, further away and across the Atlantic. Questions about the type of relations Bolivians establish in these new places that they inhabit, from which a "return" is much more difficult, and how they change their conceptualizations of home because of those relations, are pending and crucial to understand broader transnational movements.

Bolivian migration to Argentina has a long history and thus needs to be seen as part of a historical process that links both countries. The broader political and economic context of both countries influences the migration process. The identities built in migration processes are important for several reasons. First, the identities of the Bolivian men and women whom I interviewed are not only shaped by national discourses formulated by intellectuals and governmental leaders. Material conditions, such as participation in the labour market, working conditions, access to citizen rights, and movement from one place to another, intervene in the identification processes of people. These are very much determined by globalization processes of the economy, communication, and technology. As Arjun Appadurai reminds us, we are now living in a world of "ethnoscapes" and "deterritorialization," where a new landscape of persons is shaped in a world of people constantly moving, and "where money, commodities, and persons unendingly chase each other around the globe."[33]

In 1991, a regional economic cooperation and integration agreement was instituted among Brazil, Argentina, Uruguay, and Paraguay. The

MERCOSUR (Southern Cone Common Market) envisions the creation of a free-trade area among member countries, intraregional investment, and regional macroeconomic stabilization. Bolivia and Chile became special members of MERCOSUR in 1997, and Peru at the end of 2003.

Since the time that the field research for this paper was conducted, there have been several political developments aimed at addressing issues of immigration between and among MERCOSUR states and associate members. In December 2002, the ministers of justice and interior of these states crafted a plan for the "free circulation" of people throughout the territory of member countries.[34] This plan sought to extend the region's integration process, so far limited to trade, into the social and labour spheres as well. If ratified and fully implemented, it would allow citizens of the six countries to obtain lawful permanent residence in any other member country, requiring only documents that prove nationality and lack of a criminal record.[35] As of June 2005, the plan was not yet ratified by the member states.[36] Nevertheless, MERCOSUR remains committed to this goal. Its Socio-Labour Commission concluded in 2003 that labour problems must be addressed as a precondition for the regional integration process.[37] Based in part on this analysis, in April 2004, labour ministers of MERCOSUR member countries signed a declaration calling for "free circulation of workers."[38]

Although these policy decisions can be seen as advances, it is unclear whether they will have any meaningful impact on the lives and circumstances of Bolivian immigrants to Argentina. They have furthered a discourse of social "integration" to complement economic aspirations, yet this discourse coexists with continuing practices of "exclusion" and "xenophobia" experienced by migrant workers,[39] and it is not clear that the discourse will alter the experience of these workers, at least in the near future. As this chapter has shown, Bolivians suffer in their daily lives in Argentina, not only from physical violence (being robbed), but also from insults and stereotypes – being labelled as bolitas and criminals. The stigmatization of Bolivians by Argentines (as black, round, and small) is a reality that shows no signs of abating. This challenges the notion of meaningful social and political "integration," and is likely to impede progress in these areas even where economic systems may coalesce.

Even if the "free circulation" of people is approved in each MERCOSUR member country, what kind of "integration" and what kind of "rights" will migrants have? Furthermore, while granting "legal" status to formerly "illegal" immigrants may reduce the fear that some informants described of being reported to authorities, what other legal impediments (or socioeconomic barriers) will arise to undermine this new-found status? What consequences will such developments have on the lives of migrants?

In order to begin to talk about a comprehensive "integration" process, we have to recognize that in Latin America there are marked ethnic, regional, and national differences between and within countries. Neo-liberal reforms do not seem to be bridging the gaps and distances among Latin Americans, but rather appear to increase them. Migrants constantly remind us of these distances.

NOTES TO CHAPTER 7

1 During the summer of 2002, the Centre for Society, Technology and Development of McGill University generously supported the research upon which this chapter is based. I am grateful to Kristin Norget who encouraged, read and re-read, and gave thoughtful comments on earlier versions of this chapter. Thank you to Arlo Arizona for his patience and support in the early stages of this writing process. A warm thanks goes to Eric Dannenmaier for his comments, suggestions, and editorial assistance.

2 Karsten Paerregaard, "Imagining a Place in the Andes: In the Borderland of Lived, Invented, and Analyzed Culture," in *Siting Culture: The Shifting Anthropological Object*, ed. Karen Fog Olwig and Kirsten Hastrup 39–48 (London: Routledge, 1997).

3 This phenomenon has been described as "transnational migration," and the research described in this chapter explores certain dimensions of the phenomenon in a way that may contribute to its further understanding. See Patricia Foxen, *K'iche' Maya in a Re-Imagined World: Transnational Perspectives on Identity* (PhD diss., McGill University, 2001); Micheal Kearney, *Reconceptualizing the Peasantry: Anthropology in Global Perspective* (Boulder: Westview Press, 1996); Roger Rousse, "Making Sense of Settlement: Class Transformation, Cultural Struggle, and Transnationalism among Mexican Migrants in the United States," in *Towards a Transnational Perspective on Migration: Race, Class, Ethnicity and Nationalism Reconsidered*, ed. Nina Glick Schiller et al., 39–48 (New York: New York Academy of Science, 1992).

4 Foxen, *K'iche' Maya*, 32–33. The transnational approach builds on the notion that cultures are not located in particular places, and it offers a useful analytical framework within which to view how the Bolivian migrants whom I interviewed have developed networks, activities, social relations, patterns of living, ideologies, and identities that span borders.

5 Linda Basch, Nina Glick Schiller, and Cristina Szanton Blanc, *Nations Unbound: Transnational Projects, Postcolonial Predicaments, and Deterritorialized Nation-States* (Langhorne: Gordon and Breach, 1994); Rousse, "Making Sense of Settlement"; Patricia Pessar, *A Visa for a Dream: Dominicans in the United States* (Boston: Allyn and Bacon, 1995).

6 Domingo Faustino Sarmiento, *Facundo* (Buenos Aires: Peuser, 1955). The term *mestizo* was used during the colonial period to classify a racially mixed group, originally the offspring of a "white" Spanish conqueror and an indigenous woman, but it quickly became a cultural category determined by externalities such as speech, dress, and consumption.

7 Alejandro Grimson, *Relatos de la diferencia y la igualdad: Los bolivianos en Buenos Aires* (Buenos Aires: Eudeba y FELACS, 1999).

8 Enrique Oteiza, Susana Novick, and Roberto Aruj, *Inmigración y discriminación: Políticas y discursos* (Buenos Aires: Grupo Editor Universitario, 1997), 14; Emanuela Guano, "A Color for the Modern Nation: The Discourse on Class, Race, and Education in the Porteño Middle Class," *The Journal of Latin American Anthropology* 8:1 (Jan. 2003): 148–71.

9 Gloria Ardaya, *Las migraciones bolivianas hacia la ciudad de Buenos Aires, Argentina* (Master's thesis, Facultad Latinoamericana de Ciencias Sociales, 1978); Jorge Dandler and Carmen Medeiros, *La migración temporal de Cochabamba (Bolivia) a la Argentina: Trayectorias y impacto en el lugar de origen* (Cochabamba: CERES, 1985); Jorge Balán, "Household Economy and Gender in International Migration: The Case of Bolivians in Argentina," in *International Migration Policies and the Status of Female Migrants*, U.N. Expert Group Meeting on International Migration Policies and the Status of Female Migrants (New York: United Nations, 1995).

10 Carlos Waisman, "Argentina: Capitalism and Democracy," in *Democracy in Developing Countries: Latin America*, 2nd ed., ed. Larry Diamond et al. (Boulder: Lynne Rienner Publishers, 1999); Scott Whiteford, *Workers from the North: Plantations, Bolivian Labor, and the City in Northwest Argentina* (Austin: University of Texas Press, 1981).

11 Silvia Rivera, *Oppressed but not Defeated: Peasant Struggles among Aymara and Quechua in Bolivia, 1900–1980* (New York: United Nations Research Institute for Social Development, Participation Programme, 1987); Herbert Klein, *Bolivia: The Evolution of a Multiethnic Society* (New York: Oxford University Press, 1982); Dwight Hahn, *The Divided World of the Bolivian Andes: A Structural View of Domination and Resistance* (New York: Taylor and Francis, 1991).

12 Xavier Albó, "Ethnic Violence: The Case of Bolivia," in *The Culture of Violence*, ed. Kumar Rupensinghe and Marcial Rubio (Tokyo: United Nations University Press, 1994); Balán, "Household Economy," 9.

13 Ardaya, *Migraciones bolivianas*; Roberto Benencia, "El fenómeno de la migración limítrofe en la Argentina: Interrogantes y propuestas para seguir avanzando," *Estudios Migratorios Latinoamericanos* 13–14:40–41 (1998–99): 419–47; Alfonso Hinojosa, Liz Pérez, and Guido Cortés, *Idas y venidas: Campesinos tarijeños en el norte argentino* (La Paz: PIEB, 2001).

14 Such amnesties were decreed in 1949, 1951, 1958, 1964, 1965, 1974, 1984, 1992, and 1998.

15 Néstor García Canclini, *Globalización imaginada* (Buenos Aires: Paidos SAICF, 1999); Hinojosa et al, *Idas y venidas*, 10; Alberto Zalles, "El enjambramiento cultural de los bolivianos en la Argentina," in *Transnacionalismo: Migración e identidades. Revista Nueva Sociedad* 178:2 (Mar.-Apr. 2002): 89–103.

16 Alberto Zalles, "Enjambramiento cultural," 90.

17 Guano, "Color for the Modern Nation," 151.

18 http://www.comunidadboliviana.com.ar (19 April 2005).

19 Alejandro Grimson, "La migración boliviana en la Argentina," in *Migrantes bolivianos en la Argentina y los Estados Unidos*, ed. Alejandro Grimson and Edmundo Paz Soldán, 7–50 (La Paz: PNUD, 2002).

20 José Baldivia, "Migración y desarrollo en Bolivia," in *Población, migración y desarrollo en Bolivia*, ed. Instituto PRISMA, 65–118 (La Paz: Banco Interamericano de Desarrollo et al. 2002).

21 Stuart Hall quoted in Iain Chambers, *Migrancy, Culture, Identity* (New York: Routledge, 1994), 2.

22 Chambers, *Migrancy*, 5.

23 bell hooks quoted in Ruba Salih, *Gender in Transnationalism: Home, Longing and Belonging among Moroccan Migrant Women* (London: Routledge, 2003), 1.

24 Grimson, *Relatos*, 52.

25 *Choro* is an Argentine slang word usually used to describe people with no jobs, who are asking for money in the streets, but *choro* can also refer to members of a gang or common robbers.

26 See, for example, Pat Caplan, ed., *Food, Health, and Identity* (London: Routledge, 1997); and Anne Kershen, ed., *Food in the Migrant Experience* (Ashgate: Centre for the Study of Migration, 2002).

27 See, for example, Russel King, "Return migration and Regional Economic Development: An Overview," in *Return Migration and Regional Economic Problems*, ed. Russel King (London: Croom Helm, 1986), 1–30; Whiteford, *Workers*, 200; Dandler and Medeiros, *Migración*, 10.

28 Dandler and Medeiros, *Migración*, 12.

29 Grimson, *Relatos de la diferencia*, 128, 165–90.

30 See, for example, Foxen, *K'iche' Maya*, 61.

31 I am borrowing the notion of different and complementary resources that constitute home from Salih, *Gender in Transnationalism*, 155.

32 Arjun Appadurai, *Modernity at Large: Cultural Dimensions of Globalization* (Minneapolis: University of Minnesota Press, 1996).

33 Arjun Appadurai, "Global Ethnoscapes. Notes and Queries for a Transnational Anthropology," in *Recapturing Anthropology: Working in the Present*, ed. Richard Gabriel Fox, 94 (Santa Fe: School of American Research Press, 1991).

34 Consejo del Mercado Comun, *Acta 02/02 de la XXIII Reunión Ordinaria del Consejo del Mercado Común: Acuerdo sobre residencia para nacionales de los Estados Partes del MERCOSUR, Bolivia y Chile*; and *Acuerdo sobre regularización migratoria interna de ciudadanos del MERCOSUR, Bolivia y Chile*, Brasilia, 5–6 Dec. 2002, http://www.mercosur.org.uy (28 May 2005).

35 Ibid., 1.

36 http://www.mercosur.org.uy (28 May 2005).

37 Jorge Notaro, *Las políticas de empleo en los países del MERCOSUR, 1990–2003*, http://www.observatorio.net (28 May 2005).

38 Consejo del Mercado Comun, *Declaración de los Ministros de Trabajo del Mercosur*, Conferencia Regional de Empleo, Buenos Aires, 15–16 Apr. 2004, article 4, http://www.mercosur.org.uy (28 May 2005).

39 For a thorough study on the notion of "integration" in the MERCOSUR context, see Alejandro Grimson, "Fronteras, migraciones y Mercosur: Crisis de las utopías integracionistas," *Apuntes de Investigación* 7 (2001), www.apuntes-cecyp.org (29 Apr. 2005).

Part III:

Race and Identity in Brazil

Race, Ethnicity, and Class in Rio de Janeiro's Port:

THE COFFEE AND WAREHOUSE WORKERS
RESISTANCE SOCIETY, 1905–1909[1]

Maria Cecília Velasco e Cruz[2]

INTRODUCTION

On 1 May 1908, about 5,000 porters (*carregadores*) and stevedores joined in a public protest march. Carrying their respective union banners, they paraded through Rio de Janeiro's streets, shouting "vigorous cheers to the day." Stopping in front of lawyer Evaristo de Moraes's office, they acclaimed him as "patron of the working classes." That night, there were other May Day commemorations. At the Sociedade (later Sindicato [Union]) de Resistência dos Trabalhadores em Trapiche e Café (Coffee and Warehouse Workers Resistance Society), speeches continued late into the night amid an atmosphere of perfect harmony; the *Jornal do Brasil*'s reporter left the meeting "captivated by the refined politesse" with which he had been received.[3]

Two weeks later, however, incidents very different from this harmony and politesse shook the union. On Wednesday, 13 May, a fight broke out during a heavily attended general meeting, which had to be suspended. Reporting on the "commotions, shootings, and injuries," the *Jornal do Comércio* explained that the conflict was due to the election of foreigners to the posts of union president and treasurer, contrary to the organization's statutes. Brazilians Rozendo Alfredo dos Santos and Rufino Ferreira da Luz spoke at this meeting in protest against the new executive officers to be inducted that night, but they were loudly heckled and the escalating series of boos and curses finally culminated in violence. The fight was started by Antônio Henrique, a Portuguese, and the Brazilian,

Henrique Roseira; Antônio Henrique wound up injured, along with three other union members, one white Portuguese and two black Brazilians. At the police station, Rafael Serrato Munhoz and Gumercindo Ferro Lousada were identified as the men responsible for the injuries.[4] The *Jornal do Brasil* blamed "nationalism, always dangerous, a vast field in which the most unreasonable prejudices are, lamentably, exploited." This newspaper also reported that several revolvers and knives were found at the scene; the following day it added that the police had found more damage to the roof than to the walls, "indicating that the majority of shots were fired into the air."[5]

The *Correio da Manhã* noted that the society had only recently turned itself into a union to comply with legal requirements and that Rozendo had highlighted the legal prohibition against foreigners holding office, which had not been instituted by the society but imposed by federal law. The newspaper confirmed that the disorder increased during Rufino's speech and reported that, during the fracas, some shouted that they would not be regulated by the government.[6]

The inquest had barely begun when Antônio Henrique died of his injuries. The police then charged Roseira, Munhoz, and Lousada with murder, and thirteen union members (twelve Brazilians and one foreigner) testified at the trial. Etelvino José da Silva, a Brazilian-born black man, declared that he did not know the meeting's purpose, for he had only recently joined the union.[7] He did not pay much attention to the proceedings, for he was there only because he had been threatened with suspension from the union if he failed to show up, but he "saw Henrique Roseira, Rafael Munhoz, and Gumercindo Ferro [Lousada] threaten Rufino, after which there were loud and repeated shots."[8]

All of the other witnesses presented similar versions of the events. Five noted the rules established by federal Decree 1,637, as did another three who alluded vaguely to this law. Rozendo Alfredo dos Santos, a Brazilian-born black man, for example, gave details about the law, directly quoting its stipulations against foreign officers. Eight union members claimed that the election (held on 10 May to fill posts vacated by resignations from the executive) had been rigged by a small group, "almost in secret" or "clandestinely," for it had not been "properly announced in advance" but only on the "very day [of the vote] ... and then only in one newspaper," which prevented the majority from casting ballots.[9] The union's first secretary claimed that, "if the announcements weren't published, it was the newspapers' fault." The lack of advance notice, according to Filomeno Antônio de Araújo, a Brazilian, meant that "when the majority of union members arrived at the headquarters, the election was already over." This testimony appears to confirm the newspaper report that, on the day of the vote, there had been a "serious exchange of words," but no violent conflict, for "other members appealed for calm and it was determined that a solution would be found on the day that the winners took office."[10] Three of the eight workers added that, in addition to being poorly advertised, the election was also "fixed." According to the black Brazilian man, Rufino Ferreira da Luz, "Henrique Roseira, Rafael Munhoz, Gumercindo Ferro [Lousada], and So-and-So Aires campaigned aggressively"; not only did they request support for the eventual victors "in a threatening manner," but they "were also scrutineers on election day." Two others also referred to a "cabal," adding that Antônio Henrique and Constantino Vasquez were involved.

The witnesses unanimously identified the Portuguese Antônio Henrique, the Brazilians Munhoz and Roseira, and the Spaniard Lousada as those who had violently heckled the outspoken critics on the 13th. When it came to identifying who had fired the first shot, the witnesses disagreed. Carlos Pereira, a Brazilian, heard Antônio Henrique declare, "I'm a man and I'll fight!" to which Roseira added, "Then let's fight now!" as he fired the first shot. According to Araújo, Munhoz was the first one to shoot, but Mathias recalled that Roseira, Munhoz, and Antônio Henrique started the shoot-out, with Lousada quickly joining in. José Hermes de Olinda Costa, also a Brazilian, insisted that the first shots came from the group, but that Lousada was not involved, for he had then left the hall. Finally, four of the workers stressed that the violence was unexpected. Cândido de Almeida, a Brazilian black man, declared that the attack was a surprise and assured his interrogators that "the majority of members ... were unarmed and all of the brothers are accustomed to ensuring good order at the headquarters."

Naturally, the accused presented a different version of the events. They never alluded to the federal decree; rather, they declared that "the election upset a small number of members," not the majority, and that it had not violated the society's statutes. It was, therefore, "legal." Munhoz and Roseira confirmed Lousada's assertion that he had been absent when the fighting began, and all three denied having fired shots or knowing who had done the shooting.

There were significant changes in the statements of the five men called back to testify at the next stage of the trial. Rozendo, Mathias, Etelvino, Rufino, and Filomeno, all Brazilians and all black men (except for the latter, whose colour is unknown), spoke only to the facts alleged in the prosecution's case. Two of them declared that Antônio Henrique (the dead worker) had fired the first shots, while three claimed not to have seen who had done so. Etelvino now recounted that, during the heckling, Munhoz had pulled Roseira aside, requesting "that he not do anything and not interrupt the speaker." And Mathias declared, on Munhoz's request, "that during the heckling ... the accused not say anything insulting to the speaker, Rufino Ferreira da Luz." Rufino, in fact, was the only one to reiterate the illegality of the election. Although he did not say anything that might have incriminated the accused, he added that "when he ... spoke, many members shouted about blacks' [right] to speak, alluding to him."

What is most notable about the newspaper reports and the workers' testimony is neither the contradictions nor the references to the ethnic and racial elements in the conflict, but the repeated references to the law, both federal law (Decree 1,637) and the union's law (its statutes). The election of the Portuguese men was discussed in light of these laws. For some it was illegal and, therefore, illegitimate; for others it was legal and legitimate. The violence broke out over these two irreconcilable positions, after which questions of colour and nationality entered into the testimony. In short, the logic of the conflict is intimately tied to the relationship between this insistence on law and the expression of difference. Curiously, this is a question that historians have ignored.

The conflict is always presented as a dramatic example of the allegedly difficult relations between Brazilian and immigrant workers, or between blacks and whites. In this light, historians briefly summarize the facts, add that the union had a majority black membership, and note that the conflict led to its rapid decline.[11] This interpretation thus weaves together two distinct elements: first, that the conflict caused the union's collapse; second, that the conflict was an "ethnic" (Brazilian versus Portuguese) or "racial" (whites versus blacks) one.[12] More generally, the 1908 conflict is one of the key pieces of evidence for the argument that ethnic and racial rivalries constituted one of the Brazilian labour movement's principal weaknesses during the First Republic (1889–1930).[13] Moreover, it reinforces the specific assertion that these rivalries were most intense in Rio de Janeiro's port.[14]

Collective ethnic and racial identities, however, are produced by the symbolic construction of contrasts that cannot be understood apart from the daily life of a given social group and its interaction with other distinct groups. Eric Arnesen warns that "snap-shot histories, focusing on single, extraordinary events," such as conflict or cooperation among workers of different colours and nationalities in a particular moment, "often result in overly broad and misleading conclusions."[15] Only when relationships among workers are examined over time and within a broader social, political, and economic context can a specific incident be explained and its underlying social dynamics understood.

This chapter offers a new interpretation of the 1908 conflict and the Resistance Union's decline, one that downplays the role of racial and ethnic tensions. To be sure, there was much racist vitriol in Brazilian society, but most of it was directed by employers and their spokesmen against the highly-successful union, newly-founded in 1905. The Resistance Society (as it was then known) drew on long-standing labour practices that derived from the independent organization of slaves-for-hire; it presented itself, however, as a colour-blind institution and won significant workplace control in its 1906 strike.

Under the influence of utopian socialist lawyer Evaristo de Moraes, the society turned itself into a *sindicato* (union) under the terms of the 1907 decree. This law banned foreigners from holding office and, in modifying the society to conform to these terms, it introduced the tensions that culminated in the violence of May 1908. These factors, however, contributed little to the union's sharp decline, which was actually due to an offensive mounted against it by the coffee firms in the second half of 1908. The union's fortunes, in short, must be seen in broader historical context and within the long-term dynamics of class struggle. A detailed analysis of the ethical values that governed workers' day-to-day interactions reveals how unimportant ethnic and racial collective identities were, even as members disagreed profoundly about the appropriate strategy in their class struggle. The 1907 decree appeared to offer the union the opportunity to legalize its status and win a full collective agreement. Employers refused to accept these terms and eventually moved against the divided union, which in 1909 abandoned its efforts to take advantage of the new law. The conclusion returns to the significance of this case for broader discussions of race and ethnicity in the Brazilian labour movement.

WORKER ORGANIZATION AND EMPLOYER REACTION, 1905–06

In many European ports, the difficulties encountered by trade-union militants in organizing casually-employed unskilled workers prompted the establishment of dock-based unions. These were general unions that enrolled members from all of the waterside trades and sometimes from even beyond the docks.[16] In Brazil, workers in São Paulo's port, Santos, followed this pattern, but not those of Rio de Janeiro, who founded exclusive organizations, trade by trade, according to the tradition of craft associations.[17] The Resistance Society was one such association. Its members were day labourers and casual piece workers (*trabalhadores de tropa*) employed in coffee warehouses, on the quays, and in the loading and unloading of wagons. They worked in gangs (*turmas* or *tropas*) headed by so-called "captains." The society was founded in April 1905 with twenty-nine members but, a year later, it counted more than five hundred.[18] José Aires de Castro, a libertarian member, later recalled that by August 1906, when the union called its first strike, the number of dues-paying members had reached "seven hundred and some, ready and willing to struggle." Among those "altruistic workers," he recalled, "there were no races, nationalities, or religious or political creeds ... [for] all wanted more respect, shorter working hours, higher salaries, and more liberty, and thus the strike was called."[19]

The Resistance Society's rapid growth reflected in part the rising citywide labour movement, especially strong in the port. According to its 1905 statutes, the society shared the ideological goals of many other working-class movements. Its motto was "one for all and all for one," and its stated goals included "the unity of all workers" without "distinctions of nationality, colour, and religion." Moreover, the society declared that it would found a library for its members' education to combat "bourgeois ideas and mystifications," and that it would "spread socialist ideas in conferences at its headquarters and in public meetings."[20]

But this politicization explains only part of the union's success. In fact, the centuries-old social practices of labour organization that former slaves-for-hire (*escravos de ganho*) and freedmen had worked out among themselves opened the way for the unionization of entire gangs, including their captains.[21] In August 1918, an old worker explained to a reporter that, before the founding of the society,

> Our boss [*senhor*] was the gang captain. A captain obtained
> the workers and, for this, received four per cent of the amount
> paid [for the job], plus 400 réis per head and the leftover change
> [*quebrados*].... [This] was 60 réis for one, 80 réis for another....
> A worker earned 5$980 [5,980 réis], but the 80 réis "died." The
> Resistence Society put an end to this.... In addition, it was
> common for a porter to be lashed with a twine whip. There
> was no appeal ... they beat the black man.... This ... was a
> continuation of the slave gang [*eito*], which 13 May destroyed....
> The Resistance [Society] raised the cry for a new 13 May.[22]

In the early twentieth century, references to "modern slavery" were common in Brazilian union activists' rhetoric, a bitter critique of industrial society. However, it is clear that the old porter was not talking about a capitalist labour regime. Rather, he connected the experience of slavery directly to his life as a worker and the rituals of subordination that still existed. To say that the Resistance Society had raised "the cry for a new 13 May" was to use a richly significant symbol, for the law that abolished slavery had been approved on 13 May 1888. It meant, above all, a demand for autonomy, an end to the arbitrary authority of bosses and their representatives, the supervising workers or captains.

In short, the Resistance Society institutionalized the informal structures of the port district's workers, but introduced important innovations. The captains, who had formerly been labour contractors, retained their special status and continued to negotiate between employers and workers, but their power was significantly reduced. Since all were now members of a labour union, negotiations no longer took place between workers and bosses, but between port companies and the union. Through a corps of inspectors, the union took over the tasks of supervising, disciplining, and selecting the members of the work gangs. They were responsible for ensuring that all obeyed the hours and terms of work approved by the union assemblies. Thus, the "leftover change" no longer "died" and the twine whip disappeared.

Combining captains and their subordinates in a single institution produced an unusual union that took over one of the employers' principal prerogatives – managing the workplace – and presented itself to them as a labour contractor, regardless of employers' desires. These developments surprised the Centro do Comércio de Café do Rio de Janeiro (Rio de Janeiro Coffee Commerce Centre) during the 1906 strike, which was part of a much larger wave of strikes that swept through the port district in the second half of that year. The Resistance Society won wage increases from reluctant coffee companies, which also accepted the union's role in the management of casual labour.[23]

But the porters' victory did not come easily, for the agreement – with all of its threats to employers' traditional prerogatives – also implied changes in the relationship between porters and coffee carters, principally because of the ten-hour work day. Because unionized gangs did all of the loading and unloading of vehicles in the coffee warehouses, the agreement presupposed that carters would cease to work after 5:00 pm and would not attempt to unload coffee with other workers. On 8 October, at 6:00 pm, a group of coffee porters tried to stop non-unionized workers from unloading carts in the coffee warehouse district. Their leader was Rufino Ferreira da Luz, nicknamed "Minister," who was then the inspector-general of the society. This had happened before, but without any serious consequences. On that day, however, the police intervened and work resumed. An angry Rufino rallied his fellow union members who, waving sticks and throwing stones, drove out the carters' assistants. There were a few injuries – three carters – and the agreement remained in force.[24]

These events reveal two important aspects. First, they demonstrate the mutual dependence of coffee porters and the carters who specialized in coffee transport. The porters' agreement reduced these men's income and, when the carters founded their own union in December 1906, they naturally sought the same terms as those won by the Resistance Society. The two unions formed an alliance and struck when wagon owners rejected the reduced hours, shutting down all coffee transportation in the city. Many of the so-called "waterfront carters" (*carroceiros da praia*) who carried general cargo and did not depend on Resistance Society members for loading and unloading their cargo continued to work. Coffee merchants also learned an important lesson: workers' control of the labour market depended on the cooperation between coffee carters and porters.[25]

Second, and more generally, these strikes revealed what was for many employers an inconceivable desire of all workers (not just coffee porters and carters) to control the labour market and interfere in labour management. Defiant of authority, the subalterns made what employers saw as excessive social demands. Newspapers took notice of the 1906 movement. Some defended property rights and republican liberties, including freedom to work. Others dismissed most of the workers' demands as subversive and impertinent, denouncing oppressive unions and discussing the limits of legitimate union activity: "Outside of the workplace, yes! Let them gather in social clubs for welfare [and] ... recreation; what they want ... is an impudent demand!"[26]

An examination of this anti-union campaign is beyond the scope of this chapter, but it is important to note the repeated attacks against the lawyer, Evaristo de Moraes. From August to November, he won the release of strikers from prison and wrote numerous articles defending the legitimacy of workers' actions. Not surprisingly, opponents of "commander-in-chief Evaristo," or "the siren Moraes," lambasted him as a "fervent socialist" enchanting "millions of workers." Hostility against Evaristo increased over time and took on racial connotations. In December, one newspaper declared that, because of official negligence, the capital was subject "to the atavistic impulses of one Evaristo," a "loquacious mulatto" who "goes around flapping his Lombrosian prognathic jaw."[27]

Amid the outcry provoked by the December carters' strike, such racist outbursts focused on the association between Evaristo, "the self-taught mulatto shyster," and the Resistance Society's inspector-general, Rufino

Ferreira da Luz. Renowned African (*preto*), pervert, savage, monstrous black (*negro*), stupid boor (*boçal*), and criminal were among the adjectives repeatedly used to describe Rufino. The pair had usurped the law in the nation's capital and had forced workers "into a servile and passive obedience ... unseen even in the interior of Africa."[28] As the spokesman for the coffee interests who had benefited from slavery, the anonymous journalist responsible for these words apparently saw union dues as a latter-day version of the payments that slaves-for-hire owed their owners. "Every coffee carrier," he wrote, was obliged to "contribute monthly" and to "obey blindly, not the one who pays him, but the one whom he is forced to pay"; they were "enslaved" to work for a society that made a mockery of "man's liberty." The "so-called Resistance Society" had created "a new kind of slave" and he called on the chief of police to put a stop to its abuses.[29]

Such rhetoric, which continued to flourish through 1907, is a clear indication of the extent to which the Resistance Society's successes had upset social hierarchies. Not surprisingly, employers threw up obstacles to the union, the police continued to harass its inspectors, and by 1908, many coffee firms were ready to mount a counter-attack on the union. In the interim, however, the Resistance Society underwent an important institutional change.

EVARISTO DE MORAES, THE 1907 DECREE, AND UNION REORGANIZATION

As an outspoken critic of classical liberalism and the free play of market forces, Evaristo de Moraes had never hidden his socialist ideas. In 1904, he turned the *Correio da Manhã* into a vehicle to defend the legitimacy of strike action and the need for state intervention in the labour question; he published his articles in book form in 1905.[30] The capitalist world's "fetishistic respect for freedom to work," he explained, only produced misery and exploitation. Therefore, the state had an obligation to intervene to regulate salary levels and the length and nature of work, as well as "workers' professional organizations so that they, conscious of their importance, also feel the weight of their administrative responsibilities." Unions should be encouraged to collaborate with authorities in the task of ensuring social harmony. Arbitration boards, with both worker and employer involvement, would reduce the incidence of strikes.[31]

Another key element of his reasoning was his view of the labour movement's development. Wedded to a determinist and evolutionary view of history, Evaristo argued that strikes inexorably preceded the formation of unions, which were initially dedicated solely to fomenting conflict. This relatively brief phase was followed by the period of "true professional organization," when unions transformed themselves into "instruments of social peace and worker education." Legitimated by society and backed by government action, unions would cease to be merely spokesmen for complaints and demands; rather, they would establish labour conditions in collaboration with employer organizations and would be legally responsible for the "full execution of the contract signed in the name of their members." This had already happened in England, the United States, and Germany; it was happening in France; it would, according to Evaristo, soon happen in Brazil.[32] Such certainty also derived from his assessment of Decree 1,637, which legalized professional unions and cooperative societies in January 1907.[33] It declared that "unions which conduct themselves in the spirit of harmony . . . such as those linked to permanent conciliation and arbitration boards ... will be considered the legal representatives of the entire class of working men and, as such, can be consulted on all matters pertaining to the profession."[34]

Evaristo hailed the law in utopian terms as "socialism's most important demand." Recalling the intense class conflict that had preceded the consolidation of English trade unions, he declared:

> It is now our turn to pass through this stage of economic evolution. We [already] have regularly-functioning class associations, among them those of the stevedores and porters, which have already adopted a nearly-syndical system [of organization].... Little remains to be done. With *minor modifications*, the current societies will transform themselves into unions, regaining the strength and influence that they have lately lost to the bourgeois reaction.[35]

The lawyer saw himself as "an intellectual worker who peacefully experimented with the application of the syndical system to Brazil."[36] For this reason, he agreed to act on behalf of the Resistance Society during the August 1906 strike. He soon became a member and, for his birthday in October, society members presented him with a gold watch bearing a diamond-studded monogram of his initials and the number 1,268, his membership number.[37] He exercised considerable influence over the society, whose members respectfully requested that he take part in assemblies in which they discussed political questions. He gave them oral and written advice, signing his correspondence "friend, advocate, and member."[38]

It was likely Evaristo's idea that the society should reorganize itself according to the terms of Decree 1,637 to become what he understood as a proper union. On 7 January 1908, a general assembly resolved to transform the Coffee and Warehouse Workers Resistance Society into the Coffee and Warehouse Workers Resistance Union, a decision which led to the dispute upon which this chapter is focused. It is important to note that neither the institutional changes nor a bank failure which led to the loss of the union's reserve fund in March 1908, nor even the 13 May conflict prompted large-scale resignations from the union, which continued to function regularly.

THE EMPLOYERS' COUNTEROFFENSIVE, 1908

What caused the union's decline was, in fact, the employers' counteroffensive, which began when two coffee firms replaced coffee carters with waterfront carters. The new carters began to handle coffee bags with their own porters, thus encroaching on the unionized coffee porters' workspace. On 13 August, the union board debated the "question of the carters" and decided that no one should work alongside the "scabs"; they resolved to "move against the coffee firms, one by one." A week later, union committees visited both firms and requested that the jobs loading and unloading the wagons be returned to them. The firms refused and all of their warehouse workers walked off the job.[39]

This strike prompted an angry reaction from the coffee warehouse sector. Several dealers signed a letter to the Coffee Commerce Centre denouncing the "coercion" that they had suffered and demanding the "right to act in full liberty by employing people not affiliated" with the Resistance Union.[40] The letter reportedly prompted the union to present a new pay schedule for coffee transport and warehouse work. Thus, while Evaristo de Moraes was explaining that there was no coercion, merely the legitimate action of "a union – a class organ [established] under the terms of Law 1,637 of 5 January 1907 – which presented employers … with a type of collective work contract," forty coffee firms, including the biggest exporters, met at the Coffee Commerce Centre to decide how to act. While some called for a lockout, the firms resolved to hire a lawyer and to seek a peaceful solution.[41]

Almost at once, divisions appeared in the employer ranks. Claiming to speak in the name of their own interests and those of the coffee sector, on 29 August sixty-eight carting firms requested that the chief of police provide protection against the Resistance Union whose members were violating their right to work. A bitter condemnation of any agreement that would reserve the labour market to union members appeared in the press that day, the first of a series that again gave free reign to the reactionary racism of some owners. On 3 September the two firms against which the union had struck proposed that the Coffee Commerce Centre declare a lockout. Such a decision required unanimity and only sixty-one out of one hundred and sixty-two firms, most of them commission houses, voted in favour. Major bagging and export firms rejected the proposal and ensured that negotiations would continue.[42]

Seven days passed with no resolution. Desperate, the boycotted firms considered signing a contract and the Coffee Commerce Centre requested the union's proposal for an agreement. Evaristo seized the chance to put his ideas into practice. He proposed an eight-day truce and submitted the draft of a collective agreement, in the full modern sense of the term. To be signed by the Coffee Commerce Centre on behalf of all coffee firms and the Resistance Union (and formally notarized), the draft left out no details. It would give union members exclusive rights to work in the coffee houses; it specified pay scales and work hours, defined the responsibilities of captains and inspectors, and prescribed the behaviour of gang members. Furthermore, it proposed the creation of a permanent arbitration and conciliation board formed by three Supreme Court justices.[43]

Since the proposal merely sanctioned what in practice already existed and the arbitration board offered a peaceful way to resolve conflicts, the Coffee Commerce Centre's directors welcomed it. But real power in the centre lay in the individual firms and it soon became clear that they disagreed with the directors. The meeting held on 16 September to assess the proposal was disorderly, full of heckling, and ended abruptly without the firms' representatives having authorized the centre to negotiate on their behalf.[44] Evaristo de Moraes attributed these developments to a "reactionary minority" who "still lamented the glorious day of 13 May [1888] and could barely distinguish between the free wage worker and the miserable enslaved [worker] of former times."[45] What he did not note, however, was that some employers had turned his proposal for a collective agreement into an argument for destroying the union on the grounds that it was a humiliating and dangerous capitulation. "It would be the greatest of dishonours," declared several coffee firms, "if the manipulations of the lawyer for the Resistance Union led to victory.... A notarized agreement is serious business. Our firms represent something; we don't need the collectivity, [for] any one of us can guarantee our agreement. But, on the union's part, who will enforce it? Mr. Evaristo de Moraes?"[46]

In a society in which casual workers were assumed to be "vagrants" and blacks considered "thugs," and in which labour contracts were routinely violated, the argument was compelling. Furthermore, old images that associated blacks with slavery, savagery, and inhumanity reappeared.

After the centre's 16 September meeting, mistrust and fear of reaction spread. Although the truce was extended and work continued normally, only thirteen firms authorized the centre to sign the agreement on their behalf. At a general meeting on 24 September, the centre's members rejected it and its directors resigned. Union delegations visited coffee firms the following morning in a final attempt to get them to sign the agreement. None did so, but according to newspapers many expressed their desire to respect the status quo and continue employing the usual workers.[47]

The new directors of the Coffee Commerce Centre, however, took a hard line against the union. On the 24th they signed an agreement with the Associação dos Proprietários de Veículos (Association of Vehicle Owners) to provide workers and wagons and obtained the promise of police protection for them. The centre laid down the gauntlet: pay levels would be maintained but owners would enjoy full freedom in choosing their workers, regardless of union membership.[48]

When Resistance Union representatives met with the centre's bargaining team, it would only receive them as representatives of "free workers" and never as representatives "of such a syndicate, which it did not recognize"; it was a deliberate affront. For workers of the coffee carrying gangs, of course, "freedom" meant the existence of a union, for they could not negotiate successfully with employers as isolated individuals. The Resistance Union was their means of guaranteeing rights, dignity, and autonomy as "free men." It was impossible for them to accept, therefore, a declaration in which what they understood as slavery was presented to them as freedom. As soon as the workers left, the centre's directors sought police protection for the new carters and porters.[49]

The details of the rest of this struggle indicate that the subsequent sudden decline in union membership took place in the context of class struggle and not as the result of the alleged ethnic or racial conflict of May 1908. In the face of employer intransigence, the union failed to resort to its most powerful weapon – a general strike – and merely resumed the boycott of the firms that had fired union members. In the long term, however, this was a counterproductive strategy, for it allowed employers to deal piecemeal with union members and the carters who supported them. Having lost the most opportune moment for a strike with the boycotts and the lengthy negotiations, the union failed to react. Sensing the union's weakness, the Coffee Commerce Centre moved to crush it. On 31 October, its directors convinced bagging and exporting firms to dismiss union inspectors, for "their presence in the warehouses was inconvenient for the coffee business." The centre's victory was total.

At the end of the year, vehicle owners congratulated the centre's directors for their achievement of "freedom of work."[50] The final blow against the Resistance Union came in March of the following year, when Moraes had already ceased to advocate on its behalf and it had changed its name back to Resistance Society. This crisis was set off when the Leopoldina Railroad refused to let union inspectors enter its warehouses and started to dismiss all union members. In the face of this persecution, hundreds of porters quit the society. While meetings of one hundred and twenty or more workers still took place in February and March 1909, scarcely sixty showed up at the meeting of 27 November, during which the man who had betrayed workers to the railroad company was expelled.[51]

RACE, ETHNICITY, AND LEGAL STRATEGIES

According to the standard interpretation, competing ethnic and racial identities contributed mightily to this defeat in the class struggle. A closer look at the internal dynamics of the Resistance Society/Union and the culture of its members reveals a considerably more complex story. A first clue about the meaning of the 13 May 1908 conflict comes from the complete silence about it in the Resistance Society's minute book. This register was, in fact, first compiled in July 1913. It begins with the January general assembly at which the Resistance Union was constituted and its directors acclaimed; then there are no minutes recorded until 17 June, when the board considered the means of helping unemployed members who had fallen behind in their dues. However, the directors listed in the minutes of 8 January had, in fact, been elected much later, on 22 March. Among them were the union president and treasurer who subsequently resigned, which necessitated the by-election of 10 May at which the Portuguese men were elected. In other words, the minute book constructs a history that suppresses the memories of the May conflict.

The conflicts of these months and the absence of records – perhaps a deliberate silencing – suggest that a certain disorder prevailed in the union's political and institutional life. Having functioned since 1905 on the basis of nondiscriminatory membership, the society had established traditions of not taking race, nationality, or religion into account, and of allowing all members to stand for election to office. Accepting a law that banned foreigners from elected office (Decree 1,637) drove a wedge into the membership. In the tense environment that saw Brazilians and foreigners defy the decision of a general assembly, there were certainly deep concerns about the direction that the union was taking. How could assurances that the conversion from society to union was merely a nominal one be accepted when it meant the exclusion of some members from eligibility for office? After all, wrote a lawyer hired by a committee of members "injured" at the "unjust comments" made about the conflict, "they were all workers, united for the sole purposes of social elevation and defense of collective interests." "Naturally, they were deeply hurt by the label of *foreigners*."[52] It was, therefore, necessary to clear the air and put an end to the doubt about who could participate in the collectivity and how they could do so.

When tempers cooled and the new president took office, the board faced this very question. A committee composed of Evaristo de Moraes and two black workers took on the task. The workers included Antônio Pereira, wounded on 13 May, and Rozendo, who had vigorously defended the law that day. To the article in the internal regulations that affirmed that neither colour nor nationality were barriers to membership, they added the following explanation: "There will be no categories among members, for all are equal, subject to the same duties and enjoying equal rights, save in the case of holding administrative office ... which grants them the rights and obligation inherent in the said offices."[53] This subtle reference to the differences produced by Brazilians' legal privileges in election to office was modified by the sixth article that listed members rights: all could "enjoy the benefits, protection, and advantages guaranteed by the 5 January 1907 law, by the statutes, and by this regulation."[54] In the assemblies at which these amendments were put to votes, the directors assured members that the old motto of "one for all, all for one" remained in force and that the new union was the same old Resistance Society.[55]

When it comes to egalitarian ideals, there is often great distance between talk and action. The groups that came into conflict in 1908 might have publicly denied the importance of race and nationality, even as they continued to antagonize each other in daily interactions. There is, however, no evidence of this and the union's minutes reveal a pattern of joint action and solidarity, not of hostility and segregation by race or nationality. For example, at the assembly of 22 July 1908, Rufino Ferreira da Luz explained that "the comrade general-inspector was upset at having to work in a gang without having been sent by an assembly." Clarifying his statement, he added: "Since he was elected to and invested in office by an assembly," only another assembly "could order the inspector-general to work." Besides revealing the value that workers placed on the prestige and dignity associated with authority and the organization's hierarchies, this incident saw the much maligned black worker, Rufino, back up one of his most vehement opponents in the May 1908 conflict, the white porter, son of immigrants, Rafael Serrato Munhoz, then inspector-general.[56] This incident was not an isolated case. On 31 July, the Spaniard, Gumercindo Ferro Lousada, requested assistance to travel to Europe for medical treatment. Three Brazilians who had opposed him in the May conflict – one white, one black, and one whose colour is unknown – spoke in favour of his request, which was approved.[57] Two weeks later, another board meeting demonstrated that the conflict had not been a watershed for the organization. Men who had been on opposite sides in May agreed on how the union should resist the threats coming from coffee firms and waterfront carters: they included Constantino Vasques, the "plotter" behind the annulled election – a white man, and probably a Spaniard; the white Brazilians Munhoz and Carlos Pereira; and the black Brazilians Rufino, Rozendo Alfredo dos Santos, and Antônio Pereira.[58]

In short, there is no sign of division by race or nationality. Few of the foreigners directly implicated in the conflict quit the union afterward, and many of them continued to participate in its decisions and management. The Portuguese José Fernandes Ribeiro, the president elected and deposed as a result of the conflict, was still a member of the Resistance Society in 1916, when he served as first secretary, and then as board member. The same goes for José Gomes Ferreira, who, together with his compatriot Ribeiro, had first tried to found a porters' society in 1904.[59]

Such information is particularly significant, for it offers evidence of the institution's everyday life in which, were they important, exclusionary collective ethnic and racial identities would have been produced, naturalized, and reproduced. Notwithstanding the offensive references to Rufino's colour in the heat of the debate on 13 May 1908, workers did not face each other as "whites" and "blacks." In addition to the friendly relations between workers of different colours readily visible in other sources, it should be added that Rozendo was also black, and that hostility toward him was much less. Nor is it entirely clear that workers faced each other as "Brazilians" and "foreigners." The lines were not so simple, for there were Brazilians among the "foreign" party. While there is much more research to conduct in the almost two hundred surviving cases of conflicts between members that came to the board's attention before the 1930s, all indications are that the construction of ethnic and racial hierarchies did not take place in this union.

Moreover, coffee porters placed a high value on order and decorum. Union regulations specified fines to be levied on members "who, in assemblies, conduct themselves inappropriately, promoting disorders or tumults, failing to respect the presidency." "Shameful facts and inappropriate actions" would not be recorded in the minutes.[60] This explains the absence of references to the conflict in the minutes, as well as the assertions in the inquest that the majority of members were unarmed and that the violence was a surprise. To be sure, fights among union members were common enough. Physical violence to settle personal, political, or work disputes was a daily occurrence in the port district, something accepted, to some extent naturalized and valorized. When Antônio Henrique's shouted, "I'm a man and I'll fight," he was expressing values widely held in the community even as he violated union regulations. What was surprising, shameful, and improper about the May 1908 conflict was that it took place in a general assembly with complete disregard for the society's highest governing body and its presidency.

What lay at the root of this conflict was a different cultural experience of political relationships to the law. In this respect, a world of different experiences separated the black Brazilians from their foreign comrades, especially those who had arrived in the post-1890 immigrant wave. Coffee porters repeatedly asserted that "there are documents for everything," an indication that black and mixed-race workers (the Resistance Society's majority) had interpreted Evaristo de Moraes's message in light of their historical experience and that of their slave forebears who had dealt with the legal system. They had certainly heard of many cases of a hard-won freedom lost for lack of proper manumission papers or of blacks and mulattoes enslaved because they could not prove their free status. They certainly knew the value of statements duly notarized in wills or of notes written by owners to their heirs in cases of contested manumission.[61] Well aware of the written word's power, of documentary proof in the law's eyes, these freedmen and sons of freedmen were quite willing to follow their lawyer and to see the law as a significant arena for their union struggles. In the past, legal proceedings had often been used in favour of freedom, and they expected nothing different.

Thus, the Brazilian workers reorganized their society into a union under the terms of Decree 1,637 and sought a notarized collective agreement, hoping to win from their employers the full recognition of their gains. Indeed, they advocated this as the solution for all workers; on 24 May 1908, the Resistance Union invited "national [Brazilian] workers" to meetings which led to the founding, in June, of the Associação Econômica dos Operários Nacionais (Economic Association of National Workers), whose goal was to encourage Brazilian workers to "demand their rights before the duly constituted authorities."[62]

But they failed to understand the full implications of their actions. The Resistance Union's strategy of using the legal spaces that the new law had opened carried with it serious risks. Not only did it require the union to abandon one of the society's dearest principles – the equality of all members – it also assumed (wrongly, as it turned out), that employers would accept the new labour regime. The disagreement over the union's strategy persisted through the entire period that the union was under attack by employers. In the end of September, numerous workers demanded that the union call a general strike against all coffee warehouses. They took their message to the streets and some were arrested, including Munhoz.[63] The board, however, steadfastly held its course.

The union's crisis, therefore, was dominated by disagreements over political strategy. Some union members, while recognizing that the legal regime offered opportunities, found the price paid for adapting the union to the terms of Decree 1,637 too high. Excluding brothers from union office violated the core principle for which the society had always stood. Defeat at the hands of employers prompted the decision that made it possible for the membership to overcome their divisions. On 6 February 1909, a general assembly approved (with only two dissenting votes) the board's resolution to turn the union back into the Coffee and Warehouse Workers Resistance Society and to remove the January 1908 revisions from its statutes.[64] In the course of their struggle, the workers had learned that, while it was one thing to use the spaces in the law for the benefit of individuals, it was quite another matter to use them to consolidate collective gains in the class struggle. They abandoned their pursuit of the chimeras that Decree 1,637 offered. Rebuilding their society was more important.

Both the gradually-building crisis of the Resistance Society and the fact that this crisis did not completely destroy it can be explained through recourse to Albert Hirschman's theory of loyalty as developed by Alessandro Pizzorno. According to Hirschman, organizations have two kinds of members. The first are those with "low loyalty" to the organization, for whom leaving is essentially costless. They come and go, participating as they see fit, but have no strong ties to the organization. The black man, Etelvino José, who attended the 13 May 1908 assembly only because he had been threatened with the suspension of his membership, is a good example of this kind of member. The second kind of members have "high loyalty" to the organization, and for them leaving is personally difficult. They only quit when they become deeply dissatisfied, and they are the first to return when the organization resumes functioning in a way that matches their desires.[65] Raphael Serrato Munhoz was clearly a loyal member. An advocate of libertarian ideas, he strongly disagreed with the strategic direction laid out by Evaristo de Moraes, argued against him at the 13 May assembly, and unsuccessfully advocated a general strike at the height of the owners' offensive against the union.

He left the organization in April 1909 after the Resistance Union failed to respond to the Leopoldina Railroad's attack. He was also one of the first to return. At the 16 November 1910 assembly, he was once again an active speaker, supporting the nomination of the black worker, Raimundo Elias da Cruz, to the post of inspector-general.[66]

The very possibility of his return reveals the existence of a third kind of members, defined by Pizzorno on the basis of Hirschman's analysis as "identifiers" (*identificadores*), people for whom exit is not possible for they personify the organization. Unlike members with high degrees of loyalty who join organizations because they approve of their goals, such individuals identify themselves with the organization, and draw much of their very identity from the group. Such "identifiers" may be humble members, even illiterates, who remain silent in assemblies, but the organization is in their hearts and souls, and for them, leaving is impossible; if they departed, they would, in a sense, cease to exist.[67] The Coffee and Warehouse Workers Resistance Society's longevity – founded in 1905, it still exists today – was ensured by the ongoing struggles of several highly-loyal members and many more "identifiers," poor black and mulatto men, who, along with some equally poor white men, turned it into their way of struggling for freedom and citizenship in postslavery Brazil.

CONCLUSION

This close analysis of the 1908 conflict raises grave doubts about the limits that racial and ethnic rivalries allegedly placed on the labour movement on Rio de Janeiro's docks. This is not to say that such rivalries never manifested themselves – we know far too little about port workers to make such an assertion – but it is important to recognize that a conflict which appears on the surface to follow ethnic and racial lines actually turns out to have possessed very different and much more complex origins.

The historians who have seen race as central to the 1908 conflict appear to have interpreted the evidence in light of a hegemonic model of racism. If scientific racism was widely accepted among educated elites and deeply rooted in institutional practices, if the dominant classes were racist and considered themselves white, so the reasoning goes, then all whites were racist, regardless of their social position. Certainly some coffee merchants and their spokesmen were racists. They vented their spleen in newspaper articles with pejorative adjectives, untruths, distortions, and deprecating remarks; they presented Africa as the ultimate symbol of barbarism. There is no doubt about their prejudices and the fact that they created a clear border between themselves – whites – and the inferior Other – blacks – in which skin colour marked inferiority.

Their worldview, however, stood in sharp contrast to that of the workers. Workers were committed to the overthrow of racial hierarchies and the dismantling of these boundaries. They stressed equality; they envisaged a world in which race, national origin, and religion were unimportant; they created a culture of universal sociability that stressed solidarity. They did not seek to construct distinct ethnic or racial class identities, and focused all their attention on an inclusive class project of a wider struggle for liberty. Despite the racialized climate of the time, they sought to construct a colour-blind institution.

To argue for the centrality of race in 1908 wrongly assumes an automatic or necessary connection between the existence of different cultures and the expression of corresponding distinct ethnic or racial collective identities. Although cultural features are always used to create social dichotomization between members of a specific "race" or ethnic group and outsiders, it is important to distinguish culture from collective identities. As K. Anthony Appiah has argued, "with different cultures, we might expect misunderstandings arising out of ignorance of each others' values, practices, and beliefs; we might even expect conflicts because of differing values or beliefs.... Once we move from talking of cultures to identities whole new kinds of problems come into view. Racial and ethnic identities are essentially contrastive and relate centrally to social and political power."[68] In other words, the conflicts between groups that bear opposed racial and ethnic identities do not arise from misapprehensions but from refusals. They take place because the Other is different, and because, for being different, the Other is not accepted. Ethnic and racial conflicts are, therefore, more idiosyncratic than the ones arising strictly from cultural estrangements; they are deeply rooted and not easily resolved in the short term.

If the black Brazilians who controlled the organization's power positions had fought because of their hostility to foreigners, they would not have supported Lousada, treating him as a comrade, nor admitted foreigners or foreigners' allies among the few who discussed union strategies in May. If Munhoz had fought out of a refusal to accept orders from black men, he would not have continued to serve as inspector-general responsible to a predominantly black assembly. Munhoz, Vasquez, Ribeiro, Rozendo, Rufino, and many others who disagreed about Decree 1,637 stood in solidarity with each other during the day-to-day class struggle, because the 13 May 1908 conflict was a political one, not an ethnic or racial one.

This does not mean that we should romanticize or reify class identities, or that racial or ethnic tensions were absent from the Resistance

Society. On the contrary, these tensions are clearly visible in Rufino's speech and in the foreigners' discontent. But the existence of such tensions, without corresponding collective racial or ethnic identities, leads to a final conclusion. Ethnic and racial collective identities are not primordial facts; rather, they are social constructions that emerge in specific contexts. They are contingent; they are not uniform and they change over time. Objectively multicultural or multiracial contexts do not necessarily give rise to contrasting collective identities. Thus, historians should not automatically assume their existence; rather, their existence must be established empirically.

NOTES TO CHAPTER 8

1 Translated by Hendrik Kraay.
2 I thank PRODOC/UFBA-FAPESB for financial support to microfilm Resistance Society minutes and documents and Hendrik Kraay for the fine editing of the original manuscript. I am indebted to Fred Judson and Maryon McClary, of the University of Alberta, for their kind hospitality in Edmonton. All of the newspapers cited here were published in Rio de Janeiro.
3 Jornal do Brazil, 2 May 1908.
4 "Gazetilha," Jornal do Commercio, 14 May 1908.
5 Jornal do Brazil, 14 and 15 May 1908.
6 Correio da Manhã, 14 May 1908.
7 As in other legal documents of the time, the trial transcript does not indicate the race of individuals, which does, however, appear in other sources. Whenever available, this information is provided.
8 This and the following testimony is drawn from processo 720, Raphael Serrato Munhoz et al., 1908, Arquivo Nacional, Rio de Janeiro (ANRJ), m. 883.
9 In fact, I located only one announcement, in the labour column of the Jornal do Brasil, on the election day, 10 May 1908.
10 Correio da Manhã, 14 May 1908.
11 Sheldon L. Maram, Anarquistas, imigrantes e o movimento operário brasileiro, 1890–1920, trans. José Eduardo Ribeiro Moretzsohn (Rio de Janeiro: Paz e Terra, 1979), 30–31; Boris Fausto, Trabalho urbano e conflito social, 1890–1920 (São Paulo: DIFEL, 1979), 36–37; Sidney Chalhoub, Trabalho, lar e botequim: O cotidiano dos trabalhadores no Rio de Janeiro da Belle Époque, 2nd ed. (Campinas: Unicamp, 2001), 158–60; Roberto Moura, Tia Ciata e a pequena África no Rio de Janeiro (Rio de Janeiro: FUNARTE, 1983), 47.
12 "Ethnic" is here used in a broad sense, referring to the invocation and manipulation of notions and symbols of cultural difference with the aim of fixing boundaries, creating enclaves among working-class groups whose cultures of origin (nationalities) are different. This meaning of the term "ethnic" is common in labour history.
13 Maram, Anarquistas, 30–31; Chalhoub, Trabalho, 59–60.
14 Fausto, Trabalho urbano, 36–37.
15 Eric Arnesen, Waterfront Workers of New Orleans: Race, Class, and Politics (New York: Oxford University Press, 1991), x.
16 On European port workers, see Sam Davies et al., eds., Dock Workers: International Explorations in Comparative Labour History, 1790–1970 (Aldershot: Ashgate, 2000).

17 Maria Lúcia Caira Gitahy, *Ventos do mar: Trabalhadores do porto, movimento operário e cultura urbana em Santos, 1889–1914* (São Paulo: Editora UNESP and Prefeitura Municipal de Santos, 1992); Maria Cecília Velasco e Cruz, "Tradições negras na formação de um sindicato: Sociedade de Resistência dos Trabalhadores em Trapiche e Café, Rio de Janeiro, 1905–1930," *Afro-Ásia* 24 (2000): 243–290; Maria Cecília Velasco e Cruz, "Solidariedade versus Rivalidade: A formação do sindicalismo estivador brasileiro," *História Unisinos* 6:6 (July–Dec. 2002): 29–62; Fernando Teixeira da Silva, *Operários sem patrões: Os trabalhadores da cidade de Santos no entreguerras* (Campinas: Editora da UNICAMP, 2003); Maria Cecília Velasco e Cruz, "Puzzling Out the Slave Origins in Rio de Janeiro Port Unionism: The Strike of 1906 and the Sociedade de Resistência dos Trabalhadores em Trapiche e Café," *Hispanic American Historical Review* 82:2 (May 2006): 205–45.

18 On the Sociedade de Resistência dos Trabalhadores em Trapiche e Café (SRTTC)'s founding, see Cruz, "Tradições negras" and "Puzzling."

19 *Na Barricada*, 4 Nov. 1915.

20 *Diario Official*, 17 June 1905.

21 This and the following paragraphs summarize material presented more fully in Cruz, "Tradições negras" and "Puzzling."

22 *A Razão*, 23 Aug. 1918. In 1905, 1,000 réis (one mil-réis) was worth US$0.32.

23 On the 1906 strike, see Cruz, "Tradições negras" and "Puzzling."

24 *Jornal do Commercio*, 8 Oct. 1906; *Jornal do Brasil*, 9 and 11 Oct. 1906; *Correio da Manhã*, 11 Oct. 1906.

25 *Jornal do Commercio*, 20 and 21 Dec. 1906.

26 *Correio da Manhã*, 7 Sep. 1906.

27 *Jornal do Commercio*, 11 Dec. 1906.

28 *Jornal do Commercio*, 19, 20, and 21 Dec. 1906.

29 *Jornal do Commercio*, 23 Dec. 1906.

30 Evaristo de Moraes, *Apontamentos de direito operário*, 2nd ed. (São Paulo: LTr Editor and EDUSP, 1971).

31 Ibid., 9–19.

32 Ibid., 103. See also Joseli Maria Nunes Mendonça, "Evaristo de Moraes: justiça e política nas arenas republicanas (1887–1939)" (PhD diss., UNICAMP, 2004).

33 *Correio da Manhã*, 22 Dec. 1906, 8 Jan. 1907, 4 June 1907.

34 *Coleção das leis da República dos E. U. do Brasil de 1907*, vol. 1 (Rio de Janeiro: Imprensa Nacional, 1908), 17–22.

35 *Correio da Manhã*, 21 Jan. 1907 (emphasis in original).

36 *Correio da Manhã*, 29 Dec. 1906.

37 *Jornal do Brasil*, 25 and 26 Oct. 1906; *Correio da Manhã*, 27 Oct. 1906.

38 Antonio Pereira to Evaristo de Moraes, 1 Nov. 1907; Evaristo to "Comrade Directors and Board Members," 11 Mar 1908; Evaristo to Brothers Júlio, Rozendo, and Moraes Rego, 14 Sep. 1908, Sociedade de Resistência dos Trabalhadores em Trapiche e Café, Rio de Janeiro (SRTTC).

39 Minutes, Conselho, 13 Aug. 1908, "Livros de atas de assembléias e conselhos" (LAAC), SRTTC.

40 *Gazeta de Noticias*, 25 Aug. 1908; *Jornal do Commercio*, 27 Aug. 1908.

41 *Jornal do Commercio*, 27 Aug. 1908.

42 *Jornal do Brasil*, 31 Aug. 1908; Minutes, 5 Sep. 1908, "Livros de atas das reuniões do conselho administrativo" (LARCA), Centro do Comércio de Café do Rio de Janeiro (CCCRJ).

43 Minutes, 16 Sep. 1908, "Livros de atas da assembléia geral" (LAAG), CCCRJ.

44 Ibid.

45 *Correio da Manhã*, 8 Oct. 1908.

46 *Jornal do Commercio*, 18 Sep. 1908.

47 Minutes, 23 Sep. 1908, LAAG, CCCRJ; *Jornal do Brasil*, 26 Sep. 1908.

48 Minutes, 24 Sep. 1908, LARCA, CCCRJ.

49 Minutes, 5 Oct. 1908, LAAG, CCCRJ.

50 Minutes, 31 Oct. and 30 Dec. 1908, LARCA, CCCRJ.

51 Minutes, 27 Nov. 1909, LAAC, SRTTC.
52 *Correio da Manhã*, 17 May 1908; *Jornal do Brasil*, 17 May 1908 (emphasis in original).
53 Minutes, Assembléia Geral Extraordinária, 20 May 1908, LAAC, SRTTC.
54 Minutes, Assembléia Geral Extraordinária, 29 May 1908, LAAC, SRTTC.
55 These regulations were discussed and approved, article by article, in several assemblies between 20 June and 18 July 1908, LAAC, SRTTC.
56 Minutes, Assembléia Geral, 22 June 1908, LAAC, SRTTC.
57 Minutes, Conselho, 31 July 1908, LAAC, SRTTC.
58 Minutes, Conselho, 13 Aug. 1908, LAAC, SRTTC.
59 Election Returns, 19 Mar 1916, 10 Mar. 1917, LAAG, SRTTC; Cruz, "Tradições Negras" and "Puzzling."
60 Minutes, Assembléia Geral Extraordinária, 17 July 1908, LAAG, SRTTC.
61 Sidney Chalhoub, *Visões da liberdade: Uma história das últimas décadas da escravidão na Corte* (São Paulo, Companhia das Letras, 1990); Keila Grinberg, *Liberata, a lei da ambigüidade: As ações de liberdade da Corte de Apelação do Rio de Janeiro no século XIX* (Rio de Janeiro: Relume-Dumará, 1994); Eduado Spiller Pena, *O jogo da face: A astúcia escrava frente aos senhores e à lei na Curitiba provincial* (Curitiba: Aos Quatro Ventos, 1999); Joseli Maria Nunes Mendonça, *Entre a mão e os anéis: A lei dos sexagenários e os caminhos da abolição no Brasil* (Campinas: Editora UNICAMP, 1999).
62 *Jornal do Brasil*, 24 May 1908; and 10, 21, 23, and 25 June 1908; *Correio da Manhã*, 24 May 1908.
63 *Jornal do Brasil*, 30 Sep. 1908; *Correio da Manhã*, 1 Nov. 1908; *O Paiz*, 1 Oct. 1908.
64 Minutes, Conselho, 28 Jan. 1909; Minutes, Assembléia Geral Extraordinária, 6 Feb. 1909, LAAG, SRTTC.
65 Albert Hirschman. *Saída, voz e lealdade: Reações ao declínio de firmas, organizações e estados* (São Paulo: Editora Perspectiva, 1973), 81–105.
66 Minutes, Assembléia Geral Extraordinária, 16 Nov. 1910, LAAG, SRTTC.
67 Alessandro Pizzorno, "Algum tipo diferente de diferença: Uma crítica das teorias da "escolha racional," in *Desenvolvimento e política e aspirações sociais: O pensamento de Albert O. Hirschman*, ed. Alejandro Foxley, Michael Mcpherson, and Guillermo O'Donnell, 366–87 (São Paulo: Vértice, 1988).
68 K. Anthony Appiah, "Race, Culture, Identity: Misunderstood Connections," in *Color Conscious: The Political Morality of Race*, ed. Appiah and Amy Gutmann, 88 (Princeton: Princeton University Press, 1996).

9 The Brazilian *Mulata*:

A WOOD FOR ALL WORKS

Jennifer J. Manthei[1]

INTRODUCTION

Colonization and slavery in Brazil generated constellations of social identities and relations based on colour, class, region, and gender. Over time,
the images attached to these social roles have been reinterpreted and
deployed by different social groups with varied political goals in specific historical contexts. This chapter discusses the Brazilian *mulata* (a
female of both African and European heritage), whose highly sexualized
image represents a "dense point of power," an intersection of colour and
gender identity that reflects historical discourses of social stratification.
The mulata image crystallized as a cultural icon in early twentieth-century literature and continues to circulate in Brazilian culture, providing
a discursive resource for constructions of individual, group, and national
identity. Existing literature on the mulata describes how she has been
appropriated by the elite in projects of national identity, challenges to
social mores, and international commerce.[2]

In these critiques, the authors address ways in which the women are
victimized, yet argue that women may also actively engage the mulata
image for personal gain. The "hot mulata" is constructed in contrast to
the *branca* (white woman) and *negra* (black woman) as sexually desirable, and may use her powers of seduction to survive or improve her circumstances – thereby contributing to the perpetuation of the stereotype.
Recently, Donna Goldstein has suggested that darker women who hope

189

to seduce lighter, wealthier (and older) men effectively "participate in their own sexual commodification"; however, they interpret the mulata image as empowering, not only as a potential source of social mobility but also as a refutation of colour prejudice.[3]

This chapter follows in this vein of addressing nonelite perspectives, exploring how contemporary populations representing various colours and classes define, interpret, and deploy the mulata image in daily life. It is based on ethnographic fieldwork conducted in 2001 that investigated the meanings and functions of the mulata among adolescent girls and young women in a medium-sized Brazilian city. This study demonstrates how girls representing different social locations draw on historical discourses of the mulata, in somewhat ironic ways, in the process of negotiating positive moral identities. The research shows how eliciting on-the-ground perspectives and lived experience allows us to develop a richer, more complex understanding the dynamics of social identity and social relations in Brazil.

BRAZILIAN NATIONAL IDENTITY: THE INSTRUMENTAL MULATA

The 1930s marked the beginning of a particularly important moment in the development of the *mulata* as a salient marker of culture and the nation. During this period, the literati drew on existing cultural and literary images of the highly sexualized mulata and bent them to particular political projects. In the process, they not only consolidated the "hot mulata" as a twentieth-century icon but also bound her inextricably to discourses of national identity.

From the late 1800s to the 1930s, Brazil was characterized by major social, political, and economic changes in the form of coups, the abolition of slavery, World War I, industrialization, and urbanization. Europe's decline and Brazil's new economic independence suggested that Brazilians could change the role assigned to them by Social Darwinism and European culture, and control their own destiny.[4] The major stumbling block to negotiating a new national identity and international role was scientific racism, the vehicle through which European elites sought to legitimate the dominance of core nations over those on the periphery.[5] The premise of scientific racism was that European success and dominance were due to their superior racial heredity and climate. Countries with tropical climates and large non-white populations were doomed to underdevelopment, backwardness, and dependence on Europe. Thus Brazil was condemned to the status of an inferior nation in the world's presumed natural order of inequality.[6]

Because the legitimating ideology for European dominance was articulated through a discourse of race, racial theory became the forum for the contestation of exploitation as well as the justification for a new order in which Brazil had the potential to become a core nation. Such a change required a radical reinterpretation and negotiation of Brazilian history, culture, and identity; this challenge was met by sociologist Gilberto Freyre when his *The Masters and the Slaves* was published in 1933. Freyre was not the first to propound many of the themes in his works, but he managed to consolidate various elements of national thought in a very attractive package that was so successful as to provide the cornerstone of twentieth-century theories on race and Brazilian national identity.

At least overtly, Freyre's works represent an inversion of scientific racism. At the core of his theory is a positive reinterpretation of miscegenation (racial mixing). According to scientific racism, miscegenation was degenerative, resulting in a species inferior even to Africans. In contrast, Freyre argued that the three races that had formed Brazil (the Portuguese, Africans, and indigenous populations) each represented quality genetic and cultural stock. When they came together through biological and cultural miscegenation, each contributing its best attributes, they formed a superior race well adapted to the tropics as well as a superior culture. As Freyre wrote, "perhaps nowhere else is the meeting, intercommunication, and harmonious fusion of diverse or even antagonistic cultural traditions occurring in so liberal a way as it is in Brazil."[7] Thus miscegenation became the key to a new, positive national identity, and is both the product and proof of Brazil's much touted "racial democracy."

Freyre's miscegenation is based on sexual relations between Portuguese men and indigenous and African women. Sexual contact with indigenous women provided an initial "lubricating oil" for colonization, but it is the African that truly draws together the nation.[8] At the heart of Freyre's argument lies the mulata. She is the bridge between the races, the biological and social link. Freyre's mulata is not only the product of racial and cultural mixing, but also the vehicle. Her role is to unite whites and blacks, primarily through sexual relations. Thus her sexual availability is critical to Freyre's theory of superiority, national unity, and social harmony through miscegenation. This deployment of the mulata built on long-established constructions of the mulata as sexual "fair game" in contrast to the protected and controlled white women and the undesirable black women. As Freyre states, the traditional expression "a branca to marry, a negra to work, and a mulata to screw" reflects the Portuguese "sexual preference for the mulatto."[9] Freyre's conception of national identity, based on his own northeastern slave plantation heritage, effectively codifies the branca-negra-mulata system, and highlights the white male master–female slave of colour relationship.

It is important to note that Freyre does not consider the mulata responsible for her sexualized status; she is merely the object of the supersexual Portuguese man's desires, further corrupted by the institution of slavery. Slave status may also encourage a certain sexual masochism and complicity in her, and she may gain advantages through sexual relations with her masters but, Freyre asked rhetorically, "does this mean that we are to hold these women responsible for the precocious and disordered sexual life of the Brazilian young?" He responds that this is absurd; the mulata is no more responsible for sexual relations with her masters than the domestic animals that bear a similar fate with the owners' young sons.[10] In fact, Freyre asserts that, by nature, the mulata has little sexuality. At any rate, the mulata's own sexuality is largely irrelevant. Freyre portrays her as an object – a tool for Portuguese sexual use, an instrument for miscegenation, and a device to deploy in an assertion of national identity.

Arch-conservative Freyre was not the only writer renegotiating national identity through race, class, and gender in the early twentieth century. In the 1920s and 1930s, preoccupation with national identity swept the arts in the forms of southeastern Modernism and northeastern Regionalism. Visions of the Brazilian national essence varied substantially; however, there were commonalities in discursive resources. Modernist writers rebelled against the perceived degeneracy and neuroses of Europe, as well as the Brazilian bourgeoisie's slavish imitations of European styles.[11] They sought to differentiate themselves by celebrating something distinctly Brazilian; that "something" was symbolized by the people, the masses. However, for these writers, the poor person, the African Brazilian, or the Indian represented a symbolic device, "not a real human being of flesh and blood to defend socially."[12] In fact, Modernist writers fortified negative racial stereotypes of the Naturalist style that animalized, sexualized, and exoticized *negros* (blacks) and *mulatos* (mulattoes). The Brazilian Modernists, following a European Primitivist trend, used these symbols of a culture ruled by nature, instinct, and feeling in rebelling against what they saw as the "falsity" of European culture.[13] In the process, they portrayed African Brazilians as exotic, naïve, animalistic, instinctual, strong, violent, and hypersexual.

In these and later twentieth-century works, the mulata was a ubiquitous stereotype centred on sexuality and extramarital relations. As David Brookshaw puts it, "she is not allowed to exist either as a wife or mother, for she is a symbol of sexual license."[14] She is ever the mistress, portrayed as an object for male consumption. Her only power lies in her sexuality; she is a seductive temptress with an animal sexuality and sensuality. Teófilo Queiroz analyzed representations of the mulata through major Brazilian works, and found repetitive images that include flowing hair; cleanliness; a firm body with abundant breasts; musicality; an easy, rich laugh; and sensual and seductive movement. Her personality is characterized by a hearty good nature, the willingness to work hard, and having little to say regarding political or intellectual matters. She lacks restraint, particularly sexual restraint; in fact, she appears to exist outside of normative social mores, so her promiscuity may be judged either immoral or amoral. Although she is portrayed as independent – she will not be owned by a man through marriage – she is centred on pleasing men and tends to pass from one to another.[15]

In short, the written mulata is animalistic, nonintellectual, dependent on sex and seduction, sexually available, and appropriate for affairs rather than marriage. Unlike Freyre, these members of the literati elaborated discourses that attribute an inherent hypersexuality to mulatas; she is not merely a tool, but an active seductress. Thus responsibility shifts from the white men to the females of colour.[16] The combination of her sexual availability with no moral inhibitions and ascribed lasciviousness combine to construct the mulata as an object of sexual desire for white men.

An excellent example of the literary mulata is Gabriela in Jorge Amado's *Gabriela, Clove and Cinnamon* (1958). She is a highly sexual creature, utterly incompatible with the institution of marriage. In the novel, Amado uses Gabriela to poke fun at bourgeois values; she symbolizes the "true" Brazilian – inherently sexual, animalistic, outside of conventional mores. His later and overtly political *Tent of Miracles* (1969) retains the image of the hypersexual mulata while simultaneously resurrecting Freyre's instrumental mulata. The novel features a sea of mulatas, all anxious to be impregnated by the main character; they are the vehicles (no longer passive) through which races and cultures will mix, levelling Brazilian society and solving all problems.[17]

In effect, Freyre and Amado, speaking from opposing political camps, dovetail in their deployment of the mulata in asserting and naturalizing social orders predicated on colour and gender. The symbolic versatility of the mulata is essential to the persistence of her image across time and ideologies. In fact, Maria Fonseca has described the mulata as a "wood for all works."[18] The plastic image of the mulata lends itself to many uses, and has been appropriated, modified, and deployed for a variety of purposes. She retains certain stable elements (such as her sexual role), yet her secondary elements may be renegotiated to match particular historical

Table 9.1: Participant Women by Age and Class

	Very Poor	Poor	Not Poor	Totals
Ages 10–14	10	9	7	26 (33%)
Ages 15–19	10	11	8	29 (37%)
Ages 20–25	9	9	5	23 (29%)
Totals	29 (37%)	29 (37%)	20 (26%)	78

contexts and the needs of particular agents. The cultural salience and political density of the mulata image raise the question of her role today – how is she constructed, by whom, and for what purposes?

Research exploring the meaning of the mulata image in the everyday life of participants representing colour and class diversity reveals a considerably more complex picture than that of the literary stereotypes. The study investigated whether the mulata is a salient social category today, when the image is deployed, by whom, and why. It is based on ethnographic fieldwork in Juiz de Fora, a medium-sized city in Minas Gerais, a central state with socioeconomic indicators comparable to national averages and racial, cultural, and economic diversity. It should be noted that Juiz de Fora is not a tourist destination, and the image of the mulata may operate within a very different political economy than in Rio de Janeiro, São Paulo, or cities in the Northeast.

The research focuses on adolescence as a particularly intense moment of identity formation. The primary sample consists of seventy-eight girls and young women aged ten to twenty-five, with additional interviews with twenty adult women, thirty boys, a handful of men, health workers, and educators, and the local authority for minors. The interviews began with a discussion of education and employment aspirations and experiences, and issues concerning dating, sexuality, marriage, and motherhood. The second section addressed colour terms and categories, perceptions of race relations and prejudice, the role of colour in partner preferences, and colour stereotypes, with an emphasis on the mulata.

In order to capture economic diversity, the majority of the sample was drawn from three different neighbourhoods, representing Very Poor (largely insufficient access to basic needs), Poor (minimal but fairly stable access), and Not Poor (access to more than basic needs). As shown in Table 9.1, the Very Poor and Poor, who are representative of the largest segments of the Brazilian population, constituted the majority of interviewees.

Table 9.2: Percentage of Participants by Colour and Class

	Very Poor	Poor	Not Poor
Lighter	29%	56%	95%
Darker	71%	44%	5%

Using open-ended questions and visual aids (photos of models from fashion magazines), the study elicited participants' definitions of colour terms. These definitions were analyzed and organized into a spectrum characterized by a combination of fluidity and firm boundary markers. The net outcome was a binary system based on "good appearance" (*boa aparência*), here labelled Lighter and Darker, for the principal difference between good and bad appearance is the degree of blackness. Crossing the binary colour categories and the tripartite class categories demonstrates the high correlation between colour and class shown in Table 9.2. The data generated through these interviews was disaggregated in order to investigate discursive and experiential patterns according to the colour and class of the participants. In short, the research was designed to elicit and analyze multiple perspectives regarding the mulata image, embedded in broader discussions of colour, class, and gender.

MULATAS AND NEGRAS:
HEAT, SAMBA, AND BEAUTY

Within the Darker category, participants distinguished between mulatas and negras primary along the lines of skin tone and hair – comparatively darker skin and "bad hair" determine a negra, while comparatively lighter skin and "good hair" determine a mulata. "Bad hair" is associated with unkemptness and slavery; "good hair" is considered more beautiful or attractive. There is a high level of fluidity between the categories. Beauty products have had an effect on the mulata-negra border; as one participant stated succinctly, "[h]air straightening can change a negra into a mulata or even a *morena* [tan or light brown woman]." Thus a person may be designated in either category depending on her access to or use of products and grooming practices at any particular moment. It was a rare participant indeed who had the necessary combination of features that could prevent her from crossing the line.

This fluidity is reflected in the fact that, although the participants distinguished between mulatas and negras when describing a spectrum, in practice they tended to collapse them into a single category. However, the manner of blending varied according to the participant's colour. In daily practice, Darker participants almost always selected mulata (or its equivalents) as a polite term, rather than negra or *preta* (black woman), which they consider highly offensive, racist, and even illegal if spoken to a person's face.

Lighter girls, on the other hand, tended to collapse the mulata-negra distinction into the category negra. As one girl stated, "they're all the same thing.... Putting them all together, they are all negras." They often used mulata to be polite in the presence of Darker people, but generally used negra or preta in everyday life among other Lighter people. Of course, Lighter participants in the lower classes had much more occasion to use the term mulata.

Thus both populations describe physical features that distinguish mulatas and negras on a spectrum yet their practical use of terms in everyday speech is more a matter of manners. The participants' differential use of colour terms and categories in daily life is paralleled by a split in deeper symbolic associations. Although there are commonalities in Lighter and Darker participants' image of the mulata, the manner in which it is invoked is markedly distinct. Discussions of the meaning of the term reveal that the mulata is both embedded in and differentiated from the broader category of Darker women, which in turn is constructed in contrast to Lighter women. Across colour and class, the principal themes associated with the mulata revolve around heat, sensuality, and beauty. However, there are significant differences in attitudes toward the mulata, patterned primarily by the colour of the participants.

One of the most common attributes associated with the mulata is "heat." There is a strong association of Darker people in general with heat, which has a number of interrelated meanings. For example, heat is associated with emotions, especially anger, so that "hot" (*quente*) people are known for their tempers. A few participants (mostly Lighter) said that Darker women are considered more hot, meaning argumentative and even violent: "'Hot' means somebody more *brava* [fierce, angry, ill-tempered] ... most of the fights between women are by negras. Because *negros* are hotter, more *bravos*." "Negras are known to fight" and "they like to talk bull, they like to pick fights with everybody."

However, the participants differentiated between negras and mulatas on this point: "Negras are known to fight. Mulatas less ... [negras] are jealous of the brancas who get the men's attention." Although the mulata is a Darker woman, she is generally excluded from this element of heat; the stereotypical mulata is considered highly congenial (*simpática*), a major component of her attractiveness. Mulatas are known to be fun, good company. They are open and friendly, "good for dancing, taking a walk, talking," and "they know their place." To be a mulata carnival queen, congeniality is a requirement; asked her secret to success in 2001, Kíssia Gallo answered: "A lot of *simpatia* and samba in your feet."[19] Thus the mulata is distanced from the general category of Darker women in that her heat does not imply a fiery temper.

Heat is also associated with resilience. The stereotype of Darker women being hot is part and parcel of Darker people's reputation for resilience, strength, and stamina (*resistência* and *força*). These attributes allow them to work hard, endure difficult conditions, and stay healthy. They are preferred for heavy physical labour: "People don't say it out loud so much, but it's understood that negras are good for working.... They are resilient. Physical labour, carrying a 50-kilo sack, security, they get a *negão*." "African blood is stronger" is a common sentiment. "Negros are strong. They have strong health, they have strong blood. You hear it all the time. They're stronger than us." Their endurance has further advantages, according to a middle-aged woman: "You see [Darker] people my age, and they still like to go out.... Across the street, there's a woman, 60, she goes out dancing... It seems like negros have ... more desire to want to live.... This is strength for them. I don't have strength for anything, and they do.... I think the colour negra is more ... resilient."

Heat and stamina come together in the mulata's association with sexuality and sexual stamina. Indeed, this was the most common usage among the participants. Some had not heard that Darker people are hotter but thought that it was true; most had heard of the association before and agreed. It should be noted that Darker participants were somewhat more muted in volunteering or agreeing with the association.

Heat had a high connotation of sexuality among the participants; being hot means being good in bed. Being hot or good in bed means knowing how to show interest in the man, which boosts the man's ego and improves his performance and enjoyment. As a Poor, twenty-four-year-old receptionist explained: "I think the main thing is what a man does with a woman so she can show him what she's feeling. Doing things is also important. But it's like this, the person shows interest in what they're doing. Kiss, pet, feel that it's good, take an interest ... that really satisfies."

Being considered hot is generally desirable: "It's good to be considered hot. [Men] like it. I'd like to be considered hot. It's good for the ego." However, it can be a disadvantage as well. A "hot" woman is not always well spoken of – she may be considered conceited or get a bad reputation: "It's a compliment but ... [if] the guy goes and says, 'Wow, that one over there is really good in bed,' it would be praise, but at the same time it'd be sort of [bad] for the woman. Like he just got her to screw him and that's it. It's good and bad at the same time." There is also a question of taste – the idea that men of better social standing may look down on "hot" women:

> It depends on the situation. Sometimes people think it's good (to be hot).... But in other situations it's really bad. Because ... the man you're with can think bad things.... Men who are better off ... who don't like rowdiness ... they call those women something else.... He thinks the person is more provocative, an easy lay.

Sexual heat is highly associated with women with darker skin; they have more sexual appetite, are fiery and have stamina (*fogo, foguenta*) for bed. According to an adult Lighter woman, there is a continuum from colder brancas to warmer morenas to hot mulatas and negras. Darker women are "women that like sex, are more fiery, have more stamina, they are stronger." Only one Lighter participant contested darker women's exclusivity in sexual hotness:

> I've heard that [darker women are hot] but I wouldn't trade myself for any morena. I think I'm really hot too. They do say it though. Same as my husband. He used to think so too, and I asked him about it, since he had experiences with morenas, and he said the same thing. He wouldn't trade me for them. Not all morenas are hot, some are even cold.

Another Lighter participant (Not Poor) put a negative spin on the Darker woman-heat association, elaborating on the mulata and negra as having out-of-control sexual appetites, and blaming this heat for the overpopulation in slums. She equated the poor with Darker women, and asked why they have so many more children than whites. "It can only be heat!" was her answer, along with the more common idea that the poor cannot afford other forms of entertainment and thus resort to sex.

However, the majority of Lighter participants were likely to express enthusiasm for the mulata's prowess: "[Are Darker women hot?] They are. Boy, are they! Very hot ... They are electric ... they dance ... they even say that darker people are better in bed." The role of the hot mulata as the superlative sex partner was described explicitly by two men (both Not Poor Lighter). One paralleled the expression "a branca to marry, a negra to work, and a mulata to screw" in his summary: "The mulata isn't in the kitchen, nor in society. She's in the bedroom ... wild, sexually insatiable, physically stronger." The other stated that the mulata is the Brazilian man's dream, sex object, or fantasy. He explained that part of men's attraction to mulatas is their facility to have pleasure. Yes, they are hot, good in bed, but the main thing is that they really enjoy sex, and they show it. Her pleasure becomes his pleasure. It is a man's dream to feel like the greatest lover, to cause the woman so much pleasure. Mulatas have so much pleasure that it is a real ego boost for the man.

In summary, the "hot mulata" stereotype was more strongly expressed by Lighter, wealthier populations. The mulata has the strength of the Darker woman but is spared her temper; her heat is directed toward sexual stamina, which is valued in terms of pleasing men.

The ability to dance samba, which requires both sensuality and stamina, is the characteristic most frequently associated with mulatas: "About mulatas really knowing how to dance, they really do know how to dance samba." "The mulata is really something, quite an impression, a cultural being. Samba is her strength, she shows the world. It is her spice." Darker women in general are known as good dancers; they have "samba in their feet," in their blood: "It's really in negras' feet. The thing pretas do best is dance samba." "It's hard for a branca to dance samba. For a morena, it seems like they already have that swing, that something sensual." "Yes, you hardly ever see brancas dancing like [mulatas]. They really have that characteristic. It seems like they [are born with] that talent."

The correlation is highest when it is a mulata, because she is considered attractive, sensual, in a way that negras are not. When mulatas dance samba women are impressed and men aroused: "Negras too. But it's really more the mulatas." Darker girls themselves associated mulatas with samba and asserted or defended their own ability to dance samba as a matter of pride. "I think mulatas have a lot of samba in their feet. It's skin colour – like I'm a *mulatinha* – and having samba in your feet. To dance samba is a talent. You learn it at home, growing up."

The ability to dance samba was highly valued among many participants of different classes and colours, and strongly correlated with mulatas and negras. Samba is in their feet, in their bodies. The link between movement and body type were strongly associated: "Usually, if you take thirty people, fifteen brancas and fifteen morenas, you'll see the difference in their bodies.... I don't know about genetics, but it makes a difference. The delineated body. The swing of the person." Physically, mulatas are judged to have "more body" (to be more curvaceous), bigger breasts, and no cellulite. Mulatas are known to swing their hips and wear tight, short clothes to show off their bodies. These features are part of what sets them apart from negras as attractive.

However, some Lighter participants contested the image: "Mulatas sway their hips, gyrate. They dance easily. They are famous for it. But it's not true." Another denied exclusivity: "Negras have samba in their feet. But some whites can dance too." And a third claimed samba for herself: "They say that brancas don't know how to dance samba. But I dance samba great!"

Although Darker women as a group are considered hot and good at samba, the mulata stands apart because she is also considered pretty. As one young man (Not Poor Lighter) put it, the mulata has "the strength of the negra and the beauty of the branca." Negras are considered hot and good at samba, but not pretty, so men do not go after them:

> When you talk about the mulata, you always think of that ideal mulata, pretty, with pretty hair, a pretty body, that skin. When you think of mulatas, you never think about an ugly mulata. Now, when you say "negra," you immediately think of that negra … of slavery, in the time of slavery, the kitchen, fat, all that…. The mulata is like a … differentiated portion of the dark race.

Most people consider mulatas to be pretty, well kempt, and sexy. One Lighter young woman sang the mulata's praise:

> There's a mulata here … my mouth hangs open. She is really pretty, very well sculpted, her face, very painstaking. There are really pretty Brazilian women, but these days, those girls who use a ton of makeup are wrecking themselves. And mulatas don't need any of that. If they are well kempt, their hair and everything, they don't need makeup.

Although many of the darker girls categorized themselves as mulatas and the vast majority considered mulatas beautiful, they rarely made an overt connection for themselves. This is not surprising: first, because it would be immodest to say "I am a beautiful mulata," and second because self-identification of colour along a spectrum (branca-morena-mulata-negra) functions in a distinct realm from the more elaborate associations of the mulata image, which was deliberately discussed separately in the interviews. One participant did provide an exception: "I, for example, like being [a mulata]. Because everybody on the street thinks ... 'Wow, what a pretty mulata.' Everybody likes them, because here ... a mulata is a very pretty thing."

However, the attractiveness of the mulata was tempered by colour prejudice. One Darker participant mentioned that some lighter men do not find the mulata sexy because they are racist: "[Are mulatas sexy?] Yes, for some men. But there are a lot of racist men." This factor was suggested more often by Lighter girls, who tempered their assessment of the mulata's attractiveness. She is pretty, but only as far as negras go; men may like Darker women for sex, but "I think that, for beauty, they look for somebody lighter." She is sexy, but not enough for men to pursue them actively: "They say that they're really hot. They react more. And the man can do it more times. Men do not necessarily go after darker women for this reason. But if they end up with one, they like it." And the subtle implication is that they are not for everybody, only men who are into "that sort of thing" – a more adventurous sexuality: "But in general the negra's blood is hotter. I think they awaken more desire in men, for those who like ... for those who are interested in negras." In fact, the men cited above, exalting the mulata's sexual prowess, were also quick to explain that they themselves had no interest in her.

The limitations of the mulata's attractiveness are evident in discourses of colour and partner preferences. Nearly all of the participants cited colour as critical in choosing partners; however, the explanations provided by Lighter and Darker participants were markedly different. Darker girls cited personal taste as the major factor in colour preferences. They did not discuss hierarchies of colour in relation to taste; however, they acknowledged a general valorization of individual phenotypical traits that effectively place Lighter girls (and to some extent mulatas) at an advantage. Only the negra was explicitly ranked as unattractive and undesirable. In contrast, the Lighter girls were absolute in declaring that partner preferences are determined by a strict colour stratification – of which they personally approved or disapproved – that designates Darker populations as appropriate for friendship, employment, and possibly for men's sexual adventures (if he likes "that sort of thing"), but not for serious or public relationships.

HOT MULATAS AND SEXY BLONDES

The mulata shares characteristics common to the broader category of Darker women, such as strength, stamina, sexual heat, and the ability to dance samba. However, the stereotype of the mulata sets her apart as congenial, pretty, sensual, and attractive in ways that negras are not. The mulata is also defined in relation to the branca. Traditionally, brancas are considered models of formal beauty, appropriate for marriage (to *brancos* or white men), procreation, and public presentability. Their sexuality was strictly protected/controlled. Brancas are sometimes referred to as "cold" and snobby, especially by Darker participants. However, the Darker participants also tended to differentiate between brancas and *louras* (blondes), and sometimes clarified that blondes are worse than brancas. They explained that blondes are worse "[b]ecause most blondes are much more snobby. They want to be noticed, show off."

Lighter participants, on the other hand, have little recognition of the snobby branca stereotype. They are familiar with the "dumb blonde" stereotype, which they dismiss as a fairly innocuous media product. One participant stated that "Men prefer blondes but only marry brunettes." Another said that "[b]londes are dumb, brunettes are intelligent. Blondes are pretty, but hollow. Brunettes don't call attention to themselves, but they are informed, intelligent." These self-validating reactions index a certain level of resentment of blondes' success with boys, but the stereotype does not seem particularly salient in their lives.

For Darker girls, on the other hand, the loura was a significant social entity in daily life. The loura does not represent the traditional formal beauty and sexual reserve of the branca. The image of the loura, described by the Darker (and poorer) girls, is the cheap bottle blonde – easy, flirtatious, forward, and an object of sexual desire. This new loura, the "sexy blonde," is probably inspired by the hegemony of movies, sitcoms, and pornography from the United States. The imported nature of the loura was cited by a number of participants, and linked to a national obsession with things American.

Thus the mulata stands apart from the negra and the loura stands apart from the branca as sexualized objects. Both are known to purposefully call attention to themselves by wearing short, tight clothing; both change their hair to achieve a new level of attractiveness; and both are associated with sexuality. In this sense, the loura has significantly invaded the cultural space of the mulata. She is even encroaching on samba. As one participant noted, the loura can dance samba "because the rhythm that they dance ... they are bottle blondes, it's a hot rhythm. And only they have the know-how." Louras may now join the ranks of the sensual: "Louras, negras, mulatas, are more ... are better at samba, *pagode*. And the brunettes, redheads, they don't like it much." Modern products and beauty work also function to reduce the particular cultural role of the mulata:

I think that, in the past, mulatas had attributes – thighs, bum
– that men liked. Now everybody looks like that. Back then, there
was a big difference between the skinny white Europeans and the
tropical mulatas – naturally. Today, if you're white, you get a tan.
If you're skinny, you work out. If your breasts are small, you put
in silicone.

In summary, many traditional elements of the hot mulata stereotype persist in contemporary Brazil – particularly the connotations of sexuality,
sensuality, and beauty. However, there are now many challenges to her
exclusivity in these categories, wrought not only by the new sexy blonde
but also shifting behavioural norms in the general population that encourage Lighter women to take on characteristics previously relegated
to Darker women. These changes have the effect of modifying colour
and gender constructions and effectively curtail the cultural space of
the mulata.

CANNED MULATA: EXPORT QUALITY

The mulata's presence in daily discourses, the instances in which her
image is invoked, and the importance of these moments for identity
construction are also markedly different for Darker and Lighter girls
and women. While categorizing the models, an adult woman (Not Poor
Lighter) did not use the term mulata at all. "It's funny. I don't use the
mulata category much.... Here, in general, in daily life, it's rare to say 'mulata.'" Indeed, for the Lighter and wealthier, the term mulata has a limited
space. First, mulata is a polite term for negra, which they may have little
occasion to use. Second, the deeper mulata image is far removed from
daily life, a media commodity and symbol of national identity restricted
to carnival and tourism. For these participants, the mulata is a product
– canned and bland.

Darker women have extremely little presence in the media, which is
dominated by the white model of beauty. A cross-section of participants
pointed out how explicitly racist the media is, and made the common
pronouncement that Darker women are rarely depicted in telenovelas
(television dramas), and then only as maids. However, there are exceptions to the brancas-only media rule. For example, Oswaldo Sargentelli
made a career out of mulata shows – cabarets, traveling shows, and
television programs – in the 1960s and 1970s. According to Sargentelli,
"mulatas have thin waist, thick thighs, naughty little-girl face, good teeth,
wide laugh, and very good smell; they shake and jiggle, making everyone's
mouth water." In some areas, white actresses cannot compete: "I adore

white women, even those American ones with their amazing mammaries, but the mulata has no match when she sambas. She kills."[20]

None of the participants mentioned Sargentelli being accused of racism and exploiting Darker women in the 1980s. Rather, older participants remembered only how he popularized the mulata as a consumer product. As one adult woman (Not Poor Lighter) stated: "So people think of her that way. Because it is the image that is sold. Completely commercial ... Sargentelli was a businessman with more than ten, twenty mulatas – but only marvelous, pretty women, and only mulatas. So 'Sargentelli and His Mulatas' was an attraction everywhere. So that's how it started."

Another exception to the whites-only media rule comes every February when the mulata is trotted out for carnival, the yearly celebration of national identity for which she is appropriated. During the year, the mulata does not sell products or represent a media model of beauty during the rest of the year. But during carnival, there is a sudden invasion of mulatas for their entertainment and symbolic value: "On TV, they talk more about blondes. But now that it's carnival, there's only morenas. Morenas and negras in the samba schools, mulatas, like that.... They say on TV: 'Ah, here comes the Beija-Flor mulata.' They really say that. 'Full of samba in her feet.'"

As Alzira Rufino writes, "the media only recognizes [mulatas] the three days of carnival as an invitation to bed."[21] The association mulata-carnival-sex is strong: "Here in Brazil, if you say mulata, you immediately think of carnival. More sensual, more sexual. Really good at samba." [Do guys like that?] "I think it really appeals to their fantasies. Mainly because of carnival. The concentration of mulatas without clothes, I think it stimulates their fantasies." The correlation can be quite blatant. During 2001's carnival, a television commercial for condoms featured a branco walking happily down the street during carnival; he sees a sexy Darker woman leaning against a building and broadcasting a come-hither message. The man's little devil says "Yes," his angel says "No," but they both say "Forget it" when they realize that he does not have any condoms. Not only does the advertisement portray carnival as sexual playtime for brancos, with the mulata laid out like a toy, but also the Darker woman-promiscuity-disease correlation is starkly presented; it is not the mulata who demands a condom.

Although there is an element of sexual adventure for Brazilian brancos with mulatas during carnival, the majority of Lighter, wealthier participants were very clear in describing the mulata as a product for foreigners. Brazilians themselves do not appreciate the mulata; they prefer blondes.

As one particularly eloquent woman (Lighter professor of international law) explained:

> [T]he taste of Brazilian men is very associated with a more American culture than ... our African roots, the mulata. These days, the blue-eyed blonde is more attractive ... than the mulata herself. The mulata is for the foreigners.... Now, the Brazilians want blondes.... The mulata became more associated with foreigners who come here, who want to meet a mulata.... [The space of the mulata] is more restricted ... to prostitution, restricted to foreigners, tourist cities. [Mulatas] use this – the part of being a mulata and pretty – they value it. But in the day-to-day, I think she isn't valued, for being a mulata. I think they value the blonde a lot more.
>
> The mulata is more associated with carnival in Rio de Janeiro, in Bahia, and the foreigners who want to see a mulata. So she ends up a tourist attraction at certain times of the year for certain groups of people. (It does not help her in daily life.) I think that the image of the mulata is very worn out. These days a new image of beauty is being formed, not associated with the mulata, for Brazilians.... The youth want that Americanized image of the girl.

Among the Lighter/wealthier participants, the association of mulatas with tourists was very strong. In fact, when asked about the mulata and beauty, some quickly segued to foreigners that come for carnival or popular tourist destinations. "When foreigners come to Rio ... they adore a mulata." Advertisements for travel to Brazil are full of darker women in "dental floss" bathing suits.[22] The national image is so tied up in the mulata that mulata and *brasileira* may be used synonymously: "The Brazilian woman is the mulata is the Brazilian woman. It's a symbol." And foreigners come for the Brazilian experience – sex with a mulata: "It seems that out there, they think of Brazil very much as the mulata and carnival.... Tourists really go after mulatas. We hear this a lot, see it a lot."

The mulata industry is not only about shows; as Rufino notes, "[a]mong the social and economic roles permitted for negras from slavery to the present, we should add one more: sexual bait for tourists."[23] This perception was corroborated by a participant's observation: "I was in a restaurant in Copacabana and there were some foreigners, so they passed around those photo albums with prostitutes – all mulatas. So they want

9.1. One of the Research Subjects "Producing Herself," 2001
Note: The research subject is surrounded by her siblings (left) and the ethnographer's children (in the house). Source: Photo by Jennifer J. Manthei.

mulatas." Nor is the mulata experience restricted to Brazil. Although Lighter, wealthier participants joke that Brazil's primary export is samba, carnival, and mulatas, the truth in this statement is that mulatas are serious business. Rufino discusses the exploitation of darker girls and young women not only in the nightclubs and sexual tourism industry within Brazil, but also in the traps set to lure them into prostitution abroad, especially in Europe, often through offering jobs as dancers or au pairs, or as catalogue brides.

The market command of "export-quality mulatas" appears to valorize Darker women's beauty. However, the recognition of their beauty is not accompanied by commensurate wages. Furthermore, it is clear that the valorization of mulatas is highly conditional. As Donna Goldstein points out, "[b]lack female sexuality is valorized and considered erotic because it is suspended in a web of power relations that make it available in a particular way. Blackness becomes valuable only in specific situations where sexual commodification is the operational framework."[24] The mulata's attraction lies in her position as product for sexual consumption and her availability to white men, be they Brazilian, American, or European.

In short, for Lighter and wealthier participants, the mulata is not generally a part of daily life. She has salience as a symbol of national identity, but primarily as a product for entertainment, a media image, commodified for carnival and tourism. Furthermore, she is packaged mainly for foreigners, and not for a domestic market; Brazilian men prefer blondes. As the professor of international law stated succinctly: "The mulata is losing her place to the blonde. I don't know if it was like this before, but I think it's a change. The mulata is not at all valued in Brazil. In reality, the foreigners value her. Not the Brazilians. For export, preferably. Brazilians want to consume the white."

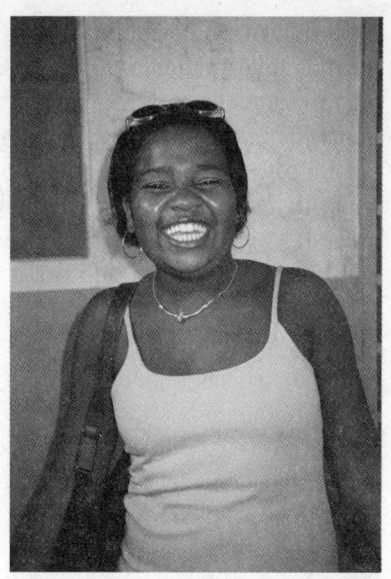

9.2. One of the Research Subjects in Her Street Clothes, 2001
Source: Photo by Jennifer J. Manthei.

In contrast to the distant, canned mulata described by the Lighter, wealthier participants, the Darker girls' image of the mulata is an immediate, important, and integral element of daily life. The participants rarely said, in so many words, that they are or want to be pretty, sexy mulatas (with the exception cited above). Nor was it common for participants to state explicitly that they transition between the categories of negra and mulata. However, the elements are all there. As described earlier, Darker girls spend time and money trying to achieve or maintain mulata status. The negra/mulata colour line is fluid, and girls may transition during the day (through the beauty work of hair, clothing, and makeup). This transition is usually accomplished for the "street" (going out in public). For example, one primary participant dressed moderately well for the street to get to work (as a maid), dressed down for work, and then dressed up again for the return home. But if she and her friends were going out socially, they spent hours in preparation to "produce themselves" (*produzir-se*) (Figures 9.1 and 9.2).

The transition was illustrated in concrete terms by an unusually uninhibited participant. At her house, she was in her "home" appearance. When asked to explain the difference between a negra and a mulata, she pulled out a picture of herself dressed up for her son's baptism and said, "I'm going to show you something that you can say, 'Look, it's a mulata.' The way I am now is preta, ugly *negra*, a real monkey [laughing]."

In discussing Brazilian adolescence, Fonseca emphasizes the importance of appearance, and the manner in which pervasive social messages regarding race, beauty, intelligence, and value often intensify fears regarding social worth. Girls may learn to hate and do battle with their bodies for limiting their dating options and economic opportunities.[25] Thus it is hardly surprising that Darker girls engage in extensive beauty work, most of which centres around hair. Hair is almost an obsession, loaded with symbolism, all indexed by the term "bad hair."[26] For Brazilians, hair is a major differentiation between mulata and negra – between pretty and ugly. In the constellation of colour components, it is also the element most readily acted upon.

For Darker girls, this beauty work is not usually about the colour and beauty line of "good appearance," which is beyond their reach. Rather, it is a second colour/beauty line that offers a positive self-image for Darker girls. Through this image they can see themselves as sexy, attractive, and coveted by men. Achieving mulata status is a positive goal, a means of social validation. This transformation is echoed in the Community Leader's view of Sargentelli's mulatas:

> Oswaldo Sargentelli, he exports mulatas.... It's like this: They are negras who don't value themselves. They have an inner beauty, a tremendous force to succeed, to be somebody. So this man, he went deep into them, brought this out.... He managed to discover the mulata that existed inside those negras. So they turned into professional mulatas.

CONCLUSION

Interpreting the importance that Darker girls and young women place on achieving the attractiveness associated with mulata status raises complex questions. In analyzing Brazilian literature, Queiroz describes the mulata image as "insidious" because it is such a pervasive and ostensibly positive image that masks exploitative social relations.[27] Put succinctly, if a mulata's only power lies in her sexuality, which functions to oppress her, then exercising her power reinforces her oppression. When considering the commercial and export mulatas, it is not difficult to theorize their involvement (often labelled "complicity" or "consent"), for limited rewards and privileges, in hegemonic discourses that ultimately exploit and oppress them. But is this the most interesting, useful, or enriching interpretation? And what of the girls and women who are far removed from these industries, who are not "professional mulatas"? Obviously, we may still theorize that the way they appropriate the mulata image in daily life functions to perpetuate stereotypes of Darker women and sexuality. But shall we say that they suffer from "false consciousness"? Do they have a "partial view"? Are they "surveilling" themselves? Are they "investing in their own unhappiness"? Must we insist that this subaltern agency merely folds back into oppression?

Theoretical models are useful for describing systems of power and exploitation; however, they provide only a partial view from a particular vantage point. If we, as researchers, assume that such a perspective is more complete, a "view from the top," we imply that it supersedes the agency expressed by low-status populations negotiating lived experience. That is, we assert that our own perspective is bigger, smarter, and better. According to Mary Louise Pratt, it is precisely this assumption of higher authority that academics need to eschew in order to develop more democratic and heterogeneous understandings of social relations: "What the new approaches show is that there is a big picture, and everyone sees it, not just the intellectuals. But everyone, including the intellectuals, sees it from where they are."[28]

Indeed, Pratt highlights the importance of qualitative methods that elicit multiple perspectives, because "[w]hat is important and revealing … is not necessarily how metropolitan intellectuals assess a situation … but what the actors in the situation think."[29] Rather than fit other voices into an existing framework, we should seek out alternative frameworks in the process of enriching and complicating our understanding. In listening to multiple voices engaging and deploying the mulata image, we may step away from formulaic interpretations and appreciate diversity, complexity, and fresh ironies. When viewed from this perspective, the mulata is truly a "wood for all works," serving different purposes for populations of diverse social locations and goals. In the girls' perspective, based on their everyday, lived experience, achieving mulata status is empowering. Their mulata shares elements with the elite/tourism model, but does not serve the same function. These girls' conception of being a mulata is not about using sex or sexuality for a living; indeed, they plan to get ahead through hard work and determination. Being a mulata is not merely accommodating oneself to received identities – adopting a "class taste"; on the contrary, the girls aspire to become lawyers, doctors, dentists, or veterinarians. For these girls, achieving mulata status means improving their self-image, feeling attractive, improving their social status – not a small consideration for adolescent girls. Thus an alternative interpretation, which corresponds to their own lived experience, is that they have "swallowed the fire," and adapted the mulata image for their own social projects.

Using the expression "to swallow the fire" is a means of acknowledging agency on its own terms. It reflects the researcher's reward for pursuing the (ephemeral) "emic perspective"; it makes sense of an Other's perspective. If the perpetuation of the ostensibly harmful mulata image by mulatas is an irony explained, it is but one in a series. The research discussed in this paper also elicited parallel issues around discourses of racism/nonracism and the importance of colour preferences in dating and marriage. Specifically, the research examined why Darker adolescent girls choose to portray Brazilian society as nonracist, whereas Lighter girls decry pervasive racism, and why Darker girls emphasize the importance of colour in partner preferences as a matter of personal taste, and Lighter girls attribute preferences to systematic racism. These apparent ironies make sense in the context of adolescents negotiating their identities through discourses of dignity and hope.[30] I would stress that an essential element of the researcher's role is to emphasize meaning over irony, respect multiple perspectives, and appreciate the complexities and downright messiness of identity politics.

NOTES TO CHAPTER 9

1 The research for this chapter was funded by The Jacobs Foundation and Ida Feldman.
2 David Brookshaw, Race and Color in Brazilian Literature (Metuchen: The Scarecrow Press, 1986), 17–78, 159–64; Marco Frenette, Preto e branco: A importância da cor da pele (São Paulo: Publisher Brazil, 2001), 70; Giorgio Marotti, Black Characters in the Brazilian Novel (Los Angeles: Center for Afro-American Studies, University of California, 1987), 362–72; Jeffrey D. Needell, "Identity, Race, Gender, and Modernity in the Origins of Gilberto Freyre's Oeuvre," American Historical Review 100:1 (Feb. 1995): 51–77; Teófilo de Queiroz, Jr., Preconceito de cor e a mulata na literatura brasileira (São Paulo: Ática, 1975); Alzira Rufino, "Violência e turismo sexual," in Mulher negra: Preconceito, sexualidade e imaginário, ed. Fátima Quintas (Recife: Fundação Joaquim Nabuco, Editora Massangana, 1995), 145; Aluysio Mendonça Sampaio, Jorge Amado, o Romancista (São Paulo: Editora Maltese, 1996), 48–63.
3 Donna M. Goldstein, Laughter Out of Place: Race, Class, Violence, and Sexuality in a Rio Shantytown (Berkeley: University of California Press, 2003), 122–27 (quote 127).
4 Thomas E. Skidmore, Black into White: Race and Nationality in Brazilian Thought (Durham: Duke University Press, 1993).
5 Kabengele Munanga, "Teorias sobre o racismo," in Racismo: Perspectivas para um estudo contextualizado da sociedade brasileira, ed. Carlos A. Hasenbalg, Kabengele Munanga, and Lilia Moritz Schwarcz (Niterói: Editora da Universidade Federal Fluminense, 1996), 43–66; Skidmore, Black into White, 27–32.
6 Carter A. Wilson, Racism: From Slavery to Advanced Capitalism (Thousand Oaks: Sage Publications, 1996), 24.
7 Gilberto Freyre, The Masters and the Slaves: A Study of the Development of Brazilian Civilization, trans. Samuel Putnam, 2nd rev. English ed. (Berkeley: University of California Press, 1985), 78.

8 Ibid., 182, 79.

9 Ibid., 13–14.

10 Ibid., 395.

11 Thomas E. Skidmore, "Gilberto Freyre and the Early Brazilian Republic: Some Notes on Methodology," *Comparative Studies in Society and History* 6:4 (July 1964): 495.

12 Brookshaw, *Race and Color*, 93.

13 Ibid., 91.

14 Ibid., 164.

15 Queiroz, *Preconceito*, 1975.

16 Ibid., 26.

17 Jorge Amado, *Tent of Miracles*, trans. Barbara Shelby (New York: Alfred A. Knopf, 1971).

18 Maria Nazareth Soares Fonseca, *Brasil afro-brasileiro* (Belo Horizonte: Autêntica, 2000), 213.

19 Mauro Silva and Aimée Louchard, "Palmas para as Rainhas da Alegria," *Raça Brasil* (February 2001): 56.

20 Oswaldo Sargentelli quoted in Alessandra Dalevi, "In Praise of Mulatas," *Brazzil, Brazilian Entertainment* (online publication), *http://www.brazzil.com* (April 2002).

21 Alzira Rufino, "Violência," 145.

22 Ibid., 144.

23 Ibid.

24 Donna Goldstein, "'Interracial' Sex and Racial Democracy in Brazil: Twin Concepts?" *American Anthropologist* 101:3 (Sep. 1999): 570.

25 Fonseca, *Brasil*, 218–20.

26 Ibid., 218

27 Queiroz, *Preconceito*, 11.

28 Mary Louise Pratt, "Intellectuals and New Social Movements: Where To? What Next?" *Organization* 4:4 (July 1997): 600.

29 Ibid., 599.

30 Jennifer Manthei, "Reading Race: Adolescent Girls in Brazil" (PhD diss., University of Arizona, 2004).

Part IV:

Community Identities

10 The *Cah*:

PLACE AND THE IDENTITY
OF THE CHEMAX MAYA

Denise Fay Brown[1]

INTRODUCTION

At the thirty-five kilometre mark on the straight, flat highway running east from Valladolid toward the Caribbean coast of the Yucatan peninsula, the road appears to end at the doors of a double-spired colonial church. Although today the road veers to the north, around the main square and around the town itself, at one time it did end at the main square of the town of Chemax. This square, even today, serves as a receiving area for outsiders. Buildings mark its perimeter, forming an L-shaped public space containing a treed, grassy area with a kiosk along one axis of the L and an apparently empty gravel and dirt lot along the other. At the apex is the small roofed structure of the bus stop. This perimeter comprises the main commercial area of the town – most of the buildings are storefronts or the homes of the non-Maya storeowners. In recent years this commercial area has grown, gradually extending off the main square and down two side streets. Butcher shops, bakeries, a shoe store, several general merchandise stores, a pharmacy, a dry goods shop, a photography studio, a cantina, offices of some political parties, and a small restaurant share the main square with the recently-restored colonial church, the imposing structure of the municipal government, and the *ejido* offices.

The roof of the church affords a panoramic view of the residential area of the town, in which the house lots are set off from the streets by high piled-stone fences. Visibility from above is obscured by the dense arboreal growth of the home gardens, in which women are responsible for cultivation of medicinal and aromatic herbs, coffee, fruits, chiles, flowers, and other items of household use. In contrast to the main square, the streets of the town are shaded and picturesque. Pedestrian and bicycle movement is still more common than motorized vehicle traffic. During the week, women and children predominate in the streets, since men's work takes them outside of this main settlement. Yucatec Maya is the only language heard, and most women wear the *hipil*, a white cotton dress heavily decorated around the neck and hem with brightly coloured embroidery. The town is extensive in size, due to the relatively large house lots, which result in an unusually low-density population for such an urban setting. The small government-run hospital is located about five blocks from the centre. The junior and senior high schools are located at the eastern edge of the town, on the highway. The residential school is found at the southern edge, and several primary schools and kindergartens are located throughout the town. There are two karstic depressions near the main square, but there is no open *cenote* (sinkhole with open water) in the town. Although there has been no archaeological reconnaissance of the settlement area of Chemax, clearly it has pre-Hispanic origins and has been continually occupied since well before the arrival of the Spanish. It is probable that the settlement pattern of the downtown area and at least one main artery follow a pre-Hispanic blueprint. Given the size of the population, the size of the forested area under the mandate of the town (ejido), and the area of the settlement itself, not to mention the prominent regional reputation of Chemax among both Maya and non-Maya, this may well be the most important contemporary Yucatec Maya town in existence today. Chemax people cultivate and express a strong identity with their town, and this is the focus of this chapter.

Questions surrounding the role of identification with a place in the overall construction of individual and group identities emerged on the academic scene within the context of discussions of population mobility, transnational communities, and impermanence of settlement. Identity construction is complex, based on colliding parameters of similarity and difference. Sameness is important, as are boundaries. Stability of identity is important, as is flexibility and adjustment to changes that affect identity. Places are usually physical or material entities, like a birthplace, and at the same time they are depositories of memory, expectation, and affection. Place identity, therefore, was first understood as a sentimental attachment of an individual to a place. However, those who share a place identity also form a group, and it is this construction of group identification with a place that is the focus of this chapter.

If the place is more than just a physical settlement, then what are its more ephemeral components? Arjun Appadurai describes places or "localities" as "life-worlds constituted by relatively stable associations, relatively known and shared histories and collectively traversed and legible spaces and places."[2] Appadurai's places are unique, separated from others through differences. These differences underwrite relationships with these Others and are social constructions that can reflect more than benign "difference."

Early studies of place stressed the meanings that localities have for individuals, and the role of these meanings in a sense of belonging and in the development of the individual's personal identity. These have been called the "experiential dimensions of place," those that "evoke some sense of belonging to a social group and provide a sense of group identity."[3] Anne Buttimer states that "people's sense of both personal and cultural identity is intimately bound up with place identity," which has many dimensions including those of a "symbolic, emotional, cultural, political and biological" nature.[4] While aspects of one's self-identity may be related to one's place of origin or residence, at the same time, statements about that place and its inhabitants become prophetic in the sense that aspects of that place are reinforced through such statements and "become transformed into part of that place" in a curious dialectic.[5] Place is a lived space, a space defined and shared by members of a cultural group, but experienced by the individual. In the words of Edward Relph, in seminal work on place published in the late 1970s, "the spatial organization of the village has in fact been made unselfconsciously to correspond with a whole variety of social beliefs and practices; each member of the culture is aware of the significance of the various spatial elements of the village and responds to them accordingly." He adds: "There is for virtually everyone a deep association with and consciousness of the places where we [*sic*] were born and grew up, where we live now, or where we have had particularly moving experiences."[6] Following Relph, George Revill proposes that place provides the certainty that "comes from possessing the means to describe oneself," and the security that "comes from doing this in a way that is shared by the group and unavailable to outsiders." For Revill, certainty and security are very desirable ingredients in identity formation. In sum, a place is a locality, imbued with shared meanings by a group; it is an arena for activity and experiences, to which the individual feels a sense of belonging and with which the individual identifies; it is also a mechanism of self-conceptualization.[7]

More recent authors have criticized these early notions of place as overly static. The meanings of places are not fixed, but are constructed and manufactured. Rather than a place existing as an unchanging entity with which individuals identify, the place is a reflection of social relations. It is part of the spatial manifestation of the community, and as such reflects changes in the community. As in the community itself, there is a dialectical process in motion in the definition of place: internal pressures work toward the conservation of the existing structures, while other pressures exist to change and innovate. That is to say, there is a tension between the stabilization of the meaning of the place, and the reconstruction and modification of that meaning. Doreen Massey suggests that the definition of places be "amplified to take account of the construction of the subjects within them." This creates a dialectic, or "a double articulation."[8] Appadurai recognizes the dangers of focusing on the physical expression of the place without consideration of its social construction when he warns against the tendency to "freeze" some members of society into certain places. In a discussion of the term "native" in anthropology, he proposes that "what it means is that natives are not only persons who are from certain places, and belong to those places, but they are also those who are somehow incarcerated, or confined in those places."[9] As mentioned above, in his later works Appadurai emphasizes the construction of difference in understanding "place."

According to John Allen, underlying differences will include levels of governance and relationships of power. He understands the formation of communities (of sameness) as an act of "self-enclosure" and sees it as an active and not a passive identification. In his words, "a sense of who belongs is achieved not by a collective construction of who is recognized as present, but rather by a set of rules which imposes a like-mindedness ... delimited sharply so that anyone wishing to be part of it must conform to the prescribed rules of conduct." A place so constructed becomes a physical location, shared memories and history, and a set of practices with subscribers. In some cases, these will underwrite the management of resources, in what could be seen as a strategy against control over resources by the more economically or politically powerful.[10] This understanding of place as a social construction and as a set of practices led Akhil Gupta and James Ferguson to explore the relationship between place construction and resistance:

> To be part of a community is to be positioned as a particular
> kind of subject, similar to others within the community in some
> crucial respects and different from those who are excluded from
> it. In insisting that these identities are not "freely" chosen but
> overdetermined by structural location and that their durability

and stability are not to be taken for granted but open to contestation and reformulation, we wish to draw attention to the crucial role played by resistance.[11]

The processes of construction of the place and of the group, the members of which share an identity with this place, are codependent and dialectical. In addition, these processes of group or place formation or construction may have a covert political agenda, in the sense of intentions of "self-enclosure" or "resistance."

Chemax appears on official maps as a municipality with a predominantly Yucatec Maya-speaking population. With approximately one million native speakers, the Yucatec Maya constitute the third largest indigenous group in Mexico (after the Nahua and the Zapotec, as measured by the number of speakers of the language). Identity with a place (called *cah*) is salient in the Yucatan region. This identity is much more than a sentimental attachment, and in fact constitutes practices, institutions, and hierarchies that place the local Maya in many complex ways.

Since 1980, when the research began, a consistently strong "place identity" with Chemax was observed.[12] This identity encompasses a group with the self-referent of *"eetcahal Chemax,"* which loosely translates as "those who share the township of Chemax," with *"cahal"* here glossed as "township." Cahal boundaries are not contiguous with municipal boundaries, although they both share the name – Chemax. Furthermore, those from Chemax identify themselves by this name regardless of their place of residence or work at a given moment. When asked in Maya who they are, these individuals do not identify themselves in the first instance by their state, language, or family. They identify themselves as being eetcahal Chemax ("coinhabitants of Chemax"). The place of "place" in this self-identification is the focus of this chapter.

What does it mean, then, to be "from Chemax"? What does one have to do in order to claim that one is "from Chemax"? The concept of "place" is relevant to understanding this problem. The individual whose identity includes affiliation and association with Chemax as a place is claiming affiliation with, and participation in, a social as well as a spatial unit. The place name, Chemax, should therefore evoke a series of shared expectations and meanings that have developed through time. At the same time, these expectations and meanings will be subject to pressures to change, due to pressures on the social construction itself. The remainder of this chapter examines some of the implications of cultivating, maintaining, and claiming affiliation with Chemax: What are the advantages to affiliating, what happens if one loses one's affiliation, what does this affiliation mean to outsiders, and what does outside affiliation mean to the eetcahal Chemax, or those from Chemax?

The placement of Chemax in the political geography of the Yucatan peninsula and the region's recent history situates Chemax in the contemporary dominant Mexican political system. In this political order, Chemax is constructed from the outside, by those culturally and physically removed from the setting. More important, however, is how Chemax is a place defined and constructed from the inside, by its inhabitants and affiliates. This discussion relies on a conservative viewpoint derived from a definition of the eetcahal Chemax based on concepts inherited from the past and maintained by the elders and others politically involved at the local level. The definition of the eetcahal Chemax relies not only on its internal workings and requirements, but also on the construction of the non-Chemax Others who fall into a cultural hierarchy. That is to say, concepts of cultural superiority and inferiority shape this social construction. The final section turns to the impact of recent changes in the eastern Yucatan on Chemax and on the definition and structure of Chemax as a place and as a social group. These changes have important implications for the placement of Chemax vis-à-vis Others and, therefore, also in the construction of the place and in the placement of its affiliates.

CHEMAX: A BRIEF HISTORY

Chemax today is a municipality in the state of Yucatan. It has an area of 1,028 square kilometres and a population, according to the 2000 census, of 25,085 inhabitants. The inhabitants are primarily Yucatec Maya, and they are culturally conservative as indicated by the fact that 97.3 per cent of them report themselves as native speakers of Yucatec Maya, and 35 per cent claim to be unilingual Maya speakers.[13] They live on a flat, karstic plain, characterized by little topographic relief, a porous limestone landscape with thin soils and little surface water in the form of lakes and rivers. The waterways are underground river systems and the most important water sources are sinkholes or cenote formations in which the ground collapses to expose the water table. In Chemax, the cenotes and wells have a depth of between twenty-four and twenty-six meters and constitute the region's only water sources. The main agricultural activity in the tropical forests that characterize the area is slash-and-burn agriculture. Mechanized agriculture is virtually impossible on this rocky landscape. In 2000, the majority of the economically active male population reported agriculture, hunting, or ranching as their primary economic activity.[14] This self-identity prevails, even though many now leave the cah on a temporary basis to seek cash income opportunities in the nearby Maya Riviera tourist corridor.

Chemax also marked the easternmost point of Spanish colonial penetration. The regional centre of Valladolid, thirty-five kilometres to the west of Chemax, represented the eastern stronghold of the Spanish (although stronghold may be an overstatement), establishing a non-Maya presence in the eastern Yucatan throughout the colonial period, the nineteenth century, and right to the present day. Chemax is mentioned in the colonial records from the sixteenth through the nineteenth centuries, and had a population of 7,500 inhabitants in 1828. On the central plaza of Chemax is a Catholic church built in the late eighteenth century, and a large government building called the *cuartel* (barracks) or *palacio municipal* (city hall), undated but possibly built during the late colonial period.[15]

Changes in taxation systems and land tenure regulations, political insecurities at the national level, and demographic pressures all contributed to the outbreak of a war in the Yucatan in 1847 in which the Maya fought to rid themselves of outside rule. One of the peculiarities of this war, commonly called in English the War of the Castes, was the abandonment en masse by the Maya of most of the large settlements in the peninsula, and the movement of population into the forested areas to the east of Valladolid and Chemax.[16] According to Salvador Rodríguez Losa, a Yucatec historian, by 1893 only 2,784 settlements were still inhabited in the entire peninsula, compared to 6,200 in the years immediately prior to the war.[17] The population had moved eastward into an area then dubbed "*Cruzob* Territory" by Mexican authorities, referring to a cult of the talking cross (*cruz*) that had emerged during the uprising.[18]

By the end of the century, the fighting had ended and Mexican government authorities began to make new inroads into the eastern, forested areas of the peninsula. Chemax was located on the cusp between, to the west, the jurisdiction of Valladolid on the frontier of government control and, to the east and south, the forested areas inhabited by many Maya agriculturists, places virtually impenetrable to representatives of the official system. The efforts of the government of Porfirio Díaz to pacify and colonize this region in the late nineteenth and early twentieth centuries have been well studied by Herman Konrad, who describes the frustration of government planners who wished to populate and exploit the tropical forest areas. Strategies adopted by the government included granting land concessions to survey companies and sales of the tropical forest lands to outside national and international interests.[19] In 1902, the territory of Quintana Roo was separated from the state of Yucatan. This move institutionalized the perceived distinction between the so-called pacified population of the peninsula (to be included in the state), and the rebel areas destined to stay under direct federal government control until such time as they were "pacified." The boundary between Yucatan and Quintana Roo runs as close as twenty kilometres to the east of Chemax and, in fact, was surveyed using the town's church towers as landmarks. Chemax's placement on the edge of Maya rebel territory, but with a perhaps tenuous classification as "pacified," was thus permanently marked. For the non-Maya of the peninsula, Valladolid was the easternmost point of Mexico's order and the first major settlement east of Valladolid, Chemax, represented the entrance to "rebel" Maya territory.

During the twentieth century, the presence of the Mexican state increased in Chemax with highway construction, the imposition of the municipal government structures which overlaid existing political and social institutions, the introduction of the *ejido* system of collective land tenure through which the agriculturists of Chemax obtained formal recognition of the forest held by the cah, and the gradual incursion of state education and health institutions. Non-Maya returned to the nodal settlement of Chemax. A few recovered their ranches held in private tenure before the War of the Castes, while others took on the role of commercial middlemen dealing in forest and agricultural products such as honey, chewing gum, game, pelts, and corn. This presence of outside people and institutions has generally been tolerated, but while Maya political, social, and economic organization adopted elements of outside structures, the institutions of the cah have remained strong and integral. The tension between systems provoked spatial contestation and social conflict throughout the twentieth century.

In recent times, non-Maya Yucatecans describe Chemax as a place of political unrest. Memories of rebellious actions in Chemax remain vivid. Today, these actions involve a rejection of ruling national and regional political parties. In the early 1980s, violence broke out in the town when an opposition candidate, widely reputed locally to have won the municipal elections, was impeded from taking office in the municipality by state authorities. Such violent confrontations happen with sufficient regularity in Chemax to confirm, for many urban Yucatecans, the stereotype of the town as a dangerous place. Indeed, while I was doing fieldwork there in the early 1990s, I was repeatedly warned about Chemax's dangers and once even asked whether I had taken out life insurance. As recently as 2004, a local candidate for senate was murdered for political motives, according to both local and state-level opinion. Due at least in part to such political dissidence, Chemax was slower than other municipalities to receive government-sponsored infrastructure, such as telephone service, which further hindered the incorporation of Chemax into the political mainstream and reinforced the idea of the eetcahal Chemax as resistant to full participation in the official political system. In short, Chemax was, and still is, situated in a strategic yet ambiguous geographical and social space vis-à-vis colonial and national projects designed to incorporate the Yucatec Maya into the Mexican nation-state.

In the conventional usage of non-Maya Yucatecans, the population of the peninsula is divided into two groups: Maya and non-Maya, although the terminology may vary. The Maya refer to themselves as "*macehual*" and to the non-Maya as "*dzul*"; the non-Maya call their male counterparts "Mayas" and call Maya women "*mestizitas*," or refer to them generically as "indios." These are primarily ethnic references. In addition to these, the Maya from Chemax are identified, and self-identify, with a place noted for violent rebellious acts and bordered by forested areas. Much of this forested area lies within the boundaries of the territory of Quintana Roo, which only obtained full statehood in 1974.

In short, Chemax is an indigenous (Maya) place on the border of forested rebel territory, seen to be not fully pacified. The Chemax Maya evoke images of renegade, non-conforming, unpredictable, and violent people who steadfastly cling to their Maya ways while rejecting outside authority. In my experience, the Chemax Maya do not spend any time dispelling these beliefs about them held by outsiders.

CHEMAX AS A PLACE CONSTRUCTED FROM WITHIN

To claim to be "from Chemax" attaches a certain stigma (or status) to the speaker from the perspective of other people in the region and state. However, what does being "from Chemax" mean to the speaker? How does one lay claim to being an eetcahal Chemax, and what advantages does this claim bring? In the course of this research, in answer to the question "what is Chemax to you?", most of those interviewed in the study area replied "*ing cah*" (my town), even if they were not living in the town when interviewed. The term "cah" signified more than the physical locality; it referred to a wider construct that included the locality itself, but transcended its physical boundaries.

To lay claim to Chemax as one's cah requires involvement in a series of activities, events, or groups, most of which have a spatial dimension expressed in the main settlement of Chemax. Chemax thus becomes a practice as well as a place. All eetcahal Chemax will ideally participate, at least as spectators, in the annual *cha'an*, which is a town revitalization ritual. They will be known by sight on the streets of Chemax, an indication that they spend time in the centre and have social networks there. They will strive to have a house plot in the main settlement, which then becomes a concrete spatial representation of their place (and that of their family) in the cah as well as a metaphor for town affiliation. Male cah affiliates are required to be prepared to take on duties for the defence of the cah, both of the membership and of the physical spaces – the locally-controlled militia institution, the *Guardia*, has come into play in the recent past in moments of political strife, organizing local men in defensive brigades. Male eetcahal are also involved in the construction and maintenance of these physical cah spaces, including the central park area, the streets, wells and cenotes, and forest. They are expected to be agriculturists, and continuance of their cah affiliation through fulfillment of these obligations will give them access to the forested lands from which they fashion agricultural plots. With the military, ritual, and social institutions centred in the cah, the eetcahal receive protection from outside threats (both ritual and material), are guaranteed social order, and receive productive spaces for subsistence activities.

According to local conventions and expectations, to be eetcahal Chemax means that one believes in and subscribes to these practices, complying as fully as possible with the obligations and receiving rights to the benefits. There is no need to be born in the central settlement of Chemax and there is no need to reside permanently in Chemax. In fact, agriculturists will maintain a habitable structure in a forest hamlet near their plots, since it is usually not practical to commute from the central settlement to the plots, given the considerable distance. However, to claim that Chemax is "my town," one must strive to participate in defined activities and to meet expectations. In defining Chemax, some local individuals spoke of "*u t'aan cah*," the "voice of the cah." Another individual, in trying to explain his affiliation with Chemax, said "*Tu chikilbesahba ti cah*," which may be translated as "one comes and registers oneself within the limits of the cah."[20] People feel themselves to be under the "orders" of the cah. Clearly, these are references to a social unit of cah that includes, but is not exclusive to, the spatial form of the town. This is a place in the sense of a social construction, which manifests itself physically. The constructed spaces corresponding to the social groups and institutions to which the eetcahal must subscribe are found in the town. The political institutions are represented centrally in the cuartel building, formerly the barracks of the Guardia; as is the land-holding institution, now subsumed under the ejido rubric and its related central office; and the ritual institutions (churches, temples, and ritual spaces). The two-week annual ritual of town revitalization is represented by a central space, a vacant lot during all but those key two weeks during the year. The families of the region are spatially represented in Chemax by their houses and plots, regardless of the fact that many of the houses sit unoccupied for most of the year.

The most important collective manifestation of the eetcahal Chemax is the annual town revitalization ritual, which takes place during the first two weeks of June. It corresponds with the celebration of Saint Anthony of Padua, and hence culminates on 13 June, this saint's day. The cha'an is organized by a well-defined group of seventeen men, known as the *combite*. It includes a committee of thirteen *diputados*, as well as a sacred head of the cha'an, called the *kulebi mayol*, two *ahkin*, and one *dzulas-tancia*.[21] Each member of the committee has collaborated for years with the cha'an organizers and placed his name on a long waiting list in order to become an "authority." The committee meets several times during the year and the organizers focus their day-to-day efforts on the main events of the celebration, which include daily bullfights and processions, and nightly dances with live music. But this is a sacred celebration. All of the activities take place in the public spaces of Chemax, notably the downtown central space and the streets. The most central ritual point is marked by the planting of a ceiba tree, which since pre-Hispanic times has represented the axis-mundi joining the multiple layers of the cosmos (Figure 10.1). The most visible evidence of the cha'an is the transformation of the downtown main park area into a three-storey corral-like structure built around the ceiba tree, which accommodates as many as 3,000 spectators. The square area formed by this structure is the scene of ritual "bullfights" and processions of the combite carrying ritual paraphernalia, including red flags to mark the four corners of this space, the ceremonial lances used to sacrifice the bulls, the decorated banderillas to jab into the neck of the bulls for entertainment, and a pig's head on a tray decorated with cut paper and carried *on* the head of one of the combite members (Figure 10.2). The nightly dances take place in a large public space situated behind the cuartel, while the processions featuring live music, conch-shell horn-blowing, exploding fireworks, dancing, and drinking take place along the town streets. The church itself becomes a depository of sacred images and the pivotal point for daily processions to and from the homes of local ritual leaders, while the church authorities attend to the masses in celebration of Saint Anthony.

The outward appearance of the constructed spaces of the settlement itself, together with the nature of the spaces constructed especially for the cha'an, become physical representations of the town meaningful to a discerning outsider, and are therefore of considerable importance to the

10.1. The Bullfight, Annual Festival of Chemax, 2004
Note: The trunk of the ceiba tree is visible in the foreground.
Source: Photo by Denise Fay Brown.

eetcahal Chemax. In addition, the number of people attending and participating in the cha'an indicates the strength of the social unit. According to informants and to observations of the event, the size and the success of the cha'an is an indication of the cah's vitality and importance to the eetcahal Chemax. At the same time, their own participation is part and parcel of this social construction. This becomes a moment to both (re)construct the cah's image and to revel in its importance. To be "from Chemax" is not, therefore, simply to be born in the place and have sentimental attachment to it. Identifying with Chemax and taking pride in that identity have to do with the image of Chemax as an important and organized place, and members' participation is inherent in this image. For this reason, the cha'an, as the public manifestation of Chemax, is a source of pride for the eetcahal Chemax, young and old.

Chemax and the eetcahal Chemax do not, however, exist in isolation. There is a wider world in which the cah, its members, and its institutions are situated. There are other *cahoob* (the plural of cah) in the region and people from Chemax attend (and comment at length on) the cha'an of other settlements. They also travel outside of the cahal. Agricultural work requires frequent and often long-distance changes of residence. In the recent past, tapping of chicle (from which chewing gum is made) was an important economic activity in the area, and contracted chicle workers spent months in the tropical forest in camps many kilometres from their

10.2. The Procession of the Combite, Annual Festival of Chemax, 1994
Source: Photo by Denise Fay Brown.

towns. Today, hundreds of young men and women leave Chemax for the Caribbean coast where they find work in the burgeoning tourist sector. Through these travels, eetcahal Chemax come into frequent contact with eetcahal of other places. In fact, even within the municipal boundaries of Chemax, there are eetcahal of other places. XCan is a settlement in the municipality that lost its status of cah following its abandonment during the War of the Castes. As it was gradually resettled, XCan residents attended the cha'an of Chemax and participated in other institutions there. Recently, however, XCan began to celebrate its own cha'an again, reflecting its people's efforts to secure their resource base and to build their own eetcahal.

The identity with the place of Chemax is an important marker. While all may be ethnically Maya, self-identifying as *macehualob*, they carefully distinguish themselves through their identity with a place. They claim place identity, and this identity reveals compliance with the activities and practices mentioned above – it is not an identity that refers simply to a place of birth or residence.

PLACEMENT OF THE CHEMAX MAYA: THE IDEA OF THE OTHER

What would happen if an individual decided that he did not want a cah affiliation, if he decided that he would not participate in the activities that lead to the maintenance and construction of the place as a social unit, and would not claim to be an eetcahal? To live in Chemax today without cultivating an affiliation to the cah might cause some difficulties in terms of defence of rights, protection from malicious gossip, burial in the case of death, and clemency in issues to do with public spaces. These are some of the practical benefits that come with Chemax affiliation. Of course, the official institutions of the municipal, state, and federal governments do not require a Chemax affiliation in order provide services. One can live in Chemax without cultivating this affiliation. Nonetheless, the majority of adult Maya males of Chemax invest some time and energy in cultivating their eetcahal affiliation or, in a very few cases, maintain a previous affiliation and place identity. This is not the case, however, for the minority non-Maya population of Chemax who do not claim eetcahal status.

The economic and political activities, language affiliation, and ethnic identity of the non-Maya in Chemax in most cases lead them to look toward Valladolid, the regional centre to the west of Chemax, for their place identity. In fact, in a way that mirrors the mechanisms that cement Chemax affiliation, many non-Maya families from Chemax strive to own a house in Valladolid or in Cancun (to the east), in order to consolidate their identity outside of Chemax. It is important to note that the Maya-speaking majority in Chemax refers to them as "*dzul*," translated by some as "dog," indicating the special social space allocated to them within the society.[22] In addition, they are ascribed a particular place within the physical settlement of Chemax. This is the plaza or downtown area of the town surrounding the main square. They are not free to settle anywhere in the town itself, and occupy a special space in the cah. They are often called "*los de la plaza*" (those of the plaza), a reference to both their physical and social placement in the town. They are not eetcahal. Instead they are almost trapped in the downtown space, restricted from penetration into the physical and social spaces of the cah.[23] The eetcahal Chemax distinguish themselves from this ethnic group within the cah, the members of which do not seek Chemax affiliation.

The eetcahal Chemax also distinguish themselves from another group. The importance of cah affiliation becomes more transparent when seen in the contrast between the Chemax eetcahal and those human beings who are not "under the mandate of a town," known locally as "*indios.*" This seemed odd to me, since the Maya people of the peninsula are considered by outsiders to be native people or Indians. However, in conversations taking place in the Maya language, individuals living in the bush would often be called "indios," used with the negative connotation of savagery or lack of civilization. Living in the bush, they are not affiliated with a town, or a cah. Town affiliation is therefore an essential component of what the Maya understand as "civilization." To surrender oneself to a town, and to therefore meet the duties and obligations centralized in a main settlement, is referred to as "*tu kububaob*," which comes from the verb *kukuba*, which means "to turn oneself over without reservation."[24] The eetcahal have done this, whereas in contrast, indios have not. Place affiliation therefore underwrites an essential distinction between the "civilized" and the "primitive" for the Chemax eetcahal. As such, the definition of the eetcahal Chemax relies not only on the internal workings and requirements of town residence, but also can be understood through the construction of the non-eetcahal Chemax Others and the idea of cultural hierarchy or ranking.

The contrast between the Chemax affiliate and an individual with no affiliation represents more than a simple comparison of places, such as that discussed by James Fernandez as leading to "a celebration of local identity by means of a contrastive place."[25] This concept also transcends the simple construction of a local identity by "emphasizing differences and stressing uniqueness rather than seeking similarities," as proposed by George Nicholson.[26] These conceptions are based on the importance of boundaries in the definition of the Other and the construction of place and place identity. In the Chemax example, establishment of the boundary of Other is based on more than just cultural difference, since it includes the idea of cultural superiority. The distinction between one with a town affiliation and one without is seen as a reflection of the cultural development of the individual, employing the ideas of superiority and inferiority, and the idea of cultural ascendancy.[27] In Chemax, the resulting social hierarchy is linked to place construction and identity.

This social construction of the indio as a contrastive identity for the Chemax eetcahal may have emerged from, or was reinforced during, the War of the Castes. During that period of violence, much of the population of the peninsula fled eastward to establish settlements in the forested zone, abandoning many previously-registered settlements. When the armed conflict ended, some of these migrants returned and re-established their membership in their original towns, others formed new towns or *cahoob*, while still others affiliated with towns near where they were living. Due to this, the number of eetcahal Chemax grew enormously in the first half of the 1900s. However, some of the Maya population opted to remain in the forest and refused to affiliate with a town. The inhabitants of Chemax knew of these people through three kinds of direct contacts: chicle workers met these small groups in the forest while collecting the product; agriculturists came upon these groups in the forest while engaged in farming activities; and, most notoriously, these groups raided the larger settlements. Recollections of direct experience and stories of contacts with indios among many old people in Chemax emphasize that they spoke the same language as the people from Chemax, although they dressed differently in loincloths or *uit*. They wore an earring to mark their identity, and they raided the hamlets and towns for goods and women. Some Chemax elders recall that the people generically-known as indios were also referred to as *sureños* (people from the south), *compas* (because they would refer to the Chemax people as *compadres*, a term of fictive kinship), *cruzob* (because they belonged to the cult of the speaking cross), or *tatiches* (because they wore an earring). According to these elders, these indios lived in small settlements in the forest, without authorities (*sin autoridad*); that is, without the institutional or, by extension, the spatial constructions of a cah.

The construction of the sureño as a primitive Other, without a cah or place affiliation, in a situation of needing to steal women and goods, serves to reaffirm the cultural placement of the Chemax Maya. The sureños are portrayed as economically, politically, and socially marginalized. These judgment criteria reinforce the placement itself, and underwrite the idea of cultural hierarchy. One of the implicit messages to the eetcahal Chemax is, perhaps, that stepping outside of the system will cause one to become a primitive sureño, an indio. They also construct local Others, the non-Maya, as dzul – relegated spatially to the plaza area of the cah. Place affiliation, therefore, signifies not only an identity, but also the relative social positioning of the eetcahal Chemax. Doreen Massey has identified this as cementing the individual in a place of "stability and authenticity" in terms of the "articulation of social relations," which are relations of inclusion and of exclusion. In Chemax, as in her research findings, the construction of place and identification with place secures and stabilizes these meanings.[28] Place construction and identity also reinforces and situates difference within a hierarchy of power relations.

In sum, place identity with Chemax has a special significance to state agents who see Chemax as a place full of renegades. In contrast, the eetcahal Chemax construct affiliation as a series of rights and obligations, which transcends the idea of place identity as a simple identification for sentimental reasons. Place affiliation with Chemax to the Maya means, precisely, that the individual is *not* a renegade. Chemax affiliation differentiates the eetcahal Chemax from a primitive status ascribed to individuals who do not live "under the orders of a town," those referred to as "indios." It also distinguishes them from the non-Maya dzulob. Therefore, the idea of cultural hierarchy and ascendancy implicit in this construction of place and Other affords those with the identity a superior status over others. In the context of the regional sociopolitical system, those with cah affiliation to Chemax consider those with other cah affiliations to be social equals, although their different cah affiliations mean that there are boundaries among them, and they are understood to be Others. Non-Maya Others have a "place" in this social system. At a larger scale of analysis, however, it is clear that Chemax is itself nested in a broader sociopolitical system, and the role of the eetcahal Chemax in that system is changing.

THE CHANGING PLACEMENT OF CHEMAX

The territory of Quintana Roo became a state in 1974, and shortly thereafter major developments in tourist infrastructure along the Caribbean coast drastically changed the demographic, political, economic, and social profile of the area that lies to the east and south of Chemax. In the space of two decades, the forested area of refuge for Maya agriculturists was transformed into a major destination for international tourism. Cancun, now one of the largest cities in the Caribbean, is a metropolis of non-Maya migrants to the zone. From the standpoint of Cancun, Chemax is a poor, small, indigenous town with no attractions for the tourist. Although the eetcahal Chemax provide a labour supply to the tourism industry, especially construction work, they have no special status in Cancun. These changes signal the end of remote forest settlements, along with the sureños, tatiches, and cruzob Maya. With only the memory of these indios to provide a contrast and a benchmark to lower-status human beings, how will the self-definition of the Chemax people change?

In the context of such changes, identity with the place becomes even more salient. This is especially true when definitions of this place are "situated" and defined in terms of power relations. Chemax is the cah, or power centre, of the Maya socio-spatial system. However, at the same time, Chemax is a peripheral place in the cultural landscape of the regional, national, and international interests operating to the east. That is to say, whereas Chemax is the pinnacle of a local hierarchy of social status, cultural development, and power relations, it is powerless and occupies the bottom of a hierarchy of places from the perspective of official and tourist sectors. These meanings are contradictory. The place of Chemax within each of these meaning systems is different, and therefore the place identity associated with Chemax is also different.

Young people in Chemax have better opportunities than before to seek their livelihood outside of the cah. They have the option of dissociating themselves from the construction of the eetcahal identity, which is based upon the integrity of the cah. They can abandon the construction of Otherness and difference connected with their "locality," that place of shared history and memory, a place full of legible spaces and places.[29] But if they are to leave a shared space of relative certainty and security,[30] they would find themselves in another place, to be placed and positioned by the Others there. In the new location, both physical and social, they would most probably be marginally positioned, for the indigenous, rural populations in the Americas, in general, are relegated to such powerless and voiceless spaces. In sum, while in the Maya context, the eetcahal is a status to be sought; in the larger regional, national, and transnational contexts, however, the status of the native person from Chemax emerges from a marginal situation in a non-Maya setting.

In fact, the eetcahal Chemax identity continues to be strong despite the growing economic and cultural influences from the Maya Riviera region. Those who work in that region face the encounter of place identities. Nonetheless, as long as the cah of Chemax remains the primary locus of place identity, then it will provide a place of dignity for the eetcahal Maya of the region. Perhaps that is one reason why ties to this place remain strong today. Together with increasing participation in the Maya Riviera tourist economy, house construction in Chemax and attendance at the annual festival are on the increase. This signifies a continued adherence to two of the key expressions of eetcahal status described above: representation of the family in the nodal cah settlement through the maintenance of a house plot, and participation in the annual festivity of cah revitalization. Although the wealth generated by eetcahal Maya now comes from beyond the forests of the cah, the strategy of "self-enclosure" continues. Wealth is invested in the physical, ritual, and social construction of Chemax.

CONCLUSION

Michael Keith and Steve Pile emphasize the political nature of space, stating that spatialities "express asymmetrical relations of power."[31] Space and place can be used as a tool and strategy to resist dominant power relations. However, this can become confounded as individuals develop conflicting affiliations and multiple-stranded place identities in the modern world, with "differing engagements."[32] This was not the case in the more tightly-knit social units and relatively isolated spaces of the past. With new needs, the boundaries of social groups can become porous, and community cohesion and participation can lessen as a result, especially as local institutions lose autonomy in the face of outside forces, agencies, and institutions.[33] Such pressures precipitate changes in the social relations, and in the spatial manifestations of those relations. In Chemax today, place identity remains strong and continues to be asserted, even in spite of increasing diversity within the cah that may eventually challenge the conventions that support the social construction of that place. The physical appearance of Chemax is changing, with new architectural styles and building materials. In a parallel way, the social and symbolic construction of Chemax evolves through time. But still, today, affiliation to this place, together with the commitment to shared meanings and memories, continues to provide a strong basis of individual and group identity and integrity.

NOTES TO CHAPTER 10

1 This chapter is based on research made possible by the Canadian Social Sciences and Humanities Research Council and the Regents of the University of California. The author wishes to acknowledge the collaboration of many people from Chemax who have expressed interest in this research and helped in data collection, analysis, and review of the findings. However, any errors and omission are the responsibility of the author.

2 Arjun Appadurai, "Sovereignty without Territoriality: Notes for a Postnational Geography," in The Anthropology of Space and Place, ed. Setha Low and Denise Lawrence-Zuñiga, 338 (Oxford: Blackwell Publishing, 2003).

3 Michael Godkin, "Identity and Place: Clinical Applications Based on Notions of Rootedness and Uprootedness," in The Human Experience of Space and Place, ed. Anne Buttimer and David Seamon, 73 (New York: St. Martin's Press, 1980).

4 Anne Buttimer, "Home, Reach and the Sense of Place," in The Human Experience of Space and Place, ed. Anne Buttimer and David Seamon, 167 (New York: St. Martin's Press, 1980).

5 James Fernandez, "Andalusia on Our Minds: Two Contrasting Places in Spain as Seen in a Vernacular Poetic Duel of the Late 19th Century," Cultural Anthropology 3:1 (Feb. 1988): 21–35.

6 Edward Relph, Place and Placelessness (London: Pion Limited, 1976), 13, 42.

7 George Revill, "Reading Rosehill: Community, Identity and Inner-City Derby," in Place and the Politics of Identity, ed. Michael Keith and Steve Pile, 137 (London: Routledge, 1993).

8 Doreen Massey, Space, Place, and Gender (Minneapolis: University of Minnesota Press, 1994), 8.

9 Arjun Appadurai, "Introduction: Place and Voice in Anthropological Theory," Cultural Anthropology 3:1 (Feb. 1988): 16–20.

10 John Allen, Lost Geographies of Power (Oxford: Blackwell Publishing, 2003), 172–73.

11 Akhil Gupta and James Ferguson, "Culture, Power, Place: Ethnography at the End of an Era," in Culture, Power, Place: Explorations in Critical Anthropology, ed. Gupta and Ferguson, 18 (Durham: Duke University Press 1997).

12 Research was conducted through participant observation, simple observation, open-ended interviews, focused interviews with elders, documentary research, as well as discussion of findings with local individuals as the research progressed. An ethnographic summary is found in Denise Fay Brown, "Yucatec Maya Settling, Settlement and Spatiality" (PhD diss., University of California, Riverside, 1993).

13 Mexico, XII Censo General de Población y Vivienda 2000: Estado de Yucatán, Table 1: "Población de 5 años y más por municipio, sexo y grupos quinquenales de edad, y su distribución según condición de habla indígena y habla español," www.inegi.gob.mx (15 May 2005).

14 Mexico, XII Censo General de Población y Vivienda 2000: Estado de Yucatán, Table 7: "Población ocupada por municipio, sexo y ocupación principal, y su distribución según sector de actividad," www.inegi.gob.mx (15 May 2005).

15 Carol Dumond and Don Dumond "'Pueblo y comarca' of Chemax," in Demography and Parish Affairs in Yucatan, 1797–1897, ed. Carol Dumond and Don Dumond, 44–48 (Portland: University of Oregon Anthropological Papers no. 27, 1988); Richard Perry and Rosalind Perry, Maya Missions (Santa Barbara: Espadana Press, 1988), 181.

16 For more information on the "Caste War," see Don Dumond, The Machete and the Cross, Campesino Rebellion in Yucatan (Lincoln: University of Nebraska Press 1997).

17 Salvador Rodríguez Losa, Geografía política de Yucatan, vol. 2 (Mérida: Universidad Autónoma de Yucatán 1989), 231.

18 Cruz means "cross" in Spanish, while the suffix -ob forms a plural in Maya. This hybrid word referred to the Maya followers of the cult of the cross.

19 Herman W. Konrad, "Tropical Forest Policy and Practice during the Mexican Porfiriato, 1876–1910," in Changing Tropical Forests, ed. Harold Steen and Richard Tucker, 123–43 (Durham: Forest History Society, 1992).

20 Alfredo Barrera Vásquez, Diccionario Maya Cordemex (Mérida: Ediciones Cordemex, 1980), 97.

21 These terms are used in Maya, although some of them have Spanish origin. Diputados, for example, in Spanish means "deputies." With the help of the Diccionario Maya Cordemex, Kulebi mayol may perhaps be glossed as "the director from the wooden step"; ahkin as a "priest of the cult of the sun"; and dzulastancia as "leader," Barrera Vásquez, Diccionario, 416, 348, 148, 401, 893.

22 Barrera Vásquez, Diccionario, 867.

23 This is discussed in more detail in Denise Fay Brown, "Ethnicity and Constructed Space in a Maya Town in Yucatan, Mexico," paper presented at the Annual Conference of the Canadian Society for the Study of European Ideas, Montreal, 3–5 June 1995.

24 Barrera Vásquez, Diccionario, 416.

25 Fernandez, "Andalusia," 32.

26 George Nicholson "Place and Local Identity," in The Politics of Attachment, ed. Sebastian Kraemer and Jane Roberts, 123-43 (London: Free Association Books, 1996).

27 Barbara Ching and Gerald Creed, Knowing Your Place: Rural Identity and Cultural Hierarchy (New York: Routledge, 1997), 30.

28 Massey, Space, 120.

29 Appadurai, "Sovereignty," 338.

30 Revill, "Reading Rosehill," 137

31 Michael Keith and Steve Pile "Introduction, Part 1: The Politics of Place," in Place and the Politics of Identity, ed. Michael Keith and Steve Pile, 1–21 (London: Routledge, 1993).

32 Liz Bondi, "Locating Identity Politics," in Place and the Politics of Identity, ed. Michael Keith and Steve Pile, 84–101 (London: Routledge, 1993).

33 Elvin Hatch, Biography of a Small Town (New York: Columbia University Press, 1979), 269.

Creating Identity Out of Place:

AN INDIGENOUS COMMUNITY IN ARGENTINA

Marjorie M. Snipes[1]

INTRODUCTION

The concept of identity is of fundamental concern to all human sciences because it gives shape to the subjective. In anthropology it has sometimes been seen as coincidental to culture, embedded in a depiction of a society, left to the reader to assemble.[2] In other works, however, it has been used to designate active agency to the subjects of study; identity acknowledged, the subjects rise up and seem to tell their own stories through the passive hand of an author.[3] Difficult to examine, identity is likewise difficult to define. Like a shadow, it seems to take substance from the way a life is projected, or lived, requiring the presence of an outside force as much as an interior form in order to take shape. Individual and collective, internal and emergent, it takes shape from the ongoing experiences of social and physical place.

My fieldwork in the Andes of Argentina began with the goal of constructing a model of the ethnic identity of herders, how humans create a sense of self from their relationship with domesticated animals. I thought that this identity would emerge and reveal itself from working with the people of El Angosto on a daily basis, systematically studying their lives and living with them over fourteen months (1991–92) and also during shorter field seasons in 1995 and 2000. As I collected their stories and experienced their lives, this native group would teach and reveal who they are and how they see themselves. But after a time, it became clear that they did not have a collectable identity, something that could be examined and reconstructed as an artefact of personhood. Instead, this identity is a process of survival, an adaptation to changing conditions in life, based as much on what "they" do and who "they" say they are as on the mechanisms "they" use to achieve these ends. While place and setting are crucial to this concept, the presence of an outside Other conjures up the need to articulate one's identity, both individual and collective. In the projection of this sense of self, identity takes shape. Although dialogical, it is not strictly so, and interchanges are not always horizontal. The Other may exist in real and metaphorical senses, defined by interpretations of history, individual experiences, imagination, and by words and deeds. Concepts attached to "who one is" are ambiguous and malleable, not merely to allow change, but actually to court it. Within this changing context where meanings are modified by circumstances, there still emerge essential tenets, axial meanings that transcend isolated events and manifest the enduring aspects of self-recognition and projection. In this chapter I examine three institutional symbols whose collective significance as metaphorical Other ties this community to the nation-state of Argentina. While these symbols appear to be fixed in place, and while they are all examples of nation-state penetration, they allow a comparative examination of collective group identity vis-à-vis a well-defined Other, Argentina, which affords an opportunity to examine who this small herding community sees itself as in historical, geographical, and social terms. As I lived with this group of herders on the Argentine border with Bolivia, I realized that one of their central identifying characteristics was the sense that they are "peripheral" by choice.

Reflecting on the experience of what it was like to travel to El Angosto, in my field notes I wrote:

> As the truck carrying me to El Angosto edged closer to the ravine, a very faint road emerged at my feet. Worn, dusty, with rock scree, this vertical surface connecting the edge of the high altitude plains to the canyon valley far below looked unwilling, fickle, and unsteady. The smaller, more rugged and more deeply ingrained goat trails bisecting the switchback turns all the way down seemed more authentic. They looked permanent, well-traversed, guttural to this landscape. Looking out over the rugged landscape at my feet, it appeared to be the ends of the earth. The rapid descent of some 400 meters is dizzying, slow, cumbersome, nerve-wracking. Accidents are relatively frequent, sometimes resulting in deaths. Trucks slip, slide, crawl, weave, grind, trying to make a slow and steady descent on such a vertical slope. As

goats chew their cud and watch the strange sight of steel beasts roaring into the valley, it is the trucks that are alien.

Yet appearing to be on the edges of the earth, I was soon to find out that I was, instead, at the centre of a well-populated universe.

Anthropology as a discipline has recently focused more on issues of place, voice, and identity,[4] in part because our subjects now routinely talk back to us in print,[5] and also because the issue of agency has become more important to our understanding of subjects and ethnic identity. Narrative voice increasingly must account for itself by providing a connecting link between the experiences of the scientist and the local knowledge of the native.[6] Dialogical exchange sets the arena for the depiction of an Other, giving voice to multiple protagonists, instead of a subject presented as object.[7] Yet as I was to discover, the Other(s) in the equation are as metaphorical as they are real.

In trying to identify ethnic identity, social scientists necessarily come face to face with something esoterically difficult, ephemeral, comparable to Pierre Bourdieu's concept of *habitus* as a playing field on which a range of performance is exhibited.[8] It functions more as a modus operandi from which definitions of self and group emerge and adhere both to the individual and to the group. Any one person or group manages multiple shifting (and emerging) identities. Who we are is based on changing experiences that allow for individual variation, such as where we live, who we interact with, what we do for a living, what language we speak and how we speak it, where we go and what experiences we have, what we aspire to, and the institutions of which we are a part. As a result, any such attempt to corner identity and define it proves to be both elusive and enticing. Something that was left out always crops up. Clearly, ethnic identity emanates from, but is not necessarily embedded in, culture. At best, culture serves as the springboard from which ethnic identity emerges.

One of the most significant advances in our understanding of self and identity has been a growing acknowledgement in anthropology that place is central to who we are. Some recent ethnographic studies have focused on place as a marker of this collective concept of meaning.[9] Indeed, place is a central component in ethnic identity. It affords tools that are used in the construction of who we are and also serves as a poignant mouthpiece. Yet in our contemporary world where displacement is as much a component of identity as belonging, imaginary qualities adhere to place as much as the physical components. A "sense of place," to use a title of a recent work, is at the heart of who we are, and this understanding, this "sense," has as much to do with a group's history and experiences as it does their sense of physical boundaries.[10] Place becomes a metaphorical field in which we work out ethnic identity, as much imaginary as it is geographical. In this work, by focusing on three different institutional symbols through which this small community engages with the nation-state, symbols associated deeply with place, I argue that the primary function of ethnic identity is to maintain and project the autonomy of the group – not just its separation from the Other, but its ability to function as a fully coherent society.

MAKING A COUNTRY:
THE INTERACTION OF COMMUNITY AND NATION-STATE

The community of El Angosto consists of a small, dispersed agro-pastoral population of roughly two hundred individuals. Their subsistence is vested in herding goats and sheep and raising corn, wheat, and broad beans. Located on the extreme northwestern perimeter of the country of Argentina, this area was formally designated Argentine in 1925, with the international Diez de Medina-Carrillo Treaty between that country and Bolivia. The primary border designation is the Río Grande de San Juan on the western edge and border posts (*hitos*) on the northern extreme, first erected during 1939 to 1940, fifteen years after the border was officially established. The total land area comprising El Angosto is roughly 102 square kilometres, most of which is located within a very expansive, arid, and rugged river valley that slopes precipitously from the eastern plateau (at 4,200 metres) to the Río Grande below (at approximately 3,640 metres). It forms a discontinuous geographical phenomenon on an east-west axis, at the farthest northwestern extreme of Argentina. The township seat, which boasts the school, nurse and police stations, and civil registry, as well as four households, sits at an altitude of 3,750 metres. Transportation is challenging, compounded further by flash floods in the rainy season (December-March) that wash away roads and scatter boulders down the hillsides.

Argentina is a country historically defined by political centralization. The current geopolitical designations were formalized in 1816, when the country declared its independence. Each province is divided into departments, with local capitals where limited decision-making occurs. Jujuy, the province in which El Angosto is located, is known colloquially as the "Andean Province." Yet the concept of "Andean" has more than geographical connotations in this area, as the Andes mountains extend through several provinces on the western side of Argentina, including San Juan, Mendoza, and Neuquén, provinces having little cultural continuity with Jujuy.

One of the goals of my research was to understand what "Andean" means to non-Andeans, as collective ethnic identity emerges from this dialogue between community and nation-state. Stereotypes and preconceptions affect the quality of dialogue and the image mirrored back to the community. What the Other thinks of these highlanders directly affects how they identify themselves. And one of the most potent Others to Angosteños is the nation-state itself. Their own sense of being "Andean" was not quite like the definition of "Andean" projected by the nation-state.

The recent political past for this region has been tumultuous. During the military governments (1966–73 and 1976–83), indigenous cultures were officially depicted as a threat to national identity; not only did their underdevelopment hold back national political, social, and technological development, but their marginal status on social and geographical frontiers also threatened national security.[11] As a result, the military governments emphasized drawing peripheral areas (read, indigenous areas) into the metaphorical centre (Buenos Aires and the larger urban zones) through numerous public works projects in remote areas. The far reaches of the national territory were approached as areas to be settled and developed. During this period El Angosto experienced two very significant things. First, the military government had an actual presence in the community, including frequent gendarme border checks and visits from politicians who came to El Angosto to speak with community leaders. They served as an official acknowledgement that El Angosto mattered to Argentina. Community members felt as if they were being heard and watched over. As Héctor C. said of the military years, "they did more for us than [anyone had] before." Insulated from the urban accounts of disappearances that most define this period of history for many Argentineans, Angosteños as a whole experienced a very different relationship with the nation-state during the military years. In fact, they felt that the government was genuinely interested in national border areas and internal development, leading them to feel more positively toward the nation-state at that time and more integrated into Argentina.

In addition, there was significant infrastructural development from 1976 to 1983 and in the immediate aftermath of the military government. The one road into El Angosto, connecting it with Santa Catalina, little used and quite dangerous for large vehicles, served as a connection to the nation-state and a symbol of dialogue between here and there, urban centre and periphery. During these years it was moved and widened to its current state; although still precarious, this represents an improvement over the older road down the mountainside. The national government developed road and communication lines to better penetrate the hinterlands and draw them toward the centre. The border with Bolivia, long established on paper by the 1925 treaty, saw increasingly frequent patrols, reflecting the government's geopolitical agenda, and people living on the periphery saw themselves as actors on a national stage. However, when the military government stepped down in 1982–83, returning the country to civilian rule, the national agenda changed. Instead of seeing themselves as "liberated" in 1983 with the election of Raúl Alfonsín as president, this particular community experienced a rather dramatic and immediate return to isolation from the rest of the nation in all areas except that of the school, an institution with which they have a specifically strong local identification.

A most significant symbol of both national and local identity, the school (the Escuela Lucía Rueda), was officially recognized in 1941, two years after it was founded on 12 June 1939. First established from the efforts of one local woman (from Santa Catalina) committed to educating her "own people," Lucía Rueda, this school originally subsisted on local initiative. Housed in three very small, cramped adobe buildings (built by the villagers themselves), the school boasted little formal curriculum and only a limited number of students (Figure 11.1). Most supplies came through charitable donations made to Rueda after her talks and fundraising events in urban areas, including Buenos Aires, more than thirty hours away by vehicle. Although community accounts extol the quality of education and the dedication of this pioneer teacher, the process of bringing this school into the national educational system was a rather long one. From 1941 to 1986 the Lucía Rueda School operated through the efforts of government-assigned teachers, but continued to be housed in the original structures that required upkeep from the local inhabitants. The community, rather than lament the loss of their little rural school's autonomy, was gratified to see it finally acknowledged by the nation-state as worthy of an official faculty that would include Rueda. In 1986, as the whole country was in the throes of recovering genuine grassroots nationalism and democracy, the provincial government of Jujuy sponsored the Emer Plan for "remote areas," areas separated from urban centres, to include the construction of newly standardized and self-contained school buildings. Initially, for the community, this symbolized progress, development, and a future for El Angosto as being "significant to the nation" yet again. The school installed indoor plumbing, electricity, a fully functioning kitchen, and dormitories for its majority population of boarding students. The government appeared to be pulling El Angosto again into its centre.

11.1. The Lucía Rueda School (National School #369), 1995
Source: Photo by Marjorie M. Snipes.

Concurrently, outside of El Angosto and unknown to its residents, a rather large national tourism movement developed aiming to open up the entire northern area to the rapidly developing urban populations in the south. The cultural differences of these northwestern peoples were being promoted as "folkloric"; they were charming and quaint reminders of the past, and obstacles to be overcome in the pursuit of creating a greater national good. This left an interesting social stigma attached to the province of Jujuy as a whole.

Maryon McDonald, in her study of Brittany, has argued that the less secure the integrity of national identity, the more ambivalent the state feels about minority cultures within its borders.[12] What to do with socio-cultural minorities in its midst is a political concern and how minorities choose to interact with the state involves repeated "imagining and reimagining."[13] Yet while ethnic identities are created in specific socio-historical contexts, the changes and adjustments are rarely equilibrating. On a national stage, governments and policies often change more rapidly than citizen response and often the cultural differences that exist at geographical areas of national frontier are the most troubling because they directly reflect limitations in the definition of the nation-state.[14] In the pursuit of national development and international competitiveness, Argentina has tried to create a recognizably authentic national identity based on centre needs and centre history.[15] Given the government's perceived position against indigenous minorities (designating them as non-existent or simply underdeveloped, defining them in noncultural terms or even resettling indigenous inhabitants on reserves), consequently there has been the rise of an intellectual class, both indigenous and nonindigenous, who have become self-styled culture brokers working to salvage this Andean culture perceived as endangered. Among other things, the history of their cultures has been altered to fit the needs of the tourist trade on both national and international fronts. Possibly in part due to paternalistic feelings of protection and the romantic notions of Andean peoples as "living fossils,"[16] as well as a need for vindication against erasure, there has developed in the Andean area an institution of folklore.[17] It has become a trade commodity, allowing certain very specific towns (those located on the main road, Route 9) to develop by selling not just local culture but the idea of a pan-Andean culture. Besides artefacts, including so-called "Inca pottery," some of which is based on designs from coastal Peru (Paracas/Nazca), which is popular as a consumer artefact because it is very colourful and stylized, but which historically never made its way into these areas of the highland Andes, there is also for sale and use the idea of something authentic and autochthonous, but it is quaint and charming, and non-threatening. It makes for a strange kind of cultural voyeurism.

Through commodification, this folklore is available as an adornment, an authentic artefact or a story lifted into another context. Its significance lies in the imagination that surrounds it. "Andean," as it is used, is a multiple referent. When it pertains to a stylized, imaginary historical lifestyle, it is a positive consumer item, both as tourist art and also as an historical footnote.

There are two towns on the main road to the Northwest that serve as tourist hubs: Humahuaca is known for folkloric shows, ethnic foods, and Quechua language classes, as well as tourist markets where visitors can purchase handcrafted items deemed to be authentic local handicrafts depicting an (idealized) Andean past; the other town, Tilcara, has some of these same things to offer, but because it is located at a slightly lower altitude and is a bit less arid, it is physiologically less stressful to those traveling through looking for relaxation and entertainment. Tilcara has a fine museum of Andean archaeology, constructed and maintained by the University of Buenos Aires, with attached seminar rooms for students and visiting faculty, interesting local ruins that have been prepared for visits and working excavations, and many vacation homes for rent. The charm of Tilcara is its intellectual identity. It is an artists' colony of sorts, with many travelers coming up from Buenos Aires and even from Europe to stay and work "in the Andes" surrounded by very beautiful houses and exquisite scenery. It is charming and quaint and provides the scholar and artist a place in which to contemplate and reflect. This is the nostalgic "Andes" of history that is so popularly consumed by Others.

In the early 1990s Jujuy television produced a weekly series called *"Nuestro Jueves"* (Our Thursday) in which a crew of urban producers and journalists traveled out into the far reaches of the province, presenting beautiful scenery, interesting novelties, and significant challenges associated with these remote areas. Although the show had some educational value, it served primarily as an apologetic for the provincial state of underdevelopment. It often included the coverage of politicians whose main reason for going there was simply to have been there, earning the respect of the urban voters who form the majority population by being seen as proactive, involved, and concerned about internal development, and interested in aiding minority regions to reach the standards of national/provincial urban culture.

So where does this leave places like the "real" El Angosto in the national imagination? Most highland communities, Andean by default, fall short of being anything like these imaginary places. Lacking amenities such as running water and electricity, staff available for the tourist industry, and without folkloric assets such as exploitable Incan ruins, markets, local handicrafts, restaurants, and interesting dances (albeit with a picturesque view and altitude), highland places such as El Angosto fail to conform to the predications of "Andean." As Thomas Abercrombie notes, "prevailing urban notions romanticize Indians, stripping them of their complex understandings of history and power relations and projecting them as living fossils into the ... past, thus taking a version of one-half of the rural-dwellers' own ambivalent identity sources for the whole."[18] Not Andean on the Other's terms, they are instead considered marginal, lower-class, left behind remnants of an imagined (glorious) history. Under these circumstances, the outside/external concept of contemporary "Andean" becomes something archaic, preserved, and endangered. While well-educated individuals bemoan the fact that minority Andean culture is in imminent danger of being erased, and have in response created institutes of Quechua, and other forms of denominated folklore such as dance and music institutes and pseudocultural television series, the contemporary carriers of cultures of the highlands (actually a variety of Andean cultures) continue to struggle to be recognized by national institutions. In fact, these individuals are so thoroughly disconnected from the Other's notion of "Andean" that their cultures are rarely considered viable at all. Instead of engaging in a multi-ethnic population, the nation-state exerts a dominant culture onto the populace with the goals of unifying such variation, treating other (rival) cultures within its borders as inert objects to collect and to preserve in museums for educational purposes and for diversion. This procedure is accomplished through ignorance of vast populations and cultural diversity, where centre power single-handedly defines the identity of the collective whole within its imaginary borders.

PERIPHERAL TO WHAT?
THE COMMUNITY RESPONDS TO THE NATION-STATE

In El Angosto people have a clear concept of themselves, something that translates effortlessly into a key principle of their ethnic identity: here they speak of *"haciendo patria,"* a phrase meaning literally building and promoting a nation, doing some service for one's homeland. In itself the phrase connotes feelings of warmth and sacrifice, of collective belonging and solidarity; however, this term is actually a relational term, a phrase that expresses a dynamic relationship between people and place. Defined by context, *hacer patria* is purposefully ambiguous; *patria* can refer to both the nation-state and the smaller community homeland. While it can be used to depict them as working sacrificially on the frontier as Argentine citizens, it also harbours a meaning of working for the good of their own community, making, in effect, their own new country. The meaning intended is blurred and in process, contingent, emergent from the situation, conveying a sense of autonomy and distinct cultural marking. It expresses their identity as relational, in the process of becoming, and under their control. Unlike subcultures embedded within a wider recognized or inevitable context (such as American Indians within the United States or First Nations people in Canada living under laws and regulations specified for them by the Other, or with an autonomy granted them by the Other), these individuals have maintained an autonomy from the centre by virtue of their challenging geographical location, the sensitive nature of their location on the national border, and their understanding and attitude about who they are. They do not see themselves confined within national perimeters, except by choice, and they engage with the nation-state through very specific institutions that provide a clear barometer of how they feel at that time about the state and how they see themselves in relation to it.

This phrase, *"haciendo patria,"* is not used solely to express one or the other meaning (whether, for example, they see themselves as working sacrificially on the periphery for Argentina or whether they see themselves working for the good of their own community in order to challenge the state), but to express their intent to identify themselves depending on changing context. Who they are depends not only on where they live, who they have been in the past, and what they have experienced as a group of people, but also on what they are currently experiencing. Taking in the messages given off by the Other, they respond through an image that conveys control and begs translation of context. "*Hacer patria*" is a very powerful ethnic identity marker because it preserves their sense of autonomy as a culture. Reapproaching the three institutional symbols through the eyes of the local inhabitants allows us to glimpse their collective sense of self.

11.2. Don Gualberto W., 1991
Source: Photo by Marjorie M. Snipes.

As previously described, the primary road into El Angosto was improved during the years of the military government. The community is very proud of this symbol of progress, often pointing out that they live in a challenging area where only hearty and capable people can live. One older informant, Gualberto W., often referred to individuals in his community as "authentic mavericks [*pura gaucha*] out there on the edges of settled places willing to sacrifice themselves" (Figure 11.2). The construction of this road, a vast improvement over the earlier one, symbolized to the community that they were important to the government. After all, no one at that time owned a vehicle, so the nation-state had desired access to them and had taken on the initiative to make it possible for development and communication to ensue. When governments changed, however, the road was left to symbolize not Argentina but a particular historic time period when the nation-state had taken an interest in El Angosto. The road, however, did not fall into disrepair, even though seasonal rains routinely leave vast gullies carved through the switchback turns. The community responded to subsequent government neglect by doing what work they could to repair the road with hoes and shovels, showing first their autonomy and ownership of the road, and then demanding that the government send machinery to clear areas that they could not mend. I was witness to many conversations regarding what should be told to the government about the state of the road. In each case, the speaker expressed the sense that the current government lacked legitimacy because of its failure to maintain the roads, that it was too inept to understand the significance of nation-building, and too young and inexperienced to perceive the national importance of this border region. Instead of feeling sorry for or feeling empathetic toward the government, it seemed to make them frustrated, feeling that they alone had the responsibilities and likewise the choice of caring for Argentina or dismissing it. Nationhood seemed to rest with them and in these cases they would use the term "*hacer patria*" to represent an internal resistance to the status quo. The feeling that was expressed was that "the government may ignore us, but we hold the reins of nationhood in our hands because we occupy the frontier." Here the Other was seen as unworthy of the hard-won identity of "Argentine."

In effect, the road is a symbol of enormous success to the people of El Angosto. This one symbol, more than any other, has been appropriated as their own, with the intention of symbolizing the past and future and their importance to the nation. They do not claim it as their own, but rather use it as a badge of identification that legitimizes their important role to Argentina, whether or not it is substantiated by any current national power-holders. It is tangible proof that they matter, and it has been incorporated into their identity in the form of pride and legitimacy.

The international border adds a further dimension to their identity. Prior to 1925, there had been a series of discussions and agreements between Bolivia and Argentina culminating in a treaty of 1889–93. This treaty, however, was inexact and was not easily reconciled with the interests of the two countries.[19] As a result, in 1925, after more than a decade of study and negotiation, emissaries from the two countries met to sign a revised pact, the Diez de Medina-Carrillo Treaty. The immediate effect of this within the area of El Angosto occurred only officially and only on paper. Inhabitants of the area were apparently unaware of the agreement, or at least unaffected by it. During my entire time in the field, Gualberto, the landowner of Buena Esperanza, the one landholding that was divided by the changed international border, at that time in his late seventies and extremely knowledgeable and aware of historical changes, repeatedly told me that Buena Esperanza had been divided in 1941. When I objected and showed him historical evidence that this treaty had actually been signed in 1925, he told me that the date was wrong, that it had occurred instead in 1941. After several attempts to discuss this with him, a very sociable and open informant otherwise, he sternly said that the papers I had (photocopies from the Ministry of the Exterior) were wrong.

In anthropology, one thing that we consistently try to employ in fieldwork is cultural relativism, and I struggled to understand how and why Gualberto, an exceptionally intelligent and gifted informant, could have mistakenly remembered the date of something so significant. To Gualberto, whose land was cut apart by the arrangement and whose family had long held Bolivian title to lands in the vicinity, and to other local landowners as well, this was a vital matter.

During many wanderings to interview and also to shepherd herds of goats and sheep, I would think about the political boundaries, trace them in the air as I looked down on the Río Grande de San Juan that marks the western border, and wonder how any extra-local news would travel in such a far-reaching place. Since Angosteños pay close attention to any news about landholdings spread by word of mouth from travelers and also through the ubiquitous radio (available during most of the past century in El Angosto), news of such magnitude would have quickly caught the attention of all affected parties, especially those whose lands were divided. However, it is also true that had the government not followed up words with actions, then the inhabitants would be essentially unaffected by the treaty for two reasons. First, many herding families continue today to use lands in both countries, even perceiving them as private landholdings (although they hold no titles); second, the fiscal relationship with Argentina does not appear to have ever been established in this area, for these affected lands were officially designated as *tierra fiscal*, government-owned lands, until 1998, when Gualberto, five years before his death in 2003, paid back taxes and had a portion of his inherited land officially recognized by Argentina, something of which he was enormously proud. Through their dependence on herd animals and pasturage, they are transhumant and have dispersed grazing lands. Knowing their citizenship as Argentines or Bolivians made no difference to the herders who continued to cross the river in the same places where they had always crossed. Property taxes are a very sensitive matter in this region because they have long been neglected by both residents and provincial collectors. Most landowners have neglected to pay property taxes,[20] so the outcome of the international negotiation had no real impact on their actual, daily lives.

So why did Gualberto (and others) think that the treaty was signed in 1941? In the historical publications regarding this treaty, the authors note that *hitos* (border markers or posts) were first erected on the northern extremes (an area not denominated by a naturally-occurring geographical phenomenon) between 1939 and 1940, but Gualberto said that some surveyors had come through the area making maps and demarcating the international frontier in 1941. This is apparently what happened, as the establishment of the international border was an historical process itself. There were numerous additional protocols and amendments to the original 1925 treaty as it was implemented on the ground.[21] Surveyors began the process of specifying the actual frontier in these more remote regions in 1939, but this process took several months and in some spots even years as precise border locations were renegotiated between governments. To some extent, this explains Gualberto's memory of the events. There was a lengthy delay between the treaty's signing and its enactment. Actions, not words, created change for the inhabitants of El Angosto, so their understanding of historical events was based on different criteria.

This particular event, the modification of the international border, something interpreted differently from the nation-state's perspective by Angosteños, adds another important element to this community's identity: action matters more than agreements. Daily work and inhabitation accentuate the legitimacy of the people who live there as holders of those lands, and as individuals able to ignore laws and rules that are not or cannot be implemented, or which are seen as illegitimate. It is not that they recklessly resist law and order, but rather that they see themselves as necessarily making their own rules as they live their day-to-day lives. The distant and external Other (the nation-state) can make decisions that affect the lives of Angosteños, but these Andeans perceive that they also live beyond the reach of the state. They are pioneers in their own place, living significant lives. The external Other can speak; indeed, the Angosteños associate the state with talk and more talk. However, the machinery of the nation-state typically does very little in these hinterlands. The Angosteños do not feel pressured by the centre because it is virtually non-existent in their daily lives. They see themselves as solely responsible for the lands that are theirs, lands that belong to them through generations of use regardless of the international border. Gualberto so treasured his land title, showing it to me while tears rolled down his face because, "finally, the documents are in order for [the good of] my children." The nation-state did not represent an imminent danger to Gualberto, and he himself had never been concerned about it, but he had lived as an autonomous highlander long enough to be well aware that future governments could change their relationship with his children, and he did not want to leave them with an ambiguous land designation. He knew that the state operated through words, documents, and treaties, while he, as an Angosteño, lived by action and deed. He took it upon himself to protect both the land and his legacy.

A final symbol of the nation-state, an institution that prompts direct and immediate dialogue between Angosteños and the centre, is the small primary school built in the town centre of El Angosto, where only four families actually reside. Embraced as a symbol of progress, hope, pride, and autonomy, the school's history makes it the most volatile institution in El Angosto. In remembering the years immediately after the school's 1939 founding, older adults speak with pride of the quality of education that they received, and of Lucía Rueda's commitment. Not only was she formally educated outside of El Angosto, exposed to places far beyond, but she chose to return and to devote herself to this community and their future. They do not interpret this as charity, but as a noble act of self-sacrifice and recognition of the worthiness of their culture, investing her future and her legacy with that of their own. As one older informant remembered:

> Lucía Rueda was a contemporary of mine. She was very good. She worked all by herself with fifty-five to as many as sixty students. In this time period a student knew how to act socially. Now some students do not know this. At that time a student had to do what was right.... Señorita [Lucía Rueda] taught ... but ... fiercely and all by herself with only one cook. And now with so much constant trouble.... It is very little that the student learns today. There is no curriculum, no programmed schedule to teach subjects each day. They teach only a little bit. A student who has hopes of going far, it works against [him or her].

The original school represented the future of this community in past times. Today's community appropriates the school as a symbol of self-worth, pride, and autonomy, while careful to note that the values espoused by the new (outsider) faculty and the abilities that they manifest are not the same as they could expect from a highland woman of their own culture.

The school has a meaning that contains both the past and the present.[22] Unlike the border and the road, the school involves day-to-day contact with outsiders, emissaries of the Other, and policies over which the Angosteños have virtually no control. Interestingly, though, the real locus of disagreement is not in the policies but in the emissaries themselves (the teachers), often depicted by community members as illegitimate and unworthy of teaching at their little school.

In 1986 the Jujuy Ministry of Education erected a prefabricated school building, an exact replica of all other highland schools, with all the so-called bells and whistles imaginable to highland peoples: infrastructure for running water, electricity, an indoors incorporated kitchen with stoves and a refrigerator, electric heat, lights, and a main office directly inside the front door. There was also a huge solar generator housed in its own adobe shed to provide the electricity for these amenities. The engineers in charge of the project left it functioning smoothly, an affirmation to the community that they were valued by the nation-state, which saw its own future connected with that of El Angosto. Such luxuries for their children represented both the seriousness and the long-term investment attached to them. El Angosto mattered.

As the years passed, however, the equipment fell into disrepair, and when community members requested that their political leaders send engineers to fix the generator, they were given empty promises that entailed years of waiting with no results. Instead of feeling marginalized and unimportant, they responded by expressing their frustrations to the rotating groups of teachers and directors who came and went, very rarely serving more than one year in the community. This very rotation, something that had not occurred during Rueda's long tenure (1939–50), was visible proof to them that this institution, which very clearly belonged to the community, had been corrupted, abused, and exploited by illegitimate outsiders. For their part, the teachers often complained about the isolation, lack of reliable transportation, and difficulties dealing with the local community, seemingly unaware that the locals did not see them as individuals, but rather as representatives of the amorphous Ministry of Education.

The school continues as a sore issue in the community, although the recent renovations (1996) have brought a new solar generator, an additional building for a kindergarten, and a greenhouse where the agronomy teacher works with his students to raise prized vegetables such as lettuce, radishes, and carrots, shared frequently with community members and served daily to their children. As a symbol of pride and progress, the school is negotiated as a product (constructed and earned) of both state and community. Whose property it is shifts back and forth, argued about or uneasily accepted by the parties involved. Over the years I have seen individual teachers and principals begin their academic year excited and impassioned and then watched as the community tightened its grip over these people through boisterous community meetings and very crippling gossip, showing that El Angosto is an autonomous community and does not need to be saved through the efforts of an outsider. One teacher, passionate about her sense of mission at the school and disillusioned by the reality she faced, asked me to intervene on behalf of the community. She encouraged me to go to the Ministry of Education in San Salvador de Jujuy to show them that "a person of importance had taken a special interest in El Angosto and that she was making sacrifices to be here." I felt saddened that this request on her behalf was so far removed from the reality that Angosteños perceive each day. After generations of life in a challenging environment, they could never imagine an outsider, no matter how valued, ever being able to truly represent them.

CONCLUSION

Each of these institutions – the school, the border, and the road – is interesting in and of itself, but by examining them together it becomes obvious that Angosteños symbolically associate place not as a unified and inert context, but as a history that symbolizes different experiences; they manipulate these institutions to maintain their autonomy. Scholars have long studied ethnic identity as something shifting, but here it is actually manipulated to ensure autonomy. Angosteños are not trying to eradicate state institutions, but seek instead to use them as vehicles for their survival, allowing the maintenance of these symbolic institutions to serve as a testing ground for the legitimacy of the rapidly-changing governments and political positions that claim to represent the nation-state. The road is identified as their own, and they forcefully insist that the state help them maintain it; the border, an imaginary denomination by the state, is defined with a different history in El Angosto than that of official documents, and is experienced as something whose importance and continuity lies within the community's own hands; the school is an open dialogue, a place where each party gives, receives, and interprets information about the Other. It is through these three institutions that Angosteños gather up the materials and the proofs of who they are today. They do not see themselves as peripheral, unless they choose to, and instead of making them feel isolated and marginal, it infuses them with pride that they alone hold down these vital frontiers through their own efforts and their own choice. They remain autonomous, at best seeing themselves as doing a good deed for a government unable to appreciate it. And they intentionally project the possibility that they might not always choose to do so. Their ethnic identity partially lies in their eager orientation towards an unknown and open future.

Periphery is an internal and imaginative state, even when it is written upon the ground. The ability to distinguish contiguous space is an imaginative exercise, whether or not there are geographic shifts in landscapes. The fact that El Angosto is located on a national periphery and its people well aware that the nation-state perceives them as a homogenous group in a sensitive place, gives them real power as an alternate and competing polity. Rather, the use of identity is adaptive – it allows them to survive and also infuses the national consciousness with imagination.

While incoherent and indistinguishable to the Other, the identity of the inhabitants of El Angosto keeps them open to possibilities and open to the future. They have a sense of being caretakers of something valuable. Never fully feeling the power of the state, they value themselves for the maverick work of living there. They see themselves as capable, valuable, and enduring. This promotes their cultural survival.

In each of these situations, three essential tenets recur. First, ethnic identity emerges from, but is not dependent upon, place: Angosteño residents' identity emanates from their understanding and manipulation of periphery; where they are matters in that it allows them to continue to see themselves as autonomous, able to choose to enter and exit the nation-state at will. Using both history and current experiences, the people here speak through the institutions present in their community; they use these symbols as mouthpieces ultimately to proclaim their own independence as a cultural group. While living in this place grounds them, it is not sufficient as a definition of who they are. They are not "that group that lives over there"; rather, they are the collection of individuals who have had to struggle together under similar situations. As in Basso's account of the Navajo, these people have drawn meaning from the land and their lives are written all over the landscape.[23] While they do not self-identify as "Andean people," a pan-ethnic identity that incorporates linguistic and geographical elements, something Javier Albó also found among a study group of highland Aymara who were self-subsistent,[24] they do recognize the impact of this identity marker when they interact with outside Others, and they manipulate it as needed in order to affirm their cultural rights.

Second, ethnic identity has an ambiguous form but is associated with an active voice: who they are is based upon what they have achieved in their past and where they focus their concern for the future. Rather than use a list of characteristics that defines them, Angosteños use a metaphoric verb (*hacer patria*) as a motto that emphasizes action, independence, and choice. Who they are is not a completed action but a work in progress. Evidence that they have been considered worthy of the nation-state's interest in the past is used to delegitimize those who currently hold posts in the government. For Angosteños, the state has established nothing that was not first developed by Angosteños themselves. Once the nation-state took over the institutions and changed them, the community remained concerned about their future and remained involved in the evolution of these institutions, in effect holding the government to standards that it no longer enforced.

Finally, ethnic identity is responsive: although their identity has been demoted to a great degree by the government and many "intellectuals" who do not see them as amorphously "Andean," Angosteños continue to maintain a separateness. Capable of adapting to a new dialogue and ever-changing governments, they have a grounded sense of who they are and intend to be. As is evidenced in the story of Gualberto, formal land titles meant nothing to him as a community member, for all his legitimacy was tied up in the history of his grandfathers' occupations of land more than a century ago; however, he was willing and able to engage in a new discourse in order to preserve what he considered the natural order of things. Angosteños' designation of themselves responds to how they are seen and depicted by the Other. It changes them over time, but it does not cause them to lose the sense of being something collectively different. They remain intact.

More than any other thing, this characteristic bodes well for their survival. Not intimidated by the potential power of the state, and unaware of the extent of use and abuse of their "Andean-ness" in other towns, Angosteños see themselves as part of a wider context in which they must negotiate their lives. While this may not guarantee their cultural survival, it gives them an advantage that they have used repeatedly during the past century. As Gualberto told me one evening through a story about his father, "among them the head men of this zone were a Sr. Ramírez and Wáyar, my father. These men had huge contracts [for alfalfa crops] by which they earned enormous amounts of money. That is how my father earned money. With that he bought mines, he bought everything. Before, animals were highly valued. A lot. And it was the basis of everything [I have now]." As I read between the lines, Gualberto was telling me that he had been through significant changes before, he had his own (glorious) past, and that he was proud to be a highlander. Surrounded by national mass media and even academic scholarship proclaiming the demise of the Argentine Andes, I saw through Gualberto that there was no reason to take such a fatalistic view of a people who continued to draw sustenance from the same lands claimed by earlier generations. Able to adapt to changing contexts, Angosteños are not "living fossils," but agents who have proven again and again that they have a deep awareness of where they fit into the larger picture, a picture that over time has only been enriched by the presence of these highland peoples.

1 I thank the people of El Angosto, especially the Wáyar family, for the many years of friendship that they have shown me as we have shared each other's lives. I also thank the University of Calgary for hosting a wonderful and inspiring conference, Hendrik Kraay for his astute editorial suggestions, each of the presenters, and my session organizer, Denise Brown, for their insightful comments, and the University of West Georgia for providing research support.

2 For example, Bronislaw Malinowski, *Argonauts of the Western Pacific* (Long Grove: Waveland Press, 1984); Roy Rappaport, *Pigs for the Ancestors: Ritual in the Ecology of a New Guinea People* (New Haven: Yale University Press, 1984); Annette Weiner, *The Trobrianders of Papua New Guinea* (Fort Worth: Harcourt Brace College Publishers, 1988); Dennis Werner, *Amazon Journey: An Anthropologist's Year Among Brazil's Mekranoti Indians* (Englewood Cliffs: Prentice Hall, 1990).

3 For example see Paul Radin, *Crashing Thunder: The Autobiography of an American Indian* (New York: Appleton, 1926); Jean L. Briggs, *Never in Anger: Portrait of an Eskimo Family* (Cambridge: Harvard University Press, 1970); Anne Chapman, *Drama and Power in a Hunting Society: The Selk'nam of Tierra del Fuego* (Cambridge: Cambridge University Press, 1982); Sharon Gmelch, *Nan: The Life of an Irish Traveling Woman* (Prospect Heights: Waveland, 1991).

4 See the special issue of *Cultural Anthropology* 3:1 (Feb. 1988); and esp. Arjun Appadurai, "Introduction: Place and Voice in Anthropological Theory," *Cultural Anthropology* 3:1 (Feb. 1988): 16–20; James Clifford and George E. Marcus, eds., *Writing Culture: The Poetics and Politics of Ethnography* (Berkeley: University of California Press, 1986); Stephen Feld and Keith Basso, *Senses of Place* (Santa Fe: School of American Research Press, 1996); Akhil Gupta and James Ferguson, eds., *Culture, Power, Place: Explorations in Critical Anthropology* (Durham: Duke University Press, 1997).

5 Edward W. Said, "Representing the Colonized: Anthropology's Interlocutors," *Critical Inquiry* 15 (Winter 1989): 205–25.

6 See Clifford Geertz, *Local Knowledge: Further Essays in Interpretive Anthropology* (New York: Basic Books, 1983).

7 See Mikhail Bakhtin, *Rabelais and His World* (Cambridge: MIT Press, 1965); Michael Holquist, ed., *The Dialogical Imagination* (Austin: University of Texas Press, 1981).

8 Pierre Bourdieu, *Outline of a Theory of Practice* (Cambridge: Cambridge University Press, 1977).

9 Tim Ingold, *The Appropriation of Nature: Essays on Human Ecology and Social Relations* (Iowa City: University of Iowa Press, 1987); Keith Basso, *Wisdom Sits in Places: Landscape and Language Among the Western Apache* (Albuquerque: University of New Mexico Press, 1996); Hugh Raffles, *In Amazonia: A Natural History* (Princeton: Princeton University Press, 2002). See also Denise Fay Brown's chapter in this volume.

10 Feld and Basso, *Senses of Place.*

11 Diana I. Lenton, *Los Indígenas y el Congreso de la Nación Argentina: 1880–1976* (Buenos Aires: UBA Papers, n.d.).

12 Maryon McDonald, *"We Are Not French!" Language, Culture, and Identity in Brittany* (London: Routledge, 1989).

13 Terence Ranger, "The Invention of Tradition Revisited: The Case of Colonial Africa," in *Legitimacy and the State in Twentieth-Century Africa*, ed. Terence Ranger and T. O. Vaughan, 62–111 (Oxford: Palgrave MacMillan, 1993).

14 Anna Lowekaupt Tsing, *In the Realm of the Diamond Queen* (Princeton: Princeton University Press, 1993); Setha Low and Denise Lawrence-Zúñiga, "Locating Culture," in *The Anthropology of Space and Place: Locating Culture*, ed. Setha Low and Denise Lawrence-Zúñiga, 27 (Malden: Blackwell Publishing, 2004).

15 Many historical sources attest to this; see D. F. Sarmiento, *Life in the Argentine Republic in the Days of the Tyrants; or, Civilization and Barbarism* (New York: Hafner Press, 1868); H. S. Ferns, *Argentina* (New York: Frederick A. Praeger Publishers, 1969); James R. Scobie, *Argentina: A City and a Nation* (New York: Oxford University Press, 1971).

16 Thomas A. Abercrombie, "To Be Indian, To Be Bolivian: 'Ethnic' and 'National' Discourses of Identity," in *Nation-States and Indians in Latin America*, ed. Greg Urban and Joel Sherzer, 95–130 (Austin: University of Texas Press, 1991).

17 For example see Leticia Muñoz Cobeñas, *Arte indígena actual: Noroeste Argentina* (Buenos Aires: Ediciones Búsqueda, 1987).

18 Abercrombie, "To Be Indian."

19 IGM, *Informe final de la comisión mixta demarcadora de límites Argentina-Bolivia* (Buenos Aires: Instituto Geográfico Militar, 1953), 40.

20 Andrés Fidalgo, *¿De quién es la puna?* (San Salvador de Jujuy: El Diario, 1988).

21 IGM, *Informe final*, 88–90.

22 See Marjorie M. Snipes, "The 'Gaze' of the State: School as Contested Territory in the Argentine Andes," *Studies in Third World Societies* 56 (Aug. 1995): 113–46.

23 Basso, *Wisdom*.

24 Javier Albó, "¿Khitipxtansa? ¿Quiénes somos? Identidad localista, étnica y clasista en los Aymaras de hoy," *América Indígena* 39:3 (1979): 477–527.

12 Becoming Nature's Defenders:

FASHIONABLE IDENTITIES AND SUBVERSIVE COMMUNITY IN THE MAYAN BIOSPHERE RESERVE, GUATEMALA

Julie Gibbings[1]

INTRODUCTION

> *For more than 100 years, we have guarded our ruins and protected the forest and wildlife.... Although the community has had proposals for timber concession and has been pressured by different organizations, we have opposed felling [trees], because we believe that trees are not only a source of life for us, but for the entire world. For this reason we must unite ourselves as good Peteneros and honest Guatemalans to rescue and protect the flora and fauna that is left.*[2]

In this self-stylized representation as a community of "nature's defenders," Antonio Aldeco, a leader from the village of Uaxactún, located in Guatemala's Mayan Biosphere Reserve, illustrates the importance of local actors in the global environmental cavalcade. From this quote, the mantra "Think Globally, Act Locally" can almost automatically be conjured. The idea that belonging naturally to a place constitutes the basis for community and responsible environmental stewardship has now become a central tenet of some versions of environmentalism and conservation. This chapter challenges these orthodoxies by raising new questions and developing theoretical frameworks through insights from the village of Uaxactún. Although it is often not recognized, the articulation of the role of local peoples in the preservation of the environment is also involved in

257

the production of new subjectivities and identities around the environment. It should not be surprising that the proliferation of environmental initiatives, institutions, and discourses has not only produced new ways for governing human behaviour in relationship to the environment, but that these same strategies of governance are important sites where new environmental identities are produced and negotiated.

Identities as nature's defenders can be understood as fashionable in the double sense of being both in vogue and malleable. In one sense, these identities are fashionable because they symbolize an important and positive relation to new strategies for governing human behaviour in relationship to the environment. If environmentally destructive regimes are to overcome environmental doom, nature's defenders must fill the role of environmental liberators guiding the way to freedom and salvation. In another sense, what counts as defending nature is highly malleable. The notion that one is defending nature can coexist with a range of political agendas from an emphasis on the roles of tradition and local knowledge to an embrace of modernity and science; it can just as easily oppose the state or ally with it. While the categories of who counts as nature's defenders might become fixed, precise, and received, the content of these identities (what counts as defending nature) might be fluid and malleable. Identities as nature's defenders gain their power not from the fixity of these categories, but from the very malleability of the changing features of that ostensible essence. This malleability and "trendy" character is what enables Uaxactuneros to subvert what it means to be local through what it means to defend nature, and in doing so to contest political hierarchies and to demonstrate the point that there is no essence of "community" or "being from here."

These new fashionable environmental identities are also tools for negotiating norms and forms of governance produced and regulated within transnational environmental discourses, ideas of national citizenship, and local communities. As Aldeco's comments illustrate, identities as nature's defenders often articulate the global, national, and local simultaneously. Uaxactuneros, according to the village leader, are at once embedded in their local environments, are good national citizens, and are protecting and preserving the world's resources.

The relationships between these three discourses, however, are fraught with tension because each discourse has slightly different norms for what counts as "community," and because power is constituted in the production of these new subjectivities. Control over who counts as "nature's defenders" is important to the production and maintenance of certain political hierarchies, while what counts as defending nature is essential to political strategies for reinforcing, negotiating, and subverting these same control strategies. When people articulate different ideas of what it means to be "local" and to defend nature, identities and the hierarchies involved in the production of those subjectivities are being negotiated.

Far from the "fortresses of conservation" that excluded people living in so-called "untouched" landscapes, ideas about the place of people in transnational environmental discourses changed radically in the 1980s and 1990s.[3] With the new emphasis placed on the needs of the people and role of local knowledge in preserving biodiversity, "community" has become a focal point for conservation efforts and identities embedded in place have become a hallmark of the "environmentally friendly" actor.[4] The notion of community as a source of legitimacy and a means of achieving effective and lasting developmental change touches on deeply entrenched romantic notions of communities as "natural," "organic," and fixed entities. These romantic notions of community make it appear self-evident that rural people in the non-Western world live together in discrete "villages," share common and fixed identities, and are committed to each other by coresidence, kinship, and shared poverty in ways that people in the urbanized, industrialized, "developed" West have lost.

Community is in many respects defined by the negation of modernity and becomes an unproblematic grab bag of all that is not modern: unincorporated, resistant, incommensurable, originary, authentic, or simply alternative. It is commonplace to find assumptions that communities are based on face-to-face interactions, sharing, and equality, whereas Western society is based on individualism, consumption, and hierarchy. Local systems of knowledge ostensibly are based on sustainability, harmony, and reciprocity with nature, whereas Western science is destructive, exploitative, and patriarchal.[5] Far from defining a negative relation to modernity, however, community is defined by the failure of modernity, or what modernity lacks.[6] Therefore, for environmentalist critics of modernity and development, community and locality become an alternative and sustainable space, resistant to colonialism, the state, capitalism, and ecological domination.[7] Identities of "dwelling-in-place" and belonging to community thus become privileged actors in the saga of environmental destruction and salvation.

In the Mayan Biosphere Reserve, the new logic of locality and environmental authenticity is illustrated by representations of harvesters of three non-timber forest products: chicle, the natural resin used in chewing gum; *xate*, ornamental palm fronds; and *pimiento*, allspice berries. While harvesters of non-timber resources were once portrayed as unlawful and living in struggle with the forest, following the creation of the Maya Biosphere Reserve, they were represented as the most avid supporters of forest protection. In a scholarly monograph published in 1990, one anthropologist suggested that "the *chiclero* [harvester of chicle] is supposed to be dangerous, prodigal, hard drinking, and locked in struggle with the forest," adding that, according to local customs, "tapping trees is profane."[8] Yet, only a few years later he claimed that these same people relate the forest to community, the home, and family, which "reinforces the sensation that working in the forest is appropriate. In many ways, Peteneros enjoy being in the forest."[9] In this way, harvesters reportedly have a "sacred" and loving relationship with the forest. Moreover, harvesters promote these same values in future generations, since "they teach children not to be afraid of insects, nor to squash them automatically, but to carefully remove them from where they are not wanted. They were only afraid of snakes and kill them if they suspect they are venomous." Likewise, other conservationists hold that harvesters' belief in "reciprocity with nature" incites them "to fight for the conservation and regeneration of secondary forest resources."[10] In this way, local peoples, including Uaxactuneros, were portrayed as a homogeneous and harmonic community of forest dwellers naturally rooted to place and, thus, having an authentic relationship to nature.

At the same time that antimodernist environmental discourses celebrate community-as-resistance, community has become a site of government action.[11] Within a relatively short period, what began as language of resistance and critique was transformed into an expert discourse; community is now something programmed by community development officers through the technical means of community resource management plans. Communities became zones to be investigated, mapped, classified, and documented. Through the integration of community resource management, community is transformed from a sustainable space outside of modernity into the locus of modern forms of power where diverse tasks of government are removed from state bureaucracy and dispersed through various community associations and agencies. In the context of advanced liberalism, states, organizations, and agencies often prefer to govern through the "entrepreneurship of autonomous actors – individuals, families, firms, and corporations," than through "society."[12]

Transnational environmental discourses, thus, do not necessarily make the state or national discourse irrelevant, but coincide with the governmentalization of the state apparatus that scholars have associated with the contemporary phenomena of advanced liberalism. Michel Foucault's concept of "governmentality" illuminates this process of governing through community at work in the formation of disciplines directed at the welfare of the population and the governance of human conduct. He distinguished governmentality from sovereignty, which is concerned with territory, legitimacy, and obedience to law, and from disciplines, which are elaborated in institutions such as prisons, schools, armies, and hospitals. He defines governmentality as a mode of pastoral power aimed at the welfare of the population by establishing an "economy at the level of the entire state, which means exercising toward its inhabitants and their wealth and behaviour a form of surveillance and control as attentive as that of a head of a family over his household and his goods."[13] The goal of government became not simply the exercise of authority over the people within a territory or the ability to discipline and regulate them, but also the fostering of their prosperity and happiness. In this way, transnational discourses and the state's imperative of governing to discipline and to promote the long-term welfare of its population may coalesce around the production of communities as sites of government.

Attempts by the Guatemalan state to govern through community were dramatized during the counterinsurgency campaign. This period of rural terror, roughly 1980 to 1983, involved village massacres, selective torture and assassinations of rural leaders, burning of houses and crops in wide swaths, and the displacement of the Indian population of the highlands. Yet, during this period of brutal violence, the military also came to recognize that the highlands would not be secure without the end of extreme exploitation there; as a result the military government sought the incorporation of the indigenous populations, investment in development at the local level, and the construction of nationalism by encompassing the different levels of society into a national project.[14] These strategies of governing and incorporating the countryside included the military's policy of establishing model villages and civil patrols.[15] By incorporating the population into the counterinsurgency state through civil patrols and administering development through these model villages, the military effectively sought to construct communities as sites of governance.

Between 1987 and 1990, shortly after Guatemala's precarious transition to democracy in 1985, the Guatemalan state mandate in El Petén turned from felling trees in the name of progress to guarding them from progress in the name of biodiversity. What was at stake in this transformation, which culminated with the creation of the Mayan Biosphere Reserve in 1990, was not simply the salvaging of nature, but also the rebirth of narratives of the nation and new attempts to construct stability and order through the incorporation of part of the population.[16] By 1998, after the organization and mobilization of sectors of the population for access to forest resources and the signing of the 1996 Peace Accords, the Guatemalan government began to implement a policy of community forest concessions in the Multiple Use Zone of the reserve that, like the military counter-insurgency campaign, sought to govern through community. The community forest concessions involved establishing twenty-five-year contracts between the state, an accompanying non-governmental organization (NGO), and a legally-recognized community organization for the sustainable management of timber and non-timber resources. Thus individual villages did not have legal title to the land, but rather they had rights to the sustainable use of forest resources for a period of twenty-five years.

The village of Uaxactún, located twenty-three kilometres north of the famous Tikal National Park in the Maya Biosphere Reserve, was granted a concession by the Guatemalan government.[17] The concession was awarded in the context of significant political conflict both within the village and between some villager leaders, forestry and petroleum companies, NGOs, and the state. Through a period of political confrontations with the state, intense negotiations surrounding an overlapping petroleum concession claimed by Perez-Compac Inc., and the disruption of internal relations of power, leaders from Uaxactún organized and petitioned for the concession between 1993 and 1999. In June 1998, the majority of the villagers of Uaxactún formed a legally-recognized organization, called the Organización Manejo y Conservación (Conservation and Management Organization, or OMYC). This organization came to represent the community in its process of soliciting, and later, managing the concession, and served as the village's representative to other political organizations involved in conservation and development in El Petén. Since Uaxactún was awarded a concession in December of 1999, OMYC, along with an accompanying NGO, Naturaleza para la Vida (Nature for Life), have been in charge of developing management plans and environmental impact assessments, and administering the extraction of timber resources. In short, OMYC, with its democratically elected officials, functions like a community business and development enterprise by both employing villagers in the extraction of forest resources and reinvesting profits in community development projects. Uaxactún was awarded the largest concession, a sizeable 130,000 hectares, due both to its historic control over the forested area and its emphasis on the extraction of non-timber resources.

Yet, in contrast to both romanticized representations of an organic community as "place-bound" and the technical representations of community as a site of governance, in the village of Uaxactún local forms of community and governance are grounded in histories of migration, transculturation, and locally-negotiated systems of resource use.[18] In Uaxactún, local forms of governance developed around the harvesting of three non-timber forest products, chicle, xate, and pimiento, and around subsistence agriculture as well.

The opportunity for employment harvesting non-timber resources brought many itinerant workers to Uaxactún, resulting in a seasonal ebb and flow of people, which also often led to permanent or semipermanent residence in the village. These migrants arrived from different parts of Guatemala, as well as from Belize and Mexico, bringing with them culturally and ethnically distinct experiences. The village, like much of the department of El Petén, contains a diversity of indigenous and non-indigenous or *Ladino* peoples. Research conducted by anthropologists in El Petén and Uaxactún since the creation of the Mayan Biosphere Reserve in 1990, confirms that the village is culturally and ethnically hybrid. The work of these scholars suggests that the mixture of indigenous and Ladino belief systems demonstrates that Uaxactún is not only culturally hybrid, but also that the cultural content of places often moves along with people, enabling its articulation anew in different geographical contexts.[19] These studies, however, tend to equate transculturation with homogenization. By overshadowing relations of power within the community and by homogenizing culture, differences between indigenous villagers' beliefs of saints, deities, and rituals in relationship to *milpa*, or cornfields, and those who do not believe in the same spirit world tend to get erased. Yet, these studies nonetheless enable us to see how lines of collective meanings and differences generate multiple identifications with place.

As a culturally and ethnically diverse community of migrants, Uaxactún is also a counterpoint to received orthodoxies of the "place-bound" and culturally homogenous indigenous rural communities in Guatemala and other parts of Mesoamerica. While it may be true that indigenous identity draws upon being from "here" or being "local" in particular ways, migration does not necessarily involve the loss of local ways of interacting with the world or in the loss of Mayan identity.[20] Indeed, the received understandings of indigenous identity as locally bound, tied to a specific landscape, also tends, as Diane Nelson suggests, to "become an incarceration and a double bind, so that any indigenous person who leaves their community, the rural area, and the manual labour association with the village is vulnerable to accusations of inauthenticity and ladiniza-tion."[21] Villagers in Uaxactún defy these accusations and demonstrate that in the process of migration place identities are mobile and multiple. Uaxactuneros articulate more than one place-identity, self-identifying as being from other parts of Guatemala, such as Cobán or El Oriente, in particular contexts, and as a "Uaxactunero" in others, or even as being from both simultaneously.

In the context of migration, these same multiple place identities also suggest that there is no clear opposition between being from here and not being from here. When people have a sense of belonging to more than one community, the lines between being from this place and from another place may be shifting and ambiguous, as well as contextual. This may be especially true among newer migrants and those who have tended to live in the area seasonally.

These shifting lines of inclusion and exclusion in Uaxactún developed in tandem with local systems of harvesting non-timber resources to pro-vide the rules and norms governing relations within the community. The vast tracts of forest were controlled by local economic and political elites who were responsible for hiring and managing harvesters in these areas. These forested areas are divided up into several regions centred around the villages of Uaxactún, Dos Lagunas, Carmelita, Yaxha, Melchor de Mencos, and Libertad. Although the state has never recognized this sys-tem of resource use, each of these working regions "belonged" to certain local elites, which then subdivided them into smaller territories. The customary boundaries within working regions were fluid and negotiated by economically powerful local elites, whose members gained control over key areas of the forest through their personal relations and political influence both inside and outside of the community. Around these key areas controlled by the local elite, small- and medium-sized contractors established their camps and territories. These boundaries were negoti-ated rather than permanently fixed, and they occasionally overlapped.[22] In turn, seasonal migrants and semipermanent and permanent residents established working relationships with individual contractors who pro-vided access to the forests resources.

Migration, cultural and ethnic hybridity, and locally negotiated sys-tems of resource use thus suggest that Uaxactún does not bear much resemblance to romantic representations of homogenous communities "dwelling-in-place." Moreover, Uaxactún's complex systems of negotiated resource use, shifting boundaries, and mobile people means that the vil-lage does not easily lend itself to becoming a site of governance by state bureaucracies and resource managers.

However, after the creation of the Mayan Biosphere Reserve in 1990, the construction of governable, spatially fixed communities was precisely what the Guatemalan government would attempt through community forest concessions. These contracts between the state and community sought to replace systems of negotiated resource use with the institutionalization of community-based sustainable management plans through a series of controls and incentives. These community forest concessions in the Mayan Biosphere Reserve are what Ann Stoler and others have called "laboratories of modernity," wherein the mechanisms of modern government were tested and refined.[23] They consist of a highly developed Foucauldian panopticon, employing surveillance, documentation, confession, techniques of "pastoral power," and dividing practices. Through these techniques community was to be constructed as a site of government that would be spatially fixed and grounded in state-sanctioned forms of management rather than unofficial, locally-negotiated systems.

This technique of governing and shaping community as fixed to place is a complementary practice to what Juanita Sundberg has called the "migrant-as-culprit" discourse prevalent in the Mayan Biosphere Reserve. According to her research in El Petén, migrants are represented as "desperate and backward" people who practice "inappropriate agricultural techniques because they are unfamiliar with the lowland environment."[24] By casting the migrant as matter out-of-place, fixed or "sanctioned" communities are cast as matter-in-place and as the sources of true environmental conservation.

Through demarcating categories of who defends nature and who does not, who has authentic relationships with nature and who does not, the national body politic also becomes neatly divided into good and bad citizens. These divisions, moreover, become a rationale for promoting the welfare of the entire population through the exclusion of negative elements and the political inclusion of others. The policy of community forest concession satisfies the desire for creating community in place with nature, in contrast to migrants, in the name of the welfare of the total population.

REFASHIONING IDENTITY AND REMAKING COMMUNITY

The establishment of a community forest concession in Uaxactún in December of 1999 brought into action the disciplines and pastoral power of governmentality that would attempt to construct a sanctioned community of nature's defenders. The system of forestry concessions signalled state plans to remap the forest areas and communities in the Multiple

Use Zone of the Mayan Biosphere Reserve. By replacing a system of customary arrangements for resource use with formal lease agreements, official maps (complete with legal boundaries) would replace local unofficial maps embedded in histories of local forest product extraction. Instead of forms of measurement based on travel times between places and footpaths through the forest, these new maps would have abstract forms of measurement based on Geographical Information Systems. The state also sought to make the population as visible as possible through surveys and census counts, as well as by plotting housing arrangements, patterns of resource use, and population birth and death rates. The visibility produced from this knowledge of people and resources in Uaxactún enabled the state to monitor changes in the population, including immigration and changes in resource use. Through these new official maps, charts, and surveys, space was made into an abstract entity, and nature and population were made visible and available for governance by the state and NGOs.[25]

As an abstract entity with its own statistical influences on the economy and nation, the village also appears as a spatially fixed entity comprised of "place-bound" villagers. According to a census conducted in March 2001, there were 688 inhabitants living in the community, and 524 or 76 per cent were "natives" of Uaxactún.[26] This census, however, merely captured the community at a fixed moment in time as if history and movement had stopped altogether.[27] To get an indication of how census data may not capture the true nature of Uaxactún, one can simply draw on some of this same data. For example, in 1991 the Consejo Nacional de Areas Protegidas (National Council for Protected Areas, or CONAP) registered 638 people living in the community with an "indeterminant number of people that live temporarily in the community."[28] Even in statistical representations that attempt to capture population growth and migration, the population in question remains nameless, and thus the statistical figures can only capture a totality of immigration and emigration, of birth rates and death rates, and other demographic characteristics. The actual movements of people in and out of the village cannot be enumerated. Through this character of anonymity and totality, the village is made to appear as a reified entity, emptied of living, moving people, and "imagined, serially, synchronically, and as a self-portrait."[29]

The distorting effects of abstraction are evident when census data attempts to measure belonging. In 2002, local directors of the community forest concession estimated that Uaxactún's population was approximately 1,500. The discrepancy between the state's record of 688 inhabitants and that of the local directors of 1,500 suggests that villagers also consider people who live in Uaxactún seasonally and those who are currently living outside of the village as legitimate members of the community. Membership in Uaxactún, thus, continued to be much more fluid than can be captured in state census data.

Moreover, census data, as recent scholars have demonstrated, does not simply describe reality, but produces those same realities.[30] In addition to the identity-shaping techniques of a census which sought to create a spatially-bounded and enumerable population, the concession required that the majority of the villagers live permanently in the community, which was prohibited from accepting new immigrants.[31] Legally fixing the population to place, these requirements were enforced through control posts and watchtowers for surveillance of the area.

By fixing Uaxactuneros to the geographical place of "Uaxactún," the concession norms sought to create boundaries and limits, an inside and an outside, to better measure belonging. These techniques of enframing the population fashioned not only divisions between inside and outside, but also between members and nonmembers. This rigid classificatory system hardened the boundaries of belonging and nonbelonging. The divisions between insiders and outsiders in the concession norms were also understood among villagers as the right to exclude "outside" harvesters of the same resources that they planned to manage.[32]

The enframing of the population, legally enshrined within the concession contracts, ensured that multiple identities embedded in histories of migration had to be purged in favour of a singular identity of "being from here." Whereas many villagers articulate multiple-place identities, these migrant identities were to be superseded by a singular identity or at the very least a hierarchy among them. This rigid classificatory system hardened the impermissibility of more than one origin or of more than one belonging. A single common form of community had to replace multiple modes of identification that were determined contextually. Charles Taylor has called these demands that citizens adopt a singular identity a form of "inner exclusion." Based on a rigid formula of politics and belonging that refuse to accommodate any alternatives, these forms of "inner exclusion" imperiously demand the subordination of other aspects of citizens' identities.[33] The subordination of migratory, multi-place identities does not simply reflect, but also constructs, the dream of a singular form of community bounded to place.

This desire to "fix" Uaxactuneros to place represents the desire for a unitary subject belonging to only one community, defined empirically and even geographically. This vision of a "unified" subject is the desire of a complete self, one that is rational (therefore, unchanging) and able to be joined by a single idea of a common good. The desire for the unified subject is also part of the liberal dream of multiculturalism characterized by an ahistorical multiplicity of discrete and insular cultural identities.[34] Indeed, divided, fragmentary, and shifting subjects confound attempts to construct the dream of a united nation rationally managing its resources. Moreover, the fixing of identities as "nature's defenders" in place hinged upon the presence of other actors, against whom this identity could be defined; "nature's defenders" defined themselves in opposition to the antienvironmental excesses of the lower-class migrants. By marking migrants' destructiveness as the truth of the self, as an index of the social category to which they truly belonged, identities as "nature's defenders" could be articulated.

The marking of these categories of who counts as nature's defenders requires the production and management of new environmental subjectivities. The concession processes included modalities of positive intervention, management, and policing that sought to produce "nature's defenders" through modes of subject formation, which would embed ecological modes of thought in the population. In this way, power was constituted not only in the construction of divisions between who counts as nature's defenders and who does not, but in the management of new environmental subjectivities, and the modes of ecological thought became important sites for the maintenance of political hierarchies.

The processes of creating forestry inventories, management plans, and environmental impact assessments were precisely this form of epistemic policing, both framing the definition of ecological risks and certifying what would count as scientifically acceptable knowledge of the natural world.[35] By incorporating the population into enumerating and codifying resources for the inventory and in defining what counts as ecological risk according to already delimited criteria, these procedures also worked to embed regulatory and environmental modes of thought and values into the actions of organizations and individuals. According to Paul Rutherford, procedures such as environmental impact assessments "promote the implementation of environmental management programmes not simply through direct coercion, but through a governmental rationality that established norms and procedures which channel problem solving in a particular direction, and which stimulate administrative agencies and other social actors to be both innovative and effective in the implementation of ecological goals."[36]

Moreover, compliance with the Management Plan and respect for the territorial limits of the concession would be undertaken through self-surveillance of the boundaries of the concession, and through internal and external reviews by the community, an NGO, and CONAP, the National Council for Protected Areas. These procedures constituted a normalizing strategy in which new relations of power came into existence through a cluster of positive norms of self-control and external self-regulation. These positive norms and policing of specific practices of the population are constructs of what is considered normality and abnormality, but they also alter perceptions of normality and abnormality.[37]

These processes of inclusion and exclusion delimited the rules under which a community could legitimately participate and sought to relinquish other modes of belonging to a community. In effect, the prohibitions surrounding resource use and the admittance of new migrants, as well as the positive norms of environmental governance, produce identity along the culturally intelligible grids of being "nature's defenders" in a bounded community. Moreover, the conceptual network of requirements constituted the limits and signs by which potential concessionaries could perform their identities, and thus as a system of power it came to make the subjects that it purported to represent.

These "fixed" communities become hardened into essentialized political realities through their role in organizing the allocation of economic and other benefits, and the expectation of such benefits. In Uaxactún, the awarding of the concession occurred amid intense political pressure by NGOs and the state whose projects were justified on the basis of providing technical assistance to communities in the design and management of the forest. These pressures culminated in rumours that the community would suffer the same fate as many other communities in the Mayan Biosphere Reserve, forced displacement to a location outside of the reserve.[38]

These forms of coercion coexisted alongside the inclusionary developmental aims of governmentality, or what has been called "pastoral power."[39] These means of incorporating part of the village population into surveillance activities in the reserve – monitoring the natural resources, enforcing laws, and preventing and controlling forest fires – sought to instil the *desire* in the population to preserve the reserve's natural resources in the name of the nation and, as the village leader suggested, the entire planet.

FLUID BOUNDARIES AND SUBVERSIVE COMMUNITY

The production and management of new subjectivities around the environment and the demands for community identity grounded in place could not, however, completely erase other conceptualizations of community grounded in local systems of resource use and migration.

Uaxactuneros are able to creatively reconstruct a domain of community within and against the logic of liberal political theory and rational politics by making malleable the content of what it means to defend nature and by strategically misappropriating the norms of environmental management.

The proposal to generate additional income through harvesting a new resource – timber – resulted in ardent debate within the village over what counts as defending nature. The idea of harvesting timber was first discussed by villagers as early as 1993, but it continues to spawn debate and shifting lines of division within the community. On the one hand, some villagers misappropriated arguments made by some ecologists working in the region. Whereas the conservation ecologists have argued that selective harvesting of timber may not be sustainable due to regeneration problems, and others have stated that "more research is necessary to learn how to log sustainably without damaging non-timber forest species and the natural forest ecosystems over the long-term," villagers who opposed the extraction of timber asserted that it would result in irreparable damage to the forest resources.[40] Villagers including Antonio Aldeco and Camila Rodríguez, who had historically been most involved in organizing access to the forest for the extraction of chicle, misappropriated these conservation languages, arguing that forest regeneration is impossible and that timber is, in fact, a non-renewable resource. Those in favour of harvesting timber, and who were aligned most clearly in favour of the new concession, including Benedin Garcia, Fernando Quixchan, Diego Arias, and Bernardo Castro, appropriated arguments made by foresters to argue that timber would provide a new source of income for community development. Moreover, while recognizing that xate and chicle had maintained the village in the past, they cited another set of ecologists whose work suggests that xate and chicle have been overexploited.[41]

The point is not that Uaxactuneros "misunderstand" how the environment "really" works, but that in these performances the power of science is appropriated through (sometimes erroneous) interpretations that reclaim the power to create meaning. By refashioning scientifically acceptable knowledge of the forest, what counts as defending nature becomes a means to negotiate the terms of the forestry concessions. Through shifting alliances of opposition and agreement among community members, they engage debates among foresters and ecologists at the regional level. In taking part in these debates, not only did Uaxactuneros alter meanings associated with the sciences of forestry and ecology and contribute to reaching a consensus about the norms and languages utilized in establishment of systems of governance, but they did so within the context of local relations of power and in ways that reclaimed control over the production of new environmental subjectivities. Through the establishment of norms and languages around the forest that would produce and regulate human interactions with nature, they sought to rearticulate scientific paradigms through local conflicts and relationships.

In March 2000, a few months after the concession had been awarded, the directors of Tikal National Park orchestrated a *"xatero* bust" to bring to light how many harvesters from Uaxactún were collecting xate illegally within the boundaries of neighbouring Tikal National Park.[42] Through local informants, the resource guards for Tikal National Park captured a busload of *xateros* (harvesters of xate) returning at the end of the day. A few days later, the Tikal National Park directors organized a meeting with the OMYC (the community association), xateros, and representatives of an NGO and of CONAP.[43] Unexpectedly, the villagers confessed to the illegal harvesting in the meeting. They pleaded that areas around Uaxactún had been overharvested and even drew a map demonstrating the areas where they would enter into the park. At the same time that they confessed, they also declared that they were not damaging archaeological sites or ecological systems by harvesting resources. They also recalled the 1998 fires in which Uaxactuneros risked their lives to protect the Mayan Biosphere Reserve's forest, which includes Tikal National Park. The directors of the national park agreed to let Uaxactuneros harvest in the park during limited times and in a controlled fashion. They even offered Uaxactuneros a space in the visitors' centre for women to sell crafts, and pledged to collaborate with villagers in a xate reforestation project.

By confessing their wrongdoings and by reciting particular notions of defending nature, Uaxactuneros did not fully submit to the norms and languages of scientific management as suggested by Foucault's notion of confessional techniques of power.[44] Rather, Uaxactuneros frustrated attempts by archaeologists and ecologists to control the norms of resource extraction and they were able to reclaim fluid, shifting boundaries and local maps of resource use. In other similar negotiations, the villagers gained access to resources in the neighbouring biological corridor and in the industrial concession, La Gloria. Through these negotiations, villagers have won recognition of fluid territorial boundaries. In defiance of the need for legibility, legality, and regulation for state forms of governance, the villagers have reconstituted a system of moving, and often overlapping, boundaries of resource use.

These fluid boundaries and the failure of several attempts by the state to regulate and to manage the extraction of non-timber resources are illustrative of the creative defiance of rules and regulations that reconstructs a subversive form of community. Outside of management plans, environmental impact assessments, and state surveillance, xate, chicle, and pimiento extraction are reborn as domains of subject formation that eschew the attempts to create a good citizenry out of nature's defenders. The construction of these domains is a refusal to act as "nature's defenders" as imagined by environmental managerialism, a refusal to be what the state and transnational environmental discourse has attempted to make them. This refusal is a kind of resistance strategy directed at the very terms of environmental governmentality.

This spurning of identities was also embodied in a form of subversive community that contravenes the fixing of people to place and the hardening boundaries of belonging. During my fieldwork, rumours of migrant indigenous families living in Uaxactún circulated endlessly.[45] These rumours were often uttered simultaneously with fears that, if discovered, this violation of the concession contract's terms would result in the displacement of the community from the reserve. The anxiety produced around the desire to comply with state regulations and contradictions with multi-place identities constructed in a fluid, indeterminate form of community coalesced around these rumours. Faced with forms of governmentality that attempted to "fix" Uaxactuneros, the villagers re-embedded these signifiers of community in narratives of migration and difference. These rumours of indigenous migrants made the power behind the sign of "being from here" visible and audible, but those circulating these stories remain invisible, evading both detection and authorial presence.[46]

In an interview, a prominent member of the community explained to me that, indeed, migrants living in the community did have a place in the concession. These xateros and *chicleros*, he said were "Amigos de Uaxactún" (Friends of Uaxactún) who, although not permanent members of Uaxactún, lived in the community for a year, or perhaps even two or three. The Amigos de Uaxactún, he went on, would then be allowed to attend and participate in community meetings with a voice, but without a vote. When I searched through the community's minutes from meetings, statues, and other documents, I came across a reference to the Amigos de Uaxactún. Yet what I discovered was a fund for donations from family and friends of a North American conservationist working in the community. When I asked others, my friend's eloquent solution to hardened boundaries of belonging was revealed to be a fabrication. In this strategic fashioning of the Amigos de Uaxactún and in the rumours that circulate endlessly among community members, there lies a place for the representation of a form of hybrid and fluid community, a taboo from the perspective of the state and NGOs that nevertheless manages to find a displaced form of representation. As Homi Bhabha observes, this strategy "is a non-repressive form of knowledge that allows for the possibility of simultaneously embracing two contradictory beliefs, one official and one secret, one archaic and one progressive, one that allows the myth of origins and the other that articulates difference and division."[47] In these forms of representation, fashionable identities as nature's defenders coexist alongside subversive forms of community disrupting state attempts to construct a fixed and governable form of community.

CONCLUSION

Even while the forms of governmentality might attempt to remake identity in Uaxactún by replacing customary maps with official maps and by fashioning the community as an abstract and fixed entity with hardened boundaries of belonging, these forms of government and identities can never be simply imposed by the state and other governmental organizations. The misappropriation of scientific discourse, the negotiation of fluid boundaries, and the rumours of migrants are all tactics of subversive resignification of what counts as defending nature. Through these acts, Uaxactuneros render malleable the content of their new subjectivities and take some control over the production of new environmental subjectivities. Thus, in the redefinition of identities' content, the tensions between transnational, national, and local forms of community are worked out.

Representations of being naturally from a certain place as the cornerstone for the environmentally friendly actor are in turn displaced and rendered multiple. In these processes, Uaxactuneros question the myth of community as an original and natural place where individuals' identities are fixed and essential. Instead, Uaxactuneros illustrate that there is no essential "Uaxactún" or any essential "community" or "nature's defenders" – communities are not fixed and given, but mobile collectivities, spaces of indeterminancy, of becoming, and of determined contextually. Yet, the fact that sometimes these performances will continue to go wrong, to be misapplied or misinvoked, enables the negotiation of identity.

The production of these subjectivities is also wrapped up in strategies of governance. The divisions between those who defend nature and those who do not, between migrants and communities bound to place, are crucial to the maintenance of hierarchies and systems of governance based on exclusion. The "Amigos de Uaxactún" may illustrate one tactic for subverting and negotiating these hierarchies and for demanding a more inclusive and democratic ideal of caring for the environment. Yet, without state and transnational recognition of the multiplicity and mobility of people's identities, the rumours of indigenous migrants to the village are likely to remain just that: invisible and lacking authorial presence.

NOTES TO CHAPTER 12

1 I would like to thank Florencia E. Mallon and Jim Handy for commenting on earlier drafts of this chapter and the International Development Research Council and the John G. Bene Fellowship for making this research possible. Research for this chapter was conducted between July and November 2002. All participants in this study have been given pseudonyms.

2 Pamphlet for tourists visiting Uaxactún, Field Notes, Oct. 2001.

3 For perspectives on the movement to incorporate the communities into conservation, see David Western, R. Michael White, and Shirley C. Strum, eds., Natural Connections: Perspectives in Community-Based Conservation (Washington: Island Press, 1994). For a more critical perspective and overview, see W. M. Adams, Green Development: Environment and Sustainability in the Third World, 2nd ed. (London: Routledge, 2001); Arun Agrawal and Clark C. Gibson, eds., Communities and the Environment: Ethnicity, Gender and the State in Community-Based Conservation (New Brunswick: Rutgers University Press, 2001); D. Western, R. M. White, and S. C. Strum, eds., Natural Connections: Perspectives in Community-Based Conservation (Washington: Island Press, 1994).

4 The view of community as actors with a vested interest in the long-term sustainability of resources arises from the tragedy of the commons debate. See Garrett Hardin, "The Tragedy of the Commons," Science 162 (1968): 1243–48; Bonnie McCay and James Acheson, The Question of the Commons: The Culture and Ecology of Communal Resources (Tucson: University of Arizona Press, 1987); Elinor Ostrom, Governing the Commons: The Evolution of Institutions for Collective Action (New York: Cambridge University Press, 1990).

5 See, for example, Vandana Shiva, "Reductionist Science as an Epistemological Violence," in Science, Hegemony, and Violence: A Requiem for Modernity, ed. Ashis Nandy, 132–56 (New Delhi: Oxford University Press, 1998).

6 For a similar analysis, see Akhil Gupta, Postcolonial Developments: Agriculture in the Making of Modern India (Durham: Duke University Press, 1998).

7 See, for example, Murray Bookchin, The Ecology of Freedom: The Emergence and Dissolution of Hierarchy (Palo Alto: Cheshire Books, 1982).

8 Norman B. Schwartz, Forest Society: A Social History of Peten, Guatemala (Philadelphia: University of Pennsylvania Press, 1990), 224, 181.

9 Norman B. Schwartz, "Una perspectiva antropológia de El Petén de Guatemala," in Trece maneras de contemplar una selva tropical: La Reserva de la Biósfera Maya de Guatemala, ed. James D. Nations and Ingrid Q. Neubauer, 18 (Washington: Conservation International, 1999).

10 Conrad Reining and Carlos Soza Manzanero, "Illuminating the Petén's Throne of Gold: The ProPetén Experiment in Conservation-Based Development," in *Timber, Tourists, and Temples: Conservation and Development in the Mayan Forest of Belize, Guatemala, Mexico*, ed. Richard Primack et al., 366 (Washington: Island Press, 1998); Schwartz, "Perspectiva," 18, 20.

11 Mitchell Dean, *Governmentality: Power and Rule in Modern Society* (Thousand Oaks: Sage Publications, 1999); Nikolas Rose, *Powers of Freedom: Reframing Political Thought* (Cambridge: Cambridge University Press, 1999); Suzan Ilcan and Tanya Basok, "Community Government: Voluntary Agencies, Social Justice, and the Responsibilization of Citizens," *Citizenship Studies* 8:2 (2004): 122–44.

12 Rose, *Powers*, 139.

13 Michel Foucault, "Governmentality," in *The Foucault Effect: Studies in Governmentality*, ed. Colin Gordon, Graham Burchell, and Peter Miller, 92 (Chicago: The University of Chicago Press, 1991).

14 Carol A. Smith, "Conclusion: History and Revolution in Guatemala," in *Guatemalan Indians and the State: 1540–1988*, ed. Carol A. Smith, 273 (Austin: University of Texas Press, 1990).

15 See Diane M. Nelson, *A Finger in the Wound: Body Politics in Quincentennial Guatemala* (Berkeley: University of California Press, 1999); Finn Stepputat, "Urbanizing the Countryside: Armed Conflict, State Formation, and the Politics of Place in Contemporary Guatemala," in *States of Imagination: Ethnographic Explorations of the Postcolonial State*, ed. Thomas Blom Hansen and Finn Stepputat, 284–312 (Durham: Duke University Press, 2001).

16 Julie Gibbings, "Becoming Green Citizens and Other Subjects: Community Forest Concessions in the Mayan Biosphere Reserve" (master's thesis, University of Saskatchewan, 2004). See also James D. Nations and Michael Saxenian, "Guatemala Reserve is a Model Biosphere," *Forum for Applied Research and Public Policy* (Spring 1998): 95–98; Victor Perera, "Guatemala Guards Its Rain Forests," *The Nation* (1991): 54–56. On the rise of environmentalism in Guatemala see also Susan A. Berger, "Environmentalism in Guatemala: When Fish Have Ears," *Latin American Research Review* 32:2 (1997): 99–116.

17 Fourteen community concessions and two industrial concessions were granted between 1994 and 2000.

18 On this point, see also Denise Fay Brown's chapter in this volume.

19 Sofía Paredes Maury, *Surviving in the Rainforest: The Realities of Looting in the Rural Villages of El Petén, Guatemala* (n.p.: Foundation for the Advancement of Mesoamerican Studies, 1997); Schwartz, "Perspectiva," 19–20.

20 See Jim Handy, "Democratizing What? Some Reflections on Nation, State, Ethnicity, Modernity, Community and Democracy in Guatemala," *Canadian Journal for Latin American and Caribbean Studies* 27:53 (2002): 63; and Orin Starn, *Nightwatch: The Politics of Protest in the Andes* (Durham: Duke University Press, 1999).

21 Nelson, *Finger in the Wound*, 130.

22 Barbara L. Dugelby, "Governmental and Customary Arrangements Guiding Chicle Latex Extraction in Peten, Guatemala," in *Timber, Tourists, and Temples: Conservation and Development in the Mayan Forest of Belize, Guatemala, Mexico*, ed. Richard Primack et al., 166–67 (Washington: Island Press, 1998).

23 Ann Laura Stoler, *Carnal Knowledge and Imperial Power: Race and the Intimate in Colonial Rule* (Berkeley: University of Califronia Press, 2002), 97. See also Nelson, *Finger in the Wound*, 97–100.

24 Juanita Sundberg, "NGO Landscapes in the Maya Biosphere Reserve, Guatemala," *Geographical Review* 88:3 (1999): 395–97.

25 For a discussion, see Bruce Braun, *The Intemperate Rainforest: Nature, Culture, and Power on Canada's West Coast* (Minneapolis: University of Minnesota Press, 2002); James C. Scott, *Seeing Like a State: How Certain Schemes to Improve the Human Condition Have Failed* (New Haven: Yale University Press, 1998).

26 Georg Grünberg and Víctor Hugo Ramos, *Base de datos sobre población, tierras y medio ambiente en la Reserva de la Biosfera Maya* (Santa Elena, El Petén: CONAP and CARE, 1998).

27 Cesar Vinicio Montero Suárez, *Informe de PPS Comunidad de Uaxactun* (Flores, Peten: CONAP, 2001).

28 Ibid., 4.

29 Benedict Anderson, *The Spectre of Comparisons: Nationalism, Southeast Asia, and the World* (London: Verso, 1998), 37.

30 See Benedict Anderson, *Imagined Communities: Reflections on the Origin and Spread of Nationalism*, 2nd ed. (London: Verso, 1991), 163–86; Ian Hacking, "How Should We Do the History of Statistics?" in *Foucault Effect*, ed. Gordon, Burchell, and Miller), 181–96.

31 Consejo Nacional de Areas Protegidas, "Normas para el otorgamiento de concesiones de aprovechamiento y manejo de recursos naturales renovables en la Zona de Uso Múltiple de la Reserva de la Biósfera Maya," in 15–98 (1998), titulo III, 7–12; Steven Gretzinger and José Román Carrera, *Procedimientos simplificados para el otorgamiento de Concesiones Forestales Comunitarias en la Reserva de la Biósfera Maya, Guatemala* (Santa Elena, El Petén: Proyecto CATIE/CONAP, 1994), 4.

32 Instituto de Derecho Ambiental y Desarrollo Sustentable, *Estudio y monitoreo de los impactos sociales en unidades de manejo forestal comunitario de Peten, Guatemala: Caso I. Uaxactún* (Petén, Guatemala: Fundacion Naturaleza Para la Vida and Fondo Mundial Para la Naturaleza, 2002).

33 Charles Taylor, "The Dynamics of Democratic Exclusion," *Journal of Democracy* 19:4 (1998): 148–50.

34 For an excellent critique of multiculturalism, see Homi K. Bhabha, *The Location of Culture* (London, New York: Routledge, 1994).

35 Paul Rutherford, "The Entry of Life into History," in *Discourses of the Environment*, ed. Eric Darier, 55–60 (Oxford: Blackwell Publishers, 1999).

36 Ibid., 57.

37 Michel Foucault, *The History of Sexuality*, vol. 1 (1976; repr. New York: Vintage Books, 1990), 144.

38 These fears were discussed openly during the meetings around the Plan Estratégico 1999, conducted by the community association (the community was awarded in the concession in early 2000), Naturaleza Para La Vida, *Plan Estratégico de la Sociedad Civil OMYC de Uaxactún* (Petén, Guatemala, 1999).

39 Hubert L. Dreyfus and Paul Rabinow, eds., *Michel Foucault: Beyond Structuralism and Hermeneutics* (Chicago: Chicago University Press, 1983), 214.

40 Conrad C. S. Reining et al., *Productos no maderables de la Reserva de la Biósfera Maya, Peten, Guatemala* (Washington and Flores, El Petén: Conservation International and Propeten, 1992), 115; R. E. Rice, R. E. Gullison, and J. W. Reid, "Can Sustainable Management Save Tropical Rainforests?" *Scientific American* (April 1997): 44–49.

41 Barbara L. Dugelby, "Chicle Latex Extraction in the Mayan Biosphere Reserve: Behavioral, Institutional, and Ecological Factors Affecting Sustainability" (PhD diss., Duke University, 1995), 67–113; Reining et al., *Productos*, 79–92.

42 Sofia Paredes Maury, interview with the author, 7 Nov. 2002.

43 Sofía Paredes Maury and Eduardo González Vassaux, *Primera Reunión sobre Actividades Extractivas en el Parque Nacional Tikal* (Tikal, El Petén: Antropología y Historia, Ministerio de Cultura y Deportes, 26 March 2000).

44 See Foucault, *History of Sexuality*, 59, 61–62.

45 According to the technical justification for the concession, since 1990 the community permitted the entry of only twenty families. This figure was used to suggest that the community had already made a commitment to closing its doors to immigrants, Sociedad Civil "Organización Manejo y Conservación," *Justificación técnica solicitud Concesión Forestal Comunitaria de Uaxactun* (Peten, 1998). Since the awarding of the concession, the community has officially expelled one family. Sociedad Civil "Organización Manejo y Conservacion," "Letter to Juan Cucul" (Uaxactún, Flores, 2000). However, according to villagers, this was after the individual set fire to part of the concession area.

46 See Ranajit Guha, *Elementary Aspects of Peasant Insurgency in Colonial India* (Delhi: Oxford, 1983), 251–77.

47 Homi K. Bhabha, "The Other Question," in *Literature, Politics and Theory*, ed. Francis Barker, 168 (London: Methuen, 1986).

Contributors

GREGG P. BOCKETTI is assistant professor of history at Transylvania University in Lexington, Kentucky. He received his Ph.D. in History from Tulane University in 2004 with a dissertation entitled "The Creolization of British Sport in Trinidad and Brazil, 1870–1940." He continues to work on the history of culture and sports of Latin America and the Caribbean.

MARIA EUGENIA BROCKMANN DANNENMAIER is a Ph.D. candidate in anthropology at McGill University in Montreal, Canada. A native of Bolivia, she studies the role of indigenous social movements as expressions of national identities and as popular critique of the democratic state and its claims to the rule of law. In the 1990s, she worked with PARTICIPA, a non-governmental organization based in Santiago, Chile, dedicated to strengthening participatory democratic rights in South and Central America.

DENISE FAY BROWN studied at McGill University and the University of Calgary before moving in 1983 to Mexico where she researched and taught on themes relating to traditional resource use, rural development, indigenous issues, educational issues, and cultural landscapes. She received her Ph.D. in social anthropology from the University of California at Riverside in 1994. Presently she is the director of the

University of Calgary's Latin American Studies Program. Her current research focuses on change and transformation of social structures and cultural spaces in the Yucatec Maya zone, including the role of tourism in these changes.

MARIA CECÍLIA VELASCO E CRUZ is associate professor of history and social sciences at the Universidade Federal da Bahia, Brazil. She received her Ph.D. from the Universidade de São Paulo. She has written articles on Brazilian labour history and is currently finishing a book on stevedores and porters in Rio de Janeiro.

JULIE GIBBINGS is a Ph.D. candidate in Latin American history at the University of Wisconsin-Madison. Her dissertation research is on race, nation, and geography in nineteenth-century Guatemala. She received her M.A. in history from the University of Saskatchewan in 2004.

LOUISE H. GUENTHER received her Ph.D. from the University of Minnesota in 1998. She was a Fulbright scholar in Brazil in 1995–96 and a senior associate member of St. Anthony's College, Oxford, at the Centre for Brazilian Studies in 2001–2. She is the author of *British Merchants in Nineteenth-Century Brazil: Business, Culture, and Identity in Bahia, 1808–1850* (Oxford: Centre for Brazilian Studies, 2004). She has taught at St. John's College in Santa Fe (New Mexico) and United World Colleges in India and Canada.

RONALD N. HARPELLE teaches history at Lakehead University. He is the author of *The West Indians of Costa Rica: Race, Class and the Integration of an Ethnic Minority* (Montreal: McGill-Queen's University Press, 2000). He is also the co-director of *Banana Split* (Shebandowan Films, 2003), a documentary film about the world's most popular fruit.

HENDRIK KRAAY is associate professor of history and political science at the University of Calgary. He received his Ph.D. from the University of Texas at Austin in 1995. He is the author of *Race, State, and Armed Forces in Independence-Era Brazil: Bahia, 1790s-1840s* (Stanford, 2001) and has edited or co-edited three books on Brazilian and Latin American history. In 2004, he was a visiting professor at the Universidade Federal do Rio de Janeiro. He is currently writing a book on civic rituals in nineteenth-century Brazil.

JENNIFER J. MANTHEI is an assistant professor in the Sociology and Anthropology Program at the University of Illinois at Springfield. She received her Ph.D. from the University of Arizona in 2004 with a dissertation entitled "Reading Race: Adolescent Girls in Brazil." Her research interests include constructions of social identity, inequality, medical anthropology, adolescence, and Brazil.

STEPHEN NEUFELD is currently pursuing his Ph.D. in Latin American history at University of Arizona where he is continuing his work on a cultural history of the Porfirian military. Formerly a student of William French (University of British Columbia) and Christon Archer (University of Calgary), he is a graduate of the Oaxaca Summer Institute VI directed by his current advisor, William Beezley. His historical interest in Mexico focuses on issues of subject construction, gender, and the performative nature of the late nineteenth century military.

MARJORIE M. SNIPES is associate professor of anthropology at the University of West Georgia, where she teaches courses on Latin America, animals and culture, and anthropology of religion. She has done fieldwork in Argentina and is privileged to have worked with informants who, over the past fifteen years, have expressed no surprise at her interest in them. Instead, as one very dignified Andean man told her, "I always knew someone would want to write about my extraordinary life."

Index

Turning Points

OCCASIONAL PAPERS
IN LATIN AMERICAN STUDIES SERIES

ISSN 1716-9429
Christon I. Archer, general editor

This series is a joint venture with the Latin American Research Centre at the University of Calgary (LARC), and is intended to reflect the wide range of issues with which the Centre is concerned. Since the signing of NAFTA, political and economic linkages between Canada and Latin America have increased greatly, a trend which has seen Alberta companies investing heavily in the new opportunities that have arisen. Turning Points will focus on such topics as Latin American economics, trade, and politics, as well as history, literature, and anthropology. The publications will stem mainly from papers resulting from conferences and scholarly research.

Trade Negotiations in Agriculture: A Future Common Agenda for Brazil and Canada?
· Edited by William Kerr and James Gaisford · No. 1

Relocating Identities in Latin American Cultures
· Edited By Elizabeth Montes Garces · No. 2

Negotiating Identities in Modern Latin America
· Edited by Hendrik Kraay · No. 3